Intricate Relations

Intricate Relations

*Sexual and Economic Desire
in American Fiction,
1789–1814*

KAREN A. WEYLER

University of Iowa Press
IOWA CITY

University of Iowa Press, Iowa City 52242
Copyright © 2004 by the University of Iowa Press
All rights reserved
Printed in the United States of America

Design by Omega Clay

http://www.uiowa.edu/uiowapress

No part of this book may be reproduced or used in any form or by any means without permission in writing from the publisher. All reasonable steps have been taken to contact copyright holders of material used in this book. The publisher would be pleased to make suitable arrangements with any whom it has not been possible to reach.

The University of Iowa Press is a member of Green Press Initiative and is committed to preserving natural resources.

Printed on acid-free paper

LIBRARY OF CONGRESS CATALOGING-IN-PUBLICATION DATA
Weyler, Karen Ann.
 Intricate relations: sexual and economic desire in American fiction, 1789–1814 / Karen A. Weyler.
  p. cm.
 Includes bibliographical references and index.
 ISBN 0-87745-884-7
 1. American fiction—19th century—History and criticism. 2. American fiction—18th century—History and criticism. 3. Economics in literature. 4. Sex—Economic aspects. 5. Property in literature. 6. Desire in literature. 7. Sex in literature. I. Title.
PS374.E4W49 2004
813'.2093553—dc22   2004047893

04 05 06 07 08 C 5 4 3 2 1

For Ronald and Shirley Weyler

Contents

Acknowledgments ix

INTRODUCTION. *Intricate Relations* 1

1. A Manner Unquestionably More Agreeable
   The Politics, Aesthetics, and Praxis of Epistolary Fiction
   29

2. Unlawful Embraces
   Sexual Transgression, Madness, and the Ascendancy of Medical and Narrative Discourse
   75

3. A Speculating Spirit
   Economic Anxieties and Opportunities in Early American Fiction
   105

4. Gentleman Strangers and Dangerous Deceptions
   140

EPILOGUE. *Looking Forward to Antebellum Fiction* 183

Notes 189

Bibliography 241

Index 261

Acknowledgments

MY MOST PROFOUND DEBT in writing this book is to Philip Gura, who directed *Intricate Relations* from the time my research began. He continues to be an inspiration. Others whose advice and assistance I appreciate include the late Everett Emerson, Mary Kelley, Townsend Ludington, Richard Rust, David Shields, and Linda Wagner-Martin. I owe a special debt to the late Robert Bain, who first introduced me to Charles Brockden Brown and his coterie and whose wise counsel I still miss. My friend and colleague Karen Kilcup provided practical advice and help when I needed it the most. My editor, Arnold Friedman, was thoughtful and meticulous. Prasenjit Gupta, acquisitions editor, and Charlotte Wright, managing editor, and everyone else at the University of Iowa Press, provided useful advice and were a pleasure to work with. For unflagging moral support, I thank my good friends both in and outside of academe: Catherine Mattingly, Katie McKee, Susan Ryan, and Felicia Wheeler.

Grants, fellowships, and awards provided me with much appreciated research support along the way. I'm grateful to the University of North Carolina at Chapel Hill for an off-campus dissertation research fellowship and for a Smith Graduate Research Award. Wake Forest University awarded me a Research and Publication Faculty Development Grant that allowed time for revision and helped me obtain the images for this book. A Summer Excellence Research Award from the University of North Carolina at Greensboro enabled me to complete revisions to my manuscript. I owe special thanks to the American Antiquarian Society for a Stephen Botein Fellowship in the History of the Book, as well as for the tremendous experience of two seminars in the history of the book, one led by Mary Kelley and Robert Gross, and the other by Ann Fabian, all of whom helped me think about books and readers in new ways. Staff members at the American Antiquarian Society—especially Joanne Chaison, Marie Lamoureux, and Caroline Sloat—were enormously helpful during my visits there.

Permission to reprint revised versions of previously published essays was kindly granted by New York University Press and the University of North Carolina Press. Chapter 2 originally appeared in *Sex and Sexuality in Early America* (New York University Press, 1998). An earlier version of chapter 3 appeared in *Early American Literature*, Volume 31.3 (1996): 207–42, copyright © 1996 by the Department of English at the University of North Carolina, Chapel Hill. It appears here by permission of the University of North Carolina Press.

Finally, I deeply appreciate the love and encouragement of the extended Weyler and Romine families. My parents, Ronald and Shirley Weyler, are simply the best. Despite their deep suspicions about my long years of graduate school and my refusal to get a "real job," my brothers, David and Tim Weyler, have also provided crucial support. The screamin' Weylers are always guaranteed to amuse, distract, and otherwise sustain me. To Scott, Olivia, and Isabella Romine—thanks for your patience in all matters and the joy you bring me.

Intricate Relations

Introduction
Intricate Relations

The relations in which men, unendowed with political authority, stand to each other, are numerous. An extensive source of these relations, is property. No topic can engage the attention of man more momentous than this. Opinions, relative to property, are the immediate source of nearly all the happiness and misery that exist among mankind. If men were guided by justice in the acquisition and disbursement, the brood of private and public evils would be extinguished.

To ascertain the precepts of justice, and exhibit these precepts reduced to practice, was, therefore, the favourite task of Engel. This, however, did not constitute his whole scheme. Every man is encompassed by numerous claims, and is the subject of intricate relations. Many of these may be comprised in a copious narrative, without infraction of simplicity or detriment to unity.

Next to property, the most extensive source of our relations is sex. On the circumstances which produce, and the principles which regulate the union between the sexes, happiness greatly depends. The conduct to be pursued by a virtuous man in those situations which arise from sex, it was thought useful to display.

—Charles Brockden Brown, from "Walstein's School of History: From the German of Krants of Gotha"[1]

IN 1799, masquerading as a reviewer of the philosophy and works of the fictional European historian "Walstein" and his coterie of scholars, Charles Brockden Brown obliquely identified the salient concerns of the earliest American novels. In this sketch, the unnamed reviewer examines Walstein's theory of the moral and ethical purposes of writing history. Engel, one of Walstein's most promising students, argues that the task of the moral historian—and that historian may deal in fact or fiction—is to explore the "intricate relations" of, and between, sex and property. "Moral historian" is a weighty label, but it is one that most novelists would have embraced as they explored sexual and economic relations, the double axes around which virtually all early American novels revolve. Sex and property, broadly construed, constitute in the novel homologous forms of exchange and expenditure, whether social, emotional, sexual, or financial, attendant upon citizens of the early Republic. In a republic anxious about burgeoning individualism in the 1790s and the first two decades of the nineteenth century, the novel foregrounds sexual and economic desires and explores ways to regulate the manner in which they are expressed and gratified. Understanding how these issues underlie the novel as a genre is fundamental to understanding the novels themselves and their role in American literary culture, for novelists used fiction as a means of intervening in public discourse with compelling narratives that synthesized the sexual and economic anxieties associated with the rise of bourgeois consciousness and culture.

Certainly, in the two hundred years since Charles Brockden Brown described the mission of the novel, critics have recognized the importance of sex and property with regard to individual novels,[2] but the overwhelming concern of the early novel, as a genre, with the intricate relations of sex and property has been rendered nearly invisible over time by virtue of its very familiarity.[3] I hope in *Intricate Relations* to complicate and invigorate our understanding of the literary history of the early Republic era, taking into consideration what nineteenth-century French historian Ernest Renan argues in "Qu'est-ce qu'une nation?"—that the essence of a nation is not merely what a people remember and share in the present, but rather what they have collectively forgotten.[4] What Renan means by this seemingly paradoxical claim is that the essence of a nation is that which is so common, so ordinary, so shared by a people that it needs little or no explanation and hence risks being forgotten by later generations. By reading fiction written by Americans between 1789 and 1814 alongside medical theory, political and economic tracts, and pedagogical literature of all kinds, I hope to re-create and illuminate the larger, sometimes opaque, cultural context in which novels were written, published, and read. Placed within such a cultural context, the prevalence of the epistolary mode and the repetition of such tropes as self-discipline, seduction, female madness, and economic speculation—some of the most common, indeed repetitive, elements of the early novel—suggest not aesthetic failures, but rather indicate loci of cultural anxiety and energy, heuristics developed by and within the early novel as a means of mapping and reforming social relations.

Fiction serves for the early national era as a literary repository of cultural anxieties concerning sexual relations and the acquisition and disposition of property of all kinds. Fiction provided a forum for articulating these anxieties and a means of exploring how economic and sexual desires especially might be mediated in order for the Republic to function smoothly. Through rigorous attention to self-discipline, reflective interiority, female chastity, and the proper acquisition and display of symbolic capital and real property, the novel explores the regulation of the complicated relations of, and between, sex and property. By contrast, the failure of such self-regulation leads to gambling, uncontrolled economic speculation, seduction, even to madness—all to the detriment of the individual, the family, and the Republic. While sex and property are not made perfectly analogous in fiction, both are sites of desire, expenditure, and exchange. In novels where sexuality and adherence to gender norms partly figure public worth, and female chastity in particular becomes a sign of value, a form of property, and another means of exchange, the already tangled relationship between sex and property becomes immeasurably complicated.[5] As a genre, the novel exposes the sexual divide opening up in the early Republic, making it clear that while bourgeois white women ruin themselves from failure to regulate a moral or sexual economy (and indeed the ability to regulate such economies becomes a sign of bourgeoisness), social ruin for men chiefly stems from unsound financial expenditures—e.g., gambling, excessive luxury, speculation, and counterfeiting. These factors become appreciably more discernible when the novel is placed in the larger Anglo-American literary context of the late eighteenth century. I am, then, necessarily concerned in *Intricate Relations* with the relationships between fiction and other modes of discourse. Situating fiction amidst other popular genres illuminates how writers of fiction synthesized and iterated many of the concerns expressed in other forms of discourse, a strategy which helped legitimate their chosen genre and make it a viable venue for public discourse in the decades following the Revolution. In this introduction, I will sketch out the contours of the literary and cultural landscape into which fiction written by Americans first emerged.

The Novel, Its Cultural Context, and the Changing Face of Print in the Post-Revolutionary Era

Following the political upheaval of the American Revolution, a tremendous struggle for cultural authority ensued in the newly-formed United States. To read popular works from virtually any prose genre in that era is to learn of a culture that feared it faced an ethical declension of vast dimensions, a declension in which the fate of the state hinged on the state of the individual and family, and vice versa. Economic and moral virtue were at the heart of these anxieties. During the turbulent years of the late 1780s and the 1790s, a broad range of economic issues assumed foremost importance in American thought. Regardless of whether or not it ever actually existed, republicans mourned the loss of the self-sacrificing civic virtue idealized during the war years, a loss manifested, they thought, by uncontrolled economic speculation.[6] Vexed questions concerning debt, currency, land speculation, foreign trade, and luxury fostered doubts about the viability of the American republican experiment. At the center of these economic conflicts were the role of the male individual and his economic relationships with other individuals. Especially perplexing was the problem of amassing capital: How could one make money and yet balance individual economic desires against larger civic interests?

Simultaneously, increased economic and geographic mobility contributed to the breakdown of traditional communities,[7] leading to crises of authority at both the family and national level. Religious, conduct, and pedagogical works urged the importance of self-control and rigorous examination of the self, yet at that exact time, birth rates from pre-marital conceptions rose to a level that would be unmatched until the 1960s. Members of the clergy struggled to address these issues in the pulpit as well as in print, yet the process of clerical disestablishment begun well before the Revolution continued to undermine the power of the clergy.[8]

As communal, parental, and religious authority waned, the printed word became ever more widely available, affordable, and influential. A combination of events brought about this change: the proliferation of small presses and improved transportation networks increased the number and range of works in circulation. While the price of books held fairly steady at this time (most single-volume novels cost around a dollar; multivolume works cost more), the growing popularity of lending and subscription libraries made it possible to read at a relatively modest cost far more books than most people would previously have been able to purchase for their private use.[9] Further, the kinds and amount of writing done by Americans increased dramatically during this time. Religious and pedagogical works, medical texts, and political and economic theory were popular in British America throughout the eighteenth century, but in the pre-Revolutionary period, most of these works were either imported from Britain or reprinted from British sources. In the post-war years, American printers published growing numbers of works by American writers in these same genres. Increasingly, these were the works of professionals, e.g., medical doctors such as Benjamin Rush and educators and ministers such as Enos Hitchcock. Through what we might call the professionalization of public discourse, we can trace a broad reconstitution of cultural authority as writers in these discourses sought to diagnose the ills of the new United States based on their professional authority. By way of contrast, fiction writing required no professional credentials other than those occasionally offered up by the putative author of a text, usually some claim to truth or experience.

Fiction, poetry, drama, and the essay—what we today consider the "literary" genres—were still non-professional discourses, since there were no professional men or women of letters in the United States able to support themselves at this time solely by their writing, a situation that could not occur until after the circumstances of authorship and publishing changed significantly. Factors that would enable a class of professional writers to develop included the passage of a federal copyright law, advances in printing technology making books cheaper to produce, and improved transportation networks enabling publishers to place substantially more books in substantially more readers' hands.[10] While national copyright was assured with the passage of a 1790 law, the slow (albeit steady) progress of these other factors during the early national period prevented even Charles Brockden Brown and Susanna Rowson, the most prolific authors of novels, from being able to live solely off the proceeds of fictional productions. Even so, as a non-professional discourse, fiction likely seemed to aspiring writers a relatively accessible route to publication, as well as an attainable venue for participation in civic discourse, despite the fact that the novel was a contested form of narrative.

Unquestionably the novel was the subject of considerable cultural criticism in the British colonies and later in the United States, particularly during the 1780s and 1790s and especially in periodicals published in New England, but this criticism of the novel needs to be placed in perspective. Not unique to the United States, this criticism closely parallels the objections that, earlier in the century, had been directed toward British fiction. The nature of this criticism varied, but much of it centered around the dangerous power of the novel to move readers' emotions and the romantic, unrealistic expectations that critics believed fiction promulgated among its readers. Critics of the novel especially feared its seductive impact on susceptible young readers, an anxiety masterfully dramatized in Tabitha Tenney's *Female Quixotism* (1801). This censure of fiction has been explored in detail by such scholars as G. Harrison Orians and Cathy N. Davidson and indeed has at least been mentioned by virtually everyone who has ever written about the novel. Michael T. Gilmore wonderfully sums up the gist of early attacks on the novel when he writes, "To them [cultural critics], the novel resembles a coquette who lured readers into a claustrophobic world of desire and self-indulgence, the antithesis of the public domain of rationality and men."[11] What is less often noted about these attacks against the novel, however, is that much of this criticism was directed specifically toward foreign imports, rather than fiction in general, for American criticism of British and continental manners and morality was often articulated as criticism of *foreign* fiction.[12] Further, while the cultural attacks against the novel illustrate the battle waged by competing forms of cultural authority—the relatively democratic power of print in the guise of the novel versus ministers and other conservative cultural elites—these attacks were part of a battle being waged against the novel that tacitly had already been conceded to fiction as a form of narrative. This may seem a paradoxical statement, but it can be illustrated easily.

While virtually all recent critics of early American fiction eagerly identify the novel as a contested, transgressive form of narrative, virtually no one has discussed the strange disparity between public criticism of the novel and the extensive use to which writers of other genres put fictions. And only recently have scholars begun giving sustained attention to how fiction permeated early American writing in another sense. American literary periodicals, which first appeared in the Revolutionary era, routinely serialized longer fictional works and used short, romantic fictions as space fillers. Even those periodicals that inveighed most bitterly against the novel were guilty of using fiction to attract readers and bulk up their numbers, just as those same periodicals were likely to include advertisements for their sale. Robert B. Winans argues, in fact, "By the 1780's and 1790's, the amount of fiction printed in the magazines far outweighed the number of essays denouncing it."[13] Further, Keith J. Fennimore claims that "by the turn of the new century, some form of imaginative prose had become staple fare in each issue of virtually all domestic magazines across the young republic."[14] Even advice manuals and conduct literature frequently use short fictional narratives for didactic purposes, to illustrate the wages of sin. Letter-writing manuals likewise use brief fictional narratives to illustrate, for example, how a young man might engage in a very proper epistolary courtship. Yet *these* uses of sentimental fictions evoked no public outcry, either with regard to their use or with regard to the public's avid consumption of them. Fiction and fictions permeated the literary life of

Americans during the early national era, and the only place fiction seems to be absent, in fact, is from sermonic literature. If nothing else, the sheer number of novels being printed in the United States illustrates the growing importance of fiction to its readers; whereas in the 1780s only about twenty-five novels were printed in the United States, two hundred novels were printed in the 1790s alone, a figure that includes American productions as well as reprints of British and continental fictions but excludes imported editions.[15] The records of lending libraries likewise substantiate the novel's appeal in both the late colonial and early national periods, for existing records indicate that novels consistently made up a majority of books borrowed.[16] Throughout the early national period, figures of cultural authority—the clergy in particular—were fighting a losing battle against the cultural legitimacy of fiction, a battle which was ultimately conceded by the 1820s. Given these facts, it seems clear that while the novel itself met with considerable hostility from some camps, the American anti-novel sentiment has perhaps been overemphasized by late twentieth-century literary critics who themselves value the seemingly transgressive precisely because it seems transgressive. Criticism of the novel as a genre thus needs to be viewed in context. Fictions saturated the national literary culture of the early Republic, and fiction (and the novel in particular) was likewise saturated with American cultural issues.

Fiction played a strange dual role during this era, becoming both a locus of anxiety about an uncontrolled populace as well as a site for expression of these anxieties. As a medium of popular culture, the novel provided the perfect forum through which to address social concerns, particularly when these anxieties centered around the rising generation in the early Republic era—those young men and women whose fathers and grandfathers had fought in the Revolutionary War, a circumstance which many novels emphasize, for fiction problematizes the mode of behavior proper to citizens of a republic, especially with regard to economic and moral issues. I am especially interested in the role which narrative, particularly fictional narrative, plays in this reconstitution of authority during the early national era, for fiction, perhaps more consistently than poetry and drama of the time, synthesizes concerns about economic and sexual virtue simultaneously explored in medical, political, economic, and pedagogical texts.

Sexual and economic relations, the axes around which most novels revolve, come to serve as litmus tests for the propensity of the new Americans toward virtue and vice or, in a broader sense, toward communal benefits versus self-gratification. White women, increasingly limited in public discourse to the role of republican wife or mother, were shut out in many ways from the practice of liberal values, as the virtue of self-discipline preached in religious and pedagogical texts displaced economic aspirations that advancing liberalism encouraged for men.[17] In novels written before 1814, these sexual and economic stories largely efface other troubling national issues—particularly such issues as slavery and policies toward Native Americans. Recently, Cynthia S. Jordan, in *Second Stories: The Politics of Language, Form, and Gender in Early American Fictions*, Teresa A. Goddu, in *Gothic America: Narrative, History, and Nation*, and Julia A. Stern, in *The Plight of Feeling: Sympathy and Dissent in the Early American Novel*, have argued persuasively for the shadowy presence of the gothic in early fiction, a mode of writing which, given the historical association of the gothic with political criticism, enabled writers to acknowledge, sometimes overtly and sometimes covertly, these troubling racial issues. While overtly gothic novels such as the works of Charles Brockden Brown or Ann Eliza Bleecker's *The History of Maria Kittle* (1793), the earliest captivity novel, sometimes foreground racial issues, most often racial issues tend to be relegated to subplots, to "second stories," to borrow Cynthia Jordan's wonderfully descriptive phrase.[18] Not until the second and third decades of the nineteenth century, when the circle of sympathy expands to include the concerns of the poor, servants, blacks, and Native Americans, do these second stories consistently move to the foreground. What most American writers foreground most consistently in novels published before 1814 are sexual and economic relations, as they struggle to find ways to accommodate advancing liberal interests within a larger cultural frame that continued to privilege republican ideals.

Constituting the Novel in Early America

As Jeffrey Rubin-Dorsky points out in his essay "The Early American Novel," in *The Columbia History of the American Novel*, "early American fiction" and "early American novel" are problematic and potentially misleading labels.[19] Here, I would like to clarify what I do, and do not, mean by those phrases, for the citizenship status of authors, length, and date and place of publication are all factors that complicate any definition of early American fiction. American novels were not written in isolation, however, so it is likewise important to understand their relationship to other works of print in the early national period.

By "early American fiction," I mean simply extended works of fiction written prior to 1814 in English by people with some claim to an American identity, e.g., through birth or extended residency in British North America or, later, the United States, conditions which would lend them familiarity with the social and cultural situation of the newly formed United States. While *Intricate Relations* focuses on the novel, "novel" as a descriptive label had much more fluidity in the eighteenth century with regard to length than it does today. Several early American texts that identify themselves as "novels" are quite short, perhaps only thirty or forty pages in length—barely a novella in contemporary terms. Even briefer serialized novels and short fiction flourished in newspapers and magazines throughout the early national era, although much periodical short fiction appears to be pirated from British sources.[20]

Not until sometime after the Revolution did a substantial body of work appear that properly could be labeled "early American fiction," but ascribing a fixed set of dates for the inception and ending point of this era requires considerable explanation. One thing is clear, however: early American *fiction* in the form of short fictional sketches began to appear decades before the early American *novel*; Benjamin Franklin's amusing satire, "The Speech of Polly Baker" (1747), is one such fictional sketch. The contenders for the title of first American *novel* are numerous, depending on the criteria considered. The very earliest novel-length works written by Americans and published in the United States first appeared in literary magazines before being published as books.[21] For example, the *Columbian Magazine* serialized clergyman and historian Jeremy Belknap's *The Foresters, An American Tale* beginning in June 1787 and continuing through April 1788, but it was not published independently until 1792, when it appeared in two volumes as *The Foresters, An American Tale: Being a Sequel to the History of John Bull the Clothier*. An anonymous work, *Amelia; or, the Faithless Briton*, initially serialized in the *Columbian Magazine* beginning in October 1787, later appeared as a book in 1798.[22] The work usually accorded the title of "the first American novel," however, is William Hill Brown's *The Power of Sympathy* (1789), which was marketed by Isaiah Thomas in precisely that fashion, since it was the first novel by an American to be published in the United States in book form. Yet another possible candidate is *Adventures of Alonso*, "By a Baltimore Native," Thomas Atwood Digges, which was published in 1775, but in London, rather than the colonies. Ann Eliza Bleecker's *The History of Maria Kittle*, by way of contrast, was written in 1779 and was published in the United States, but not until 1793. It is not my intent here to debate the "firstness" of any particular text; rather, I merely wish to illustrate that searching out the origins of American fiction and the novel is complicated.

What this listing of works and the years in which they appeared makes clear is that American novels—extended works of fiction written by Americans, for Americans, and about issues of concern to white, bourgeois readers—first appeared en masse only after the Revolution, at a time when European fictions were widely available but evidently were not satisfying the varying cultural imperatives of American readers and writers. Virtually all these novels explicitly appeal to literary nationalism, as numerous critics have noted, but their greater significance lies in how they, as a body of work, contribute to developing bourgeois subjectivity, particularly as related to economic aspirations and moral virtue in the post-Revolutionary era.

Although novels written prior to the second decade of the nineteenth century are certainly not ideologically consistent—some texts espouse conservative messages, while others seem subversive or even quite liberal, and still others are so unstable that they simultaneously illustrate the constraining and liberalizing tendencies present in the culture at large—*Intricate Relations* posits that broad-based, pervasive bourgeois concerns, as well as narrative style, unite these works. Around 1814, however, the beginnings of radical changes in the style and subject matter of American fiction become noticeable, with sustained attention beginning to be paid to the problems of more diverse groups of people in novels such as Sarah Savage's *The Factory Girl*. The year 1814 is also when Sir Walter Scott's historical novel *Waverley* was published, and Americans soon began to follow suit with historical works such as John Neal's Revolutionary War novel *Seventy-Six* (1823). The advent of historical fiction is important in and of itself, of course, as historical fiction encouraged new ways of imagining relationships between and among groups of people, but political events also likely influenced the direction the novel would take: Steven Watts suggests in *The Republic Reborn* that the War of 1812, which took place between 1812 and 1815, marks the transition between Revolutionary-era republicanism and the liberal democracy of the nineteenth century.[23] Although there is no abrupt demarcation in early American fiction between republicanism and liberalism, certainly this gradual political and cultural shift registers over several decades in fiction with regard to both subject matter and modality, as I argue throughout *Intricate Relations*.

The differentiation between early and antebellum fiction becomes even clearer by the 1820s, when technological innovations, improving transportation networks, and changing conceptions of authorship made the situations of the author and the reader dramatically different from what they had been thirty, twenty, or even ten years earlier. Further, by the 1820s, the novel as a genre had lost its subversive edge. Reviewers and other cultural commentators no longer perceived novel reading as pernicious, and many writers during this decade comment on the sea change that public perception of fiction had undergone. Indeed, the historical fiction of Sir Walter Scott and James Fenimore Cooper made novel reading positively respectable.[24]

Working from this understanding of the novel, *Intricate Relations* focuses on the longer fiction written between the Revolution and 1814 by writers with some familiarity with the American scene, while seeking to explore their cultural context. These writers shaped their novels for bourgeois American audiences, but they continued to see themselves as members of a vibrant transatlantic—especially Anglo-American—literary culture. They obviously drew upon British fiction, but popular nonfiction genres such as medical, political, economic, and advice literature also influenced them as they explored issues of concern to Americans.[25] For most ordinary eighteenth-century readers, the literariness of a text was seldom an issue of conscious concern. As Larzer Ziff and others have asserted, literary culture "had not yet separated from political culture," and "influential writers in the 1790s took literature to include all written knowledge."[26] Eighteenth-century readers read widely across genres, as diaries and journals of the time attest. Evidence in the form of newspaper and periodical advertisements, as well as publishers' advertisements bound into the backs of books, also suggests readers of the early national period were much less concerned with the distinctions between genres than are literary critics in our own era. In late eighteenth-century newspapers, for example, novels were advertised alongside political, economic, and religious works; frequently there was no differentiation between fictional and nonfictional works except by subtitle, if that. They were simply "books for sale."

Literary critics, by virtue of the profession, are trained to categorize texts, yet critical privileging of fiction, poetry, and drama as "literature" risks stripping these texts, especially novels, from their cultural context. Today, any literate person can pick up and read a copy of *Charlotte Temple* or *The Coquette*, with some readers enjoying these novels more than others, of course. Understanding the relationship of the novel to other contemporaneous forms of print, however, enables a richer understanding of the novel as it expressed and shaped the culture of the early national era, for the novel is the literary genre most closely connected to non-literary writings in genres such as conduct and pedagogical literature, sermonic literature, and medical and economic discourse. As Walter L. Reed argues in *An Exemplary History of the Novel*, "the novel is the literary genre which gives the greatest weight to those human fictions—economic, political, psychological, social, scientific, historical, even mythical—which lie beyond the boundaries of the prevailing literary canon. Literary paradigms are not simply modified in the novel, they are confronted by paradigms from other areas of culture."[27] Reed suggests here that fiction as a genre explores and critiques those other "fictions" and systems of belief by which we structure and organize our social reality.[28] Certainly this claim holds true for the early national era, particularly with regard to social and economic issues, when fiction repeatedly confronts the issues of inheritance, of acquiring capital and property, and of the social and political implications of seduction and marriage. Through its role as a synthesizer of social and cultural concerns and its attention to gender roles and responsibilities, fiction served as yet another venue for public discourse about issues troubling Americans.[29] By reading novels alongside and against medical, political, and economic theory, as well as advice, sermonic, and pedagogical literature, *Intricate Relations* explores how fiction consolidated the concerns expressed in these disparate forms of narrative.

Gender, Public Discourse, and the Sentimental

There are good reasons for the rising popularity of fiction with readers at the end of the eighteenth century. As Cathy Davidson explains, fiction required no special skills of its readers beyond basic literacy, for they did not need either knowledge of foreign languages or a classical education in order to enjoy fiction.[30] Although novels were not yet inexpensive by standards of the day, growth in the number of circulating and subscription libraries meant fiction was increasingly obtainable for readers of middling financial status. But fiction was also a form of print culture to which middle-class women and men could readily aspire *as writers*. Especially for women writers, fiction offered certain advantages over other forms of participation in public life.

While both elite and non-elite men were able to engage in pamphleteering and political speech, for most women—and especially those of the middle class—these were not attractive options for participation in public life due to the hostility that such acts provoked. Male novelists such as Charles Brockden Brown, Enos Hitchcock, and Samuel Relf, for example, participated in political culture through pamphleteering, joining other writers in the public sphere who wrote openly about such issues as international commerce and luxury, speculative economic practices, the role of institutions in the new nation, and the problem of authority in general. Relatively few women participated in print discourse, however, other than through the genres of pedagogical and conduct literature, captivity narratives, poetry, or fiction; even fewer women writers engaged in specifically civic discourse. There are important exceptions, of course, such as Judith Sargent Murray and Mercy Otis Warren, but these women are exceptions rather than the rule. As Linda Kerber has pointed out, women who entered into public discourse—particularly openly political discourse—exposed themselves to ridicule and charges of unbecoming masculinity, particularly from the Federalists.[31] Given the general cultural proscription against women's public speech, the *site* of political speech mattered as much as did the *content*. Political oratory, Sandra M. Gustafson reminds us, was equal in importance to print in producing a national culture during this period, but even though women in elite seminaries might be taught the principles of oratory, the general cultural taboo against women speaking publicly meant that this mode of civic discourse largely excluded women except as audience members for male speakers. The threat of censure clearly limited women's participation in overtly politicized cultures of oratory and print, while lack of access to publication networks compounded the difficulty of getting into print.

Consequently, when women did directly address political issues, they tended to do so in venues other than traditional print culture. The vibrant correspondence of Abigail and John Adams, and Milcah Martha Moore's commonplace book, for example, suggest that women were indeed actively writing about political topics. But they were more likely to do so in private venues of letters and manuscript culture, which, while they still involved "publication" in the broadest sense of the word—the circulation of literary works—differed greatly from print publication. In manuscript culture, writers created works for smaller, private audiences, circles of friends and mutual acquaintances through whom the "publicity" of a work—its readers and readings—could be more easily circumscribed.[32] Of course there was considerable overlap between manuscript culture and the literary salon; salons and literary groups such as those in which Judith Sargent Murray and

Mercy Otis Warren participated likewise nurtured vibrant literary cultures and a space for political discussions, but the quasi-private nature of these salons, while encouraging female participation, also meant that few women outside the cultural and political elite had access to such outlets.

Recently, both Grantland S. Rice and Edward Watts have argued that the American novel flourished in a space opened by the growing inadequacy of an earlier tradition of disinterested authorship. Rice suggests that, as a result of the waning influence of the tradition of civic commentary in the post-Revolutionary era, fiction may have been more attractive than other forms of written discourse as a means for women (as well as for men) to enter into the marketplace of ideas.[33] This seems especially likely given the broad-based appeal of fiction to American readers, whether bourgeois, elite, or working class. Along similar lines, Edward Watts describes fiction as the antithesis of the seemingly stable tradition of disinterested authorship and literary eloquence prized by republicanism. He has convincingly argued for the relevance of applying post-colonial theory to the novel, claiming in *Writing and Postcolonialism in the Early Republic* that fiction, especially metafiction involving self-conscious narrators and elaborate strategies of authenticity, enabled writers to "reveal the deeper American chaos beneath the façade of order, both political and linguistic, thrown up by republican textuality," a kind of textuality inherited from the British tradition.[34]

Although published fiction offered less command over readers and readings—especially given the challenges to authorial control highlighted by Watts in the texts that he discusses—it nonetheless offered writers the opportunity to reach a wide audience and a space through which to intervene in public discourse on issues important to this same wide audience of middling Americans. I do not mean to suggest that writing fiction entirely insulated the woman writer from public criticism: Marion Rust, for instance, has described the demeaning, gendered attack that William Cobbett (aka Peter Porcupine) directed toward Susanna Rowson in a satirical review of her works.[35] Fiction, however, offered women writers relatively more leeway than many other forms of public discourse, and clearly the tradition of anonymous or pseudonymous authorship that persisted into the early Republic worked to the advantage of female authors. During this era, novels especially were likely to be published anonymously. Fiction thus offered a refuge of sorts for American women writers, while the preface that routinely accompanied the novel simultaneously defended authorship, as the author customarily sought to distinguish her creation as an exception to the dangerous romanticism generally promulgated in fiction. For these reasons, fiction, and sentimental fiction in particular, emerged as an important, accessible, and popular vehicle for middle-class women's public voices.

Enhancing the appeal of sentimental fiction for American writers was the fact that it was a well-established genre in British literary culture. Throughout the entire colonial period, most books in English-speaking North America were printed in Great Britain;[36] the same holds true for sentimental fiction as a subgroup, which had an extensive importation history in the colonies well before Americans began printing and/or writing their own sentimental works. Although the publishing history of British fiction in the American colonies dates from Benjamin Franklin's landmark 1744 edition of Samuel Richardson's *Pamela*, it wasn't until the latter part of the eighteenth century that it became economically feasible, or common, for American printers to tie up their presses printing long works of fiction—hence the continued importance of imported novels over the next few decades.[37] British sentimental fiction continued to be popular even in the post-Revolutionary era; by this time, however, many novels were printed in the United States, often in heavily abridged and edited versions designed to appeal to American readers, as Leonard Tennenhouse has noted with regard to American editions of *Pamela* and *Clarissa*.[38] In these respects, the British novel laid important groundwork enabling American fiction to emerge.

As Americans in the post-Revolutionary era began expressing desire for a literature of their own, fiction, and sentimental fiction in particular, was perfectly poised to enable writers of less privilege an attainable, appealing means of access to the public sphere. Further, for American writers, sentimental discourse itself was a valorizing agent, legitimizing female novelists' participation in public life, for the sentimental focuses on social relations while nonetheless valuing and legitimating individual experience, whether male or female. Janet Todd has usefully described sentimental works as those that seek to evoke pathos, often through "conventional situations, stock familial characters, and rhetorical devices."[39] "The sentimental work," she adds, "reveals a belief in the appealing and aesthetic quality of virtue, displayed in a naughty world through a vague and potent distress" (3). Post-Revolutionary America, a time and place fraught with concerns about virtue of all sorts, was ripe for such sentimental discourse, as novelists used sentimentality as a modality to depict and work through cultural anxieties. Of course not all early American fictional works are sentimental, but one can fairly say that the majority of fiction, and especially that produced by women writers, is avowedly sentimental.[40]

Although sentimental fiction generally centers on the home and domestic life, writing sentimental fiction did not limit writers to speak only of the home, for there is no distinct demarcation in the novel between the private and the public spheres, between the domestic and the outside world; family affairs affect the larger community and the state, just as national events inevitably impact the family. Indeed, the permeability of private, domestic life is of major concern to American novelists. As Sharon M. Harris argues in her introduction to *Redefining the Political Novel: American Women Writers, 1797–1901*, the sentimental and the political in early American literature are not antithetical, for "the family, in its patriarchal structure and values, is a microcosmic representation of 'the state.'"[41] Today, the very familiarity of marriage and seduction plots, however, sometimes works against modern readers perceiving the other sexual, economic, and political concerns of fiction, especially given that eighteenth-century sentimentality required circumspection and discretion. This cultural shorthand and circumspect coding of the language of eighteenth-century fiction nonetheless would have suggested to contemporaneous readers an array of cultural anxieties and problems, as I argue throughout *Intricate Relations*.

My own interest in decoding these sentimental texts has been inspired by and responds to the substantial accomplishments of the past twenty-five years of scholars working in both early American and antebellum literature. Here, I want to sketch an overview of important recent studies of sentimental fiction and suggest how my own understanding of the early American novel, and of sentimentality in particular, both converges with and differs from that of other critics. Certainly the watershed event in the study of the early novel was the 1986 publication of Davidson's *Revolution and the Word*, a work with which anyone who has since studied early American fiction must contend. Davidson's work was part of a larger project of feminist scholarship in the 1970s and '80s that sought to recover women writers, and indeed Davidson was wildly successful in doing so. Her sophisticated combination of feminist, new historical, and history-of-the-book approaches offered fresh ways to read what seemed to be time-worn sentimental fiction, and her editorship of Oxford's Early American Women Writers reprint series made many of these texts easily obtainable for the first time. By assessing the importance of sentimental fiction to its readers and emphasizing its advocacy of education for women, *Revolution and the Word* laid the groundwork for critical reevaluation of fiction written in America prior to 1820, while the reprint series encouraged modern readers, especially those interested in women's literary history, to revisit these texts. Throughout her work with early American fiction, Davidson argues that the sentimental novel was a genre largely written by women, for women, and about women's experiences. Consequently, she claims, "The sentimental novel as a form mediated between (and fluctuated between) the hopes of a young woman who knew that her future would be largely determined by her marriage and her all-too-well-founded fears as to what her new status might entail—the legal liabilities of the *feme covert*, the threat of abandonment, the physical realities of repetitive pregnancy, and the danger of an early death during childbirth" (121–22). By arguing that American sentimental fiction is "ultimately about silence, subservience, stasis [the accepted attributes of women as traditionally defined]" (147), Davidson explores how the promises of equality espoused during the Revolution failed women in the early national period. Certainly much of the appeal of Davidson's work stemmed from her willingness to entertain feminist, subversive, indeed revolutionary, readings of these novels that ran counter to the previous wisdom concerning early American fiction espoused by much earlier critics such as Lillie Deming Loshe and Herbert Ross Brown, who had little good to say about the sentimental, or women's writing in general.[42]

Davidson's work has engendered numerous reappraisals of early American sentimental fiction, most importantly for my purposes the work of Julia Stern and Elizabeth Barnes, both of whom consider, but in different ways, the significance of sympathy and sentiment in the novel. In *The Plight of Feeling*, Julia Stern explores the affective history of the Federalist epoch as suggested by five novels written during the era. Stern reads William Hill Brown's *The Power of Sympathy*, Susanna Rowson's *Charlotte Temple*, Hannah Foster's *The Coquette*, and Charles Brockden Brown's *Wieland* and *Ormond* as works of self-conscious theatricality that expose the foreclosure of liberty for all in the post-Revolutionary era. Stern argues that these explicitly political works suggest "that the foundation of the republic is in fact a crypt, that the nation's noncitizens—women, the poor, Native Americans, African Americans, and aliens—lie socially dead and inadequately buried, the casualties of post-Revolutionary political foreclosure" (2). In greatly simplified terms, where Stern sees sentiment, and sentimental fiction in particular, as revealing the gap between the rhetoric and reality of revolution, Elizabeth Barnes sees sympathy as, much later, bridging this gap, for sympathetic union first enabled writers to imagine a unified America. Only partly about early American fiction, Barnes's *States of Sympathy: Seduction and Democracy in the American Novel* takes on the important work of synthesizing critical discussions about the sentimentality of early American and antebellum novels. She sees sympathy as linking these disparate works and argues that sympathy, "the act of imagining oneself in another's position," was "crucial to the construction of American identity."[43] Barnes proposes that such sympathetic identity depends on a sense of affinity between people: "[O]thers must be shown to be *like* the reader" (2), and it is affinity, in her reading, rather than democracy, that enables sentimentality throughout the nineteenth century. In other words, Barnes argues, "[S]entimental literature teaches a particular way of reading both texts and people that relies on likeness and thereby reinforces homogeneity. In the sentimental scheme of sympathy, others are made real—and thus cared for—to the extent that they can be shown in *relation* to the reader" (4). Barnes's and Stern's understanding of the working of sentiment and sympathy in the early Republic reveals the complexity of this literature; while sentiment makes sympathy possible, it does not guarantee it, and sentimental fiction may at times most potently document the grief that results from the *absence* of true sympathy. Taken together, the works of Davidson, Barnes, and Stern represent the most important, sustained attention to the sentimental element of early American fiction in recent years. Each has contributed immensely to the projects of historicizing and theorizing about early American fiction. In different ways, all three emphasize how the novel enabled readers to see America through the eyes of white women, denied full citizenship in the Republic yet nonetheless expected to bear the largest share of the burden of representing the symbolic virtue of the United States. And, more so than Davidson or Barnes, Stern shows how the boundaries of sentiment in the early Republic expanded to enable aliens and non-whites to become visible, however briefly.

While I read the novels of the early Republic as no less political than do Davidson, Barnes, or Stern (or Rice or Edward Watts, for that matter), I diverge from them in reading the genre, as a whole, as less generally subversive. This different way of seeing emerges in part from *Intricate Relations*' embrace of the novel *as a genre*; *Intricate Relations* explores how early fiction as a body of work enabled writers to articulate widespread cultural anxieties about sexual and economic relations and how these might be negotiated in the best interests of the individual, the family, and the Republic. The individual novels that I discuss here—some three dozen, a mixture of works that will be familiar to contemporary readers, along with some that might be less familiar—cohere in interesting ways and unearth important aspects of the literary landscape into which fiction written by Americans emerged. Early American fiction reflects the values of its time, as novelists—both male and female—experimented with narrative authority as a means of commenting on rapidly-changing social conditions. While this fiction has the potential to be subversive and many novels are indeed so, the relentless, repressive conservatism of some novels less studied today, and the confused politics of still others, suggests that fiction attracted writers across the political spectrum. Vocalizing neither wholly republican nor wholly liberal ideology, the novel as a genre sought ways to accommodate the tenets of liberalism, especially economic individualism, without compromising the individual virtue so esteemed by republicanism. In this sense, the novel exposes the halting, sometimes progressive, sometimes oppressive, development of bourgeois subjectivity.

Further, sympathy across the genre of early American fiction, as I understand it, tends to be carefully circumscribed. Although Stern compellingly contends that the novel makes visible the social invisibility of certain kinds of non-citizens (e.g., those who are non-white, non-American, or non-male), her engaging close readings of these selected works most vividly emphasize the withholding of rights from white women, who play much larger roles in these texts than do Native Americans, African Americans, or aliens, who most often exist on the margins of the novel.[44] Like Stern, I see these concerns emerging in the novels of the early Republic, but I locate them several decades later, in the 1820s. Most typically, American novels before 1814 emphasize the dilemmas facing young women, and these are largely the dilemmas of white women of the middling and upper classes. Only occasionally does fiction address the concerns of lower class women, and even then it is in a prescriptive manner.[45] The subjects of fiction and hence of affinity—white men and women of the middling and elite classes—thus mirror to a large extent their readers. In these respects, sentiment and affect in early fiction operate differently than in antebellum fiction as understood by such critics as Jane Tompkins and Philip Fisher, for the sentimentality of nineteenth-century fiction has different subjects and objectives.[46] The sentimental novel of the early Republic era is not at all about female power turned outward in order to effect change in the family and ultimately in the state itself (e.g., *Uncle Tom's Cabin*); rather, it is more likely to be about female energies turned inward, in order to discipline the self. Sentiment makes different demands upon the writer and reader of early American fiction, then, for it requires only that the writer be able to sustain sympathy for characters who share traits and dilemmas akin to its readers. Children, slaves, Native Americans, and the poor—important subjects of nineteenth-century sentimental fiction—are implicitly excluded from republican political discourse, as Michael Warner has pointed out.[47] While they may appear in the context of displays of affect in the novel, they themselves are seldom empowered by these emotions, and seldom do their concerns remain foremost.[48] These groups move to the forefront in the novels of the 1820s and later in the works of such writers as James Fenimore Cooper, William Gilmore Simms, Lydia Maria Child, and Catharine Maria Sedgwick, but in earlier American fiction, their members are for the most part of secondary or tertiary concern. Fleeting sympathy is directed toward these disenfranchised groups and individuals, but not until the nineteenth century do we find in fiction the kind of democratic sympathy and sentiment that Barnes, Fisher, and Tompkins describe.[49] Instead, as I argue throughout *Intricate Relations*, the creative energy of most novelists writing during and about the early Republic is directed toward issues confronting people like themselves, Americans of the middling classes, and hence the overt emphasis in their fiction on property, inheritance, and the relationships among sexuality, marriage, and social standing.

Although writing fiction, especially sentimental fiction, a genre that could readily accommodate discussions of such issues, may have been more appealing to many female writers than authorship of explicitly political works, a certain amount of criticism of the novel and fiction writing in America was in all likelihood directed toward keeping women out of public discourse.[50] Much criticism of the early novel focuses on the susceptibility of the American reader (especially the female reader) to its negative influences, but, in attacking fiction and the sentimental, critics were also attacking one of the few venues for public discourse accessible to women. As Peter Stallybrass and Allon White explain in *The Politics and Poetics of Transgression*:

> Patterns of discourse are regulated through the forms of corporate assembly in which they are produced. Alehouse, coffee-house, church, law court, library, drawing room of a country mansion: each place of assembly is a different site of intercourse requiring different manners and morals. Discursive space is never completely independent of social place and the formation of new kinds of speech can be traced through the emergence of new public sites of discourse and the transformation of old ones. Each 'site of assembly' constitutes a nucleus of material and cultural conditions which regulate what may and may not be said,

> who may speak, how people may communicate and what importance must be given to what is said. An utterance is legitimated or disregarded according to its place of production and so, in large part, the history of political struggle has been the history of the attempts made to control significant sites of assembly and spaces of discourse. (80)

Given the prominence of the home and domestic life in the creation of republican ideology, the family home—the site of production and consumption of fiction, as well as a favored subject—was in no way a free space. Indeed, at that time the home was as politicized a space via the discourse of republican wife- and motherhood as any of the sites of corporate assembly that Stallybrass and White list. While sentimental discourse itself may have authorized women to write, enabling them to use the home as site, inspiration, and setting of their work, the appropriation of the novel by female voices at times elicited venomous reactions in American public life; critics, both contemporaneous and throughout the first three quarters of the twentieth century, often responded by dismissing these and later female-authored sentimental texts precisely because of their domesticity, begetting a vicious cycle in which the domestic was itself devalued because of its prominence in these texts, and so on. These attacks on the novel signal not just a reaction against fiction per se but perhaps more importantly an attempt to control who speaks, when, where, and with what authority.[51]

How, then, did female writers and male writers of less privilege negotiate within a paradigm of republican ideology that effectively excluded them or limited their rights as citizens and, further, within an environment not especially nurturing of domestic productions? *Intricate Relations* argues that the repetitive tropes of early American sentimental fiction (and indeed many of these novels feature similar plots, themes, and characters) themselves speak to the uncertain status of the fiction writer—whether male or female—in the early Republic era. Over and over again, American novels feature plots revolving around self-discipline, seduction, female madness, and economic speculation, and it is these broad-based, pervasive, and intertwined concerns that give shape to *Intricate Relations*.

One way to understand this repetition is as an important feature of the genre "contract" of the sentimental novel in the United States. As Fredric Jameson has suggested, "Genres are essentially literary institutions, or social contracts between a writer and a specific public."[52] A subgenre such as sentimental fiction operates under a special kind of genre contract that shapes readers' expectations and interpretations of a text. Hence certain tropes appear repeatedly, as if their very repetition legitimates the novels in which they appear. Fiction writers of less privilege—regardless of sex—typically negotiate within the paradigm of these understood conventions (although they at times question these same conventions), while stylistic differences and ambiguity are more likely to appear in the writings of more privileged (e.g. male, educated, and urbanized) writers like Charles Brockden Brown and Hugh Henry Brackenridge. Fulfilling the genre contract—even if that contract was itself under attack—thus represented one way for writers of less privilege or status to legitimate their role as authors.

Another, more interesting way to understand this repetition is as the expression of widespread cultural anxieties about the intricate relations of sex and economics that Brockden Brown identifies in "Walstein's School of History." Placed within a meaningful interdisciplinary, Anglo-American context, the prevalence of the epistolary mode and the repetition of such tropes as self-discipline, seduction, female madness, and economic speculation signal not aesthetic failures but loci of cultural anxiety and energy. Fiction functioned as an accessible forum through which to articulate cultural apprehensions and explore how various economic and sexual aspirations might be muted, mediated, or controlled in order for the Republic to function smoothly. Sexual and economic relations are explored by and within the novel as heuristics, as means of mapping and reforming these same sets of relations. The flexibility and plasticity of the novel made it the perfect genre to express the ambiguities and the social and cultural anxieties of America in the post-Revolutionary era. As Mikhail Bakhtin explains, "The novelistic word . . . registers with extreme subtlety the nicest shifts and oscillations of the social atmosphere; it does so, moreover, while registering it as a whole, in all of its aspects" (300). By exploring the relationships between fiction and other modes of discourse, we can better understand how early American writers used the novel as a vehicle for participation in public discourse.

Fiction makes up only one piece in the puzzle that represents a national literary culture, and a literary culture is only one aspect of a national culture. Other types of books, magazines, pamphlets, and newspapers likewise contributed to the development of a literary culture, with newspapers playing one of the more important roles. Yet, building upon the work of Benedict Anderson in *Imagined Communities*, Nancy Armstrong and Leonard Tennenhouse have suggested that fiction's contribution may have been equal to, or perhaps even greater than, the influence of newspapers in creating national cultures.[53] Certainly fiction, like national newspapers, enabled writers to *imagine* a United States and explore the problems besetting individuals and the nation. Fiction alone in the post-Revolutionary United States could not create a national cultural identity, nor could it alone resolve complicated issues surrounding gender relations, economics, and sexuality, for fiction was only one mode of writing in a sophisticated system of print cultures encompassing newspapers, magazines, pamphlets, and the local, national, and international book trades. Yet fiction readily incorporated the authority of other kinds of discourse and made their power its own. Reading early American fiction alongside and against other modes of discourse, including religious and pedagogical writings, and political, medical, and economic theory, highlights the contested nature of the emerging bourgeois culture of the early national era. Taken together, these very different kinds of narrative reveal that a contested struggle for cultural authority was taking place; this juxtaposition of genres reveals the intricate, and conflicted, workings of discourses of power and authority about the individual, institutions, and the nation, for fiction of this era explicitly takes as its subject the formation of economic and sexual desires, especially as related to the emerging middle class. Further, fiction's ability to appropriate the authority of other modes of discourse both informed and enabled its engagement with contemporary issues and furthered its contributions to the creation of a national culture. A brief overview of the chapters of this work will suggest some of the ways these intricate relations among sexual and economic desires manifest themselves in early American fiction, as well as how gender informs them.

The first chapter sets the context for my study by examining the prevalence of epistolary fiction during the early national era. While the novel as a genre brought readers into close relation with the text and its characters, the very process feared by cultural critics of the novel, epistolarity brought the reader even further into the text, suggesting intimacy in the midst of an increasingly impersonal public world. Yet writers of epistolary fiction were in many ways the most conciliatory with regard to the qualms proffered by critics, pointing to their novels' kinship with the advice tradition in a way that harmonized with republican ideals. Choosing to write epistolary fiction, I argue, was an ideological choice, as well as an aesthetic one. Early American letter fiction emphasizes self-scrutiny and self-discipline as means of promoting a Lockean educational paradigm that ideally would produce a republic of readers prepared to govern and protect themselves in a world filled with dangerous strangers. The pervasiveness of the epistolary format during the early national era typifies a complex cultural ideology and methodology concerning education, habit, discipline, and character formation, all of which depended upon advanced literacy and writing skills. I read epistolary fiction against a context of pedagogical literature of all kinds, including British works such as John Locke's *Some Thoughts Concerning Education*, Adam Smith's *The Theory of Moral Sentiments*, and Isaac Watts's *Logic* and *The Improvement of the Mind*, as well as a wide range of American religious and secular advice literature. William Hill Brown's *The Power of Sympathy*, Judith Sargent Murray's *Story of Margaretta*, Hannah Foster's *The Coquette* and *The Boarding School*, and Sukey Vickery's *Emily Hamilton*, I argue, all reveal their origins in the aforementioned pedagogical literature, modeling a program of self-knowledge, self-discipline, and self-control—traits that would come to be central to bourgeois subjectivity and which could be attained through the kind of moral mentoring illustrated so well by epistolary fiction. By melding advice literature with the sentimental novel, American epistolary fiction attempted to render fiction palatable to figures of cultural authority, while simultaneously rendering precepts of self-discipline palatable to youthful readers.

If early American epistolary fiction shows readers the advantages of self-examination and self-regulating behavior, then other modes of sentimental fiction illustrate the dangers of failing to discipline the passions, especially sexual passions. During the early national period, when enforcement of laws governing sexual behavior declined just as the rates for premarital pregnancies climbed to a level unmatched until the 1960s, fiction offered a forum for exploring the consequences of extramarital sexual behavior in a republic anxious about the virtue of the American "fair," coded language for middling and elite white women, who were increasingly assuming the burden of symbolizing the nation itself in the national imaginary. Female insanity appears repeatedly in novels as a special kind of marker, a fictional coding of sorts, to underline unwise expenditures of sexual desire such as adultery. These lapses are invariably marked as female failings, for regardless of the fact that fornication and adultery require two individuals, the simple fact is that women, not men, go mad in early American fiction.

In chapter 2, I read Susanna Rowson's *Charlotte Temple* and *Lucy Temple*, Samuel Relf's *Infidelity*, Sally Wood's *Dorval*, and the anonymous *Amelia; or, the Faithless Briton* alongside the medical writings of Benjamin Rush, Philippe Pinel, and John Haslem. These medical theorists argue that the guilt resulting from adultery and fornication—or any serious failure to control the passions—almost invariably induces insanity. Adultery and fornication continued to be illegal in the United States, but both historically and in the world of the novel, these crimes ceased being punished through the legal system. Instead, the intense emphasis on internalized discipline in pedagogical literature and epistolary fiction suggests that responsibility for maintaining—and punishing lapses in—female virtue rested with the individual. Fiction became a surrogate for law as it assisted in the pathologizing of extramarital sexual desire and helped to provide social structure during a period of changing attitudes towards sexual morality. Fictionalized madness and death following lapses in chastity—or even the appearance of such a lapse—dramatized the costs to the individual of the loss of chastity, for chastity was the most valuable form of property that most women possessed. Criminal law might no longer publicly punish those guilty of sexual transgressions, but the novel showed readers the inevitable punishment of those who transgressed against their families and communities. By rereading the trope of female insanity through the lens of pervasive medical discourse on insanity and the laws governing sexual behavior, I conclude that there was a cultural shift in the early Republic era in the policing of white, female sexuality from a legal authority to the sphere of medical, social, and narrative authority.

Sex and property, in broad terms, constitute in the early American novel gendered but homologous forms of expenditure and exchange; whereas regulation of sexual behavior figures largely as an area of concern for women, regulation of economic behavior, encompassing the acquisition and disposition of property of all kinds, serves as a masculine corollary. In the years following the Revolution, changing economic conditions wrought both hope and disappointment in the new United States as opportunities for economic opportunities expanded, but the fabled civic virtue of the war years gave way to profit-oriented individualism. Luxury, gambling, economic speculation, and international commerce, both by-products and driving forces behind increasing materialism, became loci of anxiety to dismayed republicans throughout the United States. Luxury, in the connotative lexicon of eighteenth-century America, came to signify not only material goods, but also a sophisticated, anglicized lifestyle in polite society, the obverse of the republican ideal and as threatening in its own way to the individual and to republican conceptions of virtue as was unchecked female sexuality.

Americans began authoring their own novels at precisely the time when this post-colonial economy was in flux, and many of these novels seek to unpack this complex of interrelated economic behaviors by pointing to the possibilities and dangers inherent in a capitalist economy that placed grave demands upon trust between individuals. Novelists were not alone in their concern; poets, political writers, and belletrists, regardless of their political orientation, likewise expressed considerable anxiety about balancing economic self-interest and civic virtue. I argue, in chapter 3, that reading novels alongside political pamphlets, economic tracts, and belles lettres reveals how early American fiction synthesized contemporary economic concerns and intervened in economic discourse during the 1790s and the first decades of the nineteenth century. Consistently engaged with economic issues facing Americans of the rising middle-class, fiction helped rehabilitate international commerce as a virtuous economic practice, albeit one best displaced to other parts of the world, and at the same time imagined economic desire as a specifically masculine prerogative. Novels such as Rebecca Rush's *Kelroy* and Wood's *Dorval* legitimate trade by distinguishing it from speculation and gambling of all kinds. In these novels, the figure of the gambler and speculator points to the dangers inherent in the rising national capitalist economy and the need to balance private and civic interests; the merchant trader, however, not only benefits himself, but also advances his extended family and community. As an important form of vernacular print culture, American fiction patriotically affirmed the individual and national benefits of the newly-formed United States's trading freedom and encouraged increased American commerce with the rest of the world. Concomitantly, the participation of writers such as Rush and Wood in bringing this bourgeois agenda into being illustrates American women's vested interest in issues that extend outside the home and the domestic sphere. Yet illustrating the simultaneously liberalizing and constraining tendencies of the novel, fiction also constructs economic advancement as the responsibility and privilege solely of white men; it is a privilege, however, that is not without its dangers.

In chapter 4, I continue to explore the gendering of economic behavior in early American fiction. Whereas in the first three chapters I focus on the role of the individual in regulating, or not regulating, his or her behavior, this chapter examines the growing influence of liberal individualism by tracing the fictional substitution of an economy of credit for one of individual virtue; at the same time, this chapter considers the role of traditional institutions such as the family, community, and the prison in regulating male social and economic behavior. Economically dispossessed and profligate men play a central role in early American fiction, enabling writers of fiction to problematize the changing nature of the American economy. As communities became increasingly dependent upon credit in order to establish relationships and categorize individuals, they became less able to control the social behavior of their members. The mere appearance of wealth and mastery of polite behavior guaranteed acceptance as the American culture depicted in fiction shifted from an economy of virtue, which placed a premium on individual character, to an economy of credit, in which the presumption of social worth is predicated on credit status; the fluidity of credit likewise entailed increased geographical mobility in post-Revolutionary society. The pervasive critique of politeness in early American fiction beginning in the 1790s suggests that novelists saw politeness as the *lingua franca* of this economy of credit; rather than simply trumpet republican virtue, novels instead illustrate the dangerous deceptions that polished behavior and the appearance of wealth enable when communities institute an economy of credit and appearance. Such novels as Murray's *Story of Margaretta*, Foster's *The Coquette*, and the anonymous *The Gambler* foreground anxieties about incorrigible or unregulated men, pointing to the waning power of communities to discipline their unruly male members while exploring alternate forms of social authority. I conclude this chapter with an extended discussion of Charles Brockden Brown's *Arthur Mervyn*, a synthetic text that revolves around uncontrolled economic greed and speculation, insurance fraud, and illegitimate sexual desire among the merchant class, thereby invoking the concerns central to post-Revolutionary American culture and prevalent in the fiction of the time.

Finally, in the epilogue, I consider how sexual and economic relations, foregrounded in the novels of the early Republic era, begin to recede into the background in the early decades of the nineteenth century. The issues that dominate the fiction of earlier years do not disappear entirely, as illustrated by Sarah Savage's 1814 novel *The Factory Girl*, but they do transform. The extended attention that the novel pays to the virtuous poor, I argue, suggests the imminent expansion of the subjects of the novel beyond the anxieties that middle-class white authors of early American fiction felt on their own behalf. This expansion of subject matter includes not only the concerns of the poor, slaves, and Native Americans, but also the concerns that these groups elicited among authors, who continued to be largely white and middle class; at the same time, the imposition of bourgeois values onto these formerly excluded groups reveals the limitations of nineteenth-century liberalism. Better than any other nineteenth-century novel, Harriet Beecher Stowe's *Uncle Tom's Cabin* illustrates precisely how the anxieties that so perplexed novelists of the early Republic came to be subsumed by these new interests; at the same time, Stowe exposes the economic underside of slavery and the havoc wrought by economic speculation and gambling. Economic speculation, rather than being at the heart of *Uncle Tom's Cabin*, instead provides its genesis, as Mr. Shelby's failed economic speculations force him to sell Tom and Harry. The consequences of illicit sex, although it, like Mr. Shelby's economic speculation, takes places off-stage, likewise underlie *Uncle Tom's Cabin*. Although the context differs dramatically, sex, property, and the intricate relations between them ring as true for Stowe's *Uncle Tom's Cabin* in 1852 as they did for the novelists of the early Republic. The resonance and tremendous popularity of *Uncle Tom's Cabin* in the nineteenth century owes in part, I propose, to Stowe's astute repackaging of themes and tropes that had been an important part of the horizon of expectations for American writers and readers for the preceding six decades.

1

A Manner Unquestionably More Agreeable

The Politics, Aesthetics, and Praxis of Epistolary Fiction

> *Maria to Lucy*:
> Dear, dear! I've no patience! Stay always at home?
> You may if you please, but so will not I.
> It would mope me to death, I should certainly die . . .
> To stay prosing at home with mother and you;
> And then for amusement; perhaps we may drone
> Over Gregory's letters, or Madam Chapone. . . .
> No amusement in such stupid books can I see . . .
> Were I to read much of such stuff it would craze me,
> I hate such nonsensical trash.
> —Susanna Rowson, "Dialogue for Two Ladies,"
> from *A Present for Young Ladies* (1811)

ONE OF THE MORE curious phenomena of the literary culture of the early national period is the extraordinary and enduring popularity of the epistolary novel among American readers and writers. At the same time that the epistolary novel was waning in popularity in Britain, it was enjoying a resurgence of popularity among American readers. While British and continental novelists were experimenting with a variety of narrative devices to develop plots and convey mental states, American novelists continued to rely on the epistolary mode from the end of the Revolution until the early decades of the nineteenth century. Critics of British and European fiction have striven to place the epistolary novel in the context of the development and literary history of the novel itself, but critics of American fiction have not, by and large, known what to make of the persistence of epistolarity during the early national era.[1] Although the epistolary status of various individual works has been the subject of recent essays and book chapters, none of these addresses these underlying questions: Why did epistolary fiction persist, even thrive, in the United States, comprising more than 30 percent of the novels written by Americans between 1789 and 1814, as well as a large percentage of the British novels most favored by American readers?[2] Why did writers and readers find epistolary fiction so engaging? Finally, how did writers and readers *use* epistolary fictions? Here I propose to explore how and why the epistolary form was so ideally suited to the cultural politics and social practices of the early Republic and hence so widely appreciated by American writers and readers, for epistolarity was not only an aesthetic narrative choice, but also an ideological one: While virtually all early American novels emphasize the importance of self-examination and discipline, epistolary fiction most clearly and consistently articulates this concern, for it creates a world in which the individual's conduct is constantly mirrored, much as Adam Smith postulates in *The Theory of Moral Sentiments*. By melding the philosophical content of advice texts with the voyeuristic thrills of letter fiction, late eighteenth-century American epistolary fiction aptly expresses prevailing Lockean pedagogical theories about reading, writing, and the importance of habit formation—skills of crucial importance, especially for the bourgeois woman and the polity whose symbolic weight she was increasingly coming to bear.

As is commonly acknowledged, the eighteenth century was the great age of the letter in English-speaking America, as well as Britain and the Continent. David S. Shields has suggested that the personal letter in the United States assumed even greater importance in the 1780s and 1790s in response to a flourishing, yet increasingly impersonal, print culture. The nature of the letter underwent a change as well. As Shields explains, "With this expansion came a shift of emphasis away from the individual letter as an event of communication to the idea of correspondence in which an enduring relationship in feeling might be cultivated." Even within the arena of print, Shields asserts, the genre of the letter played a major role, for the letter "was put to service in overcoming the impersonality of print marketed to an unknown audience."[3] Thus the letter appears in political, economic, travel, conduct, and religious works, as well as in epistolary fiction, as a form universally familiar to readers and as a means to counter the formality of print. The special appeal of epistolary fiction, which emphasizes, above all else, feelings, intimacy, and relationships, can be best understood when measured against the culture-wide appeal of the familiar letter itself. Abigail Adams emphasizes the circularity of this effect in a letter to her niece, Lucy Cranch, in which she praises Samuel Richardson: "I believe Richardson has done more towards embellishing the present age, and teaching them the talent of letter-writing, than any other modern I can name."[4]

While influenced by its British antecedents, American epistolary fiction differs in important ways. Early American novels frequently emphasize the intersection of the mind and body through sentiment and sensibility, with sentiment suggesting the capacity for fine feelings and sensibility suggesting a corresponding expressiveness of the body, but never to quite the same degree as do their British counterparts.[5] As John Mullan explains in *Sentiment and Sociability* about the British novels of the mid-eighteenth century, "It is the body which acts out the powers of sentiment. These powers, in a prevailing model of sensibility, are represented as greater than those of words. Tears, blushes, and sighs—and a range of postures and gestures—reveal conditions of feeling which can connote exceptional virtue or allow for intensified forms of communication. Feeling is above all observable, and the body through which it throbs is peculiarly excitable and responsive."[6] The expression of such exquisite sensibility pervades the British epistolary novel, most obviously in works such as Samuel Richardson's *Pamela* and *Clarissa*, yet sensibility never played so large a role in any of the more popular American titles other than Susanna Rowson's *Charlotte Temple*, a novel which one would expect to dramatize the state of the physical body, given Rowson's own experiences as an actress and dramatist.

While Rowson's novel and imported epistolary fictions such as *Pamela* and *Clarissa* continued to be popular with American readers throughout the late eighteenth and early nineteenth centuries (especially in abridged formats), American writers modeled the sentimental epistolary novel to both reflect and shape civic imperatives and cultural values. Consequently, American epistolary fiction de-emphasizes the physical body and elevates instead the sentimental, yet disciplined, mind. Concomitantly, rather than accenting the process of seduction and its effect on the physical body, most American epistolary fiction emphasizes the consequences of seduction, as well as ways to prevent seduction and promote virtue through self-knowledge, self-discipline, and self-control, ideals which pervade public discourse, both fictional and pedagogical, during the latter half of the eighteenth century.[7] This kind of fiction was the perfect antidote to the criticism of fiction that prevailed during this time, much of which was inspired by followers of the Scottish Common Sense philosophers, who were suspicious of the imagination and anxious for literature to serve an elevating purpose.[8]

While virtually all of the earliest American novels take up, to some degree or another, the importance of such self-regulation, epistolary fiction most clearly and consistently articulates this concern, for it creates a world in which the individual's conduct is constantly mirrored and scrutinized, much as Adam Smith postulates in *The Theory of Moral Sentiments*. Through this focus, late eighteenth-century American epistolary fiction aptly expresses prevailing Lockean pedagogical theories about reading, writing, and the importance of habit formation. In this chapter, I intend to examine epistolarity as a deliberate aesthetic choice, representative of a secularized ideology and complex cultural methodology with regard to education, habit, discipline, and character formation—all dependent upon advanced literacy and writing skills.[9] While pedagogical materials represent self-discipline as its own reward, essential if it is to be properly internalized, fiction also suggests the civic and social value of such discipline. The civic dimension of this equation was crucial; the virtue of white, bourgeois American women was increasingly linked to the moral health of Columbia itself in the national imaginary.[10]

Epistolary fiction illustrates ways to achieve a virtuous transparency of character—an important trope in American social thought—through a process of examination and self-discipline. In such novels as William Hill Brown's *The Power of Sympathy*, Judith Sargent Murray's *Story of Margaretta*, Hannah Foster's *The Coquette* and *The Boarding School*, and Sukey Vickery's *Emily Hamilton*, letters are used to exhibit moral development (or failure) ostensibly unmediated by a narrator. Reading and writing skills embody both disciplinary tools and a means of demonstrating evidence of this requisite self-discipline, with letters providing stable representations of the female self that can be measured against cultural ideals of female behavior. While the educative focus of these novels suggests literacy and writing skills are means of empowerment for women, as Cathy N. Davidson has demonstrated in *Revolution and the Word*,[11] these novels simultaneously send readers strangely mixed messages by advocating a conservative, repressive process of self-discipline to be implemented via these same skills. For this reason, I read many of these novels as being both more complicated (and more conservative) than some other critics have recently read them. In the world of the novel, this self-control ideally empowered bourgeois women to direct social relations at a time when women were denied the opportunity to practice the liberal self-determination promised by revolutionary rhetoric, for the same writing and reading skills used to examine one's own character could also be used by the perspicuous to "read" or decipher the characters of those around her.

The deliberate aesthetic choice of epistolarity and the self-reflective conduct it typically promotes provided American writers of fiction—especially female writers—with a defensible position from which to venture into the sphere of public discourse. By marrying the philosophical content and pedagogical style of advice literature with the sentimental novel, American epistolary fiction attempted to render fiction more palatable to figures of cultural authority, while simultaneously rendering precepts of self-discipline more palatable to youthful readers. In the best, most positive cases, these epistolary fictions epitomize the optimism of the Enlightenment, with its belief in the potential of the individual to shape and represent his or her own character; but in other cases these fictions suggest an almost fetishistic obsession with discipline and appearance, with form and formality, as they become less a way of representing an authentic self than of manufacturing an idealized, self-denying, bourgeois man or woman.

The Importance of Writing in Character Formation

Throughout the eighteenth century, the western European-influenced pedagogical and medical theory prevalent in American public discourse almost uniformly emphasized the importance of self-knowledge, self-discipline, and self-control. This organic view of character formation evolved from a several-centuries-long genealogy of British and continental pedagogical and advice literature.[12] In the United States, Enos Hitchcock, a prominent Rhode Island minister, brigade chaplain in the Continental Army, and author of *Memoirs of the Bloomsgrove Family* (1790) and *The Farmer's Friend, or the History of Mr. Charles Worthy* (1793), didactic novels which themselves provide examples of self-discipline, propagated the central tenets of this discourse of discipline throughout his nonfiction works. Since Hitchcock was both a product and popularizer of this school of thought, his works serve as an excellent introduction to American interpretations of this discourse.[13]

In his 1785 sermon *A Discourse on Education,* Hitchcock uses a popular eighteenth-century organic metaphor, comparing young people to plants, to discuss the issue of character formation. He explains, "The mind, like the infant plant, is, in its first stages, feeble and tender; like that, it is capable of growth and enlargement, and may receive almost any direction, or impression you please to give it. If left untutored, it becomes the sport of every passion; but if informed, and guided by a suitable education, it will produce noble and worthy fruits."[14] Hitchcock expresses tremendous optimism about the potential for human growth and development, about the power of humans to harness the mind and the passions. "Harnessing," rather than "repressing," is indeed the optimal word to describe this view of human nature; as he elaborates, "The faculties of the human soul are in themselves noble and excellent, and capable of continual enlargement—the more the soul thinks and reasons, the more capable it becomes of that noble exercise—And it may be externally increasing in knowledge and wisdom, making perpetual advances toward perfection—Bending forward to the excellence of superior natures, unbroken by exercise and unimpaired by time—Receiving new accessions of bliss and glory from its perpetual approaches toward the fountain of all perfection" (7). Hitchcock's buoyant optimism undoubtedly springs from his hopes for the future of the United States; there is a definite political edge to his rhetoric, for he explains that without the education he believes is so necessary, "the rising generation would grow up uninformed and without principle; their ideas of freedom would degenerate into licentious independence; and they would fall a prey to their own animosities and contentions" (10). Thus his advocacy of education and self-control stems in part from his desire to see Americans educated so they may responsibly safeguard their liberties—something they can do only once their own desires are suitably directed. He later continues his organic metaphor, adding "—If the principles of virtue are early implanted in the mind they will take deep root, and produce the most happy fruits—If a foundation is seasonably laid in the mind by regular instruction, men will learn to think rationally and soberly upon subjects of moral duty, and Christian faith—they will be able to enquire candidly after truth, and determine, impartially, what is their duty" (12). While Hitchcock's *Discourse on Education* exemplifies the popular notion of harnessing the passions through relentless self-regulation, he did not originate this model of behavior. To produce a cultural ideology that stressed the importance of self-examination and regulation via writing, Anglo-Americans writing in the latter half of the eighteenth century in a variety of discourses—among them education, medicine, religion, moral philosophy, and epistolary fiction—melded together decades of British and continental pedagogical and advice literature, as well as the moral philosophy of the Scottish Enlightenment writers, whose profound influence on the American educational system peaked in the 1790s.[15] In this environment, the personal letter assumed profound importance.

The works of John Locke provide a critical starting point to trace this convergent genealogy of educational, medical, religious, and philosophical thought. Locke's works were well known in eighteenth-century British America, and his educational theories permeated American discourse about education and habit formation, not only via his own works, but also through works by other British writers of educational and advice tracts, since the pedagogical works most often reprinted in British America tended themselves to be derivative of or influenced by Locke's theories.[16] So pervasive were Locke's ideas that even Richardson's eponymous epistolary heroine Pamela is seen reading and critiquing Locke's work in the seldom-read continuation of that novel.

Although many of Locke's works are important in the formation of American culture, central to my purposes here is his *Some Thoughts Concerning Education*, first published in Britain in 1693. Virtually every commentator on Locke acknowledges the centrality of this work to American educational theory. Gillian Brown, for example, in *The Consent of the Governed: The Lockean Legacy in Early American Culture*, a brilliant exposition of his influence, claims that "Locke's *Thoughts Concerning Education* was probably the most widely read and instituted pedagogical theory in eighteenth-century Anglo-American culture."[17] As Brown points out, Locke's theories not only guided the process through which early American children were schooled to establish authority over themselves and accept responsibility for their actions, but also informed the very works they read, whether schoolbooks such as *The New England Primer*, or entertaining works such as *Goody Two-Shoes* and *Giles Gingerbread*. This schooling process became of ever-greater importance in the early national era because, according to republican thought, the perpetuation of political liberty required that individuals understand the importance of governance of the self and demonstrate this by continually assenting to, or alternatively rejecting, the laws and customs of the new nation. Immersion in Lockean thought did not end with childhood. Indeed, the influence of Locke in Anglo-America extends to adult pleasure reading during the eighteenth century, as Brown suggests later in *The Consent of the Governed*, when she explores the role of the novel in exposing the unequal limits of consent as it applied specifically to women.[18]

While Brown is interested in the novel as a popular cultural vehicle used to explore the consequences and limits of consent for women, my own concern with the relationship between Lockean thought and the novel relates to the subgenre of epistolary fiction in particular and to the cultural weight granted to writing. The epistolary mode represented a deliberate means through which novelists could explore the cultural importance of individual and social control through thoughtful, reflective behavior. The ideological underpinning of most of these novels, which rely heavily on Locke's understanding of habit and self-discipline and thus reiterate contemporary pedagogical theory, served as a legitimating vehicle to public discourse for their authors, many of whom, as women, otherwise faced significant limitations on their ability to participate in public life.

Perhaps the most significant contribution of Locke's *Some Thoughts Concerning Education* to pedagogical theory is its secular emphasis on the power of habit to shape the character. As James Axtell explains in his introduction to Locke's educational writings, Locke's emphasis on training the mind in orderly habits of thought "is the mark that distinguished the *Education* from the dross of educational writings in the seventeenth century. With Locke the emphasis on education ceased to be placed on brain-stuffing and was firmly transferred to the *process* for the formation of character, or *habits*—a word always on his tongue—of mind and body."[19] Whether referring to bodily or mental fortitude (and Locke emphasizes both), "habit" is indeed the basis for Locke's educational program. Habits of virtue must be internalized, Locke explains, "For the Time must come, when they [children] will be past the Rod, and Correction."[20] Further, "Every man must some Time or other be trusted to himself, and his own Conduct; and he that is good, a vertuous and able Man, must be made so within. And therefore, what he is to receive from Education, what is to sway and influence his Life, must be something put into him betimes; Habits woven into the very Principles of his Nature" (§42, 146). Locke's program aims to train young men to monitor themselves in order to develop a sophisticated form of internalized discipline, an internalized monitor for their own conduct that will replace the figure of the parent. To this end, he consistently advocates mental discipline as superior to physical discipline in shaping character. With just a few exceptions such as open rebellion against parental authority, Locke disdains corporal punishment, believing that beatings are the "Root from whence spring all Vitious Actions, and the Irregularities of Life" (§48, 149). Instead, Locke proposes that parents alternately use "esteem" and "disgrace" to create a habituated discipline that eventually gains such sway over a child that he literally becomes his own monitor (§48, §56, and §60). Locke's educational program, expressed most clearly in *Some Thoughts Concerning Education*, came to influence pedagogical theorists in Western Europe and the British colonies throughout the eighteenth century; Jay Fliegelman labels it "a volume whose influence on eighteenth-century English culture and especially eighteenth-century English literature can hardly be overemphasized."[21] And, indeed, one need look no further than Benjamin Franklin's *Memoirs*, or Benjamin Rush's "An Inquiry into the Influence of Physical Causes Upon the Moral Faculty," to be assured of how deeply Locke's theories concerning habits likewise permeated American thought.[22] Although Locke refers specifically to the education of young gentlemen in this work, other educational writers soon applied his theories to both sexes, as would, much later, American novelists, who would particularize this theory for female letter writers. As I will argue later in this chapter, what epistolary fiction illustrates is whether or not, and how well, young men and women have developed internalized monitors of their own passions and whether they are habituated to control themselves.

Isaac Watts, the British psalmist and logician, was one of the most important popularizers of Lockean educational thought in British America, especially with regard to the role of writing in forming the character.[23] His *Logic: Or, the Right Use of Reason*, often used in British America as a college textbook, was designed to teach his readers how to apply logic and reason to everyday life and to offer a "humble assistance to divine revelation."[24] Watts wanted to teach his readers how to use the full potential of their minds, which he believed could be realized only by rigorous reflection. For this reason, he includes in his fifth chapter a lengthy section on mental improvement, which he divides into a three-step process for his readers to follow. First, he advocates, individuals must daily reflect upon what they have learned; next they must discuss this newfound knowledge with a friend (64). Finally he recommends, "Commit to writing some of the most considerable improvements which you daily make.... And here I think Mr. *Locke's* method of *adversaria*, or *common places*, which he describes in the end of his first volume of *posthumous works*, is the best" (Watts's emphasis) (*Logic* 64). The process does not stop here, however, for one should continually review one's conduct and thoughts after weeks, months, and years, in order "*To judge of your own improvement*" (*Logic* 64). Central to the process of monitoring the self are reading and writing, which function as memory aids as well as disciplinary tools in and of themselves, a concept which epistolary novelists will emphasize.

But merely reviewing one's character is not enough; Watts emphasizes the importance of learning mental discipline, proposing that his readers "*Learn to acquire a government over your ideas and your thoughts, that they may come when they are called, and depart when they are bidden.* There are some thoughts that rise and intrude upon us while we shun them; there are others that fly from us, when we should hold and fix them" (*Logic* 66). Watts postulates the mind and the imagination as unruly entities, controlled only by means of constant attention and strict discipline:

> If the *ideas* which you would willingly make the matter of your present meditation *are ready to fly from you*, you must be obstinate in the pursuit of them by an habit of fixed meditation; you must keep your soul to the work, when it is ready to start aside every moment, unless you will abandon yourself to be a slave to every wild imagination. It is a common, but it is an unhappy and a shameful thing, that every trifle that comes across the senses or fancy should divert us, that a buzzing fly should teaze our spirits, and scatter our best ideas.... [I]n order to help a wandering and fickle humour, it is proper to have a book or paper in our hands, which has some proper hints of the subject we design to pursue. We must be resolute and laborious, and sometimes conflict with ourselves, if we would be wise and learned. (*Logic* 66)

The mental discipline that Watts promulgates is not inherent—it is something that one must laboriously learn in youth and continue to practice in adulthood. And once again, Watts asserts, reading and writing foster this mental discipline.

Watts continues to emphasize a secularized form of self-government in his popular *Improvement of the Mind*, which, although it circulated for decades as an English import, was first published in the United States in 1793. Although Watts is commonly associated with religious discourse because of his musical adaptations of the psalms, both *Improvement of the Mind* and *Logic* are essentially secular works, for while the author acknowledges that self-government is an important part of the practice of religious faith, he also believes that self-discipline is essential to give direction "to all the purposes of human life in this world."[25] Mature self-discipline, as Watts understands it, builds upon a basis of self-control established in childhood. Watts explains, "Children should be instructed in the art of self government. They should be taught, as far as possible, to govern their thoughts; to use their wills to be determined by the light of their understandings, and not by headstrong and foolish humour; they should learn to keep the lower powers of nature under the command of their reason. They should be instructed to regulate their senses, their imagination, their appetites and their passions" (*Improvement of the Mind* 71).

Watts repeatedly stresses that children must be taught to use their reason for the purpose of self-knowledge. In fact, he considers self-knowledge part of the "[foundation] of human prudence" (84). To know one's self, according to Watts, "one should be taught to consider within himself, what is my temper and natural inclination; what are my most powerful appetites and my prevailing passions . . . what are the weaknesses and follies to which I am most liable, especially in the days of youth; what are the temptations and dangers that attend me. . . . A wise and just survey of all these things, and keeping them always in mind, will be of unspeakable use to us in the conduct of life, that we may set our chief guard upon our weak side, and where our greatest dangers lie . . ." (84). The importance of self-examination, then, is that it allows us to identify our weaknesses and frailties; by identifying these weaknesses, we are better prepared to prevent ourselves from giving in to temptation.

Just as Watts promulgated and amplified Locke's educational theories, so did other writers, both religious and secular, in turn echo Watts's sentiments about the responsibility of parents to promote self-examination and control of the passions. George Burder, for example, author of *The Closet Companion: or, An Help to Serious Persons, in the Important Duty of Self-Examination*, a pamphlet published in at least ten American editions between 1785 and 1810, advocates a similar regimen of self-examination, although his program has a decidedly religious emphasis. As both Watts and Burder acknowledge, one of the chief purposes of self-discipline is to control the passions. It is important to realize that most eighteenth-century educational theorists—both British and American—recognize passions and desires, including sexual desires, as a normal part of human experience. Further, as Albert O. Hirschman points out in *The Passions and the Interests*, harnessing the passions in order to render them useful to the individual as well as the state preoccupied such eighteenth-century British thinkers as Bernard Mandeville and Adam Smith.[26] Building upon this theoretical base, the Reverend John Bennett explains in *Strictures on Female Education; Chiefly as It Relates to the Culture of the Heart*, a popular British work frequently reprinted in the United States during the 1790s, that the passions are not wicked in and of themselves, since they "were implanted in us by the Deity, as the springs of all our actions." Rather, he explains, passions like love are "not to be eradicated, but only to be properly regulated and controlled. And it will always rage with a violence in private, proportioned to the unnatural restraint laid on it before the public eye."[27] John Walker, author of *The Teacher's Assistant in English Composition* (1804), includes a sample essay on the subject of the passions, in which he similarly explains that the passions "are the very stamina of our natures, the foundation stones on which our moral character is built." But, Walker urges, "[I]t ought to be the business of rational creatures to regulate and chastise these internal tyrants! how carefully ought they to guard against yielding to their first impulses, and how ought all our education to be directed to a proper government of our passions."[28] British writer Hannah More, too, recognizes the dual nature of the passions, arguing that the passions resemble fires, "which are friendly and beneficial when under proper direction; but if suffered to blaze without restraint, they carry devastation along with them, and, if totally extinguished, leave the benighted mind in a state of cold and comfortless inanity."[29] Enos Hitchcock shares these views, claiming that the chief duty of parents is to help their children learn self-discipline sufficient to control their passions (*A Discourse* 15).

Medical theories seconded this need for individual self-control, for benefit of both the individual body and mind and the body politic. Joseph Parrish, a student of Benjamin Rush and the author of *An Inaugural Dissertation on the Influence of the Passions Upon the Body in the Production and Cure of Diseases* (1805), advocates the need for self-control, claiming that cultivation of virtue serves as a preventive for disease, both mental and physical (48). John Haslam, a physician at Bethlehem Hospital in London and author of *Observations on Madness and Melancholy*, explicitly recommends education and self-control as means of preventing insanity and other mental disorders. He frighteningly ascribes most causes of insanity to "errors of education, which often plant in the youthful mind those seeds of madness which the slightest circumstances readily awaken into growth" (237). He adds, "It should be as much the object of the teachers of youth, to subjugate the passions, as to discipline the intellect" (237). Self-discipline, he postulates, leads to a healthy mind and, in a larger sense, to a virtuous, morally healthy populace. Whether through means of parents, teachers, or some other moral "monitor," many late eighteenth-century sentimental novels advocate precisely such a program of self-examination and carefully regulated conduct, and, conversely, illustrate the dangers of submitting to the passions, as I will discuss in the next chapter.

Although this extreme emphasis on self-control may seem repressive to modern readers, it is important to acknowledge the optimism underlying it, for these writers believed in the potential for human choice and individual development—but only after careful attention to forming proper habits.[30] Furthermore, Anglo-American writers saw education as the key to creating a virtuous Republic, which could exist only if populated by virtuous men and women. As Samuel Stanhope Smith, later to become president of Princeton, wrote to James Madison, individuals could train themselves to virtue by "calling forth different ideas & engaging [the mind] in a new train. By the repeated [e]xercise of this power man might have forever confirmed his innocence; fixed boundaries in practice to all his passions & as they were created in just proportion &c have established that proportion by habit which would become habitual virtue." In a fallen world such as we inhabit, he continues, one can recover this state of virtue by "recalling the lost images of virtue: contemplating them, & using them as motives of action, till they overcome those of vice again & again untill after repeated struggles, & many foils, they at length acquire the habitual superiority."[31] By this means, Smith believed, it would be possible to create an entire American society rigorously habituated to virtue. As a professor of moral philosophy, Smith, like so many of his contemporary educators, was profoundly influenced by the Scottish moral philosophers, who believed in the moral value of education, both for individuals and society at large. This desire for a Republic habituated to virtue pervades American writing, whether political, religious, pedagogical, or fictional.[32]

Advice Literature, Letters, and the Moral Preceptor

In addition to pedagogical, religious, and medical tracts such as those I have discussed, also influential throughout the eighteenth century was the genre of parental advice or conduct literature, popularized by texts such as Dr. John Gregory's *A Father's Legacy to His Daughters* and Philip D. Stanhope's *Letters to His Son*. During the 1790s, enough copies of both of these texts were sold in American editions alone (not counting numerous British imports) to qualify them as best sellers of the eighteenth century (Mott 304). This subgenre of advice literature was extremely influential in the development of American epistolary fiction, for as a body of work, advice literature continually urges its readership to open themselves up completely to trustworthy "friends." There is a great deal of latitude given to the word "friend," for it could refer to a parental "friend," in the sense that Philip

Stanhope, Lord Chesterfield, uses it in his *Letters to His Son*, or it could refer to a friend who stands in place of a parent as a mentor. For the purposes of epistolary fiction, self-examination alone could not create the self-regulating individual. Instead, what was needed was a monitor, a mentor, or a moral preceptor—all terms commonly used in epistolary fiction—a role that could be fulfilled by the correspondent(s) of the individual at the center of the text.[33] In fact, "mentor" became so commonplace a term in these texts that it lends itself to the title of Susanna Rowson's 1794 epistolary novel, *Mentoria; or The Young Lady's Friend*.

In *Mental Improvement*, a collection of educational dialogues designed to train the mind in observation, Priscilla Wakefield models for her young readers the proper relationship between parental monitors and children and reveals evolving attitudes toward child rearing. In this work, the idealized Harcourt family gathers around the fireplace in the evenings while the children explain the natural world and various manufacturing processes to their parents' satisfaction. The rationale for these dialogues is as Mr. Harcourt explains:

> Instruction should always be rendered agreeable, in order to be beneficial to those that are to learn. The skill of a preceptor consists in gaining the affections of his pupils, and conveying knowledge in so gradual and clear a manner, as to adapt it to the strength of the young student's capacity. Many a poor child has been disgusted with books and learning, by the heavy laborious tasks that have been given him to learn by heart, before he was capable of understanding them. The spirit of improvement, that distinguishes this enlightened age, shines in nothing more conspicuously than in education. (121)

In these dialogues, the parents intently focus their attention on their children. They critique each child's explanation, manner of speaking, and demeanor, while the children gratefully accept their smallest suggestions and thank them for their attention. This friendly mentorship vividly illustrates the new attitudes towards child-rearing prevalent in the eighteenth century. As Sophia, the eldest daughter of this family, explains, "I flatter myself, that there is not one of us, that is insensible to the privilege we enjoy, by the indulgence of our kind parents; particularly that of being permitted, nay, encouraged, to open our whole bosoms to them" (122). Although to readers of today the dialogues that take place between the parents and children may seem more akin to an inquisition, this preceptor-driven dialogue is very similar to the kinds of moral inquiry found in contemporaneous epistolary fiction.

Nowhere is this program better exemplified than in Judith Sargent Murray's serialized novel, *Story of Margaretta*. In this novel, the Gleaner and his wife, Mary Vigillius, closely monitor the intellectual and moral development of Margaretta, their adopted daughter.[34] The hallmark of their educational plan is its organized discipline: one hour of each day is devoted to the study of history, one hour is devoted to conversation upon Margaretta's reading, and one hour is dedicated to compositions based upon what Margaretta has learned during the day. While Margaretta's parents engage her in Socratic dialogues very like those in Wakefield's text, their carefully constructed educational plan also requires monitoring her moral development by engaging Margaretta in an epistolary correspondence with her mother—even though they live in the same house.[35] Once a week Margaretta writes a letter to her mother, from which, as her father explains, multiple benefits ensue: "[T]he penmanship of our charge was improved; the beautiful and elegant art of letter writing was by degrees acquired; and Margaretta was early accustomed to lay open her heart to her maternal friend."[36] This latter benefit is of course the most important, for their goal is to create a perfectly transparent young woman whose inner virtue will be visible for all to see. The Gleaner goes on to explain that sound pedagogical reasons (at least to his mind) justify this part of Margaretta's educational program: "Persons when holding the pen, generally express themselves more freely than when engaged in conversation; and if they have a perfect confidence in those whom they address, the probability is, that, unbosoming themselves, they will not fail to unveil the inmost recesses of their souls—thus was Margaretta properly and happily habituated to disclose, without a blush, each rising thought to her, on whom the care of preparing her for the great career of life had devolved" (60–61). Mr. and Mrs. Vigillius carefully analyze Margaretta's letters, as they do all aspects of her moral development. Her letters to her mother are to be, in diary-like fashion, intimate and revealing, yet this revelation will subject her to her parents' scrutiny. Richard Brodhead, in speaking of a similar instance of parental scrutiny as it actually occurred decades later between Louisa May Alcott and her mother, describes this kind of interaction as a "discipline of love." Alcott's mother regularly read and commented on her daughter's diary, a process of surveillance intended to shape her daughter's thoughts, feelings, and compositional style.[37] The use to which Alcott's diary was put, as a sort of moral testing ground, differs dramatically from our current understanding of the diary as an essentially private form, in which the diary represents, as Jürgen Habermas labels it, "a letter addressed to the sender."[38] At the same time, the letter-as-moral-testing-ground enables us to imagine personal writing of all kinds in a different context, one in which personal writing was neither simply a means of communication, nor simply a means of self-expression, but rather stood for a fixed, concrete representation of the interior self that could be measured against cultural ideals of female behavior.

The scrutiny evoked by letters in the epistolary novel is crucial, for letters create a necessary mirror of individual social conduct like that Adam Smith describes in *The Theory of Moral Sentiments*. Smith suggests that the popularity in the eighteenth century of diary keeping, letter writing, and—by my extension—epistolary fiction, owes much to this "mirroring" function. The man or woman raised in isolation from other humans, Smith explains, would be unable to evaluate his or her own character or actions, for we depend on society to act as a "mirror" or "looking-glass"; we can adjudge our actions only after seeing them through the eyes of other people. Smith explains:

> [W]e either approve or disapprove of our own conduct, according as we feel that, when we place ourselves in the situation of another man, and view it, as it were, with his eyes and from his station.... We can never survey our own sentiments and motives, we can never form any judgment concerning them, unless we remove ourselves, as it were, from our own natural station, and endeavour to view them as at a certain distance from us. But we can do this in no other way than by endeavouring to view them with the eyes of other people, or as other people are likely to view them.[39]

Writing, especially personal writing that will be shared with others, continually invokes the social mirror. Letters and the self-reflective behavior they invite make their writers (whether real or fictional) hyper-conscious of "the eyes of other people." External observers of our behavior awaken what Smith has famously called "the man within the breast," who will then become qualified to serve as a spectator and interior judge of our behavior (256). Epistolary fiction, an aesthetic, belletristic rendering of these social theories, similarly creates a social world where, ideally, conduct is continually mirrored.

Like Wakefield, Murray, and Smith, the writers of numerous other eighteenth-century works invoke similar notions about the necessity of a moral preceptor, a person who will reflect one's conduct. Although Wakefield's and Murray's texts place parents in the monitorial role, other advice tracts recommend older friends as well as peers for the role of moral preceptor. In recognition of their ideological similarities, these advice works tend to be grouped in anthologies. These collections are often arranged around a theme, such as lugubrious advice literature from ailing parents. One such anthology is *The Young Lady's Parental Monitor* (1792), a reprint of a British work that includes Gregory's *A Father's Legacy to His Daughters*, *Lady Pennington's Unfortunate Mother's Advice to Her Absent Daughter*, and the Marchioness de Lambert's *Advice of a Mother to Her Daughter*, all of which emphasize affectionate bonds between parents and children. Another such anthology, edited by American publisher Mathew Carey, is *The Lady's Pocket Library* (1792). Carey's anthology also includes *Lady Pennington's Unfortunate Mother's Advice to Her Absent Daughter*, a work often reprinted in American anthologies. Lady Pennington advises her daughter to find one true friend to whom she can open her heart. To such a friend, Lady Pennington says, "let your heart be unreservedly open. Conceal no secret thought, disguise no latent weakness, but bare your bosom to the faithful probe of honest friendship, and shrink not, if it smarts beneath the touch; nor with tenacious pride dislike the person who freely dares to condemn some favorite foible; but, ever open to conviction, hear with attention, and receive with gratitude, the kind reproof that flows from tenderness. When sensible of a fault, be ingenuous in the confession; be sincere and steady in the correction of it."[40] The kind of intimate friendship that Lady Pennington advocates is precisely that modeled in American epistolary fiction, whereby correspondents must reveal themselves to one another in order to demonstrate and maintain their virtuous status, yet do so knowing that their friends will reprove them for even the smallest transgressions.

Parental Legacies (1804), yet another compendium of popular advice texts, describes similar notions of friendship in *Advice from a Lady of Quality to Her Children*, an essay translated from the French. The "Lady of Quality," too, advises her children to seek out one true friend, telling them, "But there is nothing, my children, more agreeable or useful to mankind than friendship: without this, the happiest life leaves a vacuum which can never be filled. There are a thousand cases in which we have need of counsel or assistance; a thousand situations in which we derive comfort from the sight of a friend: he is a support in our adversity; a MENTOR, to recall our wandering steps."[41] The "Lady of Quality's" advice is very much to the point of my discussion of epistolary fiction, so I will quote her description of friendship at some length:

> You must penetrate into the very soul of him whom you wish really to know: if you listen only to the public voice, you will find your judgment equally divided betwixt satire and panegyric, and you will not know which side to take....
>
> But how, you will ask, shall we get at the heart of him with whom we seek to be united in friendship? Your own understanding will teach you the way that will make you attentive to those words and actions which are purely natural, and unpremeditated; and which unfold the inmost recesses of the heart. That will teach you to watch the prevailing inclination of the person whom you wish to take into your bosom; and to attend to his different pursuits and connexions: that will shew you in that mirror of the mind, the eyes, whether there be sweetness, anger, or pride in him.
>
> It is easy to study others, when we have been accustomed to study ourselves; but unhappily, this self-inquiry is too much neglected. We read, with eagerness, books on every subject; but we do not give ourselves the trouble to search into that instructive volume, the human heart: thus it deceives us every moment; and makes us pay dearly for our negligence in this matter. (123–24)

The "Lady of Quality" thus advises her readers first to know themselves. Only then can one judge others truly, for this self-knowledge will provide one with a sort of moral yardstick by which to estimate the characters of others and to distinguish between the public and intimate personas.

American epistolary fiction shares this fixation with the idea of creating a transparent self through means of writing—writing that will make virtue visible and will enable the reader (whoever that might be) to see within the heart of the writer. Undoubtedly the fact that so many mothers in early American novels are conspicuous either by their absence or for their ineffectual roles—a fact noted by Davidson and others—explains the presence of female friends serving as surrogate monitors.[42] While Jay Fliegelman has argued in *Prodigals and Pilgrims* that one of the predominant analogies American writers used to describe the relationship between King George III and the colonies was that of the tyrannical patriarch who refused to recognize the autonomy of adult children, Michelle Burnham notes that also prominent was the analogy of Britain as the mother of a colonial daughter. In such a circumstance, it makes perfect sense, as Burnham claims, that these texts about absent mothers suggest that "the colonial daughter must be capable . . . of governing herself" (78). Yet, this language of monitoring and mentoring permeates many texts even when mothers *are* present.

A number of sociological and cultural factors particular to the early Republic may help explain the cultural preoccupation with self-discipline and the figure of the mentor, and the relationship of these tropes to the letter.

Sociological information about the decades immediately following the Revolution suggests that young women in the United States were experiencing unprecedented social and sexual freedom, subjects which I discuss in more detail in the next chapter. This freedom was a matter of grave public concern, so it is not surprising that fiction, a genre popular among young women and perfectly equipped to address such issues, should explore means of self-regulation. At the same time, other cultural forces such as increased educational opportunities for young women and the rise of seminaries and boarding schools encouraged the establishment of homosocial bonds across distances. Likewise, relocations caused by marriages, enhanced by the mobility of this society, would also have encouraged a broad cultural reliance on the personal letter. Fliegelman has summed up the changing role of the letter this way: "[T]he letter allowed one to reflect on his or her experience, to learn from it, and to reach out beyond the prescriptive world of the household and its roles. It enhanced the development of the self, just as the novel built around the letter asserted the claims of that self" (*Prodigals and Pilgrims* 29). The confluence of these and other related factors in all likelihood bolstered the popularity of epistles and the epistolary mode in America.

A combination of cultural influences, then, led to writing becoming conjoined with self-regulating conduct in sentimental fiction of the late eighteenth century. An excellent illustration of this point appears in the preface to *Dorval; or The Speculator*, where Sally Wood explicitly points to writing as an activity that will lend itself to self-regulating discipline for women. As a conciliatory gesture to conservative readers (and Wood's novels are, by and large, very conservative themselves), Wood grants that "*a female is never half so lovely, half so engaging or amiable, as when performing her domestic duties, and cheering, with smiles of unaffected good humor, those about her. But,*" she explains, "*there are some, who, forgetful of those sacred duties, or viewing them all in a circle very circumscribed, devote a large portion of time to dissipation, and such fashionable occupations, as waste many hours that might be devoted to better purposes.*" Wood argues that for such women, the act of writing might provide a reformative method of self-discipline: "*If a small share of that time [normally devoted to dissipation] were attached to the pen, I am certain no future author would agree with the Abbe Raynal, 'That America had produced but few persons of genius': Envy would be banished from society; and while a woman was drawing a picture of virtue and amiableness from imagination, she would imperceptibly follow the example and copy the portrait.*" Wood figures writing as a process of moral osmosis. Initially, the act of writing would prevent women from engaging in dissipated activities such as following fashion, gambling, or gossip, because their interests would be otherwise engaged. Further, making a logical leap, she assumes that women writers would write only of "virtue and amiableness"; in other words, if women were to write novels—as does Wood—she speculates that they would not write wicked or immoral books.[43] In fact, women writers would be rendered unable to write immoral works because of the properties that Wood supposes are inherent in writing. Finally, Wood assumes in a Lockean moment that, because women will be writing only of positive subjects, they will literally write their own characters. The only real action a woman must take on the road to virtue, then, is to pick up the pen.

For women (and men) who do not know what to write after they have picked up the pen, countless letter-writing manuals stand ready to advise would-be writers about both style and content. The letter-writing manual, a hybrid of etiquette book and what nearly qualifies as short fiction, is one of the more curious sub-genres of eighteenth-century pedagogical or advice literature. These letter-writing manuals vary greatly in style. At one end of the spectrum are utilitarian books designed for scriveners and businessmen that contain form letters that can be customized to fit the needs of a particular business. At the other end are texts that model forms of social correspondence; some of these include series of letters obviously intended for the reader's entertainment, since they do not offer practical models of correspondence.

Both British and American letters were endlessly recycled into new volumes, sometimes verbatim, and other times merely by borrowing the framework. Most of the letter-writing manuals published in the United States after the Revolution are customized for an American audience, including descriptions of American localities. Among the most popular are letters from errant children to parents, letters from daughters voicing unhappiness with their father's choice of a husband for them, courtship letters, rejection of courtship letters, letters consoling a beautiful woman disfigured by smallpox, etc. These more socially-oriented letter collections served as models for polite diction and correspondence, while simultaneously providing a form of voyeuristic entertainment.[44] In the latter respect, they continue to function much as did the earliest European collections of fictional correspondence, which led to the development of epistolary fiction. The subtitles of these letter manuals further indicate that they were intended to amuse; many, such as *The Universal Letter-Writer*, include the phrase "entertaining letters," and often these letters are sequenced together to provide mini-narratives.

Time and again, what these manuals argue is that letter writing is like a conversation—only better, because, as one manual argues quoting a Mr. Howell, "The tongue and the pen are both interpreters of the mind; but the pen the most faithful of the two: and as it has all the advantages of premeditation, it is not so apt to err, and leave things behind on a more authentic and lasting record."[45] Samuel Richardson, author of *Pamela* and *Clarissa*, the latter of which profoundly influenced early American epistolary fiction, expresses similar sentiments in a personal letter to Sophia Westcomb. Richardson writes, "I make no scruple to aver, that a correspondence by letters, written on occasions of necessary absence . . . gives the most desirable opportunities of displaying the force of friendship, that can be wished for by a friendly heart. This correspondence is, indeed, the cement of friendship: it is friendship avowed under hand and seal: friendship upon bond, as I may say: more pure, yet more ardent, and less broken in upon, than personal conversation can be even amongst the most pure, because of the deliberation it allows, from the very preparation to, and action of writing."[46] For Richardson, the significance of the letter in part rests on its physicality, on its structural stability and ability to be authenticated, for letters both arrive under seal and serve to cement friendships. Speech—at least in the pre-audio recording era of the eighteenth century—lacked this same permanence, and, consequently, as W. M. Verhoeven points out, "is harder to monitor and control" (144). Surprisingly, the premeditation inherent in correspondence also lends it greater authenticity in the minds of many eighteenth-century letter writers than does the spontaneity of speech.

Repeatedly, letter-writing manuals emphasize the expressive freedom and intimacy of the letter. The editor of *The Complete Letter-Writer*, for instance, instructs readers to "Write freely, but not hastily; let your words drop from your pen as they would from your tongue, when speaking deliberately on a subject of which you are master, and to a person with whom you are intimate" (10). Letters between friends encourage intimacy. As the introduction to *The American Letter-Writer* explains, "When you write to a friend, your letter should be a true picture of your heart: the stile loose and irregular; the thoughts themselves should appear naked, and not dressed in the borrowed robes of rhetoric; for a friend will be more pleased with that part of a letter which flows from the heart, than with that which is the product of the mind."⁴⁷ Like many other manuals, *The American Letter-Writer* espouses the curious notions that writing is somehow "freer" and more authentic than speech and that it provides a more accurate portrait of the heart. Remarkably, the authors of these prefaces seldom show awareness of the irony of claiming that letters in general provide accurate, indeed, almost unmediated portraits of the soul and heart, and the fact that they are providing their readers with generic examples to imitate.

One popular writer who took exception to this notion of writing as being closer to the language of the heart, of making the character perfectly transparent, was the Scottish rhetorician the Reverend Hugh Blair. In his *Lectures on Rhetoric and Belles Lettres*, an immensely popular work first published in the United States in 1784 and often used in colleges and seminaries, Blair ridicules the notion that writing in some way exposes a transparent heart. He says of letters (especially those exchanged between prominent people): "We expect in them to discover somewhat of their real character. It is childish indeed to expect, that in letters we are to find the whole heart of the author unveiled. Concealment and disguise take place, more or less, in all human intercourse." Arguing for the primacy of speech and the importance of elocution to both the speaker and the listener, Blair claims:

> [S]poken language has a great superiority over written language, in point of energy or force. The voice of the living speaker, makes an impression on the mind, much stronger than can be made by the perusal of any writing. The tones of voice, the looks and gestures, which accompany discourse, and which no writing can convey, render discourse, when it is well managed, infinitely more clear, and more expressive, than the most accurate writing. For tones, looks, and gestures, are natural interpreters of the sentiments of the mind. They remove ambiguities; they enforce impressions; they operate on us by means of sympathy, which is one of the most powerful instruments of persuasion. Our sympathy is always awakened more by hearing the speaker, than by reading his works in our closet. Hence, though writing may answer the purposes of mere instruction, yet all the great and high efforts of eloquence must be made, by means of spoken, not of written language.⁴⁸

That Blair, a rhetorician, should trumpet the superiority of spoken over written language is not surprising. Indeed, as Sandra Gustafson argues in *Eloquence is Power*, eloquent political speech flourished alongside a burgeoning print culture throughout the latter half of the eighteenth century, although such public oratory was largely the province of men and excluded women except as listeners, except in unusual instances such as the religious speech of Quaker women or Deborah Sampson Gannett's speaking tour.[49] Blair's praise of oratory suggests a counter-discourse to the increasing power of print in the late eighteenth century and to advice literature that fears the dangerous immediacy of seductive rhetoric, instead privileging the seeming authenticity, circumspection, and safety of the letter.[50] For women readers and writers, however, the discourse of advice literature was infinitely more accessible and employable.

Epistles and the Epistolary Novel

Why, if advice literature was both a respectable and popular genre—so popular that archive shelves today groan under the collective weight of these tomes—did readers need epistolary fiction to convince them that writing was an important element of the process of self-regulation? There are several interrelated explanations for this conundrum. First, while advice literature appears to have sold quite well in the literary marketplace, the mere number and variety of these texts sold do not necessarily equal books *read*, much less internalized. Indeed, the excellent condition of so many of these texts in research libraries today suggests that conduct-of-life works were not read as frequently and repetitively as were novels, which in many cases were literally read to pieces. Further, inscriptions suggest that many of these advice tracts were gifts—from parents to children, from brothers to sisters, or from teachers to students. Thus, these books may have been preserved for reasons other than their lasting influence upon their readers.

But perhaps more to the point, as Eliza Leslie suggests in *The Young Ladies' Mentor* (1803), a collection of historical sketches, poetry, and miscellaneous essays, is that many young readers found advice literature unpalatable, while the epistolary novel rendered similar precepts in a much more engaging fashion. Leslie explains that works "where precept alone reveals the theory of virtue . . . however excellent, are too generally tedious, and often uninteresting in the lively idea of youth; and pieces where morality is insinuated through the medium of history, or even of fiction, answer the same end, *in a manner unquestionably more agreeable* (emphasis added)."[51] A young female character in one of Susanna Rowson's dialogues in *A Present for Young Ladies* (1811), who bears a passing resemblance to Hannah Foster's Eliza Wharton, asserts a similar sentiment, satirically expressing dismay at the thought she might be expected to stay at home with her mother, where "for amusement: perhaps we may drone / Over Gregory's letters, or Madam Chapone. . . . No amusement in such stupid books can I see. . . . Were

I to read much of such stuff it would craze me, / I hate such nonsensical trash."⁵² Clearly, a segment of the American reading audience found advice literature less than engaging! By melding advice literature with the sentimental novel, however, American writers of epistolary fiction attempted to render fiction more palatable to figures of cultural authority, while simultaneously rendering the precepts of self-discipline more palatable to youthful readers.

The language of discipline, of self-control, permeates early fiction, beginning with the epistolary novel commonly recognized as America's first: William Hill Brown's *The Power of Sympathy*. This philosophical orientation operates on the level of narrative as well as plot. As Carla Mulford explains, Brown's narrative strategy of interspersing allusions to advice literature throughout his novel "provides a doubly intensive strategy by which the reader's concerns about women's issues would be engaged. By providing a layer of text from a popular advice book in the middle of his own novel giving advice, Brown could lay claim to his book's edifying function while providing the very edification he sought to render fictionally."⁵³ Brown is not the only novelist to employ this technique; indeed, his narrative strategy is quite common among epistolary novelists. Mulford explains this importance of this technique this way: Borrowing from and alluding to other pietistic and advice texts "created a literate dialogue that could function as a sort of cumulative, inclusive, and metacritical commentary on the actions taking place in their novels" (xxxii). Such a dialogue enhanced authorial control of readers' interpretations of text, an important consideration in epistolary fiction, which generally lacks a controlling narrative presence.

While sharing a common narrative strategy with other epistolary fictions, *The Power of Sympathy* differs from these other novels in an important fashion: While most subsequent novels tend to gender issues of self-discipline, construing it as a "female problem," *The Power of Sympathy* depicts self-examination and self-regulation as problems for both men and women. The novel includes numerous letters between Harrington and his friend Worthy that demonstrate the importance of self-control for young men. Harrington, passionate, impetuous, and sorely in need of self-regulation, continually rebukes Worthy for his "monitorial" role. Writing to tell Worthy that he has fallen in love with the poor, apparently orphaned Harriot and plans to make her his mistress, Harrington evinces familiarity with the discourse of self-regulation but rejects this ideology. He writes to Worthy, "I suppose you will be ready to ask, why, if I love Harriot, I do not marry her. Your monitorial correspondence has so accustomed me to re-

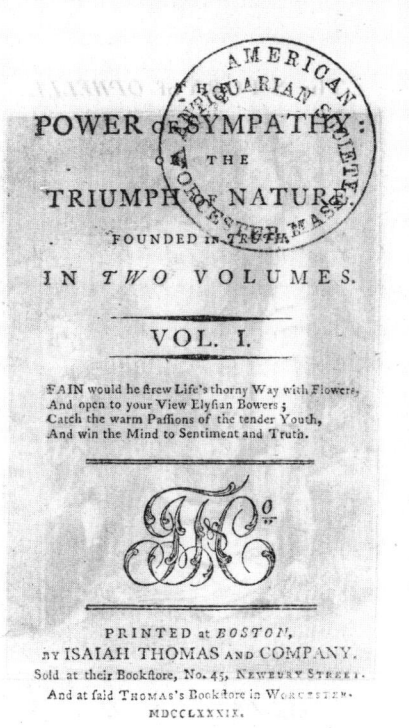

1789 frontispiece and title page of *The Power of Sympathy*.
Courtesy, American Antiquarian Society.

proof that I easily anticipate this piece of impertinence"[54] Later, however, Harriot's innate virtue convinces Harrington that he does indeed want to marry her. Yet after learning that Harriot is his illegitimate half-sister, he writes numerous letters to Worthy that reveal his increasing despondency and his diminishing self-control. In one of these letters, he begs for the monitorial wisdom he has previously rejected: "I want advice, but I am too proud to let the world know I am weak enough to be under obligation to any one else" (116). That Harrington feels a burdensome sense of obligation from his need for advice distinguishes his relationship with Worthy from the friendly monitorial role maintained by most female characters in early

American fiction. Whereas Harrington perceives being mentored as a sign of politically-charged, un-republican, un-masculine dependency, such a relationship between women is taken as a matter of course—indeed, of necessity, not as a sign of personal weakness.[55]

Further, the plot of *The Power of Sympathy* depends upon the revelations made amidst these monitorial relationships. Harriot maintains such a friendship with Myra Harrington (who, unknown to either, is her half sister). Myra describes their friendship as "a constant correspondence" and explains that Harriot "keeps no secret from me" (71). Indeed, the very openness of their friendship leads to the discovery of Harrington's near (but unintentional) incestuous relationship with Harriot, for Myra soon passes news of their courtship on to *her* older, monitorial friend, Mrs. Holmes, who knows the secret of Harriot's birth. As the moral center of the novel, Mrs. Holmes is enmeshed in relationships with all the characters in the text, and her letters to and from these other characters often center around the importance of scrutinizing one's conduct. It was Mrs. Holmes's family that took in Maria (Harriot's unmarried, pregnant mother) when her lover rejected her, and Mrs. Holmes is thus the recipient of a letter from Mr. Harrington (as the narrative styles the elder Harrington) after his conscience has slowly awakened to his transgressions. He writes to her:

> From all the variegated scenes of my past life, I daily learn some new lesson of humanity. Experience has been my tutor. I now take a retrospect of my past conduct with deliberation, but not without some serious reflection: like a sailor escaped from shipwreck, who sits safely on the shore and views the horrors of the tempest; but as the gale subsides . . . he beholds with greater concern the mischief of the storm and the dangers he hath escaped. From what innate principle does this arise, but from *God within the mind*! I assert it for the honor of human nature that no man, however dissolute, comes back to the hour of reflection and solemn thoughtfulness—when the actions that are passed return upon the mind, and this *internal monitor* sits in judgement upon them and gives her verdict of approbation or dislike.
>
> He who listens to its call views his character in its proper light. I have attended to its cry, and I see my deformity. I recall my misspent time, but in vain. . . . (96)

He continues his self-critique in a letter to the Reverend Mr. Holmes, emphasizing his awakening to his internal monitor and advising him not to upbraid him because his "heart is monitor enough" (102).

Unfortunately for Maria, the younger Harrington, and for Harriot, the elder Harrington's serious reflection takes place too late. He seems to have escaped paying for his sexual transgressions, but in this novel, as in most novels of the period, Old Testament law prevails, and the sins of the parents are visited upon the children; the public revelation that Harriot is the elder Harrington's child brings about her grief-stricken death and the subsequent suicide of his son. An old man at Harrington's funeral understands this displaced punishment, remarking: "poor youth. . . . Thou wast a promising genius, of violent passions. . . . how my heart bleeds for you! We consider thee as the dupe of nature, and the sacrifice of seduction" (128).[56]

The most important monitoring and mentoring relationship, however, takes place between Mrs. Holmes and Myra. Mrs. Holmes's letters carefully inquire about Myra's reading and activities, and she frequently suggests works for her to read, such as *Advice from a Lady of Quality*. Mrs. Holmes seldom has to reprove Myra's behavior, however, for as she explains, "You are such a good girl that I know not in what to direct you; for you leave me no room for advice—continue to anticipate the desires of my heart and to secure the high opinion you have obtained there" (82). Nonetheless, given the dangerous passions that run rampant in Myra's family, Mrs. Holmes feels compelled to clarify for her just what kind of conduct is virtuous: "We may lay it down as a principle, that *that conduct which will bear the test of reflection and which creates a pleasure in the mind from a consciousness of acting right is virtuous; And that she whose conduct will not bear this test is necessarily degenerating and is assenting to her destruction*" (98). Mrs. Holmes does not see young women as passive victims, helpless against seduction. She grants individual women agency and independence but requires that they balance their independence by exercising rigorous self-control. As she explains, "Happy they who can thus reflect—who can recall to view the scenes that are passed and behold their actions with reiterated satisfaction. They become ambitious of excelling in everything virtuous, because they are certain of securing a continual reward" (98). Self-affirmation is the reward, a pleasure which Mrs. Holmes, in a Lockean moment, asserts the well-trained heart eventually will seek on its own, rather than pursue approval from external sources. Her letters to Myra are filled with more of the same language, stressing the importance of "the test of reflection and serious examination" (99).

Other American epistolary novels use similar language to urge self-control upon readers within and without the text. *Emily Hamilton* is a case study in self-discipline, as it pulls together many of the themes prevalent in educational and advice literature, especially vigilant control of the passions and relentless self-scrutiny under the eyes of a mentor. Correspondence in this novel takes place between a number of young women, with Emily Hamilton at the center of a web of correspondence. Like most epistolary novels, this one includes the obligatory description and praise of friendship. Emily writes to Mary Carter Gray, her closest friend: "A real friend is one of the greatest blessings of life. How truly wretched must that person be, who has no one to whom he can give the endearing appellation of friend, no one, in whose generous breast he can confide his secrets, and repose his cares."[57] Mary shares Emily's view of friendship, favoring its reflective nature. In expressing her disgust with the gossip of the social world, Mary advises that "We all have something to amend in our conduct, and we should undoubtedly be wiser and better if more of our time were employed in examining our hearts, and removing our own bad qualities" (38). Mary also warns Emily, "[W]e are all liable to err, and ought therefore to be constantly on our guard" (47). Their letters act as such a guard, for each serves as a moral preceptor for the other. In particular, Mary continually interrogates Emily's romantic inclinations and urges her to channel them appropriately.

What Emily Hamilton must "amend," in particular, is her passion for Belmont, with whom she fell in love before learning that he was married. When Mary cautions Emily to be wary of first appearances, Emily graciously thanks her for the "friendly hint" (79). Emily later tells Mary that she "often blushed in secret" from her "involuntary" passion, which struck her when she was "unguarded" (134). Yet once she realizes that Belmont is married and that he and his wife are her new neighbors, she leaves town for an extended visit with her sisters. She explains, "I determined if possible to extricate myself from a passion, which could only be productive of guilt and wretchedness, if it were indulged; and knowing that the time would soon arrive that I should be necessitated to see him, and converse with him, I endeavoured to acquire sufficient fortitude to enable me to disguise the real sentiments of my heart; sentiments, which I cannot own even to you, without blushing. . . . My situation was not unlike that of a thief, who conscious of guilt, imagines himself suspected by every beholder" (135–36). Continual reflection does not end Emily's passion for Belmont, but it enables her to be resolute about controlling this passion. Yet this control is not enough for Emily. She wants to deny even knowledge of Belmont's existence but expresses frustration that "I [have] no more command over myself" (189). Eventually, Emily accepts the proposal of Charles Devas, a friend she has long admired. Mary praises this action, and urges her to be true to Devas, "though it may be some trouble to you to keep your thoughts from straying to what was once their most pleasing object" (202). As it turns out, however, Belmont is widowed and Devas drowns at sea. Belmont then courts and duly marries Emily, convinced not only that he loves her, but also that he has found a woman qualified for the task of teaching his motherless children self-discipline.

Whereas *Emily Hamilton* explores the struggles of women who safely pass through trials by moderating their passions with self-regulating conduct, Hannah Foster's *The Coquette* relates the compelling story of a woman who completely fails the test of self-mentorship, despite the warnings of friends, and later dies, readers are to understand, as a result of this failure of self-discipline. As Lori Merish has penetratingly observed, Eliza recognizes that she is being sold a bill of goods—that the domesticity, virtuous self-restraint, and discipline that Ann Richman, Julia Granby, and Lucy Freeman Sumner urge upon her effectively disguise the limitations placed upon women in the early Republic.[58] Yet the fact that her society offers Eliza so few options compels her friends and acquaintances all the more to urge her to self-reflection. In a scathing but memorable letter, even her erstwhile suitor Reverend Boyer warns Eliza Wharton: "Your own heart must be your monitor!" But she is unable and unwilling to follow his advice any more than she is able to follow that of her mother or friends.[59] Indeed, from the second letter of the novel onward, we see that Eliza is unprepared for the painful rigors of self-scrutiny. She explains to Lucy Freeman, "I have received your letter; your moral lecture rather; and be assured, my dear, your monitorial lessons and advice shall be attended to" (7). Lucy's letter unfortunately is not included in the text of the novel, but we can assume, based upon the sentiments that she expresses in her other letters, that she is an outspoken devotee of conduct-of-life literature that advocates self-scrutiny and self-discipline. Eliza does temporarily follow Lucy's advice; in her next letter, she explains, "I have been taking a retrospect of my past life; and a few juvenile follies excepted, which I trust the recording angel has blotted out with the tear of charity, find an approving conscience, and a heart at ease" (9). This is one of the few instances when readers see Eliza reflecting upon the motivations for her actions. Much later, after several missteps in conduct, Eliza will explain to Lucy that "I would fly to almost any resort, rather than my own mind. What a dreadful thing it is to be afraid of one's own reflections" (115), a state of mind that Julia Granby will label "indications of a mind not perfectly right" (121).

More often than not, Eliza's letters are externally oriented; she prefers to dwell upon exciting social events and romantic conquests, rather than upon the motivations and results of her actions. As Sanford describes her, Eliza is "gay, volatile, apparently thoughtless of every thing but present enjoyment" (18). Eliza reveals as much about herself in letter 5 when she tells Lucy of attending a dinner party, during which she chameleon-like scripted herself to appeal to the tastes of Reverend Boyer. She says of her conversation, "Mine was sentimental and sedate; perfectly adapted to the taste of my gallant" (12). But as she reveals, she gains even more pleasure from her adeptness at projecting a persona when she is at last able to retire to her chamber. Rather than engaging in sober reflection, she explains, "I have now retired to protract the enjoyment [of her social triumph] by recollection" (12). Eliza will later reject this sedate version of herself that so charmed Boyer, but at this time, she revels in the illusion of social power it produces.[60]

The extent of Eliza's individual social power and of the coquette in general is a matter of some critical dispute. Whereas I see Eliza as possessing only the illusion of social power, Grantland S. Rice argues otherwise in *The Transformation of Authorship in America*. Rice claims, "[T]he coquette, perhaps more so than any other deportment, by simultaneously embodying desire and scarcity, possession and loss, could control her own value and thus command her own price.... [T]he coquette could still be the authoress of her own worth by creating a market while at the same time providing for scarcity" (165). Rice concedes, however, that this power endures only "so long as this oscillation remained in an enduring form. Once she decided one way or the other, the coquette lost the power to control her 'market value,' since she no longer held the symbolic reigns of desire and scarcity" (166). Rice deftly describes social relations in *The Coquette* as being based upon the principle of exchange, but he overrates the power and overvalues the worth of the coquette, for Eliza *cannot* "command her own price." Eliza and the exchange value represented by her virtue, wit, and beauty are simply not worth enough (either financially or symbolically) for Sanford to marry her, and hence the appearance of choice for Eliza is as illusory as is her social power. Adam Goldgeier also follows this line of argument. In defining "coquetry" as a type of counterfeiting, Goldgeier aptly labels Eliza's use of social personas "a false autonomy." He explains, "A false autonomy (false also because the men who create it can destroy it) is granted her while the paradox that marks her two affinit[i]es renders her radically dependent" (2).

Eliza's only real choice, then, is to marry Boyer or not to marry Boyer, but her subsequent interactions with him reveal two traits that unnerve him—Eliza's levity and her resistance to criticism of her conduct. When Boyer quotes lines from Thompson describing his dream of a future life with Eliza, one marked by "an elegant sufficiency" and quiet contemplation (42), Eliza jokingly deflects this vision by questioning the definition of "an elegant sufficiency": "Perhaps you will answer as some others have done, We can attain it by circumscribing our wishes within the compass of our abilities. I am not very avaricious; yet I must own that I should like to enjoy it without so much trouble as that would cost me" (47). Eliza immediately apologizes for her sally, but it nonetheless reveals Eliza's lack of interest in restraining her desires. On another occasion, Eliza justifies her reluctance to commit to an engagement to Boyer by telling him: "Self-knowledge, sir, that most important of all sciences, I have yet to learn. Such have been my situations in life, and the natural volatility of my temper, that I have looked but little into my own heart, in regard to its future wishes and views" (28–29). Much of Eliza's reluctance to set a date for her marriage seems to stem from her dislike of anyone else scrutinizing her conduct, as would be the case were she to marry a minister. She explains, "I recoil at the thought of immediately forming a connection, which must confine me to the duties of domestic life, and make me dependent for happiness, perhaps too, for subsistence, upon a class of people, who will claim the right of scrutinising every part of my conduct; and by censuring those foibles, which I am conscious of not having prudence to avoid, may render me completely miserable" (29). Yet later, after her final parting from Boyer, Eliza laments this very lack of self-knowledge and discipline. She explains to Lucy that she desires to see her "mamma": "To her will I confess my faults, in her maternal breast repose my cares, and by her friendly advice regulate my conduct" (93–94). Eliza's mother, however, is too ineffectual to provide such advice, and Eliza does not follow even her mother's most pointed suggestions. Despite the presence of her mother, she later bemoans to Lucy her lack of a confidant, someone "to share and alleviate my cares! to have some friend in whom I could repose confidence, and with whom I could freely converse, and advise" (106).

Regardless of her protestations to Lucy, "from whom," she claims, to have "never concealed an action or idea" (87), readers learn that Eliza conceals the extent of her relationship with Sanford; indeed, as their involvement deepens, Eliza reveals even less of herself in her letters. Readers never see Eliza, unlike Emily Hamilton, writing out her anxiety or guilt over her love for a married man. Thus not only lack of self-knowledge but also Eliza's willful self-delusions render her vulnerable to Sanford's seduction.

In fact, as Eliza succumbs to Sanford's determined pursuit of her, she becomes increasingly less disposed to write to her friends. She explains to Lucy Freeman Sumner, "Writing is not so agreeable to me as it used to be. I love my friends as well as ever; but I think they must be weary of the gloom and dulness which pervades my present correspondence. When my pen shall have regained its original fluency and alertness, I will resume and prolong the pleasing task" (127). Eliza thus willfully withdraws from her circle of female friends, explaining later to Julia Granby that "Writing is an employment, which suits me not at the present. It was pleasing to me formerly, and therefore, by recalling the idea of circumstances and events which frequently occupied my pen in happier days, it now gives me pain" (134). These happier circumstances were those that could bear the scrutiny of the social mirror.[61] Unlike Charlotte Temple, Eliza does not lack confidants or friendly mentors, a point that Susanna Rowson repeatedly emphasizes with regard to Charlotte, who suffers as much from the cruel machinations of women such as Madame La Rue as she does from Montraville's actions. As Eliza herself remarks to Lucy Freeman, "Fortune, indeed, has not been very liberal of her gifts to me; but I presume on a large stock in the bank of friendship" (9).

Eliza's circle of friends has generated much recent critical discussion, with most readers harshly condemning both her correspondents and their correspondence. Dorothy Z. Baker, for example, locates Eliza's problems in the *nature* of the correspondence that circulates among Eliza's friends; Baker points to their reliance on conventional maxims and aphoristic advice, maxims which often conflict, and concludes that Eliza is always a pretender to the "beau monde, and must also be recognized as a pretender to its linguistic authority." Ian Finseth also looks at the language the correspondents use, arguing that its inadequacy is revealed through its failure "to socialize an individual [Eliza] who everyone acknowledges is intelligent and well-intentioned." John Paul Tassoni, on the other hand, discusses how the rhetoric of virtue "oppressively" shapes the dialogues among Eliza's circle of friends in *The Coquette*. As he points out, "Despite the characters' intense concerns for one another, the regard of Wharton's friends for her economic status and her virginity displaces their affectional vocabulary." Tassoni further argues that Eliza's own iteration of the discourse of virtue reflects, not her acceptance of these codes, but rather "her own fear of social invisibility: we can read her discourse as a recital geared to ensure her place among friends." That is to say, Tassoni elaborates, "[S]he procures her presence by espousing a text that her friends recognize and accept without censure."⁶² Julia A. Stern labels Eliza's circle of correspondents "the republican chorus" (72), a female community allied with an increasingly feminized Federalist clergy. Stern describes this female chorus as "self-righteous" and even "sadistic," arguing that they are as "destructive to Eliza's equanimity as the physical incursions of the libertine" (140). Donna R. Bontatibus similarly condemns Eliza's correspondents for their condemnatory attitude and for their overweening concern about her lack of an inheritance; thus, Bontatibus concludes, "Eliza's succumbing to seduction represents, in part, a self-fulfilling prophecy. Eliza's family and friends believe that she has fallen long before she enters into a sexual relationship with Sanford."⁶³ Although her mother may be ineffectual, Eliza, at any rate, unlike Charlotte Temple, has other advisors, but she lacks the will and desire to follow their advice.

Equally dangerous for Eliza, her correspondents vacillate between condemning her and making excuses for her conduct. After her break with Boyer, at the very time when her friends could most effectively urge her to examine her behavior and permanently alter her habits, they retreat and make excuses for her. Ann Richman, who has perhaps the most rigorous notions of conduct among Eliza's friends, consoles Eliza after Boyer ends their relationship. She advises her: "If the conviction of any misconduct on your part, give you pain, dissipate it by the reflection, that unerring rectitude is not the lot of mortals, that few are to be found who have not deviated in a greater or less degree from the maxims of prudence" (97)—sound advice, perhaps, but not in keeping with the rigorous notions of female conduct demanded by the sentimental novel of the late eighteenth century, where one misstep sends a woman sliding down the slippery slope of virtue.

At the opposite end of the spectrum from Mrs. Richman's gentle excuse of Eliza's conduct is Boyer's scathing response to her penitent, confessional letter, an exchange of correspondence that wounds Eliza's pride. In a previous letter to her, in which he encourages Eliza to let her heart be her monitor, he also urges: "[R]eview your conduct, and before you have advanced beyond the possibility of returning to rectitude and honor . . . restrain your steps from the dangerous path in which you now tread!"; further, he tells her, "[S]hould you hereafter be convinced of the justice of my conduct; and become a convert to my advice, I shall be happy to hear it" (84, 85).⁶⁴ Although Boyer claims in this letter that his "resolution" to break off his relationship with Eliza "is unalterably fixed," his passionate response to what he sees as her betrayal and his continuing interest in her conduct suggest that a rapprochement might not be impossible (85). What Boyer advocates for Eliza, albeit in an excessively pompous manner, is the same course of self-examination and self-discipline advocated by Eliza's female friends, as well as by writers of advice literature for over a century—self-scrutiny that demands more from Eliza than from the men of her acquaintance. That women were held to a higher standard of conduct and sexual morality is irrefutable; further, over the course of the eighteenth century, advice literature became increasingly concerned that the character—especially of women—become perfectly transparent and self-regulating. Eliza does at last review her conduct and agree that perhaps she erred, but Boyer's subsequent cold, unfeeling rejection of her—what amounts in effect to a secular execution sermon—deals a fatal blow to Eliza's pride and perversely discourages her from continuing a program of self-examination. Unseduced as of yet but using the traditional language of the seduced woman, Eliza tells Lucy: "Oh my friend, I am undone, rejected by the man who once sought my hand" (105). As she explains, "Oh that I had not written to Mr. Boyer! by confessing my faults, and avowing my partiality to him, I have given him the power of triumphing in my distress; of returning to my tortured heart all the pangs of slighted love!" (105). It was not charitable of Boyer to throw Eliza's repentance back in her face, but as Leonard Cassuto has argued, *The Coquette* generally "portrays religion as a voice that speaks without listening."[65] Neither religion nor its representatives offer consolation to Eliza.

Certainly Boyer is proud, judgmental, and prone to pronouncements, rather than dialogue, yet Eliza seems to view their relationship (and marriage in general) as a battle of the sexes in which only one can be the victor, and she sees the knowledge of herself that she has given to Boyer as the basis for power over her. Eliza's pride and vanity are wounded, not only by the knowledge that he has replaced her in his heart with another, but also because this other woman meets his strict standards of rectitude—standards which Lucy Freeman Sumner and Ann Richman also negotiate with apparent ease. Eliza's skill in presenting herself to please a specific audience thus has its dangers as well as its advantages. While it temporarily grants her power over Boyer, her power lasts only as long as she maintains this carefully manufactured image.

Paralleling Eliza's fall from virtue is Sanford's disgrace, the nature of which most critics of the novel tend to overlook. Whereas Eliza, as a minister's daughter, understands the importance of reflection but lacks the discipline to deny her desires, Sanford's letters betray no concept of such notions. Although the fate he suffers is not as severe as Eliza's—and part of the logic of the eighteenth-century sentimental novel is that women, for both cultural and biological reasons, bear the heaviest burdens in sexual transgressions—Sanford is nonetheless disgraced, even using in an ironic twist, as Fritz Fleischmann points out, the cry of the seduced, disgraced woman: "Oh, Deighton, I am undone!"[66] Sanford's wife leaves him, his debtors attach his property, his neighbors scorn him, and he is forced to become a wandering pariah, pursued, as he tells his friend Deighton, by "the upbraidings of my mind, which accuses me as the murderer of my Eliza" (164). He tells Deighton, "I shall fly the country as soon as possible; I shall go from every object which reminds me of my departed Eliza! But never, never shall I eradicate from my bosom the idea of her excellence; or the painful remembrance of the injuries that I have done her! Her shade will perpetually haunt me! The image of her . . . will always be present to my imagination! The solemn counsel she gave me before we parted, never more to meet, will not cease to resound in my ears!" (165). Thus in one of the more ironic moments of the novel, Eliza, who in life was unable to regulate her own conduct, will become Sanford's moral monitor; Sanford at last develops Adam Smith's "man within the breast," but in this case the man within the breast is not a man at all, but the shade of Eliza, the lover he wronged. Sanford's punishment is always to see himself through her eyes. Always present, this monitorial image of the fallen Eliza gains far more power over Sanford as she awakens his conscience than she ever had during her life as a coquette. This awakened conscience, we are to presume, will spur Sanford to regulate his desires. That Eliza has more power in her fictional death than in life is a stinging indictment of a society in which women bore an unequal burden of expectations as practitioners and mentors of self-discipline.

Far less popular than *The Coquette*, Hannah Foster's other novel, *The Boarding School* (which went into only three editions), should nonetheless be read as a companion novel to *The Coquette*. As Frank Shuffelton has pointed out, both novels seek to diagnose the moral ills of New England society, and both see sororal benevolence as a possible replacement for the decline of the Puritan brotherly watch (222). Like *The Coquette*, *The Boarding School* centers around exchanges of correspondence, but it is not a true epistolary novel, because it intersperses series of letters into narrated text. The many conduct works discussed or recommended in this novel—including those authored by Mrs. Chapone, Dr. Bennett, and Lord Chesterfield—foreground Foster's familiarity with the advice literature of the day, leading Sarah Emily Newton to label it a "conduct novel."[67] In sharp con-

THE BOARDING SCHOOL;

OR,

LESSONS

OF A

PRECEPTRESS TO HER PUPILS:

CONSISTING OF

INFORMATION, INSTRUCTION, AND ADVICE,

Calculated to improve the Manners, and form the Character of

YOUNG LADIES.

TO WHICH IS ADDED,

A Collection of LETTERS, written by the PUPILS, to their INSTRUCTOR, their FRIENDS, and each other.

BY A LADY OF MASSACHUSETTS;

AUTHOR OF THE COQUETTE.

Hannah Foster

Published according to Act of Congress.

PRINTED AT BOSTON,

BY I. THOMAS AND E. T. ANDREWS.

Sold by them, by C. BINGHAM, and the other Booksellers in *Boston*; by I. THOMAS, *Worcester*; by THOMAS, ANDREWS & PENNIMAN, *Albany*; and by THOMAS, ANDREWS & BUTLER, *Baltimore*.——JUNE, 1798.

1798 title page from Hannah Foster's *The Boarding School*.
Courtesy, American Antiquarian Society.

trast to *The Coquette*, *The Boarding School* not only demonstrates the importance of reflection and self-discipline, but it also instructs one how to perform these tasks.[68] Also of great importance, it demonstrates how proper writing and reading skills can translate into the skill of "reading" character. The narrator clearly sets the context for this work by explaining that after the death of her husband, Mrs. Williams opened a select finishing school for young ladies, carefully choosing her pupils and limiting their number to seven at a time. This school has multiple purposes: to provide company for Mrs. Williams's two daughters, as well as to enable Mrs. Williams to bestow larger dowries upon them—a fitting detail that the production of young, self-regulating bourgeois women should support another such commodity. Although finished with their formal education, the young women under Mrs. Williams's tutelage presumably lack the perfect self-regulation of idealized republican womanhood. Her goal is "to polish the mental part" of these young women. Mrs. Williams thus attempts "to extend and purify their ideas, to elevate and refine their affections, to govern and direct their passions. . . . while, with candour and mildness, she reproved their errors, detected their follies, and facilitated their amendment."[69] She also advocates discipline of the body—the benefits of early rising, a moderate diet, and steady industry—as facilitating mental discipline. Mrs. Williams serves not as a surrogate mother to these women, but rather, as they repeatedly call her, as their "Preceptress" (147) or "monitor" (163).

The narrative begins as one group of young ladies is finishing its term in the Williams household. As a fitting conclusion to their session, Mrs. Williams delivers to the young ladies what she calls her "valedictory address," in which she summarizes "the counsels, admonitions, and advice, which I have . . . endeavored to impress on [their] minds" (10). She divides her comments into categories such as "Reading" and "Writing and Arithmetic" (10); some of her most important advice centers around the importance of writing. She expresses now-familiar sentiments, urging her students to write daily as part of the process of self-examination (30–31). As part of a lecture titled "Miscellaneous Directions for the Government of the Temper and Manners," she urges her pupils to commit only those actions "such as will bear the test of examination and reflection" (49). She advises them to

> Let these be the criterion of all your pursuits and enjoyments. Make it an invariable practice to re-trace the actions and occurrences of the day, when you retire to rest; to account with your own hearts for the use and improvement of the past

hours; and rectify whatever you find amiss, by greater vigilance and caution, in future....

To know yourselves, in every particular, must be your constant endeavour. This knowledge will lead you to propriety and consistency of action. But this knowledge cannot be obtained without a thorough and repeated inspection of your various passions, affections, and propensities. (49)

Mrs. Williams's comments here virtually paraphrase Watts's program for self-examination in *Logic; or The Right Use of Reason* and *Improvement of the Mind*. She continues at length in this same vein, explaining that self-knowledge will protect young women from the dangers of flattery, because self-knowledge will enable her pupils to estimate accurately their merits and virtues: "In order to discriminate between flattery and merited praise, critically examine your own heart and life. By this mean[s] you will ascertain what is really your due, and what is merely the effect of this insidious art" (51). Interpolated into this lecture is the story of Flirtilla, who vainly overvalued her physical beauty due to the insidious effects of flattery and was devastated when smallpox marred her appearance. The purpose of this tale is to illustrate that had Flirtilla scrutinized and examined her true merits and regulated her conduct accordingly, she would not now be subjected to the devastating force of pity. Self-knowledge thus serves as a cultural cure-all, able to deflect flattery, resist seduction, and prevent private disappointment. Mrs. Williams reiterates these points throughout this lecture, commanding her pupils, "Examine yourselves, therefore with impartial scrutiny" (55). Espousing essentially the same advice to know thyself that Ralph Waldo Emerson would dispense some four decades later, *The Boarding School* is profoundly optimistic—and perhaps simplistic—in its understanding of the individual's relation to the world.

The latter half of *The Boarding School* is comprised of a series of letters that circulate among Mrs. Williams and the graduates of "Harmony Grove"—the name they give to her household. These letters take the place of the close companionship they once shared at Harmony Grove, replacements for the "amiable companions, among whom [they] had been used to unbend every thought" (115). Although the letters are sometimes sequenced, neither plot nor character development cements them together; indeed, many of these letters could be reordered, with little effect on the reading process. In this respect, these letters resemble the linked letters of letter-writing manuals that form mini-narratives, but coherent themes unite and distinguish the letters of *The Boarding School* as the graduates monitor one another.[70] Conspicuous by its absence, however, is the *need* for these women to monitor one another. They are so perfectly self-regulating, so perfectly self-disciplined, that they need little or no guidance from one another. Only at the onset of major life changes—marriage and the death of a parent—do they stand in need of advice. Regardless, they parrot Mrs. Williams's advice to one another, particularly her emphasis on the need for self-knowledge, as a means of demonstrating their own internalization of this code of behavior (168). Further, they critique the foolishness of false wit, flirting, and fashion. Indeed, virtually the only occasion upon which one friend must reprove another is after Sophia Manchester has scathingly criticized three beautiful and celebrated female wits. Her friend Matilda Fielding softens her criticism, reminding Sophia that "Few, you should remember, have had the advantages which you have enjoyed; and still fewer have your penetrating eye, correct taste, and quick sensibility. Let charity then draw a veil over the foibles of others . . ." (150).

What these letters display instead is their self-regulating virtue. These women need no mentoring—no reminders from friendly preceptors—because they are already models of self-regulating conduct. Although they are still quite young, they are astonishingly mature in opinion and attitude. Their letters reveal that they successfully negotiate assemblies, balls, social visits, and shopping with moderation and good sense. To today's readers, these letters may seem repetitive, sententious, and smugly self-congratulatory. Nevertheless, such self-congratulation was necessary to assure the writer as well as her correspondents of her virtue. As Michael T. Gilmore emphasizes about the early American novel, "The iterative and formulaic qualities of eighteenth-century fictions—features that seem so tedious today—contributed to the novel's communal goals" (623). And certainly epistolary fiction, above all other modes of sentimental fiction, emphasizes community feeling, or its unfortunate absence. Gilmore continues, "Where the aim was to instruct, the predictable was more effective than the 'novel'" (623).

Acknowledgment of the self-regulating status of the graduates of Harmony Grove comes in a letter from Mrs. Williams to Caroline Littleton—not on the occasion of her marriage, as is one customary ending for sentimental fiction—but rather on the death of Caroline's mother. In many other sentimental novels, the death of a mother heralds the evils about to befall her daughter, who will be left unguided by mature wisdom. This is not so in *The Boarding School*. Filled with final words of consoling advice,

Mrs. Williams's letter simultaneously acknowledges Caroline's initiation into adulthood, as she must assume her mother's role in her family. As Mrs. Williams advises her: "You must now think and act for yourself. . . . Your brothers and sisters will look up to you as the guide of their tender years" (249). Caroline will thus assume the role of preceptor or mentor for her family, and it will now be her duty to inculcate in her siblings, especially her sisters, the virtues of self-scrutiny and self-discipline. Caroline's status elevation symbolizes that of the other young women of *The Boarding School*, all of whom have successfully passed the test of town life in cities like Boston and Salem—a test that Eliza Wharton failed.

In most respects a conventional text, one minor plot strand disrupts the conservative tenor of *The Boarding School*, when the stultifyingly virtuous Williams family decides to take in a pregnant, unmarried, Irish servant girl. Maria, one of Mrs. Williams's daughters, tells of finding the desperate young woman while on a walk. Surprisingly unafraid of contaminating the impeccable morals and discipline of her pupils, Mrs. Williams takes the seduced and pregnant girl into her household as a servant in order to rehabilitate her—an action that runs counter to the prevailing treatment of the fallen woman in early fiction as a contaminating presence. The Irish girl readily explains the cause of her "fall": "Brought up in ignorance of those principles of decency, virtue and religion . . . I was ruined by a deceitful man, who, under the mask of love, and with the most solemn promises of marriage, betrayed my confidence, and left me to reap the bitter fruits of my credulity" (228). But Maria Williams diagnoses the girl's true problem, when she explains, "I found her knowledge confined entirely to domestic drudgery; that she had never been taught either to read or write" (229). Maria then vows to teach her to read, explaining, "Her tale impresses, more forcibly than ever, on my mind, the importance of a good education and the obligations it confers" (230). At the most basic level, the Irish girl's ignorance and consequent lack of alternatives for supporting herself constitute a powerful argument for women's education—a fact which Davidson has noted is part of the agenda of nearly all early American sentimental novels (*Revolution and the Word* 65–79). But on another, more symbolic level, exemplified not only in this text, but in all of those that I have previously discussed, learning to read symbolizes far more than being able to decipher letters on a page: it symbolizes the ability to decipher character, to "read" and to judge another character's actions and motivations.

"Reading" Character

While absolutely necessary, self-knowledge, as most eighteenth-century advice literature tells us, is not sufficient to enable a person to negotiate the world successfully. Isaac Watts emphasizes in *Improvement of the Mind* that children must be taught to use their powers of reason to observe those about them—"to observe more particularly, what are the peculiar tempers, appetites, passions, powers, good and evil qualities of the persons with whom they have most to do in the world" (85). In other words, what Watts wants parents or other preceptors to teach children is how to *read* character and "avoid the vices and follies which have plunged others into mischief, [and] to imitate the virtues of those who have behaved well in life" (85). Indeed, in *The Coquette*, Julia Granby is amazed that Eliza, renowned for her wit and intelligence, is such a poor reader of character. As Julia, whose "inquisitorial eye" Sanford fears (140), writes Lucy Freeman Sumner upon seeing Sanford for the first time, she "disliked him exceedingly. I am astonished that Eliza's penetrating eye, has not long since read his vices in his very countenance" (121).

Fiction itself, as some authors assert, can help women learn to read character. Mrs. Holmes of *The Power of Sympathy* advises Myra that fiction reading has value, although one must balance reading of fiction with essays, to enable the "mind to remark the difference between truth and fiction. You will then always be enabled to judge of the propriety and justness of a thought and never be misled to form wrong opinions by the meretricious *dress* of a pleasing tale. You will then be capable of deducing the most profitable lessons of instruction, and the design of your *reading* will be fully accomplished" (77). Learning to read texts, however, is but preparation for the real lesson that Mrs. Holmes wants to impart: the importance of reading character. Once skilled in the act of reading, Mrs. Holmes explains, "[Y]ou will be provided with a key to the characters of men: to unlock these curious cabinets is a very useful, as well as an entertaining employment" (77). British minister James Fordyce offers another, more chauvinistic, view of the metaphor of reading character in his conservative *Sermons to Young Women*. He claims, "Your chief business chiefly is to read Men, in order to make yourselves agreeable and useful. It is not the argumentative but the sentimental talents, which give you that insight and those openings into the human heart, that lead to your principal ends as Women." He continues, seemingly un-ironically, "Nevertheless, in this study you may derive great assistance from books."[71] While other advice manuals such as Dr.

Gregory's and even some sentimental novels, such as Sally Wood's *Amelia; or The Influence of Virtue*, advocate this self-effacing mode of womanhood, early American novels more often use the metaphor of reading character as a way to teach women to protect themselves from the gentleman strangers populating these same novels.

Novels that emphasize writing as crucial to the process of self-discipline thus simultaneously emphasize the corollary skill of reading, for skills used in deciphering texts could easily be transferred to reading character, a task of critical importance to young women in eighteenth-century fiction, and one more demanding than simply assessing physiognomy, a trope popular in nineteenth-century American fiction. As Nell Irvin Painter explains in an essay about Sojourner Truth, the ability to "decipher" other people is "a technique for survival. Once called woman's intuition, this ability to decode others without indicating what one perceives is a sense cultivated by the powerless who seek to survive their encounters with the powerful."[72] Painter's assessment of this ability certainly applies to the situations facing young women in early American fiction, for they too often meet with men who wear masks of virtue to obscure their true natures. But someone possessing self-knowledge and an understanding of the language of the heart, joined with adequate reading skills, could nonetheless penetrate a mask by means of an "inquisitorial" eye, just as does Julia Granby in *The Coquette*. True nature will shine through in a legible fashion, just as will crossed lines of text in a letter be visible to the experienced eye.

Not surprisingly, the men who wear masks are often described as "counterfeiters" of sentiment and of virtue, and indeed counterfeiting, whether of character or cash, is a preoccupation of eighteenth-century fiction. Aurelia Morely of Sally Wood's *Dorval; or The Speculator*, a novel that I will discuss at length in subsequent chapters, is astounded that her parents and friends are unable to read the true character of the villainous Dorval in his face. The inscription to chapter 8 of *Dorval* reads:

> He comes, behold, the villain in his face!
> And inward conscience mars all outward grace.
> For every deed of darkness stands prepar'd,
> And bids with smiles the honest man be spar'd.
> Avoid him, fly him; death is in his eye,
> And vile hypocrisy in every sigh.[73]

Aurelia later explains in a letter to her friend Elizabeth, "I am apprehensive, my dearest friend, that he [Dorval] is not a good character. I have marked him from his first appearance in Boston, and think, underneath all the frankness and bluntness, of which he seems to boast, that deception and deep laid plans of villainy are concealed. It is true that he could not find a better veil for his hypocrisy, than his appearance of not caring for the opinion of any one, of concealing nothing, and of speaking whatever he pleases" (40). Her parents and friends, however, are self-deluding readers; as the narrator suggests, "We easily believe what we wish" (64). Further, Dorval promises to answer their desires—whether for wealth, status, or love—and Aurelia's parents and friends thus read upon his countenance what they desire to see there. Aurelia's reading of Dorval's character proves to be accurate, for Dorval later appears in his true guise as a forger, speculator, and murderer. Aurelia, on the other hand, plainly broadcasts her own goodness and virtue, which likewise attract another good reader in the young lawyer Burlington, who is drawn to her by the fact that "Her mind was portrayed upon her face, and the emotions of her bosom legible in her countenance. She did not wish to conceal her failings, nor lay claim to one virtue that was not her own" (65). Burlington astutely reads what Aurelia's heart projects onto her countenance: that she has faults, but virtue predominates.

Emily Hamilton likewise learns the necessity of reading beyond appearances and penetrating the mask of virtue. The "amiable manners," virtuous appearance, and secure financial status of Lambert, one of Emily's suitors, initially mislead her parents (40), but Emily distrusts him. Her father contends that Emily's judgment is faulty, and he insists that she accept Lambert as a suitor. Emily wisely proceeds with caution. She tells Mary, "I must do him justice to say, he appears to be a finished gentleman" (41), but she questions this appearance, which her family and friends all too readily accept. Emily explains to Mary, "I am not apt to be very suspicious, yet I should like to know more concerning him" (41). Her intuitive reading of Lambert's character is validated when he seduces Emily's neighbor at the same time he is courting Emily, refuses to marry the neighbor woman after she has his baby, and still proposes to the rightfully indignant Emily.

Clearly, *Emily Hamilton*, *The Boarding School*, *The Power of Sympathy*, and *Story of Margaretta* captured the ethos of advice and pedagogical literature of the day, demonstrating via the epistolary mode the efficacy of external and internal moral monitors and rewarding their disciplined heroines with happy endings. Why, then, was it *The Coquette*, second in enduring popularity only to *Charlotte Temple* among early novels authored by Americans, that captured the imagination of American readers for the next century? Certainly from an aesthetic perspective the multivocality of *The*

Coquette is more successfully rendered than in most of these other epistolary fictions; in *The Boarding School*, for example, the characters are static and most letter writers sound alike and espouse virtually the same ideas.

But perhaps the best explanation lies within the words of Julia Granby and Lucy Freeman Sumner, two women in the text who *do* have proper internal monitors. After seeing Major Sanford sneak from the Wharton household in the early morning hours after an illicit assignation with Eliza, Julia writes: "My blood thrilled with horror at this sacrifice of virtue!" (142). If, for modern readers, the blood does not thrill with horror in exactly the same way, we can at least sympathize with eighteenth-century readers that unalleviated virtue and proper moral monitoring, if not "too generally tedious" like the advice literature of the day (Leslie iv), are less exciting than seeing someone struggle, even fail, because of her rebellion against the prevailing norms of behavior.

Foster's use of the word "thrill" in this instance, however, is wonderfully evocative, for the eighteenth-century meaning of this word denotes more than a titillating sensation. Rather, "thrill" in this context suggests what G. J. Barker-Benfield calls the "nerve paradigm," an important outgrowth of the Lockean-derived culture of sensibility.[74] Julia's "thrill" suggests a physical effect upon the nervous system, resulting in an enduring mental effect. Further, Julia communicates this same "thrill" to Lucy, prompting her to note that although Eliza herself failed at the business of self-monitoring and self-regulating conduct, "she shall live on in the heart[s] of her faithful Lucy" and Julia (167). While the other sentimental novels that I have discussed in this chapter demonstrate moral monitoring and even instruct one how to accomplish these tasks, only *The Coquette* actually succeeds in installing such a presence within the hearts of readers. The specter of Eliza lives on not only in Sanford's heart, but also in Lucy's and Julia's, with this specter serving as an always-present monitor. In this sense, then, *The Coquette* illustrates Foster's understanding of both Lockean pedagogy and sensational psychology, disseminated at this time primarily through such writers as Isaac Watts and the authors of advice literature. In eighteenth-century terms, *The Coquette* is a cultural tour de force, successfully deploying sentiment, sympathy, and sensibility that, when combined with the sensationalism of its true-to-life inspiration in individuals from prominent New England families, virtually guaranteed its success.

To conclude my discussion of epistolary fiction, however: What may appear to readers of the twenty-first century as an obsession with rules and order, with self-discipline and self-control, ironically also reveals the optimism and sense of human potential present in American Enlightenment thought, in this case, excitement at the notion that people have the potential to control their lives and behavior. This enthusiasm for the reformative potential of habit and self-discipline would spill over from pedagogical theory to animate the reform movements for the treatment of the insane and criminals, subjects I will take up in later chapters. Specifically, in the following chapter, I will again address the mind-body connection explored in American sentimental fiction, although at that point I will be less concerned with Locke and more interested in what medical theorists contemporary to American novelists were arguing with regard to the connection between the mind and the physical body.

The particular developments and emphases that I have noted in epistolary fiction are in many ways the natural outcomes for prose fiction grounded in Enlightenment thought. Use of the epistolary mode by Americans most often was a deliberate aesthetic, pedagogical, and ideological choice, reflecting the cultural and political importance of self-control through thoughtful, reflective behavior. The social conservatism of these epistolary texts served as a legitimating vehicle to public discourse for their authors, a vehicle akin to advice literature, yet geared toward a more daring audience—those young women and men who read fiction in spite of widespread criticism of novels by ministers and other figures of cultural authority. Illustrating the simultaneously constraining and liberalizing tendencies of fiction, the conservative behavior these texts advocated for white bourgeois women nonetheless encouraged literacy as well as writing skills—skills which were often taught separately and which were not guaranteed for young women during this time—while simultaneously underlining women's urgent need for social perspicuity in a rapidly changing and mobile society.[75]

American epistolary fiction suggests that the female reader of such texts could learn to write and to read with the same effects as modeled in fiction; hence, she would be endowed with skills that would protect her from being deceived by the pleasant appearance of and easy social acceptance granted to men of wealth and status. This pedagogical methodology suggests a far more complicated process than that represented by the reductive equation that sentimental epistolary fiction is necessarily didactic, and that didactic fiction simply tells one how to behave. The issue at stake in American epistolary fiction is that of character formation, with potentially broad cultural implications. As Jeffrey H. Richards observes, the ostensibly private decisions of female characters in sentimental novels are really not private at all, but participate in larger public conversations about virtue and vice in the new Republic, for they "are linked in the minds of commenting observers to public images of women as teachers of virtue and as icons of the republic."[76] Although in the best case, these epistolary texts show concern for presenting an authentic self, the endless repetition of the tropes of reflection and self-regulation ultimately (and ironically) suggest the pursuit of an idealized, self-denying, generic self, the consequence of the denial of liberal self-determinism for bourgeois women turned crushingly inward.

The lessening popularity of the epistolary novel in the 1810s and '20s did not mark the end of this concern for character formation. This anxiety about self-examination and self-discipline merely took on a new guise in the nineteenth century as part of the self-culture movement in a literary culture that preached self-reliance yet ironically depended on the public sphere of publication in order to teach readers how to re-create themselves as private individuals. Indeed, within the epistolary fiction of the late eighteenth century, we can trace the origins of the self-culture movement as championed by William Ellery Channing and later by Ralph Waldo Emerson, for the epistolary novel's emphasis on writing as a means of developing a disciplined interior self would metamorphose in self-culture discourse into an emphasis on reading as a means to develop one's own character, with character taking on a new signification as the ultimate marker of culture and gentility, subjects Joan Shelley Rubin addresses in *The Making of Middlebrow Culture*.[77] According to Rubin, in the nineteenth century, "character" comes to denote "integrity, balance, and restraint.... Animated by a firmly grounded sense of the self as interior, persons of character were also, paradoxically, selfless. Public-spirited and cognizant of moral obligation, they were committed more to the fulfillment of duty than to uninhibited self-expression. Possessors of character won prestige and 'reputation' by exhibiting it to others" (3–4). It is worth noting that, in Rubin's formulation, "character" bears a striking resemblance to masculine republican virtue as understood by novelists of the early Republic, a subject I will take up in the third and fourth chapters of this work. Understanding the epistolary urge present in early American fiction enables us in turn to understand the impetus among nineteenth-century writers toward self-culture and the collateral optimistic view that not only we can analyze, understand, and control ourselves, but that we can also direct our future growth.

2

Unlawful Embraces

Sexual Transgression, Madness, and the Ascendancy of Medical and Narrative Discourse

---

A conscience burdened with guilt, whether real or imaginary, is a frequent cause of madness.
  —Dr. Benjamin Rush, *Medical Inquiries and Observations Upon the Diseases of the Mind* (1812)

TWO CULTURAL ARTIFACTS, one a painting, the other a medical case history, vividly illustrate the cultural conflation of sexual transgression and madness in Western Europe and Anglo-America in the late eighteenth century and help us understand the repeated, puzzling appearance of the trope of insanity in early American fiction. The first of these artifacts is Tony Robert-Fleury's striking painting *Le docteur P. Pinel faisant tomber les chaînes des aliénés*, which dramatically illustrates changing medical attitudes toward the insane. This painting depicts Philippe Pinel, a reformer and the leading French psychiatrist of the time, removing the chains from the madwomen at the Salpêtriére, the Paris lunatic asylum. Even as Pinel frees the women, Robert-Fleury captures the instability of the moment: passive only momentarily, the women sprawl across his canvas with their clothing in suggestive disarray; drooping stockings display bare legs, and their tangled hair reveals their uncontrolled passions even as it partly conceals their naked breasts.

The second artifact is a brief medical case history drawn from Philadelphia physician Benjamin Rush's 1812 study *Medical Inquiries and Observations Upon the Diseases of the Mind*. In this case history, Rush provides a startling illustration of the cultural conflation of sexual transgression, the conscience, and insanity in the early Republic era. Discussing the powerful influence of guilt upon the conscience, Rush writes dispassionately about a tragic case of madness: "An instance of insanity occurred in a married woman in this city some years ago, of the most exemplary character, from a belief that she had been unfaithful to the marriage bed. An accident discovered that the supposed criminal connection was with a man whose very person was unknown to her."[1] The elusive and ambiguous phrase "whose very person was unknown to her" invites further question. Does Rush mean that the anonymous man was literally a person the woman had never met? Or is Rush making a (perhaps unconscious) double entendre—meaning that the woman lacked *carnal* knowledge of this man, and hence if they were guilty of anything, it was not of a physical relationship? This second possibility leaves open the option that the anonymous woman might have been guilty of emotional infidelity—that she and the equally anonymous man might have shared some degree of emotional intimacy, a state of affairs that contemporaneous American novels portray as illicit, even dangerous.[2] The fate of this woman remains unexplained, but Rush later makes the provocative claim that cases of derangement in the United States are *commonly* caused by "infidelity" (65–66).

This supposedly true episode of guilt-driven insanity is strikingly similar to the pattern of self-punishment for sexual transgression that pervades many early American novels. This self-punishment is commonly figured as "madness"—a trope that may appear to today's readers as just another tired cliché of early American fiction. Yet the very repetition of this trope demands our attention: *Why* does conscience or guilt-induced madness repeatedly appear as a special kind of punishment for sexual transgression in so many early novels, and what does it tell us about novelists' engagement with their culture and with other forms of discourse? In particular, how and why do the interests of medicine and the novel converge with regard to the exercise of female sexuality? As I will argue throughout this chapter, the convergence of fiction and medical theory in pathologizing the misguided expenditure of sexual capital outside the constraints of marriage reveals the formative role fiction played in the development of bourgeois subjectivity. Fiction of the early national period consistently explores the social, economic, medical, and political consequences of female sexuality exercised outside the bonds of marriage during a time in which there was a declension in both private morality regarding sexuality and in enforcement of laws governing female sexuality. The novel and medical discourse, working

Le docteur P. Pinel faisant tomber les chaînes des aliénés, painting by Tony Robert-Fleury. Réunion des Musées Nationaux/Art Resource, New York.

in concert, became surrogates for law as they sought to represent and to regulate bourgeois female sexuality in a conservative manner.

As historians of mental illness have demonstrated, madness and insanity are very much culturally constructed states. In *Madness and Civilization*, Michel Foucault has described the complex history of the evolution of European attitudes toward insanity.[3] To some degree, the history of American methods of dealing with insanity parallels that of Europe. Prior to the eighteenth century, in the British colonies as in Europe, the insane in many communities were treated as criminals, meaning they were incarcerated, beaten, and chained alongside common criminals.[4] In other communities, harmless madmen (and women) were boarded out in the homes of people of the town, while more violent madmen might be incarcerated in small houses. The late eighteenth century, however, was a crucial time in the history of mental illness, as physicians and reformers such as Rush and Pinel studied insanity, theorized about it, and attempted to decriminalize it. Like Robert-Fleury's painting and Rush's anecdote, early American fiction captures fluctuating cultural attitudes toward insanity, especially when coupled with the exercise of female sexuality. Cultural associations between madness and criminality obviously lingered, and contemporary fiction reflects this state of flux, with madness inevitably associated with transgression, whether as a type of mania, as found in Gothic fiction, or the guilt-driven, confessional insanity of the sentimental novel.[5] In this chapter, in order to trace evolving American attitudes towards bourgeois female sexuality, I will explore the relationships among sentimental fiction, laws governing sexual behavior, and psychiatric discourse during the period from 1789 to 1814, when fictional narratives were assuming an increasingly important and authoritative cultural role.

Much recent criticism of novels from the early national period, while acknowledging the conservative elements of the genre, has nonetheless tended to reflect the political currents of our time, privileging either the more proto-feminist texts or the more subversive aspects of other texts.[6] Indeed this critical emphasis has been crucial in creating a new audience for these texts, especially among women in the academy. This trend represents a reaction to the scholarship of earlier decades by critics such as Lillie Deming Loshe and Herbert Ross Brown who, while progressive for their time in even considering these novels, tend to dismiss their sentimental agenda and criticize what they perceive as a lack of originality.[7] Among recent critics of early American fiction, Cathy Davidson has been the strongest proponent of progressive and subversive readings of these texts, particularly in her study *Revolution and the Word*. Drawing upon the work of Mikhail Bakhtin and numerous historians of the book, Davidson persuasively argues that sentimental fiction as a genre was progressive through its advocacy of literacy skills and education for women, agendas advanced both in authorial prefaces and through the plots of novels.[8] These claims about the novel are irrefutable. Yet Davidson herself acknowledges the strange disparity with regard to the conservative plots of some sentimental novels and the sex and situations of their authors.[9]

Indeed, not all early American texts are subversive, and the *nature* of the conservatism of early American fiction needs to be carefully considered. While *The Coquette* with its multiple voices, allusions to a real-life scandal, and exposé of the economic predicament of women is a complex and fascinating novel deserving the attention that it has recently garnered, perhaps more representative of early American sentimental fiction, as a body of work, are novels little-known today like Samuel Relf's *Infidelity, or The Victims of Sentiment* (1797), the anonymous *Amelia; or, the Faithless Briton* (1798), and Sally Wood's *Dorval; or The Speculator* (1801), conservative, even reactionary, novels that treat transgressive sexual behavior in an uncompromisingly harsh manner, killing off entire families in order to portray the devastating effects of women's sexual choices. While their characters and politics are not as appealing as *The Coquette's* to today's readers—and indeed these were not the kinds of texts I hoped or expected to find when I embarked on this project, they represent a pervasive strand of conservatism in the early novel and hence a significant aspect of the nativist literary terrain of the early national era.

The dialogic nature of fiction works in complex ways, for the very "plasticity" of fiction (to borrow Bakhtin's phrase) that allowed it to be employed subversively in many texts also enabled more conservative writers to promote their own agendas.[10] What I will consider in this chapter is how several writers who are representative of a conservative strain in the early novel shrewdly exploit the possibilities inherent in fiction—the multifariousness of the novel and the composition of its audience—in this case not for a subversive purpose, but rather for a conservative one. These writers demonstrate an astute understanding of their own cultural dynamics and of the readership of fiction.[11] Revisiting these texts while armed with an understanding of how even radical politics in the novel are sometimes joined with conservative plots enables us to engage in a more rigorous and sustained critique of fiction's treatment of white, female sexuality. Specifically, I intend to address the social, cultural, and political implications of this conservatism as it manifests itself in fiction, for the very preponderance of these plots centering around female sexuality and the misguided expenditure of sexual capital demands critical attention.

Certainly fiction's interest in female sexuality has multiple dimensions. To a large extent, the novel's anxiety over bourgeois female sexuality has to do with value, in particular the woman's value in masculine eyes. Female value, in the early American novel, is largely figured as dependent on virtue. And virtue for women, as the Reverend Mr. Boyer writes to his friend Selby in Foster's *The Coquette*, depends on chastity. After Boyer has broken his engagement to Eliza, he tells Selby, "I would not be understood to impeach Miss Wharton's virtue; I mean her chastity. Virtue in the common acceptance of the term, as applied to the sex, is confined to that particular, you know" (78). Of course by raising the issue, Boyer induces Selby to do precisely that—to question Eliza's virtue; but my point in quoting Boyer here is to illustrate the relationships among value, virtue, and chastity. "The virginal woman," as Luce Irigaray reminds us, "is pure exchange value."[12] Nowhere is that better illustrated than in early American fiction, where virginity bestows a special value on a woman and is, with virtually no exceptions, an important precondition for a first marriage.

In *Writing in the New Nation*, Larzer Ziff suggests another dimension to the novel's concern with female chastity when he attributes the popularity of the seduction novel and its anxiety about female sexuality to a larger cultural concern with issues of representation. Ziff writes:

> Women were put into the position of embodying the quality of a fixed reality that had disappeared from the everyday world of getting a living; their chastity figured in the plot as a determinate value in a world in which the worth of most things was indeterminate. The novel of seduction typically concerns itself with a negative example; the woman cannot preserve the true value she represents and as a result dies. The repetition of such negative examples in popular novels suggests indulgence in nostalgia for a world that is no longer rather than an obsession with female chastity. (72)

Ziff's point about the larger issue of self-representation is well taken (and one that I myself will take up in chapters 3 and 4), for writers in just about every genre imaginable voice concerns about the potential for deceit in personal and commercial relationships. However, while agreeing with Ziff that the popularity of the seduction novel "suggests an indulgence in nostalgia for a world that is no longer," I will argue in this chapter that the popularity of the seduction novel among writers and readers also points to serious engagement with the social, economic, medical, and political consequences of female sexuality exercised outside the bonds of marriage.

Transgressive behaviors such as adultery and fornication affected both the private and public spheres, for they both disrupted the family unit and violated legal and moral codes.[13] This intersection between the private and the public—between the family and the community—helps explain the popularity of seduction and sexual infidelity as topics for novelists during the early national period. The parameters of these spheres were far from settled, as Rush's example demonstrates, and novelists, as well as medical writers, mediated between the public and private spheres, struggling to determine precisely what concerns would be "public." As I argued in the previous chapter, scrutiny of female emotions and conduct emerges as a primary concern of epistolary fiction, revealing the genre's grounding in Lockean-influenced pedagogical literature. The burgeoning medical discourse of the era also powerfully influenced writers of fiction, as novelists drew upon the authority of this discourse in order to critique fictional models of female sexuality in the absence of the requisite self-control. *Amelia; or, the Faithless Briton*, Wood's *Dorval*, and Relf's *Infidelity*, as well as better-known works such as Susanna Rowson's *Charlotte Temple* and *Charlotte's Daughter; or, The Three Orphans: A Sequel to Charlotte Temple* (best known as *Lucy Temple*) all rely upon the theoretical discourse concerning insanity in order to describe and regulate female sexuality.

While Americans were increasingly seeking companionate marriages and autonomy in choice of marriage partners, these sentimental yet profoundly anti-romantic novels emphasize that marriage, one of the most personal of human relationships, is nonetheless also an economic transaction.[14] Seduction, fornication, and adultery, then, are all misguided expenditures of sexual capital; further, illegitimate children conceivably involved expenditure in a more public, economic sense, if they became a financial charge on a local community in the absence of an acknowledged father. Yet for the most part, these novels disregard legal remedies as punishment for transgressive behavior. Instead, belated self-scrutiny, with the potential to induce madness as self-punishment for social and moral transgression, emerges as the ultimate disciplinary tool. Reading these novels alongside medical texts illustrates the convergence of these discourses in pathologizing female desire outside the bonds of matrimony, as each discourse borrows from the other in an attempt to gain authority over the bourgeois female body and mind. These novels provide insight into the fluid and dynamic relationship between psychiatric discourse and sentimental fiction between 1789 and 1814, when fictional narratives were assuming a heightened cultural position in the United States. Medical theories about insanity permeate fictional discourse at large, and it is during this time that medical and narrative authority increasingly come to complement and even supplant legal authority governing female sexual behavior.

The Ascendancy of Medical and Narrative Discourse

Unlike France, the United States has no such dramatic moment as Pinel unfettering the madwomen at the Salpêtriére to demarcate the boundaries in the eighteenth century between cruel and sympathetic treatment of the insane. Rather, medical treatises, in concert with early American fiction, suggest instead a gradual evolution in attitudes toward mental illness and self-control. In order to understand the context in which early American fiction was written and read, we must first consider the medical understanding of insanity during the early national period. Through his advocacy of humane treatment and decriminalizing the insane, Benjamin Rush played a crucial role in the reform of American medicine in the late eighteenth and early nineteenth centuries. Given his status as a signer of the Declaration of Independence, surgeon general of the Middle Department of the Continental Army, member of the Pennsylvania convention that adopted the Constitution, and treasurer of the United States Mint, Rush and his work would have been known to most literate people of the early Republic. In *Concepts of Insanity*, medical historian Norman Dain dubs Rush a "transitional figure in the history of psychiatry," claiming that his work synthesizes some of the most enduring beliefs of the time about mental illness.[15] While Rush did attempt to systematize established beliefs about mental illness, he also incorporated into his work new theories about the benefits of "moral treatment," which consisted of treating patients with sympathy, kindness, and care for their mental and physical needs.[16] There is some debate about the extent to which Rush actually originated new medical ideas, for Rush, Philippe Pinel, and William Tuke (an English Quaker reformer and founder of the York Retreat) were all experimenting with moral treatment at about the same time, and each was aware of the others' work (Dain 12–15; Caplan 5).[17] While the degree to which Rush originated new theories of mental illness is thus unclear, what remains important is that Rush was at the center of the nexus of new thought in the United States regarding the function of the brain and mental health and illness. As one of the most prominent physicians of his time, he disseminated his theories and those of his contemporaries through thirty years of teaching at the medical school of the University of Pennsylvania, his private practice, and his scientific writings.[18] Even works on insanity published by other Americans decades before Rush's clearly demonstrate his influence. Edward Cutbush's 1794 *An Inaugural Dissertation on Insanity*, for example, is little more than a pastiche of Rush's theories with footnotes crediting his lectures, as is Joseph Parrish's 1805 *An Inaugural Dissertation on the Influence of Passion Upon the Body in the Production and Cure of Diseases*. Moreover, Rush's works were not limited to a professional medical audience; learned individuals of the time such as Thomas Jefferson and John Adams were familiar with Rush's medical theories.

The literate general population would also have been cognizant of contemporary medical ideas about insanity through works such as William

Buchan's *Domestic Medicine*, which one medical historian claimed was more influential "than any other similar work ever published."[19] Originally published in Britain for a general audience, *Domestic Medicine* was first reprinted in British America in 1772 and in numerous later editions (over twenty-five times prior to 1800) both in large cities like Philadelphia and in small towns such as Halifax, North Carolina. Rush and Buchan use a number of terms to denote the spectrum of mental instability, among them "melancholy" and "mania," but they and others basically agree on general descriptions of these states, as well as the distinctions between hysteria and madness. Rush and Buchan both argue that hysteria is primarily a physical disorder, characterized by convulsions, heart palpitations, and the like (Buchan 261). Further, Rush concludes that "hysteria . . . often continues for years, and sometimes during a long life, without inducing madness" (16). Hysteria thus was not part of the continuum that led to madness. Instead, the mildest form of mental illness was considered to be melancholy, a state characterized by depression and sadness. Madness itself was a heightened state on this continuum. Rush explains that "Madness is to delirium what walking in sleep is to dreaming. It is delirium, heightened and protracted by a more active and permanent stimulus upon the brain" (12). This spectrum of mental illness terminates in mania, a state characterized by violent, often homicidal, tendencies.[20]

Most contemporary medical authorities agreed that great emotion, regardless of cause, was the most dangerous risk factor for inducing madness. Rush provides a fascinating list of the possible causes of mental illness, including intense study (36–37) and "the frequent and rapid transition of the mind from one subject to another" (37). "But," he explains, "madness is excited in the understanding most frequently by impressions that act primarily upon the heart. . . . They are joy, terror, love, fear, grief, distress, shame from offended delicacy, defamation, [and] calumny . . ." (38–39). Grief and guilt resulting from infidelity or sexual incontinence were other potential causes of madness (44; 66). John Haslam, member of the Royal College of Surgeons, Apothecary to Bethlehem Royal Hospital, and author of the 1809 *Observations on Madness and Melancholy*, concurs with Rush about these potential risk factors, and he adds "the long endurance of grief; ardent and ungratified desires; . . . prosperity humbled by misfortunes: in short, the frequent and uncurbed indulgence of any passion or emotion, and any sudden or violent affection of the mind" (210). Further, physicians considered grief to be a particularly dangerous emotion, for although it manifests itself as melancholy, Buchan explains, unchecked grief "often terminates in absolute madness" (248). Eighteenth-century psychiatry thus tended to reduce certain kinds of mental illness to a direct cause-effect relationship: great emotion stimulates the brain, resulting in corporeal effects such as fever or a lesion on the brain, which in turn produce some form of mental disturbance. Thus medical practitioners confused the symptoms and possible causes of mental illness.

Central to my argument is the consensus among physicians that the force of the conscience itself could drive people—especially women—to madness. In *Medical Inquiries and Observations Upon the Diseases of the Mind*, Rush explains that "The understanding is sometimes deranged through the medium of the moral faculties. A conscience burdened with guilt, whether real or imaginary, is a frequent cause of madness. The latter [imaginary guilt] produces it much oftener than the former" (44). Rush provides a number of anecdotes about guilt, including the story of a man who killed a friend in a duel, an example of "real" guilt, versus the aforementioned case of the woman unjustly believed to be involved in an affair, an example of "imaginary" guilt. The end result of unchecked grief and guilt could be particularly dangerous, according to the prevailing medical thought, for grief, often linked with guilt, "sometimes brings on sudden death, without any signs of previous disease, either acute or chronic" (318).[21]

Also commonly accepted by the medical community throughout the late eighteenth and nineteenth centuries was the notion that women, by virtue of their biological status, were more susceptible to mental disturbance than men. Both British and American physicians promulgated this belief. Rush claims that "Women, in consequence of the greater predisposition imparted to their bodies by menstruation, pregnancy, parturition, and to their minds, by living so much alone in their families, are more predisposed to madness than men" (59); Haslam concurs with these beliefs (245–50). This conflation of medical theory and sociological observation again suggests the permeability of the private and public spheres, as well as the ways in which male medical practitioners established decisive authority over the female body. The first novels written by Americans, for Americans, appeared at precisely this time of great flux in the diagnosis and treatment of mental illness, and beliefs like those that Rush expresses concerning privacy, the conscience, guilt, and madness emerge time and again in sentimental fiction.

Rush furthers his sociological view of madness by rejecting the notion that the insane are a public spectacle and emphasizing instead the need for privacy, even secrecy, in the treatment of mental illness. Rush argues: "Mad people should never be visited, nor even seen by their friends, and much less by strangers, without being accompanied by their physician, or by a person to whom he shall depute his power over them. The dread of being exposed, and gazed at in the cell of a hospital by an unthinking visitor, or an unfeeling mob, is one of the greatest calamities a man can anticipate in his tendency to madness" (238). For their own benefit, then, people suffering from any sort of mental illness should not be subjected to public ridicule and humiliation, as they were in British insane asylums such as Bedlam. Certainly Rush's chief concern here is humane treatment, but he goes beyond protecting these individuals and gives in to the impulse to hide mental illness as if it were still a shameful condition. He explains, "[T]here is another advantage from concealing the persons of mad people from the eye of visitors and the public.... Now, by rendering the place in which mad people are confined, private—I had almost said sacred—members of families may be sent there without its being known. Nay, they will be sent there upon the first appearance of the disease, in order to *prevent* its being known, and the disease thereby be more frequently cured" (238–39). While still stigmatized, mental illness is stigmatized *differently* in Rush's theories, for it is something that will be hidden from the community, a change from the common earlier practice of boarding harmless madmen with caretakers in the community.

Privacy from the eye of the viewer is even more important to the female sex, Rush hints, because madness has a peculiar effect upon the "moral faculties" of women. The moral faculties, for Rush, represent the will of the individual toward virtue or vice.[22] Rush reinforces the notion that mental illness is especially shameful for women, given the immodest actions in which they might engage while mentally troubled—actions at which Robert-Fleury's painting hints. This is yet another link between female sexuality and madness, in this case suggesting that only rational attention and discipline keep women's sexual natures contained. Further, Rush argues that if women's madness were hidden or otherwise kept secret, then "The obliquity and convulsions of the moral faculties, which sometimes take place in madness, would in this way never be known, or, if known, would be forgotten, or never divulged" (239). Thus women's actions should be concealed from view, if not in a prison, then in an asylum where, if they were unable to control their own expression of sexuality, it could be controlled for them.[23]

Rush, Haslam, and Buchan were progressive, however, in their view that some kinds of mental illness were curable, even preventable. Haslam, for example, explicitly advocates education and self-control in preventing insanity. He ascribes most causes of insanity to "errors of education, which often plant in the youthful mind those seeds of madness which the slightest circumstances readily awaken into growth" (237). He adds, "It should be as much the object of the teachers of youth, to subjugate the passions, as to discipline the intellect. The tender mind should be prepared to expect the natural and certain effects of causes: its propensity to indulge an avaricious thirst for that which is unattainable, should be quenched: nor should it be suffered to acquire a fixed and invincible attachment to that which is fleeting and perishable" (237). That passion could be subject to the will was a commonplace belief of medical practitioners. Joseph Parrish explicitly advocates the importance of the will in the overall health of the body and mind, arguing that cultivated virtue is "the most powerful agent in the prevention of disease" (48). This is precisely the moral message of many sentimental novels, which show by example the dangers of submitting to passion and desires, of whatever kind.

As I argued in chapter 1, much sentimental fiction advocates self-discipline through close examination of the conscience as a means of developing the will and controlling the passions. Although Richard Brodhead has located the nineteenth-century American obsession with discipline in the educational reform movement and traced it into later sentimental fiction such as *Uncle Tom's Cabin*, I want to suggest that the issue of discipline in the sentimental novel emerges concurrently with the genre in America.[24] Epistolary fiction in particular promotes the goal of self-discipline, for the prized qualities of sensibility and virtue (or the absence thereof) can easily be conveyed to readers both inside and outside the text through the process of letter writing. Clearly this epistolary communication is practice in the art of self-scrutiny; done repeatedly over time, self-scrutiny becomes a seemingly natural process rather than a learned skill. Significantly, even those sentimental novels that are not written in epistolary form usually include a number of letters that serve to reveal the transgressions of the writers, because to be most effective, self-examination must be observed by others—it must be publicly validated—a requirement that epistolary fiction readily fulfills. A more dramatic alternative to epistolary self-scrutiny, however, is the deathbed confession, a trope indispensable for the importation of medical theory into sentimental fiction. Thus guilt-driven self-examination and admission of error, given a medical context, frequently came to serve as the dramatic climax of deathbed scenes in non-epistolary novels.

This emphasis on self-scrutiny in the early American novel culminates in an overt disciplinary function, particularly affecting female characters, as they examine their conduct and emotional responses in minute detail. Recognition of significant moral failings such as loss of virtue necessitates a secularized, but nonetheless ritualistic, process of confession and self-punishment, frequently culminating in "madness" or some other disorder of the senses. This ritual of confession undoubtedly derives in part from the seventeenth- and eighteenth-century New England tradition of religious and civil confession, which is not surprising given the New England origins of so many writers of early American fiction.[25] In fiction, however, these confessions are purely secular, absent any specific religious context. Even the language used in these confessions is secularized: rather than speak of sins, women speak of "errors." The fictional emphasis on the conspicuous, even performative, nature of this confessional madness might seem in some ways to subvert the trend toward privacy in contemporary medical treatments of insanity, given that these scenes are reproduced for the entertainment of the reader. Yet these scenes function didactically, showing the reader not only the ultimate dangers of transgressive behavior, but also the "remedy" for them. As I have argued, this connection between transgressive behavior and madness is not coincidental. Rush's progressive work was indeed crucial in decriminalizing the insane and in establishing humane treatment for the mentally ill in the United States. Yet even from his intermediary position, Rush views criminal behavior itself as a potential cause for madness, particularly if the person who has broken a law feels intense guilt or remorse.

Rush's conflation of legal and moral transgression is closely related to the broad shift in the sphere of punitive action in the United States during the late eighteenth century. Prior to 1750, moral sin and crime were virtually synonymous in most of the colonies, for the function of law was to identify sinners; thus adultery and fornication were criminalized not just in New England, but in virtually all of the English colonies. Yet as legal historian William E. Nelson has pointed out, dramatic changes occurred in the legal system during the decades immediately before and after the Revolution, as accounts of adultery and fornication apparently increased, but criminal punishments for these offenses underwent a sharp decline.[26] Nelson concludes that these changing patterns of legal enforcement are not indicative "of significantly more immorality but of a new social and legal attitude toward the immorality that had always existed" (458).

It may indeed be the case that legal attitudes toward immorality were changing, but other evidence indicates that the rates of pre- and extramarital sex were increasing, perhaps reflecting decreased parental authority over their children's behavior, ranging from courtship to choice of marriage partner. In her study of courtship behavior, Ellen Rothman concludes that "Young men and women born in the years after Independence enjoyed a high level of self-determination. This meant not only that they were free to choose their own mates but that they socialized with little parental supervision."[27] Perhaps linked to increased freedom in courtship was increased choice of marriage partners. Historian Daniel Scott Smith's study, "Parental Power and Marriage Patterns," indicates that parental authority over children's marriage choices decreased over the course of the late eighteenth and nineteenth centuries. For women born to marriages between 1781 and 1840, the growing tendencies among the children of wealthier families to delay marriage, to marry out of birth order, and to remain single indicate decreased parental involvement and increased freedom of choice for young women.[28] This changing relationship between parents and children may also have contributed to the striking rise in the incidence of premarital sex during the last decades of the eighteenth century. Daniel Scott Smith and Michael S. Hindus's well-documented study, "Premarital Pregnancy in America 1640–1971: An Overview and Interpretation," convincingly demonstrates that there was a dramatic increase in premarital pregnancies, those pregnancies that resulted in a birth before the ninth month of marriage: during the time period of 1761–1800, 33 percent of all first births to married women occurred before the ninth month of marriage.[29] These factors suggest that young women were indeed exercising increased self-determination and sexual freedom—a situation that many writers of sentimental fiction regard with considerable anxiety.

Understanding contemporary theories of insanity and sociological factors indicating that young women were exercising increased sexual freedom enables us to better interpret the narrative conjunction of sexual transgression and madness in early American fiction. Given these factors, I want to argue that it is significant that the first American-authored sentimental novels appeared at precisely the time that they did, for some of these novels advocate conservative, even reactionary, notions regarding female sexuality, as novelists shrewdly negotiate the complicated politics of fiction in order to reach an audience composed of precisely those young women whose lives they wished to influence. Despite the apparent declension in both private morality and enforcement of laws governing the exercise of female sexuality, the American novel during this time assumes a compensatory function by asserting a higher standard of sexual morality. As fictional and medical discourse develops during this same time period, madness becomes increasingly prominent as the medical consequence and fictional punishment for violation of moral codes. This shift in the punitive consequences of sexual transgression is especially striking, given the fact that the law and legal issues are omnipresent in many novels of the period and that legal remedies to provide financial support for children born out of wedlock were readily available.[30] Even though fictional characters from a range of texts are arrested for forgery, debt, or murder, virtually no one is prosecuted for sexual transgressions, despite the fact that laws governing such behavior remained on the books (and for that matter, still exist today).[31] The increasing irrelevance—if not the removal—of such statutes suggests a broad cultural usurpation of legal authority by a narrative authority, in tandem with medical authority, that pathologizes extramarital sexual desire and locates punitive consequences for sexual transgressions firmly within the private sphere.[32] Many of these novels punish women for both passion and gullibility by death in childbirth, but death in childbirth is an evil that could befall any woman.[33] Madness, therefore, acts as a special kind of marker, as a fictional coding, to signal moral failings such as fornication and adultery.

Before I discuss specific novels, there is one last factor connecting insanity and sexual behavior that needs to be considered: syphilis, a disease with complex medical and sociological implications. In its tertiary stage, syphilis may result in meningoencephalitis, commonly called general paralysis or paralytic affection in the medical literature of the time. The timing of this stage varies dramatically; it typically appears from five to twenty or thirty years after the initial infection. Although there was not complete agreement among medical professionals about the exact nature of the relationship between syphilis and madness, a connection between these two conditions was established in the sixteenth century (Quétel 160–62). Numerous physicians reaffirmed this connection in the medical literature of the late eighteenth century. Based upon his experience at Britain's Bethlehem Hospital, Haslam makes the relationship between insanity and syphilis explicit in his *Observations on Madness and Melancholy*, claiming: "Paralytic affections are a much more frequent cause of insanity than has been commonly supposed" (259); he also adds that "a course of debauchery long persisted in, would probably terminate in paralysis" (208–209). In his chapter on venereal disease, William Buchan, too, makes this connection explicit, matter-of-factly listing "madness" alongside "ulcerous sore throats" and "carious bones" as the result of untreated syphilis (303). Despite medical knowledge that syphilis was commonly contracted in a variety of non-sexual ways, Buchan lists possible means of contracting syphilis only after first asserting that venereal diseases are "generally the fruit of unlawful embraces" (285). In the late eighteenth century, syphilis was, in fact, often transmitted through kissing, shared clothing or utensils, unsterilized medical implements, and through hereditary infection and breastfeeding.[34] The widespread labeling of syphilis as a "venereal" disease is significant, because this designation carried with it a persistent association with uncontrolled desire (Quétel 71–75). That, before the discovery of penicillin, insanity was a possible consequence of syphilis undoubtedly contributed to the lingering view of the insane as immoral, even criminal, despite the work of physicians like Rush and Pinel to counteract this view. Statistics are not available to indicate how many people in the late eighteenth century suffered from insanity that had its origins in syphilis. Numerous studies from the early twentieth century, however, after reliable tests for syphilis had been developed, but before the discovery of penicillin, indicate that an average of 25 percent of patients in state psychiatric institutions tested positive for syphilis.[35] It is reasonable to assume, then, that many cases of insanity in the late eighteenth century were induced by syphilis.

Certainly Americans of this time period had an avid interest in cures and treatments for what the medical literature called the "French disease" (a misleading label, since most studies indicate that a virulent strain of syphilis probably originated in North America and was transmitted to Europe by Spanish and Portuguese sailors). Worldwide, more than thirty different works on syphilis were published in English between 1780 and 1820, and many of these works appeared in multiple editions.[36] Numerous works on this topic for both general and scientific audiences were printed in the United States, including John James Giraud's *Doctor Giraud's Specific and Universal Salt, for the Venereal Disease, and All the Venereal Affections Which are the Result of It* (1797) and William Burrell's *Medical Advice; Chiefly for the Consideration of Seamen: and Adapted for the Use of Travellers, or Domestic Life* (1798).

Although no American sentimental novel explicitly details the physical manifestations of syphilis, the prevalence of syphilitic insanity places fictional depictions of madness in a charged context. The reticence of novelists is not surprising, given that even some doctors avoided discussions of syphilis. Despite knowing that syphilis frequently was contracted non-sexually and even though he intended his *Domestic Medicine* to be a practical handbook to address common ailments, Buchan initially omitted a chapter on venereal disease, owing to the unsavory nature of the topic. In later editions, he felt compelled to justify the inclusion of such a chapter: "The unhappy condition of such persons will certainly plead our excuse, if any excuse be necessary, for endeavouring to point out the symptoms and cure of this too common disease" (285). The closest novelists come to mentioning venereal disease is to hint at the debauched state of a character such as Madame La Rue of *Charlotte Temple*, whose debilitated condition requires hospitalization, or Lady Harriot Barrymore of Sally Wood's *Amelia; or The Influence of Virtue*, whose "vice had pillaged her once fair face of every charm and disease had rendered her an object loathsome," or Edward Somerton, the seducer figure in Caroline Matilda Warren Thayer's *The Gamesters*, part of whose narrative retribution is to live out the remainder of his life "prey of the disease" that he caught from the "irregularities of his youth."[37] Indeed, phrases such as "debauched state"—often read by contemporary readers as hackneyed clichés—were polite ciphers for eighteenth-century readers, hinting at a whole array of moral transgressions: drunkenness, gambling, and especially uncontrolled sexual behavior and consequent disease.[38] Novelists deal with the issue of sexual passion in a similarly coded way, leaving out the lascivious details (in part from fear of giving directions for seduction) and providing readers with just enough information for them to understand the magnitude of the woman's fall from virtue, as, for example, she becomes pregnant with an illegitimate child. Despite the delicacy with which American novelists deal with sexual issues and venereal disease, the prevalence of syphilis and the poor prognosis for treating the disease, which in all likelihood led to high incidence of syphilitic insanity, place fictional incidents of madness, especially when linked to sexual misbehavior of any kind, in a provocative cultural context.

For readers of the late eighteenth and early nineteenth centuries, then, madness as a literary trope would have served as a remarkably effective theme to underscore the criminality of the individual character's behavior, for it both flags guilty behavior and serves as a punishment in and of itself. Sally Wood's *Dorval; or The Speculator* dramatically emphasizes these elements in the novel's treatment of Elizabeth Dunbar. Betrothed to a man chosen by her parents, Elizabeth becomes one of the many victims of Dorval, a speculator, bigamist, and murderer. Dorval wears the mask of the sentimental man, and only the truly discerning can see beyond it. Despite the warnings of her dear friend Aurelia against Dorval, Elizabeth agrees to elope with him. Elizabeth is no passive, sexless creature; she readily avows that "from the moment I saw Dorval, my senses were infatuated, my reason obscured by a passion" (213). Love and passion properly directed and publicly sanctioned within the context of marriage are not proscribed in this novel. However, Elizabeth's passion is unsanctioned, for as she explains, "The *first* failing of my erring heart was concealment. Had I made a confidant of my injured mother; had I confided in my friend . . . I had never known the misery into which I have been betrayed by the worst, the vilest of men" [emphasis added] (213). In order to further his own financial and romantic ends, Dorval cruelly encourages Elizabeth's passion for him, convincing her to elope with him. Elizabeth again recognizes that it was the secrecy attendant in this relationship that rendered it so dangerous: "I heard his secret vows—fatal beginning! I consented to correspond with him—guilty commerce! I met him in private—incorrigible folly!" (214).[39] Dorval never intended to marry Elizabeth; instead, in a plot twist undoubtedly borrowed from *Clarissa*, he holds her captive in a house in Philadelphia while he attempts to seduce her. Elizabeth eventually escapes with her physical virtue intact, as she repeatedly asserts to anyone who will listen.

But fatal consequences follow her actions nonetheless, as Elizabeth's elopement is a "harbinger" of evils for her family, preceding the deaths of two of her siblings and the loss of her family's fortune (226). In the midst of her escape from Dorval, Elizabeth learns of these tragedies by overhearing the story of her family's downfall and slanderous rumors about herself. Elizabeth dramatically re-enacts this scenario for Aurelia: "I could hear no more. A kind of distraction seized me—I grew raving—a dreadful fever followed—my intellects were unequal to the trial—my reason deserted me" (217). Elizabeth's "broken heart and a guilty conscience" result in her incarceration in a madhouse in Philadelphia, where she slowly regains her rationality (218).[40] In a testimonial to the efficacy of moral treatment, Mr. Lawson, the superintendent of the asylum, provides her with books, a private room, and conversation, thereby aiding in her recovery. Lawson even reunites her with her friend Aurelia, who finds Elizabeth much changed, her beauty marred by "[h]er trembling limbs, her emaciated form, and her pallid countenance," all of which "declared how much she had suffered" (211). Despite her sympathy, Aurelia finds Elizabeth's situation distasteful: although she expresses her pleasure at seeing her friend, in a colossal understatement she ponders, "surely a mad house was a most undesirable place in which to find her" (213).

Once Elizabeth has learned of the dangers of concealed passions, duly suffered for her transgressions, and confessed them for the benefit of Aurelia's already sterling character, she can be rehabilitated—but on the condition that she was guilty only of allowing ill-judged passion to induce her to elope with Dorval, not of engaging in sexual relations with him. To this end, Elizabeth repeatedly protests her innocence; she claims that "I am wretched, frail, and weak, but not guilty.—The shame of vice has never washed from my cheek the crimson of virtue" (213). Even though Aurelia eventually becomes convinced that Elizabeth is indeed "pure and unspotted" (223), she argues that marriage is the only means to salvage Elizabeth's reputation and reconcile her with her parents. Now able to appreciate kindness and virtue, Elizabeth does not return to her erstwhile suitor, Mr. Jones, but instead marries Lawson, the superintendent of the asylum. Fascinated by her "melancholy beauty" (223), Lawson has fallen in love with her, thereby further complicating the novel's erotic equation of sexuality and madness. Is Elizabeth now the only fit mate for Lawson, given his close association with the inhabitants of the asylum? Or, perhaps more likely, is Lawson the only fit mate for Elizabeth? Certainly he is the savior of her reputation, for once they are married, she can escape the asylum, that "scene of shame and sorrow" (212) and return to her parents with her virtue "unspotted." Indeed, her friends urge Elizabeth to marry Lawson, if for no other reason than "in becoming the wife of so valuable a man, every thing like disgrace would be removed from her character, and all past disagreeable occurrences forgotten" (224). In other words, the law of coverture extends here to the moral sphere, as his moral distinction effectively eclipses Elizabeth's moral disrepute. But even more important, it seems clear that in Wood's view, Elizabeth's passion can be suitably directed only by a man who has witnessed the results of uncontrolled passions and learned how to tame them.

Misdirected passions also cause the tragic madness of a female character in Samuel Relf's novel *Infidelity*. Caroline, the female protagonist, is married to an older "man who never avowed more than a motive of expediency for his addresses, who has ever neglected the offices of a husband, and for whom . . . [she] never felt more than esteem."[41] In modern parlance, Mr. Franks married Caroline for her money in an arranged marriage, and neither is particularly happy in this situation. Although Relf coyly avoids describing the exact nature of the husbandly "offices" that Mr. Franks neglects, the narrative hints that, at the minimum, Mr. Franks does not fulfill Caroline's romantic emotional needs—hence he is at fault in this relationship as well. Amid many a subplot, Caroline remedies her loneliness by falling in love with a young neighbor, named Charles Alfred. The narrative is ambiguous about whether Caroline and her neighbor ever consummate their relationship. However, Caroline obviously has committed emotional infidelity by permitting another man to become emotionally intimate with her, as suggested by the clandestine meetings and communication between Caroline and Charles.

Upon discovering this relationship, Caroline's husband kills himself. Guilt-stricken, Caroline then begins her descent into madness, which is completed when her outraged brother kills her lover (whom he has inadvertently encouraged to pursue Caroline) in a duel. After a friend worries that Caroline "will soon fall victim to the ravages of madness," she tells Caroline's brother, "We have sent to town for Dr. R——, that patron of humanity, whose presence imparts health to the patient, and comfort to the distressed" (184). Evidently even the powers of the eminent "Dr. R——"—clearly an allusion to Benjamin Rush, given that *Infidelity* was published in Philadelphia—cannot save the adulterous, guilt-stricken Caroline. Eventually she, too, dies of grief and guilt, "the fury of madness . . . tearing her soul" (190). Lest the reader misread Caroline's madness as merely an excess of sensibility, Relf carefully ensures that Caroline herself enacts a ritualistic acknowledgment of wrongdoing, as she conveniently returns to lucidity only long enough to castigate her behavior and confess her wrongdoing.

Although seemingly a parable about the dangers of arranged marriages, another way to understand this novel is by exploring the consequences of extramarital sexuality, for Caroline's unregulated sexuality threatens not only herself but also her family and that of her lover; the novel ends with the deaths of Mr. Franks, Caroline, and her lover, Charles Alfred. The exclamation of Caroline's brother makes this understanding explicit, when he accuses Alfred: "You have murdered the character of my whole family, by insulting the chastity of my sister!" (187). Caroline's father abused his authority and exercised poor judgment in arranging her marriage, but according to the narrator, Caroline's misdirected passion exacerbates this dangerous situation.

Numerous other early American novels feature similar scenes of deathbed madness and confession—all of which are explicitly linked to sexual transgressions. Charlotte Temple, too, rages in a delirious state brought on by grief and shame. After Montraville abandons her, Charlotte writes a poignantly repentant letter to her mother, begging her forgiveness. Made melancholy by her intense solitude and the lack of a female confidant (an absolute necessity, according to the advice literature of the day), Charlotte

The frontispiece from an 1809 edition of *Charlotte Temple*.
Courtesy, American Antiquarian Society.

teeters on the brink of madness. After she gives birth to her daughter in a hovel, guilty visions torment Charlotte; she "rave[s] incessantly" and does not even recognize her own child.[42] Modifying the usual gendering of novelistic insanity, Rowson has Charlotte's seducer, Montraville, who has taken Franklin as his surname after marrying Julia Franklin, succumb to madness in the sequel novel *Lucy Temple*. According to the narrator, his sin is legible on his countenance even to "[a]n indifferent gazer," for he is guilty of "yielding to the impulse of guilty passion" (230–31). Fittingly, Montraville himself is now haunted by visions of Charlotte, and he "labour[s] under slight fits of insanity" (175). After seeing his illegitimate daughter Lucy, whose true identity is unknown to him, he becomes even more tormented, crying "Take her away, this vision haunts me forever, sleeping or waking, it is still before me" (175).

Once again, as in *Infidelity*, the sins of sexual transgressions are visited upon entire families, for Charlotte Temple and Montraville both die after their respective fits of insanity. Further, Montraville's legitimate son, Lt. Franklin, continually tempts death in the pursuit of heroism after learning that his beloved Lucy is his half-sister, and he dies fighting against Napoleon. Lucy, herself guilty of no crime, "did not shrink nor faint, nor fall into convulsions" upon learning that she has lost Lt. Franklin forever (238). She merely "[placed] her hand upon her brow, reclined against the mantel piece a moment, and then left the apartment" (238). Although Lucy grieves, she does so rationally. Rowson, like Relf and Wood, reserves fits of insanity to identify and punish those guilty specifically of sexual misbehavior.[43] Rowson later has Lucy devote herself to benevolent acts, from which she learns "the great secret of woman's happiness, to enjoy the happiness of others" (260). Despite the narrator's hard sell of this position, readers must understand that, for the narrator, this is the only fate left to the product of an adulterous liaison. (One can only wonder what Rowson, who raised the illegitimate son of her husband, William Rowson, was thinking as she wrote this novel.) Lucy's eventual death marks the end of the Temple family as well, for "the history of her family was closed with the life of its last representative" (265).

Even those characters in early American fiction who are victims of trickery or sexual violence are not free of narrative scrutiny, and they too are punished for their romantic and sexual gullibility, if for nothing else.[44] The case of Amelia, for example, the female protagonist in a novel entitled *Amelia; or, the Faithless Briton*, differs dramatically from that of Elizabeth Dunbar, Caroline Franks, Charlotte Temple, or Montraville. The title is inadvertently confusing; while Amelia is the central figure of the novel, as the title suggests, the phrase "the Faithless Briton" refers to her deceitful British lover. Lillie Deming Loshe was the first of numerous critics to dismiss this novel, which she calls one of the many "histories of seduction, too common in the fiction of the time" (61). Yet a closer look at this overtly political and very conservative novel, which, unusual for this period, was reprinted several times, illustrates the engagement of its author with contemporary issues. Amelia is the beloved daughter of a wealthy American merchant, Horatio Blyfield. She, her father, and her brother live on Long Island, where they moved to escape the hostilities of the Revolutionary War. When a battle occurs in their neighborhood, Horatio Blyfield charitably brings home Doliscus, a wounded British soldier. Doliscus, a practiced seducer and nobleman, repays Blyfield's hospitality by tricking his gullible daughter Amelia into a clandestine mock-marriage ceremony and then abandoning her. When she informs him that she is pregnant, he ripostes: "[Y]ou may be assured, that I still entertain the warmest gratitude for the favours which were there [in the Blyfield household] conferred upon me by the virtuous Horatio, and his amiable daughter" (14–15). His cruel play on the word "favours," hinting at the sexual favors he enjoyed, and the distinction he makes between the "virtuous Horatio," but the merely "amiable" Amelia, signal to Amelia that he does not regard her as his wife, but she vows "publicly to vindicate her honour, and assert her rights" (16). She intrepidly follows Doliscus to England, setting the stage for the final and fatal conflict between her family and Doliscus. After Doliscus rejects her demands for "a public and unequivocal acknowledgment of their marriage" (19), he informs her that their marriage was nothing but "a rural masquerade, at which an honest soldier . . . played the parson, and you the blushing bride—but, pr'ythee, do not talk of husband" (19). This discovery shocks Amelia into a stupor punctuated by "boisterous [laughter]" and "nervous ejaculation[s]" (20). She then gives premature birth to a son, who dies three days later.

    The rest of the novel centers around the issue of culpability: to what degree is Amelia responsible for the tragedy that befell her? Amelia continues to assert her righteous innocence; contemplating suicide, she prays, "Gracious Father! . . . I have been deluded into error; but am free from guilt: I have been solicitous to preserve my innocence and honour. . . . The treachery of him to whom I entrusted my fate, has reduced me to despair" (22). The appearance of her forgiving father prevents her from committing suicide, as he blithely instructs her: "Cheer up, my Amelia! The errors of our conduct may expose us to the scandal of the world, but it is guilt alone which can violate the inward tranquillity of the mind" (24). But guilt *does* "violate the inward tranquillity" of Amelia's mind. Racked by grief, shame, and guilt, she succumbs to a fever, which in turn sends her into a delirious, Ophelia-like state, and she dies amid "peals of loud and vacant laughter" (30) and pathetic fits of singing. In a belated acknowledgment of *his* guilt,

Doliscus allows Honorius, Amelia's brother, to kill him in a duel. This act of vengeance precipitates Honorius's own death: to escape the consequences of the duel, Honorius flees to America, where he is immediately killed at the battle of Monmouth.

The 1798 frontispiece from *Amelia; or, the Faithless Briton*.
Courtesy, American Antiquarian Society.

Responsibility and culpability are central issues in this narrative. Doliscus lied to, tricked, and seduced Amelia; based on his actions, readers sympathize with and wish to exonerate Amelia, but the narrative itself discourages this reading. Despite Amelia's innocence, the narrator deliberately dwells upon the "errors" that she committed. First, she erred by allowing passion to obscure her judgment of Doliscus's character. She compounded this error by consenting to a clandestine marriage ceremony without her father's permission. Aside from the issue of consent, this novel explicitly attacks the belief that romantic love somehow supersedes the bonds that legally and publicly unite individuals and families, as Amelia allows herself to be seduced by Doliscus's dangerous rhetoric about the privacy of intimate relationships. Doliscus dismisses the need for public rites such as the marriage ceremony and instead asserts the primacy of the private relationship between a passionate couple, arguing, "My Amelia has surely no vanity to gratify with idle pageantry; . . . the privacy of the marriage does not take from its sanctity" (11). By "privacy of the marriage," Doliscus means a secret marriage, one that is not publicly announced or sanctioned by the presence of family or friends. Although Amelia recognizes that it is the very public nature of marriage as a legal transaction that protects the individual from "the fatal consequences that might arise from the obscurity of the transaction" (11–12), her passion wins out over her common sense. Doliscus's trickery and Amelia's poor judgment and susceptibility to passion bring about the end of two families. The deaths of Amelia, her son, Honorious, and Doliscus signal the end of the family line for both the American Blyfields and Doliscus's noble British family.

As the narrator explains, the purpose of this narrative is not merely to entertain, but "to improve his readers" (2). To this end, madness once again appears as a trope to signal the dangers of unchecked passion and independent female choice. The narrator also critiques Amelia's political infidelity—her susceptibility to the blandishments of her political enemy—and her belief that private life can be effectively insulated from public life. Clearly the fate of the family is linked to the state, as the narrator sets forth in the introduction: he explains that "the great events of the late war . . . were chequered with scenes of private sorrow, and the success of the contending forces was alternately fatal to the peace and order of domestic life" (1). In "Infidelity and Contagion: The Rhetoric of Revolution," Shirley Samuels argues for a specific connection between the notion of the family and the nation during the early Republic period. "National concerns were portrayed as domestic dilemmas," she claims, "since to preserve the nation it was conceived necessary to preserve the family as a carefully constituted supporting unit. Therefore the sexual infidelity that represented the greatest threat to the family was presented as a national threat, especially after the French Revolution when women were popularly understood to be the instigators of the dread mob that came to stand for democratic rule, and Liberty came to be depicted as a whore."[45] Although Relf's narrator is much too refined to label Amelia a "whore," clearly there is a political element to his critique, for not only did she secretly choose a husband, but she chose a British nobleman, the very antithesis of her own American merchant family. While contemporary readers might be tempted to excuse Amelia given her youth and Doliscus's deliberate seduction of her, the narrator discourages such a reading. His emphasis on guilt and culpability shows us that he, at least, finds Amelia partly responsible for her situation.

Anxiety over female agency is at the heart of *Amelia* and many other early American sentimental novels. Given the manner in which the narrative encourages sympathy for Amelia, but carefully forecloses the possibility of absolving her of all responsibility for her plight, it is simply not possible to read *Amelia* as proto-feminist tract or even as a subversive text, as so many contemporary critics read *The Coquette*, another novel of seduction. In the character of Eliza Wharton, Foster complicates matters by showing readers a woman of limited means who sees her life slipping away, is desperate to marry into a higher social class, and seizes perhaps her last chance at happiness. Amelia, however, is young, beautiful, rich, and beloved by her father; she lacks nothing except maternal guidance or, failing that, common sense. And, although Amelia, like Charlotte Temple, is a naive target of deliberate seduction, this circumstance does not eliminate their responsibility for their actions. To describe them merely as the victims of seduction is to deny them agency—something that the narrators and authors of each of these texts are careful not to do. Indeed, these novels betray considerable anxiety about the issue of female agency. While each of these women is in some way victimized by her seducer, each is also partially responsible for her own fate, whether from her fateful passivity (Charlotte Temple), her passion (Amelia Blyfield and Elizabeth Dunbar), or her improperly channeled romantic sensibilities (Caroline Franks).[46] Madness as a repeated trope underscores this reading of these texts and provides a dramatically lurid fate for each transgressive woman. The delirious state suffered by each of these characters serves a necessary narrative function, for it exposes the misguided expenditure of sexual capital that costs the woman not only her reputation, but also her sanity. This delirious state represents self-annihilation, the utter negation of self, as self-punishment either for misplaced trust, betrayed consent, or transgressive behavior—consistent with contemporary medical theory. In each case, madness serves as a means to deliver a narrative verdict on the character, as well as a punishment for his or her errors.

Fiction, together with medical treatises, accordingly helps illustrate the gradual evolution of American cultural attitudes toward mental illness and self-control in the eighteenth century. There was no dramatic epiphany in American culture equivalent to that signified by Pinel's acts at the Salpêtriére and immortalized by Robert-Fleury's painting. Rather, the continued conflation by fiction writers of extramarital sexuality and madness emphasizes that this evolution in attitudes was neither steady nor coherent. While medical authorities were developing a variety of theories to explain insanity, numerous writers of fiction seized upon one particular current of medical thought that postulated a connection between extramarital sexuality and insanity, thus fictionally conflating madness and moral sin while medical theorists were themselves struggling to decriminalize madness. Punishment for sexual transgressions via the trope of madness is so common in novels of the early Republic period that it becomes in a sense almost naturalized. Seduced by the repetition of this pattern into a misleading familiarity, twenty-first-century readers do not necessarily find it surprising that the female protagonist's self-censure will drive her into a guilty and ultimately deadly delirium; the repetition of this pattern undermines the strangeness of these texts for modern readers until it simply appears to be an odd quirk of early American fiction.[47] In *Is Literary History Possible?* David Perkins writes that when texts are "seen as belonging to the past, and especially to a past about which we are informed, [they become] at once a part of a world that is not our own."[48] Situating novels among other forms of discourse helps us see anew their alienness and understand a fictional past that novelists imagined was threatened by dangerous desires.

As a genre, the novels of the early Republic have long been conspicuous, even notorious, for their reliance on thematic conventions such as conscience-induced madness. This tropical repetition does not necessarily signal a lack of originality or creativity on the part of the novelists, as critics such as Loshe once argued. Rather, tropical repetition in popular culture serves to reinforce basic cultural norms and values and helps readers "combat ambiguity," as Janice Radway argues in *Reading the Romance*.[49] Further, if the principles to guide female behavior were to be effectively instilled throughout the literate populace, then they had to be iterated in multiple texts and in multiple genres, as Carla Mulford has proposed.[50] The problem for modern readers, of course, is our distance from the cultural values and beliefs of late eighteenth-century America. In a time of social and political upheaval such as existed in the early Republic, thematic repetition represented both reliability and the reification of older social codes—shrewdly translated and exported into a new form that would effectively enthrall the exact audience of young women whom writers most wanted to reach. In some cases, fiction itself may have served as a repository for older communal values during the turbulent post-Revolutionary years, thus for a time stabilizing and perhaps enabling a sense of nationally shared cultural values.[51] These early American "tales of truth" reassure readers that those who transgress will be punished in a marked way. Because pregnancy so easily identified the female half of any pair of transgressors, female conduct was much easier to criticize than the broader social problems that beset early America. Fiction thus acted as a check upon bourgeois female sexuality, as a cultural force to counter increasingly tolerant legal attitudes toward the exercise of sexuality in general outside of marriage. Further, the lingering cultural associations between madness and criminality rendered madness a far more powerful and meaning-laden punishment for women than death during childbirth.

During a time in which there was a loosening of legislation concerning private life and sexual mores were becoming private or local concerns, rather than state concerns, fiction assumed an increasingly important role. John Zomchick has argued that "law and narrative both stand as references, guides for adjudicating between personal desires and social demands—the latter understood in the double sense of personal demand for society and social demands upon person."[52] In this instance, fiction became a surrogate for law, as it helped to provide structure and social continuity during a period of changing attitudes towards arranged marriages and sexual morality. Perhaps we should not be so quick, then, to dismiss the innumerable prefaces that argue for the moral efficacy of American fiction. Many novelists seized upon this issue of sexual transgression precisely because they could advocate a higher standard of sexual morality than that currently enforced by most state legal systems. It is important to remember, however, that these conservative fictional plots are merely that—*fictions*. As Laurel Thatcher Ulrich demonstrates in *A Midwife's Tale*, women who became pregnant out of wedlock might indeed make delivery-bed confessions, but these confessions usually elicited only the name of the father of the child being born. After this birth, women generally went on to marry the fathers of their children or to collect support payments from them and, in all likelihood, eventually to marry other men.[53]

The conservative fictions of the early national era, however, provided frightening examples that transgressive behavior such as fornication would not go unpunished, even if that crime were not highlighted by a pregnancy. Criminal law might no longer publicly punish those guilty of sexual transgressions, but the novel showed readers the inevitable punishment of those who transgressed against their families and communities. Madness following lapses in chastity—or even the appearance of such a lapse—was used by novelists to dramatize the magnitude of loss from the unproductive expenditure of virginity.[54] Thus the novel in effect made public behavior that the legal and medical systems were increasingly regarding as belonging to the private realm. Drawing upon the authority of current medical and psychological theories, fiction filled in the gap between the penal code and private morality. By training readers in the art of self-scrutiny, asserting the absolute necessity of confession, and demonstrating the horrific dangers engendered by sexual transgressions, novelists gave themselves an eminently defensible position from which to assert the virtuous nature of American fiction—a particularly important concern given the continued attacks on fiction by figures of cultural authority such as Noah Webster and Timothy Dwight. At the same time, novelists insisted on the importance of the inviolable, unmarried female body to the integrity of the nation's conception of itself, consolidating women's position in the post-Revolutionary imaginary, even as the state itself denied them the full rights of citizens.

The fluidity between fiction, "real life," and medical thought during the early national era indicates some of the ways in which early American fiction is embedded within its culture and vice versa. "Medicine," Benjamin Rush asserted in 1795, "has caught the spirit of the times."[55] The same might well be said of fiction. Novelists of the early Republic affirmed their engagement with critical and cultural issues of the day by incorporating contemporary scientific beliefs into their work and engaging in critiques of the weakening familial and public control of young women. Sentimental novels such as *Infidelity, Lucy Temple, Amelia,* and *Dorval; or The Speculator* reflect considerable cultural anxiety about female choice and sexual freedom, as they insist upon a morally and sexually normative status for unmarried white women. Their conservative plots in all likelihood contributed to, as well as were symptomatic of, the growing sexual conservatism of the early nineteenth century. During this time, fiction became an increasingly important link in the nexus of public discourse, able to incorporate the authority of other kinds of discourse and make their power its own, while the literary arts likewise influenced medical practitioners.[56] Close study of early fiction reveals the shifting balance and fascinating interplay of cultural authority. The convergence of fiction and medical thought in pathologizing female desire outside the bonds of marriage delineates the increasing power and ascendancy of medical discourse, while at the same time revealing the extent to which American writers were engaged with their culture as they explored the boundaries of the public and private spheres, and indeed, attempted to make these boundaries permeable.

3

A Speculating Spirit

*Economic Anxieties and Opportunities
in Early American Fiction*

> We thought when once our liberty was gain'd,
> And Peace had spread its influence thro' the land,
> That Learning soon would raise its chearful head,
> And arts on arts would joyfully succeed;
> 'Till all Columbia's genius 'gan to blaze,
> And in true science more than rival'd Greece:
> But *Speculation*, like a baleful pest,
> Has pour'd his dire contagion in the breast;
> That monster that would ev'ry thing devour ...
> —From *The Glass; or Speculation: A Poem: Containing an Account
> of the Ancient, and Genius of the Modern, Speculators* (1791)

IN THE YEARS following the Revolution, changing economic conditions wrought both hope and disappointment in the newly formed United States. As the idealized, self-sacrificing civic virtue of the war years gave way to more profit-oriented forms of individualism, "speculation" and its companion vices, avarice and greed, came to dismay republicans throughout the United States.[1] Americans began authoring their own novels at precisely the time when this post-colonial economy was in great flux, and these novels consistently point to the possibilities and dangers inherent in a capitalist economy that placed grave demands upon trust between widely separated and differing individuals. Novelists were not alone in their concern; poets, playwrights, political writers, and belletrists, regardless of their political orientation, likewise expressed considerable anxiety about how this changing economy would affect the moral virtue of American citizens.² The luxuries resulting from this changing economy became a locus for these fears, and luxury came to refer not only to goods procured in international trade, but also to an urbanized, sophisticated, anglicized lifestyle of unregulated expenditure that was as threatening, in its own way, to republican ideology as was unchecked female sexuality.³ Like uncontrolled sexual desire, excessive desire for luxury even becomes characterized as a pathological condition, typified in such works as *Letters from an American Farmer*, in which J. Hector St. John de Crèvecoeur likens luxury to a corrupting epidemic, the end result of which produces decadent, depraved Limas and Charlestons.⁴

Although novelists were similarly anxious about abuses of luxury, they were perhaps more concerned about the problematic issue of accumulating capital. While most early American novels exalt industry and the potential for economic advancement that the expanding, post-mercantilist American economy offered, these novels simultaneously explore contemporary economic anxieties, primarily the fear that men would attempt to make money without industry through such means as gambling, speculating, and counterfeiting. I argue in this chapter that reading novels alongside political pamphlets, economic tracts, and belles lettres reveals how novelists used fiction as a means through which to intervene in public discourse concerning American economic practices during the 1790s and the first two decades of the nineteenth century. Engaged with economic issues facing Americans of the rising middle-class, fiction contributed to public economic discourse by exploring ways to reconcile desire for personal economic advancement with larger civic interests. At the same time, fiction contributed to the gendering of the American economic system by presenting international trade as a virtuous means of making money while simultaneously constructing economic desire as a masculine prerogative. In the promotion of international trade with the East, we see American nationalism conjoined with the promotion of bourgeois interests in an anticolonialist yet economically imperialist project. And yet the liberal, democratic plots of these novels are consistently balanced by republican resolutions that reject urban splendors for rural repose. The novel thus attempts to mediate for its readers between the values of a modern capitalist society that privileges bourgeois economic advancement and the republican ideals still cherished throughout the early national era.

As I have argued, novels written between 1789 and 1814 provide a window into post-Revolutionary America that allows us to understand both the cultural values and anxieties of Americans. In the previous chapters, I considered how increased social choices and sexual freedom for young women excited trepidation among writers of early American fiction. After briefly expanding during the Revolution, public and political life had contracted for women in the post-Revolutionary years, but women still played an essential role in the American imaginary. Female virtue—meaning chastity, primarily—was a crucial component in the United States's early republican political identity and budding sense of nationalism.[5] Although these novels place many of the same demands upon male and female characters— among these demands are patriotism, fidelity, and chastity—these demands differ in one essential respect. While the primary challenge women face is to be sexually and emotionally chaste, the challenge male characters face is to be economically virtuous—meaning that they must balance self-interest and public interest. The difficulty of this balancing act clearly evoked concern on the part of writers of early fiction, for virtually every novel written during this time betrays considerable apprehension about the issue of accumulating capital. Money—particularly the presence or absence of private capital—proves a complicating factor in practically every early novel. Novels portray money being amassed in a variety of ways, sometimes legally, through inheritance or commerce, and other times illicitly, through some other means such as counterfeiting, forgery, gambling, or speculation. Yet contemporary disputes over political and economic policy meant that even a legal means of making money such as international trade carried with it overtones of ideological and class conflict. The provocative question these novels pose is this: How does one reconcile what were often conceived of as conflicting desires, making money and being economically virtuous? In other words, how does one mediate between individual and civic economic interests? The agenda of much early American fiction is precisely this regulation of masculine economic desire in a republic anxious about the dangerous effects of luxury on both the individual and national psyche. Much fiction seeks to mediate between these desires; consequently, a fictional battle emerges, pitting money earned through virtuous commerce against that acquired through gambling, speculation, or inheritance.[6]

The problem of making money is a natural one for writers of early American fiction to explore, for the task of the American protagonist is literally to become Crèvecoeur's "new man"; numerous protagonists of early American fiction are disinherited, both literally and metaphorically, perhaps as a parable for, or meta-response to, the severing of the colonial relationship with England. The response of these protagonists to this disinheritance serves as a driving force to the plots of many American novels.[7]

Charles Brockden Brown, for example, whose fiction demonstrates his avid interest in the emerging modern capitalist economy of the United States, frequently relies upon this trope, although his male protagonists chiefly seek means to *avoid* having to make their own way in life. In Brown's *Arthur Mervyn* and *Edgar Huntly*, both eponymous protagonists search for a wealthy surrogate father to adopt them and free them from the need to earn a living. Arthur Mervyn, whose father has foolishly sold the family farm in order to speculate in frontier land, is astonished by the contrast between his own poverty and Welbeck's luxurious wealth. Mervyn fantasizes, "what was the fate reserved for me? Perhaps Welbeck would adopt me for his own son. Wealth has ever been capriciously distributed.... All within me was exhilaration and joy."[8] When Welbeck's faked suicide renders this dream impossible, Mervyn then considers Mr. Hadwin as a surrogate father, thinking at his first meeting, "I could embrace him as a father, and entrance into his house, appeared like return to a long-lost and much loved home. My desolate and lonely condition appeared to be changed for paternal regards . . ." (123). Similarly, the orphaned Edgar Huntly, whose guardian uncle has his own family to provide for, seeks a surrogate father/father-in-law in Sarsefield, who has grown rich in the India trade. Ultimately, however, the events of the novels snatch their fantasy father figures away from Huntly and Mervyn, leaving both men in the same economically uncertain positions in which they began, although Mervyn's financial hopes now rest tenuously on his fiancée, Achsa Fielding. Brown's interest in these and other economic issues has been explored by a number of critics, and my own extended discussion of *Arthur Mervyn* appears in chapter 4.[9] What I am concerned with instead in this chapter is how other, less well known, yet representative, early American novels explore alternatives to inherited wealth arising from the evolving U.S. economy. In particular, my discussion will focus on Rebecca Rush's *Kelroy* (1812) and Sally Wood's *Dorval; or, The Speculator* (1801).

The majority of early American novels exhibit a definite republican bias, exalting a virtuous rural lifestyle on a landed estate, but wealth and land ownership are precisely what most disinherited protagonists lack; instead, property is extended as a tantalizing reward for a life of virtue and industry, and commerce is the means to such propertied prosperity.[10] The anonymous work *Moreland Vale* (1801) provides an excellent illustration of this trope. After toiling for years as a clerk in a counting house in Canton, China, Henry Walgrove, the male protagonist of the novel, inherits a substantial fortune; he and his wife then retire to country life. He explains why: "In the peaceful bosom of calm retirement, you do not give up the world; but you have the pleasure of enjoying the company of your friends unaccompanied by the ceremony and bustle of a town life. You have leisure to attend to the calls of humanity and to relieve the wants of your fellow creatures."[11] It is the very orderliness of rural life that provides such a happy resolution to so many early American novels, for rural life generally symbolizes a life ordered by hierarchy, where systems of philanthropy enable each individual to neatly categorize others.[12] The corollary to this praise of rural life is the relative absence of novels portraying details of life in urban industrial centers, which is not surprising since widespread industrialization did not take place until the second decade of the nineteenth century. With the exception of Sarah Savage's 1814 novel *The Factory Girl*, early American fiction paints a landscape largely free of manufacturing, populated instead by farmers, artisans, professionals such as doctors, lawyers, ministers, and soldiers, and, most interestingly, merchants.[13] Merchants and trade are the key to economic opportunity, as trade offered a proactive approach to this problem of earning an income, as well as a virtuous means of halting post-Revolution downward mobility.

Yet merchants and trade held an unsettled status among thinkers of the day. Historians studying both sides of the eighteenth-century North Atlantic such as J. G. A. Pocock, Carroll Smith-Rosenberg, and Drew R. McCoy have documented ambivalent contemporary attitudes toward commerce in general.[14] Indeed, writers from virtually every professional field in the early Republic express ambivalence that stems from two different problems, the first directly involving merchants and the relationship of trade to productive labor. The second problem centers around the consequences of international trade, chiefly the increased numbers of luxury goods imported into the United States and their effect on the psyche of consumers. These concerns about luxury were present throughout the mid- to late-eighteenth century; indeed, as T. H. Breen has persuasively argued, colonial theories that the *appearance* of luxury led to increased taxes fostered pre-Revolutionary antagonism to British commercial policies and precipitated the subsequent non-importation agreements.[15] Dramatically increased opportunities for international commerce after the Revolution, and especially with Asia after 1793, when Britain was involved in the war with France, undoubtedly fomented anxieties about the consequences of such trade.

Despite unsettled views about the effect of trade on the virtue of Americans, international commerce represented a rapid means of acquiring wealth, especially when compared with agricultural practices. In *The Social*

Structure of Revolutionary America, Jackson Turner Main indicates that the merchant class in the post-Revolutionary period offered significantly increased opportunities for social mobility, particularly in large cities such as Boston, New York, and Philadelphia. He concludes that trade, along with law, offered the most fruitful way to wealth.[16] And, while trade in theory aroused considerable anxiety among Americans, Stuart M. Blumin has argued that the *occupation* of international "long-distance" trader, removed as it was from retail trade, was both dignified and respectable in the early Republic.[17] Novels of the time such as *Dorval; or The Speculator, Moreland Vale,* and *Fidelity Rewarded; or, The History of Polly Granville,* to name just a few, use the motif of virtuous trade to illustrate the mobility inherent in the American economy, while the conclusions of these novels, which almost inevitably feature settlement on a landed estate, emphasize the return of order, social stability, and hierarchy. In a fascinating mix, then, of democratic plots and republican resolutions, novels explore how the worthy might find ways to prosper in an emerging capitalist society in the absence of inherited wealth.

In order to advance trade as a virtuous means of earning capital, however, novelists had to distinguish between those individuals who participated in honest trade and those who dealt in unsavory or potentially dishonest economic practices such as gambling and land, currency, or commodity speculation. Because many Americans still perceived success in trade as something of a gamble, novelists had to find a means to distinguish commerce from other practices on the same economic spectrum. Novelists differentiated between these practices and linked economic speculation with gambling, which is universally damned in American fiction and belles lettres. Gradually, commerce came to be understood as a moral, rational practice distinct from speculation. Furthermore, by encasing trade in a rhetoric and logic of sentimentality, fiction associated trade not only with individual benefits, but also with the economic health and security of communities and the nation at large. Men turn to foreign commerce not out of greed or desire for luxuries, but rather for reasons of sentiment or honor—to support aged parents, redeem a father's debts, or honor an engagement. In an era in which land owning continued to be exalted and trade was still slightly suspect among some political circles, fiction valorized the East India and China trade as a daring, even romantic, venture that offered the possibility of tremendous legitimate profit without unfair risk to other Americans—an important distinction that novelists carefully portray.

Nationalism, Luxury, and the East India and China Trade

The East India and China trade had a tremendous cultural resonance during the early national period, for it symbolized American entrepreneurship, as well as the United States's new freedom from the trading restraints of the British mercantile system. Partisans of free trade like minister-turned-merchant Pelatiah Webster also claimed that a vigorous international trade would actually serve to unite the new country through shared interests, thereby giving additional impetus and significance to the sea trade.[18] This imperial project thus promoted nationalism in a variety of ways, allowing the United States to define itself against both Britain and Asia. Although British mercantilist policy prohibited direct American trade with the British West Indies, the former colonies' nearest trading partner, and blocked American trade with the French West Indies colonies during the Napoleonic war, Great Britain tolerated American participation in the East India and China trade until the commencement of hostilities that later led to the War of 1812. Furthermore, the Jay Treaty guaranteed reception of American ships in important British ports throughout the trade routes to East India and China.[19]

Post-Revolutionary direct commerce with Asian countries allowed Americans to trade for their own luxuries—precisely the kind of luxuries that appear conspicuously in a number of novels. Americans would ship goods such as ginseng (used for medicinal and aphrodisiac purposes), tobacco, pitch, tar, turpentine, furs, and silver to China and East India. Export of commodities such as ginseng and tobacco was acceptable, even necessary, according to Jeffersonian political doctrine, in order to expand the agricultural basis of the new nation. In return, traders would receive tea, cotton nankeen cloth, silk, porcelain (which was so inexpensive in China that it was often shipped as ballast), pepper, and Chinese cinnamon. Americans might also ship home more exotic luxury goods, including such items as hand-painted wallpaper, lacquered trays and boxes, silk slippers, and decorative fans made from a variety of materials, such as paper, mother-of-pearl, silk, and lacquer.[20] Formerly a symbol of British mercantilist policy, tea had obvious cultural significance for Americans, as did these other conspicuous luxury items procured through free trade with the exotic Orient. The tremendous popularity of special-order Chinese porcelain decorated with patriotic motifs, especially tea sets, lends significance to mention of China plate in shipping lists, newspapers, and novels, and further signifies how American patriots valued their country's participation in the East India trade.

The conspicuous presence of these items, especially tea, in virtually every early American novel would have signaled to readers not only patriotic pride in American entrepreneurship, but also approval of American participation in international trade.[21] Further, as David S. Shields points out, the tea table "was the superintending agency in the spread of manners and taste."[22] Shields speaks specifically of the pre-Revolutionary era, but the tea table continued to be an important site of sociability in the early Republic, as well as a site that could mark the *absence* of sociability and manners. Taking tea thus was not merely about the consumption of a luxury beverage; it offered the opportunity for display of the requisite tea service as well as bourgeois values, manners, and taste. In *Kelroy*, for instance, the nouveau riche Gurnet family demonstrates the ludicrous *misuse* of luxury goods as they unintentionally caricature the polite ritual of taking tea by wearing gaudy and inappropriately lavish satin gowns. The juxtaposition of the Gurnets' social aspirations and their vernacular discourse also renders them ridiculous as, for example, Mrs. Gurnet repeatedly calls their expensive porcelain dishes "chany."[23] That the visit to the Gurnets' house was obviously intended for comic relief highlights the sophisticated cultural values and assumptions about luxury goods that Rush assumes her readers will share.

What is most significant about the goods procured through international trade, then, is not their mere presence, but how they come to be used. For instance, Henry Walgrove, the honorable merchant protagonist of *Moreland Vale*, presents to his new wife a trunk filled with Chinese porcelain, elegant fans, and silks—gifts that she generously shares with her friends. In such a situation, proper display and use of these cultural signifiers not only celebrated American trade, but also denoted consumer sophistication that in itself came to symbolize a shared culture, thus uniting the United States in ways that even advocates of free trade like Pelatiah Webster might not have anticipated.

The luxury goods procured during voyages to China and East India offered both ship owners and investors opportunities for remarkable profits. For example, in 1784–85, the first American voyage to China, that of Robert Morris's *Empress of China*, netted the owners a 20 percent return on their original investment. Other voyages generated even more profit, such as the 1785 voyage of the *Experiment*, which netted investors returns of 72 percent on their investment (Goldstein 30; Dulles 43).[24] Although such an investment was not without risk from shipping disasters, the Asian trade was a very permeable business, and ship owners were not the only ones to profit from such voyages. Merchants other than the owners or original investors might invest in a voyage by shipping cargo on the same ship. The captain and other members of the crew, such as the supercargo, also engaged in small private commercial ventures; supercargoes, for example, carried out commissions for private individuals for a flat fee or a percentage of the profits (Dulles 44–47). Thus there was considerable opportunity for individual participation in the trade with the Far East. Once in the East, individuals might also choose to remain in India or China in a managerial capacity as a commercial agent for a number of years beyond the usual fifteen- to eighteen-month round-trip voyage, a situation that frequently occurs in fiction of the time: Henry Walgrove of *Moreland Vale* becomes a clerk in a counting-house in Canton, while one of the sons of the Dunbar family in *Dorval* remains in India as an agent for seven years, amassing an enormous fortune.

The impact of the first direct voyage to China was of great importance and was widely documented in East Coast newspapers of the time such as Boston's *Massachusetts Centinel*, the *New-York Packet*, and Philadelphia's *Pennsylvania Packet*, undoubtedly providing information and inspiration to American writers of fiction. In *Philadelphia and the China Trade*, Jonathan Goldstein claims that "In private correspondence, newspaper articles, and books, two themes emerged that would be echoed down to the end of Philadelphia's old China trade: the China trade was of unprecedented economic importance for the new nation; and because of that great commercial value, the Chinese people as a whole were to be held in esteem" (31). The China and East India trade immediately burgeoned after this initial venture. Goldstein claims that "Between 1784 and 1804, as many as seven ships a year went from Philadelphia to China, and as many as thirty-one per year from the entire United States. After 1804, until the end of the old China trade in 1846, the number of American voyages leveled off at about thirty or forty per annum, with Philadelphia ships comprising about one-third of these passages" (34). The entrepreneurial possibilities inherent in international trade enthralled the imagination of writers of fiction, and merchants and the separations demanded by trade become favored characters and situations in such diverse novels as Mrs. Patterson's *The Unfortunate Lovers, and Cruel Parents* (1799), Wood's *Dorval; or The Speculator*, and Rush's *Kelroy*.

Patriotic pride in such trading ventures pervades newspapers and other writings of the 1780s and 1790s. Philip Freneau's *envoi*, titled "On the First American Ship That Explored the Route to China, and The East-India, After the Revolution," aptly captures this celebratory patriotism in the new freedom for American shipping.

> With clearance from BELLONA won
> She spreads her wings to meet the Sun,
> Those golden regions to explore
> Where George forbade to sail before.
>
> Thus, grown to strength, the bird of Jove,
> Impatient, quits his native grove,
> With eyes of fire, and lightning's force
> Through the blue aether holds his course.
> No foreign tars are here allow'd
> To mingle with her chosen crowd,
> Who, when return'd, might, boasting, say
> They show'd our native oak the way.
>
> To that old track no more confin'd,
> By Britain's jealous court assign'd,
> She round the STORMY CAPE shall sail
> And, eastward, catch the odorous gale.
>
> To countries plac'd in burning climes
> And islands of remotist times
> She now her eager course explores,
> And soon shall greet Chinesian shores,
>
> From thence their fragrant TEAS to bring
> Without the leave of Britain's king;
> And PORCELAIN WARE, enchas'd in gold,
> The product of that finer mould.
>
> Thus commerce to our world conveys
> All that the varying taste can please:
> For us the Indian looms are free,
> And JAVA strips her spicy TREE.
>
> Great pile proceed! —and o'er the brine
> May every prosperous gale be thine,

> 'Till, freighted deep with eastern gems,
> You reach again your native streams.²⁵

Despite his patriotic pride in being free of "Britain's jealous court," Freneau himself embodies the ambivalence that many American writers felt toward commerce, ambivalence that also permeates political and economic tracts of the 1790s. Although he could thrill patriotically at the freedom of American shipping, at the same time Freneau feared that the luxuries procured by this trade would foster avarice among his countrymen. Just a few years later, in 1797, Freneau printed in *The Time Piece* an extract from the anonymous work *Of Commerce and Luxury*, which questions the benefits of a developed international trade in luxury goods. While granting the necessity of economical trade, the author of this piece clearly feared that an advanced trade in luxury goods would create ever-greater disparity in wealth among the population.²⁶ This fear of altering the status quo of wealth in the new Republic was only one of the problems associated with the sea trade.

Here, I want to explore in more detail the nature of the ambivalence over trade expressed in a variety of political and economic tracts; doing so will better illuminate precisely how the novel intervenes into this topic of widespread public discussion. While Freneau worried that foreign commerce would create a wider divide between the haves and the have-nots, increasing participation in international trade also presented potential conflicts with republican political ideology, as merchants and trade became a locus for generalized apprehensions about the American economy and culture. These concerns range along a spectrum that extends from dislike of unproductive labor to the negative effects of a luxurious, speculative lifestyle. The first of these anxieties centers on the objective that all labor be productive labor. Although Scottish political economist Adam Smith considered trade to be productive labor, many American writers followed the general tenets of the French physiocrats in arguing that trade was, in fact, unproductive.²⁷ Thomas Cooper, who would later teach at the University of South Carolina one of the first American courses on political economy, argues in his 1798 work *Political Arithmetic* that the military costs of protecting international trade far outweigh its profits. But equally a matter of concern for Cooper was that "*merchants, and all the people directly employed by him, rank among the unproductive classes of society*"; Cooper includes in this group agents, factors, clerks, sea captains, and sailors, all of whom merely arrange and transport the labor of others, while producing nothing new themselves.[28] Other Jeffersonians, like the Virginian John Taylor, agreed that the sea trade, when compared with the practice of agriculture, was unproductive.[29] Hence, the nature of the wealth procured through trade was itself problematic.

Attendant to this fear about the unproductive nature of foreign trade was the belief that involvement with trade would bring about wealth too quickly when compared to the slow and steady prosperity of agriculture—no small concern in a Republic obsessed with private and civic virtue. In *An Enquiry Into the Principle and Tendencies of Certain Public Measures* (1794), Taylor describes merchants as "brokers, honourable and useful, whilst adhering to a steady line of commerce, and supplying the wants of a nation; but pernicious and dangerous, whilst speculating indiscriminately on foes and friends for the acquisition of wealth, and aspiring to exclusive privileges and prerogatives" (78). Thomas Cooper makes a similar argument, claiming

> Nor is it a slight objection, that while by the peaceful products of agriculture, gains can be made but slowly, gradually, and by the regular exertions of habitual, wholesome industry, the commercial speculator often gets rich by accident, by unfair venturing, by sudden exertions. Wealth thus suddenly obtained is in many respects detrimental to the community. It operates as a lottery: it tempts capital into trade beyond prudent bounds: it entices to unjustifiable boldness: it introduces ostentation, luxury and pride, and manners out of harmony with republican principles. (14–15)

This emphasis on agriculture as non-competitive, "habitual," and "wholesome" points to doubts that trade itself might not be wholesome and, further, that the vagaries of trade themselves are a danger. Trade is dangerous not so much from the possibility of losses but rather from the possibility of too sudden gains, a possibility that explicitly connects the merchant with the speculator, just as the mention of the lottery links trade to gambling. This association illustrates the uncertain status that merchants and trade continued to hold for some writers during the early national era, for both Taylor and Cooper associate merchants with a dangerous tendency toward avarice and greed and a subsequent appetite for a luxurious lifestyle. At the same time, Taylor, Cooper, and others feared that this poisonous desire for luxuries would spread throughout the population at large. These fears are precisely those that novelists of the early Republic era seek to counter, as I will argue later in this chapter, by illustrating the broad economic benefits of such trade.

Luxury, Gambling, and Speculation

Other Americans were also critical of the newly formed United States's easier access to the sources of luxuries, for concomitant with this changing economy were anxieties about how people would behave in an economy filled with luxuries.[30] The vituperative 1785 debate between Samuel Adams and the supporters of the Boston Tea Assembly (the "San Souci Club") exemplifies this fear about the kind of society a changing economy might produce. Even the author signing himself "One of a Number," who was himself a supporter of the Tea Assembly, links an increase in commerce with luxury; he views public amusements such as dancing and card playing at the Tea Assembly as the natural outcomes of an increasingly luxurious lifestyle.[31] Just as unproductive labor was a source of anxiety in republican thought, so too was unproductive exchange, for, at base, criticism of gambling and luxury is criticism of unproductive, even deleterious, forms of exchange. The Tea Assembly became a prime target for those concerned about such unproductive exchange. Adams, advocate for a very spartan version of republicanism, had many concerns about the Tea Assembly, particularly about the promiscuous mixing of social classes he believed such a public entertainment might entail. But more dangerous, he believed, was the possibility that card playing at the Assembly would lead to it becoming a decadent gambling den, where such speculative acts would be publicly performed and might lead "to the destruction of everything good or virtuous" (reprinted in Wood, *The Rising Glory* 138). Adams sees card playing as the slippery slope to ruin: "Those who play frequently get an itch for it, and although they may begin small, will play more largely as they are more attached to it. The gamester by being fortunate this night, is desirous to risk again: —Or by being unfortunate the last night, again plays in hopes of regaining it;—thus he is led on step by step until he has imbibed such a desire for gaming, as never to be easy but when at play" (reprinted in Wood, *The Rising Glory* 147). Benjamin Austin concurs with Adams about the potential dangers of card playing, for such gambling might lead to "the *ruin of their [the gamblers'] fortunes*, and *misery of their families* . . . for though [the] independent gentleman may claim this right, within his *private sphere*, yet a *public amusement* may prove fatal to a community, and may with propriety be *supprest as such*" (reprinted in Wood, *The Rising Glory* 151). Indeed, Austin seems to fear that private vices like gambling would no longer remain so, but would permeate bourgeois American culture, an end brought about by the luxurious lifestyle that international trade fostered. Austin's position here is typical of American republicanism in its rejection of Bernard Mandeville's equation of private vices with public virtues, for most Americans feared private vice would infect the public sphere.

Although there had always been a streak of antigambling sentiment running through the religious and literary culture of colonial Anglo-America, this rhetoric reaches a new pitch in the late eighteenth century, as gambling becomes understood as a result of luxury and as the extreme end of the continuum of economic speculation. A prime example of this confusion of economic practices is Mason Locke Weems's 1810 antigambling tract *God's Revenge against Gambling*. This volume is one of a series of morality tracts compiled and marketed by Weems, who likewise sensationalizes the dangers of adultery, drinking, and other social and religious evils in additional volumes, aptly reflecting the increasing social conservatism of the early nineteenth century and foreshadowing the more sensationalist aspects of the nineteenth-century social reform movements. In this particular volume, Weems provides lurid examples of violence and tragedy resulting from gambling; some of these are obviously fictionalized sketches, while others, Weems claims, are based in fact. One anecdote in particular strikingly illustrates the cultural association between gambling, speculation, and commerce. After enumerating the tragic loss of fortune and subsequent suicide or murder of several gamblers, Weems concludes that "this just judgment of poverty inflicted on Gamblers, is a universal truth none can deny" (34). He challenges readers to show him "one single Gambler, who *has liv'd and died rich*" (34). On the other hand, Weems himself promises he could "name . . . hundreds, and here in the town of Augusta too, to go no farther, hundreds of industrious, honest men, who started poor and now are rich" (34). Among the doctors and lawyers he mentions, Weems includes "honorable Merchants, who, thirty years past, open'd shop with hardly more than pedlars packs, and yet now drink as good wine as the *great Emperor*, and parry, with a shrug only, the loss of 50,000 dollars on a cotton speculation" (35). Clearly honest trade was not completely free of all association with speculation in 1810, but by this time, the kind of speculation involved in basically honest trade has taken on a more positive connotation— at least in Weems's view—as a legitimate risk of the marketplace.

Novel-length fictions of the 1790s and the first decade of the nineteenth century, however, are careful to isolate gambling as a seductive obsession, as a practice distinct from virtuous trade, and as an economic practice with no possibility of redemption.[32] One such novel is *The Gambler, or The Memoirs of a British Officer* (1802), which combines a number of themes popular in

Illustration from Mason Locke Weems's *God's Revenge against Gambling* (1810). Courtesy, American Antiquarian Society.

fiction of the time. The main character is, of course, a British officer who gambles away his family's fortune, is imprisoned along with his family for debt, and eventually dies from disappointment and grief. The British officer is the natural choice to represent the gambler in this text, for American readers see embodied in this soldier Britain's lack of virtue, as well as their own fears about the outcome of a luxurious, riotous lifestyle. Telling his tale while imprisoned, the officer describes himself as a man in the grip of an obsession, unable to overcome it even though he regrets his actions and the suffering they cause his family. Through its use of first person narration, the tale borrows from the genre of the conversion narrative. Despite this first person narration, the tale remains flat, and it never gains the power of a true conversion narrative, perhaps because there is no possibility of redemption for this gambler.

Another, more complicated, antigambling novel that also bills itself as a conversion narrative of sorts is *St. Hubert* (1800), which suggests that gambling results from a failure to regulate the self and control the passions. *St. Hubert* begins the conversion process by including on its title page the motto "Exemplo aliorum discite," or "Profit by example." Interestingly, in spite of, or perhaps because of, its status as a quasi-conversion narrative, the preface takes a very different tack from that of most prefaces in early American fiction. The frame narrator, no apologist, explains in the preface that he is telling his tale in the form of a novel in order to aid the "rising generation" in the face of "the many difficulties" and the "numerous temptations" they face. He prefers the novel form because he fears that "the austere manners and jesuitical denunciations which priestcraft has too often invented to answer the purposes of fraud and deception" will not appeal to the youth of his time; he goes on to condemn sermonic literature, claiming that "the awful and silent exhortations of the pulpit . . . [have] not had the salutary effect which they merited, inasmuch as they [are] too serious and . . . gloomy." Instead, the frame narrator finds the novel to be the most "captivating mode of recommending virtue in her simple and comely garb, and of exhibiting vice in her native hideous colors."[33]

The tale itself fascinatingly intertwines the seduction of sexual and economic virtue. St. Hubert, who narrates the inside narrative, is a married Frenchman led into debauchery by his friend Delaferre, who introduces him to card playing and to the widowed Madame de Trenville, who in turn seduces St. Hubert into adultery. The widow and gambling are twin seducers, each furthering St. Hubert's descent into debauchery, as St. Hubert gambles in order to be near Madame de Trenville, and she in turn encourages him to gamble. Gambling and seduction are thus made analogous threats to his moral virtue.[34] After St. Hubert has lost his entire fortune, he learns that Madame de Trenville, who is the picture of "hardened vice, of experienced seduction" (30), has merely feigned love in order to seduce his fortune away from him. Learning of St. Hubert's debauchery, his wife dies of grief and shock hastened by the loss of their money. St. Hubert then enters a religious order and practices acts of "charity and beneficence, to make [his] being not hateful in [Heaven's] sight" (36). *St. Hubert* is a relative rarity among early American fiction, because few novels show male chastity under such a tempting attack. Nonetheless, *St. Hubert* operates under sexual logic similar to that of other fictions: women still unjustly bear the burdens of sexual transgressions, even though, in this case, it is St. Hubert's innocent wife who suffers and dies.

Economic virtue is similarly under attack in Caroline Matilda Warren Thayer's 1805 novel *The Gamesters*, as Leander Anderson is seduced into vice by Edward Somerton, his corrupt and dissipated friend. Somerton is the proverbial snake in the garden of Leander's rural married bliss, using specious logic to sway Leander from virtue. Knowing that gaming is Leander's weakness, Somerton argues that there is no reason for Leander not to pursue his passion. He asks Leander, "Were [the passions] not implanted into the soul when it first animated a mortal form? You will undoubtedly answer, they were; if so, they must proceed from Deity, and is it not the height of presumption and impiety to pretend that any *evil* can flow from the *Fountain of all Good?*" What Somerton here proposes—that passions are a normal part of human existence—was widely accepted in eighteenth-century pedagogical and religious writings. However, as I discuss in both chapters 1 and 2, this same pedagogical literature also argued that it was the duty of rational humans to control the passions. Nonetheless, Somerton easily convinces Leander that he should thus "acquiesce in the will of Heaven, and not attempt to stifle the growth of that which God himself implanted in [his] soul."[35] Untested and unskilled in regulating his own behavior, Leander succumbs to this seductive rhetoric, games away his inheritance, commits suicide, and leaves his wife and son destitute.

The connection among *The Gamesters*, *St. Hubert*, *The Gambler*, and Weems's *God's Revenge against Gambling*, aside from their obvious antigambling rhetoric, is the light they shed on the relationship between gambling and speculation. Gambling is a small-scale, private form of speculation, one that wreaks havoc on the domestic life of the gambler by decimating family finances and destroying the family itself; in that sense, it eventually impacts the larger community, albeit in a limited fashion.[36] But if gambling is speculation on the domestic scale, then speculation is gambling on a large, public scale—gambling that affects the entire community and its web of economic relationships with far-reaching public implications, for it is private vice made public. No good emerges from *this* private vice, for greed and self-interest triumph over civic interests.

Indeed, medical and political discourse of the time points to culturewide apprehension about how greed and avarice were fueling speculative economic practices, and vice versa. Such anxiety is understandable considering events in Western Europe, the British colonies, and the new United States during the preceding seventy-five years. The John Law currency fiasco in France, the failure of the Mississippi Company, the South Sea bubble in England, and numerous currency and land scandals in the new United States all threatened the financial stability of the northern transatlantic community. In the early national era, the Yazoo land speculation fraud vividly exemplified the fortunes to be made by some speculators and the tremendous costs borne by others.[37] When American writers of the late eighteenth and early nineteenth centuries use the term "speculation," clearly they are viewing American speculation as part of an unfortunate transatlantic history of greed and economic fraud. In *Travels in New England and New York*, for instance, Timothy Dwight refers specifically to the "Mississippi and South Sea schemes" in the context of a discussion of American land and currency speculation.[38] And in what amounts to a mini-jeremiad on the evils of speculation, Dwight extravagantly praises the New England states for their success in commerce while condemning his greedy countrymen for their desire to profit through speculation. He finds post-Revolutionary currency speculation particularly repugnant, claiming that "At the first effusion of this evil upon the community, every sordid passion of man was stimulated to the most vigorous exertion. Wealth, for such it seemed to the fancy, was acquired with an ease and rapidity which astonished the possessor. The price of labor, and of every vendible commodity, rose in a moment to a height unexampled. Avarice, ambition, and luxury saw their wishes anticipated, and began to grasp at objects of which they had not before even dreamed" (vol. 4:261). Although at a different point on the political spectrum from many of his Jeffersonian contemporaries, Dwight, too, worries about the dangers of wealth too rapidly acquired, claiming "Sudden wealth rarely fails of becoming sudden ruin; and most of those who acquire it are soon beggared in morals, if not in property" (vol. 4:261). In addition, Dwight felt that speculation was undermining the work ethic of his country, arguing that "Fortunes, they [enterprising men] will easily believe, may be amassed at a stroke, without industry or economy, by mere luck, or the energy of superior talents for business" (vol. 1:158). Even Pelatiah Webster, a partisan for trade, similarly warned of the dangers of speculation decades before Dwight, claiming in 1779 in *A Second Essay on Free Trade and Finance* that "fortunes acquired suddenly without the *industry* of the possessor, rarely ever increase his happiness and welfare, help his virtuous habits, or continue long with him; they must commonly ruin him."[39] But what most incensed Dwight was the fact that those who bear the costs of speculation, whether in currency or land, are too often those who could least afford to lose their money: "widows and orphans" and "great multitudes of sober, industrious people [launching] the earnings of their whole lives," and "the honest purchaser, stripped of his possessions . . . left to meet old age without property, consolation, or hope" (vol. 1:159–60).

Dwight was only one of many public figures who excoriated speculation. Solomon Aiken, a frequently published anti-Federalist minister, condemned the currency and scrip speculation by Federalists during the 1790s in his 1811 fast-day sermon, *The Rise and Progress of the Political Dissension*, and concluded, "These gross and bare-faced instances of speculation, have a tendency to break down all barriers to common honesty. Hence the increase of dishonesty, defrauding and overreaching, in private and individual dealings; and consequently an augmentation of vexations and expensive law suits."[40] Speculation was not merely a private vice, as gambling was supposed to be, for speculation had wide-ranging public implications. Benjamin Rush took an even more dramatic point of view in his multifaceted work *Medical Inquiries and Observations upon the Diseases of the Mind*. He suggests that the tremendous opportunities for various kinds of financial speculation in the decades following the Revolution caused a corresponding increase in cases of insanity. Rush claims, "In the United States, madness has increased since the year 1790. This must be ascribed chiefly to an increase in the number and magnitude of the objects of ambition and avarice, and to the greater joy or distress, which is produced by gratification or disappointments in the pursuit of each of them. The funding system, and speculations in bank scrip, and new lands, have been fruitful sources of madness in our country" (66). Unregulated economic desire, then, like sexual infidelity, is another potential source of madness. However, unlike many of his contemporaries, who tended to see the flow of civic influence in one direction—from the individual to the community—and thus believed that the central issue was the danger of private vice contaminating the public sphere, Rush saw these public events as deeply influencing private life and the individual.

Even works in popular circulation expressed dismay about the greed, avarice, and ambition that seemed rampant in American culture. In his "Chronology of Facts," a satiric piece published in the *National Gazette*, Freneau labels the year 1791 "The Reign of Speculators," due to the "Banks, bubbles, tontines, lotteries, monopolies, usury, forgery, lying, gambling, swindling, &c. &c." that he saw plaguing the nation during that year. In another savage but amusing satire, Freneau constructs a plan for an American nobility based upon practitioners of speculation, ranging from the lowest rank, the "order of the Leech," to a middling order, "Their Hucksterships," to the highest order, "The Order of Scrip."[41] But perhaps most interesting is how antipathy for speculation entered the realm of popular culture in the form of song. A.W.'s *A Dandy Song*, a broadside ballad dating back at least to 1806, cleverly expresses some of the disillusionment of the age, as it heaps scorn upon the greediness of speculators who hold government offices and professionals such as doctors and lawyers. The final lines of the song aptly sum up its message: "But I'm sure you'll not be beat if I call the world a cheat, / And he that reaps the harvest is the dandy O."[42]

Stephen Burroughs, the most notorious confidence man of the late eighteenth century, vividly illustrates in his *Memoirs of Stephen Burroughs* the seductive lure of land speculation, with its promises of easy wealth, and the risks such speculation entailed. Initially employed as an agent by Robert Morris (the same Robert Morris involved in the China trade), Burroughs traveled throughout Georgia, surveying the lands still controlled by the Indians. When Morris's business concerns foundered, Burroughs opened his own office as a land agent with great success. As frequently happened to him, however, his reputation caught up with him, and the owners of various properties subsequently withdrew them from his office. Even so, Burroughs had by this time accumulated thirty thousand dollars, which he invested through a Philadelphia lawyer, but he himself was soon conned by a confidence man. When the lawyer asked for a power of attorney in order to manage Burroughs's business interests, he readily complied. Burroughs explains that "Having the most absolute confidence in the integrity of my agent, I did not hesitate one moment to comply with his desires, executed the power [of attorney], and sent it on forthwith. However, this was a fatal stroke to my fortune. By virtue of the power he sold my security in Philadelphia, realized the money, and fled to France." After this episode, Burroughs was again impoverished with nothing left to show for his labors in Georgia; his experiences illustrate the chimerical nature of the "speedy affluence" that Burroughs and others sought to realize through speculation.[43] Burroughs's narrative begs the question, of course, of whether he really was tricked or whether he is simply conning the readers of his narrative into having sympathy for him!

Greed and avarice alone did not create the national problem of rampant speculation; greed and avarice fueled ambition, and vice versa, for public speculations. Thus ambition, too, comes under attack in countless pamphlets, poems, and sermons of the early national period. Hezekiah Woodruff, for example, in his 1804 sermon *The Danger of Ambition Considered*, militates against ambition, arguing that ambition "is a selfish exercise" that "aims primarily at its own advancement."[44] John Adams, in his *Discourses on Davila*, struggles to distinguish between selfish ambition and a natural desire for self-improvement, which he calls "distinction." He argues that striving for distinction bears positive results for the individual and the state; however, he cautions about this striving, "when it aims at power, as a means of distinction, it is *ambition*."[45] What emerges in the literature of the time—both fictional and non-fictional—is the notion that ambition had to be tempered by a sense of justice and fair play for one's fellow Americans. Above all, ambition had to be regulated by industry, which writings of the day praise in its stead.[46]

Benjamin Franklin's *Autobiography*, a tale of the transformation of a private individual into a public servant and statesman, is perhaps the best known written example from the early Republic era of this tempering of ambition with industry. Although, by modern standards, Franklin's life appears to be a textbook study of ambition, "ambition" is a word he uses only twice in all four parts of his memoirs, on one occasion of which, when discussing how contemporary writers categorize the moral virtues, he explicitly links ambition with avarice.[47] Instead, the touchstones for Franklin's autobiography are those character traits that I discuss throughout this chapter: industry and virtue. As the life story he recounts illustrates, self-interest is best advanced not through ambition, but through private virtue and industry, which in turn benefit the larger community. This harmony between self and society is precisely what Franklin seeks to uncover or recover in his autobiography. Furthermore, Franklin spends a great deal of time explaining how he himself countered the appearance of ambition through his deliberate displays of modesty, the most famous of which is the iconic image of the industrious younger Franklin, aproned and trundling a wheelbarrow through the streets of Philadelphia.

Throughout his autobiography, Franklin emphasizes the importance of civic virtue, of acting in what he calls a "publick-spirited" manner. His illustrations of how to behave, such as his refusal to accept a patent on the improvements he made to the wood-burning stove, arguing that part of our public duty is to serve others by contributing to the betterment of our community, have appeared to many critics like monuments to his ego. Nonetheless, Franklin also emphasizes that in pursuing these civic achievements it is important to de-emphasize the self—not only to ensure the cooperation of others, but also to mitigate charges of self-serving personal ambition. When Franklin began raising money for the academy that would later become the University of Pennsylvania, he explains, "In the Introduction to these Proposals, I stated their Publication not as an Act of mine, but of some *publick-spirited Gentlemen*; avoiding as much as I could, according to my usual Rule, the presenting myself to the Publick as the Author of any Scheme for their Benefit" (193). For Franklin, it was not enough merely to be virtuous—one had to avoid the appearance of personal ambition and perform virtue, over and over again.

While Benjamin Franklin carefully avoids describing himself as ambitious because of the word's negative cultural connotations, and deflected potential charges of ambition by conspicuously displaying private and civic virtue, early American novelists are far freer with that term. Writers such as Sally Wood and Rebecca Rush readily associate ambition with greed, luxury, speculation, and gambling. Concomitantly, the novels of Rush and Wood are deeply concerned with the morally problematic issue of making money by means other than agricultural pursuits—a dilemma that bedevils the characters of both their books. Although we know relatively little about the life of either woman—and more is known about Wood than Rush—it perhaps is not surprising that these two women, both of whom were connected to prominent and well-to-do American men (Rush to her uncle Benjamin Rush and Wood to her father Nathaniel Barrell and her grandfather Judge Jonathan Sayward), would have been intrigued by this issue.[48] The fact that her sex would have hampered either woman in making money adds another layer of intrigue to their choice of this topic, for both women portray female economic desire as verboten, as forbidden in its own way as extramarital sexual desire. The only legitimate solution either novelist proposes to this masculine dilemma of amassing capital is trade—especially trade with the exotic East Indies.

Trade and the Fictional Gendering of Economic Desire

In order to represent trade as an ethical economic practice, novelists focused on many of the same issues that Benjamin Franklin identifies as crucial in conveying the appearance of individual virtue. Further, using fiction as a public forum through which to champion trade required novelists to distinguish between honest trade and vices such as gambling or lottery playing, as well as between honest trade and potentially dishonest practices like speculation. Novelists also had to demonstrate that one needed industry, rather than merely superior business sense or good fortune, to succeed in trade. Finally, novelists had to show the productive fruits of trade, fruits that serve a triple purpose of patriotically celebrating the United States's trading freedom while benefiting individual and public interests.

Although many novels from the early national period include one or more of these motifs, two novels in particular draw them together coherently, framing trade as a viable, virtuous means of accumulating capital, while at the same time gendering economic desire. Significantly, both of these novels are by women; juxtaposing them against one another emphasizes the diversity of fiction written by women during this era, for while Rebecca Rush's *Kelroy* emphasizes private life and the effect of individual vice on domestic life, Sally Wood's *Dorval; or The Speculator* attempts to show the impact of national economic events and trends upon the individual and upon domestic life. Yet both novels illustrate how economic transactions render permeable both the public and domestic spheres.

Kelroy is the more consciously gendered of the two novels in its exposé of the snares of ambition. Mrs. Hammond, one of the central characters of the novel, is the mother of Emily and Lucy and the widow of a well-connected Philadelphia merchant. The narrator describes her as "a woman of fascinating manners, strong prejudices, and boundless ambition, which extended itself to every circumstance of her life" (3–4). Despite her limited funds, Mrs. Hammond's appetite for luxurious living, as well as her confidence in her ability to broker economically advantageous marriages for her daughters, encourages her to "[launch] fearlessly into the wide sea of dissipation, and in the incense, and adulation of the giddy multitude" of Philadelphia (11). Indeed, Mrs. Hammond's lifestyle comes close to caricaturing contemporary notions of luxury. She has every luxurious accouterment: a city house in Philadelphia and a country estate bordering the Schuylkill River, numerous servants, expensive furniture, plate and crystal, diamonds, her own carriage, and silk and satin gowns—all of which are financed by credit, her expectations, and loans finagled from her future son-in-law. Mrs. Hammond also engages in what someone like Samuel Adams would have viewed as an extremely dissipated lifestyle: once her daughters are of marriageable age, their lives become an endless round of balls, social calls, tea parties, and card playing. Although Mrs. Hammond has no active role in Philadelphia's foreign trade, she is a voracious consumer of luxury goods, and foreign trade enables and encourages her participation in social rituals.[49] The conspicuous presence of foreign goods indicates the economic permeability of the domestic sphere, yet women like Mrs. Hammond are consumers only, unable to participate in the profit-making aspects of this trade.

Eventually Mrs. Hammond's financial extravagance squanders her remaining money, but perversely, her very poverty drives her to "feverish extravagance," both from the self-denial she has practiced in the past and the struggle she has to maintain appearances (164). Unlike the hapless Gurnet family, Mrs. Hammond knows how to use trade goods as status symbols, enabling her to maintain her place in a social hierarchy that has material wealth as its basis. Eventually, however, her creditors force her to settle some of her bills in order to avoid exposure. The final calamity that befalls her is a fire that burns down her townhouse, the insurance policy for which she had let lapse only the week before. Nearly destitute and "half wild with perturbation," Mrs. Hammond plays the lottery with money borrowed from a friend (129). She has the true gambler's mentality, always convinced that "it was possible the scale might still turn in her favour" (129). In her final venture in the lottery, the first ticket drawn is a blank, while the second ticket amazingly wins Mrs. Hammond fifty thousand dollars.

To the characters of *Kelroy*, this lottery win appears to be the stroke of fortune that saves Mrs. Hammond from financial ruin; subsequent events, however, reveal to the reader that this fortunate gamble sets in motion the tragic events of the novel's denouement. Although Mrs. Hammond's youngest daughter, Emily, is at this time happily engaged to a young man named Kelroy, Mrs. Hammond has long conspired to marry Emily to a wealthier man, a scheme she hopes will ensure her own financial stability. Kelroy was raised and educated as a gentleman, but his father lost the family fortune in "a wild speculating scheme, which he fancied would at least double his property, but on the contrary it failed, and ruined him" (36). After Mrs. Hammond wins the lottery, Kelroy believes that Emily will be financially secure under her mother's care, so he travels to India to recoup the family fortune. However, Kelroy's absence leaves his relationship with Emily vulnerable to the manipulation of Mrs. Hammond, who now has no other worries to distract her and thus can direct her full attention to wresting control of her daughter's matrimonial plans. Consequently, Mrs. Hammond and her confederate Marney intercept letters

Title page from *The Lottery*, Philadelphia, 1807 (RBD ROS 337).
Courtesy, Rare Book Department, The Free Library of Philadelphia.

between Kelroy and Emily and forge still others, severing their engagement. Mrs. Hammond then manipulates Emily into accepting the proposal of Dunlevy, a young man whose considerable fortune ensures Mrs. Hammond status and financial security for the rest of her life. Her luck runs out, however, when she has a crippling stroke during the post-wedding festivities. Unable to walk or speak, she dies, leaving in her desk incriminating evidence of the forgeries, which Emily later discovers.[50] Disillusioned and crushed by grief over her mother's treacherous betrayal, Emily soon follows her to the grave. Thus, the payoff from the ambitious Mrs. Hammond's last great gamble destroys her, Emily, and Kelroy; and in a bizarre twist of fate, a misfiring pistol later blinds Marney and blows up his forging hand.

As I earlier claimed, *Kelroy* is far more gendered in its critique of economic desire than is Wood's *Dorval*. Indeed, *Kelroy* suggests that only men may strive to improve their economic situations. Although the novel ends with Kelroy's death during a shipwreck, the narrative condones his economic desire, for his voyage to India is a financial success. Mrs. Hammond's economic desire is a vastly different matter, however. Her economic aspirations could easily have been sentimentalized—and hence made legitimate—as the story of a widowed mother who merely desires for her daughters financially secure marriages with respectable young men—an outcome which she does effect. Instead, *Kelroy* indicts Mrs. Hammond as an ambitious, greedy, grasping woman who views her daughters as commodities—as her own stock to trade—or, as Cathy N. Davidson has aptly suggested, as another investment on which she can wager (233). Indeed, the most positive spin on this situation is that Mrs. Hammond is able to guarantee herself an income only by bartering her daughters, for as Dana D. Nelson argues in her introduction to a recent reprint of *Kelroy*, "If Mrs. Hammond is vicious, so too is the situation to which she responds" (xvi). That *Kelroy* does indeed accurately represent the financial difficulties women faced during the early nineteenth century is in some ways less important than the cultural value it propagates: that economic ambition is neither becoming nor acceptable for women. In *Kelroy*, as throughout early American fiction, economic aspirations are consistently configured as masculine, and women who seek unsentimentalized economic advancement, even through marriage, virtually the only means open to them, are literally struck down, by a stroke as is Mrs. Hammond, or by death in childbirth as is Eliza Wharton in *The Coquette* (although Eliza's situation is admittedly more complicated, as I discuss in chapters 1 and 4). Foreign commerce is implicated as part of this project of gendering economic desire, for while novelists struggle to represent it as a virtuous means of accumulating capital, it is strictly a masculine occupation.

Gendering economic desire is a less important issue in Sally Wood's *Dorval; or The Speculator*, which focuses more broadly and generally on the problems of economic ambition and speculation in America during the 1790s. Although the plot of the novel revolves around a young woman, Aurelia, the title, by naming Dorval and his economic function, puts these economic issues at center stage. Further, Wood plays upon her audience's apprehensions that no type of virtue is sacrosanct, and that even model republicans and Revolutionary heroes—given the right set of temptations—can be corrupted. Equally important, Wood explicitly parallels challenges to male and female virtue, for the character of Dorval unites the seducer of female chastity with the seducer of male economic virtue, illustrating the structural similarities between sex and property in early American fiction. Rather than concentrating on the personal and the domestic, Wood's sentimental novel instead portrays how national economic trends influence the individual and impact domestic life. Just as fictional seducers were counterfeiting love to despoil the virtue of young women, so were speculators and their ilk seducing the economic virtue of the nation with promises of quick and easy wealth without industry.

Wood pairs Colonel Morely, a virtuous, patriotic merchant, with Dorval, a walking compendium of the cultural evils of the early Republic. Both men respectively epitomize the best and the worst that the new United States has to offer. Colonel Morely, a New York delegate to the Constitutional Convention, is honorable, philanthropic, public-spirited, and faithful—in short, a catalog of republican virtues. Dorval, on the other hand, is a murderer, bigamist, seducer, forger, gambler, and speculator. Hiding these evils behind a mask of sincerity, Dorval tempts Colonel Morely with the seductive allure of quickly gained, unearned wealth. By exploiting the greed lying dormant in apparently virtuous men, the figure of the speculator thus served to test the depth of that virtue, as well as to exploit the greed and naiveté of the American character.

In order to provide her readers with a context for understanding Colonel Morely's patriotic virtue, the narrator of *Dorval* describes how Morely personally helped stave off economic catastrophe for the individual and the nation in the years after the Revolution. When the war veterans were paid in devalued scrip, the colonel bought their securities for their full face value, at great financial risk to himself, in order to ensure fairness for those who had fought for their country's independence. "Determined to do every thing in his power to support the sinking reputation of his country," the narrator explains, Colonel Morely "bought up, at their original value, as many certificates and securities, as his own finances would allow. For these he paid in silver and gold, and in the produce of his lands" (13). Morely dangerously overextends himself, but his patriotic venture is vindicated when these securities are later redeemed at face value, and the country becomes more economically stable.[51] Morely's self-sacrificing virtue would have been apparent to contemporary readers of *Dorval*, since he paid many times the going rate for those securities and made no personal profit.

Even though the colonel is once again a wealthy man, happily ensconced on a rural estate, his economic ambition eventually prevails over his interest in the public good. Dorval, as agent for a Georgia land company, tempts the colonel with visions of wealth to be gained through land speculation from the Yazoo purchase. Morely enthusiastically pursues this speculation, although his adopted daughter, Aurelia, anxiously cautions him to avoid land speculation. Aurelia emerges as the true republican when she questions Morely's motives and means: "I don't know any thing of the value of land; but it appears to me, there must be some deception when it is sold for a cent an acre.... Perhaps it is the observations, I have heard my aunt make upon the evils of speculation, and the impositions, that are often practiced, that give me this disgust to the most distant appearance of speculation" (35–36). Aurelia understands that good intentions are not enough—one must avoid even the hint of impropriety. Indeed, Aurelia is the voice of sensible virtue, as she explains to her friend Elizabeth Dunbar: "I am sorry to remark, that my father seems to have an ambition, to which I thought he was superior, that of possessing great wealth. He talks as if millions of acres were not large enough for a farm, and thousands too contracted for a garden. My mother is quite delighted with the idea that every dollar, my father now pays away, will produce a hundred, twelve months hence. But every passion must have its reign; and I am inclined to say with the Preacher: 'Surely man, in his best state, is altogether vanity'" (36–37).[52] The colonel does not intend to enrich himself by bilking others, but his greedy ambition overcomes his natural virtue and reason. The narrator explains that "The time was, when [Morely] became a poor man to secure his country; but the time had now arrived, when, as he supposed, he was amassing great wealth, and this at the expense of the ruin of thousands. —He was not aware, however, though Dorval was, that such ruin would be the consequence" (50–51).[53]

Despite Aurelia's continued misgivings, the colonel and Dunbar, his partner, pursue their land speculation deals with the unscrupulous Dorval, with repercussions that Morely never anticipates. Morely and Dunbar sign a contract typical of the land deals of the time, which the narrator describes in dramatic detail: "The fatal deeds were drawn, which conveyed to these gentlemen millions of acres of land. The boundaries were specified, the lines mentioned, as marked upon the maps, and every appearance of honest and just dealings exhibited to sanctify the fraud and conceal deceit. In exchange for these deeds, which were signed by Dorval, as agent for the Georgia proprietors, bonds and notes of hand were given. One fourth of the money was to be paid in three months, one fourth in six, and the remainder in one year" (68–69). Morely and Dunbar are true speculators, for they gamble on future sales to raise the rest of the purchase price: "They had no doubt but the land would sell so well, that they should dispose of enough within three months to pay the whole" (69). Despite strenuous efforts, however, they are unable to sell the land either in the United States or Europe, and the financial burden of these debts forces Morely to undermine his personal policy of economic benevolence, driving him to call in a number of loans made to assist young tradesmen in starting businesses (84). These recalled debts are merely the first of the repercussions that emanate outward in a republic when an individual or group of citizens lacks economic virtue. Indeed, selfish focus on private interests inevitably produces such public repercussions, as the epigraph to chapter 10 makes clear:

> 'Tis avarice suggests a thousand schemes,
> A thousand plans, and fills our waking dreams,
> With hopes of gain, bids speculation come,
> And forces ruin to a happy home,
> And love of country turns to love of self,
> And centers all our pleasures in ourself. (49)

This self-focus becomes selfishness, and excessive self-interest demands the sacrifice of the public good.

When Morely fails to sell any of the land, his creditors have him imprisoned for debt in Philadelphia, where he dies repentant and cognizant of the temptations that overcame him. He explains to Aurelia:

> I now view the motives that induced me to become concerned in the Georgia purchase in a light very different from that in which I have been used to see them. Divested of that glare, which variety, avarice, and self love threw upon

them, I behold myself as nothing more nor less than a speculator, who was willing to risk his paternal inheritance and the produce of honest industry for the vain, the foolish hope of acquiring immense sums. I had a fortune sufficiently large to gratify every reasonable wish of my heart; and had I never attempted to increase it by this species of fraud, I should now have been happy; but I have followed the phantom, that enchanted me, until it has stripped me of my property, of my happiness, of the peace of my mind, and left me an inhabitant of a prison. (151)

Morely's self-condemnatory speech focuses on key issues of post-Revolutionary economic anxiety: the dangers of greed, avarice, and fraud, culminating in the cultural problem of speculation, highlighting the necessity for honest industry. Moreover, the dying Morely himself describes all speculation as merely another form of gambling—risky, vain, and foolish. Aurelia's biological father, Major Seymour (with whom she is reunited at the end of the novel), emphasizes this connection between speculation and gambling when he visits Morely's grave. Although Major Seymour recognizes "the iniquity of Dorval," he concludes that "An ambition to be wealthy was the cause of [Morely's] ruin," by rendering him susceptible to Dorval's schemes (284). He advises Aurelia's half-brother: "For, whatever arguments we may use to deceive ourselves or others, we may be certain of this, that the *man who aims at immoderate riches, without intending to give an equivalent, is building his own glory upon the ruin of his fellow creatures, and must be considered as a speculator.* Do all you can, my son, by precept and example, to discourage every species of gaming...." (284).

Not one for subtlety, Wood continues to drive home her message that speculation is merely a large-scale version of gambling through the character of Dorval. Dorval is a fascinating figure who unites in one person multiple evils, for he is a seducer of both economic and moral virtue, a male counterpart to *St. Hubert's* Madame de Trenville; yet Wood insists in a footnote to her novel that "The character and history of Dorval are not a fiction. What is related in the subsequent sheets, however romantic and melancholy it may appear, is well known by many to be strictly agreeable to truth" (62). Dorval's identity is fluid, and with each incarnation he becomes increasingly depraved. He is the consummate speculator; even his romantic intrigues are a form of speculation, for he is driven not by love or even by lust, but by the profit that he speculates he can gain from each marriage or seduction. Before the time of the novel, Dorval's avarice has already driven him to marry in secret a Jamaican heiress and to commit multiple murders. To avoid imprisonment, Dorval escapes to the United States, where he becomes the agent for a land company that typically employs "wretches . . . more cruel and more criminal than the convict who makes his exit on a gallows" (52). Dorval cleverly hides his greed and depravity behind a mask of "frankness and bluntness" that conceals "deception and deep laid plans of villainy" (40). After ruining the reputation of Elizabeth Dunbar through an elopement and causing the bankruptcy of Colonel Morely, Dorval flees to Philadelphia, where he then gambles away the money of his victims. Greed and the seductive lure of chance drive him to risk this money. In order for readers to understand the relationship between his activities as a land speculator and as a gambler—that these guises are two sides of the same coin—the narrator explains that "From one species of gaming he had descended to another far more injurious to him than speculation: in the latter he dealt with honest men, whose unsuspecting probity laid them open to imposition; but his other associates were rascals like himself, and equally artful and knavish" (130). These "gamesters" and "sharpers" entice Dorval into games of billiards, cards, and dice, with the result that "from the possession of a large sum of money, he found himself reduced to a single dollar" (130).

With Colonel Morely disposed of, only Aurelia's discerning nature and republican virtue protect her from Dorval. Attempting to recoup his fortune, Dorval once more assumes a guise of forthrightness and proposes to Aurelia, who wisely rejects him. Dorval next turns his attention to the widowed Mrs. Morely, who demonstrates her lack of perspicacity as well as her love of luxurious, dissipated living by accepting his proposal. After Dorval marries her in a bigamous ceremony, he quickly defrauds her of her money and estate, and later murders her. After his arrest, Dorval spuriously blames Aurelia for his troubles, claiming that it was her rejection of him that drove him to such lengths. Foiled in his attempt to murder Aurelia, Dorval shoots himself, but lingers for five agonizing and self-deluded days. Although Dorval indirectly wreaks havoc upon the entire community because honest creditors of those bankrupted through speculation suffer as well, he directly harms only those who are themselves culpable—those whose ambition, greed, or gullibility render them vulnerable to his enticements. However, Aurelia's republican virtue and all that it entails—her chastity, fidelity, patriotism, self-sacrifice, industry, and philanthropy—ultimately triumph over Dorval's seductive powers, as she escapes him and aids several of his victims, among them Elizabeth Dunbar and Dorval's Jamaican-born wife.

The virtue and industry of one of the younger Dunbar sons and Burlington, whom Aurelia ultimately marries, balance the greed of Dorval and Morely. Burlington and the younger Dunbar represent the hope of the rising generation of families in the novel as they earn their fortunes through industry in the East Indies. Their actions signal self-sacrifice, industry, and a sentimental justification of trade. Although they profit from their voyages, this accumulation of capital results from personal effort; further, they use this money not for vain luxuries, but to fulfill social and familial obligations. The cumulative effect of these actions is more powerful than any individual example; a brief listing of some of the events enabled by their participation in trade with Asia will illustrate my point. The return voyage from the East Indies allows Burlington to exhibit his compassion and disinterested benevolence as he endangers himself to rescue a dying, shipwrecked man, who returns the favor by bequeathing him thirty thousand dollars. One of the Dunbar sons, unnamed in the novel, because it is not who he is but what he does that is important, returns fantastically wealthy after seven years of labor in the East Indies. He has amassed a fortune large enough to settle all of his impoverished father's debts, as well as to bestow a two-thousand-dollar dowry on his sister, Elizabeth. And Major Seymour, Aurelia's biological father, returns from the East Indies with enough money to settle the debts of those individuals who befriended Aurelia and to buy her a large country estate. The juxtaposition in early American fiction of this foreign trade against gambling and speculation emphasizes the need for individuals to balance self-interest with concern for the public good of the Republic and its individual communities. Further, the difficult and virtuous labor of these merchant characters highlights Dorval's depravity and the foolishness of men like Colonel Morely and Dunbar, who seek wealth without industry.

The repetition of these sentimental rewards stemming from foreign commerce represents far more than an easy way to resolve plot difficulties: The continued presence of the East Indies and China points to this area as a free economic space rationalized by sentimental rhetoric—what Edward Said has called "realms of possibility"[54]—where Americans can fulfill their economic ambitions without harming their fellow citizens. To American novelists, China and East India represented not colonies to be subjugated, since East India was already under British control, but rather resources that could be exploited as part of an economically imperialist agenda. China, East India, and their inhabitants—themselves virtually unmentioned, which in the case of China is not surprising given the strictly limited contact between the Chinese and foreigners—represent a cultural lacuna on which economic desires could be profitably inscribed. This imperial project of displacing economic aspirations onto non-Western countries enabled white, male bourgeois and elite Americans to define themselves *as Americans* and as the representative face of the United States. In consolidating American nationalism in their image, they were able to define *their* interests as *America's* interests. Further, the goods for which they traded and the money made in such trade enabled bourgeois lifestyles—both financially and materially—in the United States.

Curiously, within the context of individual novels, participation in international commerce was for the most part a temporary expedient. While novels such as *Dorval; or The Speculator* were successful in distinguishing the merchant from the speculator and in representing trade as a valuable, virtuous, indeed patriotic, economic practice, what early American fiction generally could not envision was a life-long engagement with trade. Trade is ultimately doubly displaced—both moved to the exotic East and out of the sight of the novel and its readers, as in *Moreland Vale*. As I suggested earlier, most novels engaged with the issue of trade conclude with the return of the male protagonist from the East, bearing gifts of porcelain, fans, and silks, while an important feature of the resolution of these novels is settlement on a landed estate—what I described earlier as democratic plots joined with republican resolutions. This is exactly the situation in *Dorval*. The settlement of Burlington, Aurelia, and Major Seymour on a country estate signifies the return of social order and the reestablishment of social hierarchy, reinforced by carefully planned philanthropy. The temporary expediency of foreign commerce in fiction suggests that, while most novelists found foreign trade in the absence of inherited wealth vastly preferable to even more contested economic practices such as manufacturing, land speculation, or gambling, even their novels register ambivalence, at some level, at settling for anything less than the republican agrarian ideal. Thus we see the novel trying to mediate for its readers between the values of a modern capitalist society that privileges bourgeois economic advancement and the republican ideal that continued to hold sway over the imagination of Americans.

Despite the ephemeral nature of trade as a fictional economic solution for rising young American capitalists, the development of this theme suggests widespread ramifications for the evolution of American fiction. First, the participation of women such as Rebecca Rush and Sally Wood in actually writing this bourgeois agenda into being demonstrates American women's vested interest in issues that extend outside the home and the do-

Sally Sayward Barrell Keating Wood, author of *Dorval; or The Speculator*. Collections, Maine Historical Society.

mestic sphere, decades before novels such as *Hope Leslie*, *Hobomok*, and *Uncle Tom's Cabin* would weld sentimentality and social concerns. Writing itself allowed middling and upper class women of the early Republic to enter into the bourgeois public world of commerce—both literally through their books and metaphorically through their novels' engagement with economic practices—when other means of access were denied to them.

Additionally, the fictional emphasis on commerce also suggests something about the evolution of the novel genre in the United States. The focus on characters actively involved in commerce represents a schism with British fiction of the time and its emphasis on the landed aristocracy and non-working gentry. At the same time, the pro-commerce advocacy of American fiction pointed to the more egalitarian nature of American society and the potential mobility inherent in such a society. As a form of vernacular print culture, American fiction also patriotically affirmed the success and benefits of the newly formed United States's trading freedom and encouraged increased American commerce with the rest of the world, thereby aiding in the creation of a national identity.[55] In the rogues' gallery that was early American fiction, the virtuous merchant and businessman begin to stand out against a backdrop that warns against the speculator, the con man, the cheat, the counterfeiter, the gambler, and the seducer.

The figure of the speculator himself represents both the unbounded economic potential of the American economy and the dangers inherent in such freedom. The speculator also symbolizes the dangers of too much social fluidity and self-creation—the dark side of the myth of self-creation that Franklin's autobiography promulgates. As William E. Lenz has explained of the emergence of the confidence man in America, "he relies not on supernatural powers or charms or courts but on the fluid nature of society in the New World with its unique opportunities for self-government, self-promotion, self-posturing, and self-creation. He appears to trace his ancestry most directly from the ambiguities of the New World, which had earlier given rise to the regional images of the peddler, the Yankee, and the rustic Jonathan."[56] The same ambiguities and possibilities that could give rise to a benevolent Franklin could also give rise to a Dorval, a Marney, or a Stephen Burroughs, because it is but an easy step from Franklin's "projector" to Sally Wood's "speculator."[57]

By paralleling and merging the seducer of chastity with the seducer of economic virtue, novelists demonstrated their engagement with challenges facing Americans in a changing, post-colonial, post-mercantilist economy. The speculator serves as a cautionary figure to point to the dangers inherent in the rising capitalist economy and the problems of trust in an international economy. This issue of economic virtue was a crucial one for people of the early Republic, since the economic seduction practiced by speculators was a matter for grave public concern; once freed from the restraints imposed by the British colonial governments, speculators bankrupted countless families and communities. This anxiety about economic virtue would continue into the novels of the nineteenth century, when the confidence man, that peculiar and indigenous American version of the picaro, would emerge from the figure of the sentimental seducer and the speculator.

Gentleman Strangers and Dangerous Deceptions

As the most minute Attention to every Sentiment of Politeness and Decorum is absolutely necessary to render Public as well as Private Societies agreeable, the Managers flatter themselves that it is unnecessary to urge the strictest Observance of the following Rules; the slightest Deviation from which, they beg Leave to observe, will not pass unnoticed.

IV. Members who wish to introduce Gentleman-Strangers, can only do it with the Approbation of the Managers for the Evening, to whom they are to be introduced, so as to meet with proper Attention.

—The rules of the Baltimore *Amicable Society*, November 25, 1791

FOR MUCH of the twentieth century, critics either reviled early American sentimental fiction, damned it with faint praise, or ignored its very existence. Consequently, this denigration of the sentimental enabled literary critics to distinguish Charles Brockden Brown's more "gothic" works—with gothic being used as an adjective to suggest both their political and psychological dimensions—from novels written by other early American writers. This distinction enabled the titling of Brown as the "father of the American novel" and hence the (sole) progenitor of a whole line of nineteenth-century novelists, including Poe, Hawthorne, and Melville. While Brown's fiction has obvious continuities with nineteenth-century fiction, as critics too numerous to name here have argued, this temporal dislocation of Brown further underscored his supposed difference from other early novelists: Brown, then, came to be seen as a genius who proleptically anticipated the great American writers of the nineteenth century, while the sentimental novelists looked back to the eighteenth century and, worse, for

Amicable Society.

AS the most minute Attention to every Sentiment of Politeness and Decorum is absolutely necessary to render Public as well as Private Societies agreeable, the MANAGERS flatter themselves that it is unnecessary to urge the strictest Observance of the following RULES; the slightest Deviation from which, they beg Leave to observe, will not pass unnoticed.

I. That the Managers shall, from Time to Time, make such Rules and Regulations, for the internal Government of this Society, as they deem necessary; which, together with these following Rules, shall be posted up in the Ball-Room; and that all other Cases, not expressly provided for, by any of these Rules, be determined by the Majority of the Managers.

II. The first Ball will commence on FRIDAY, the 25th of NOVEMBER, at Mr. GRANT's NEW ASSEMBLY-ROOM, and be continued every SECOND FRIDAY, during the Season.

III. Unmarried Gentlemen, and Widowers, Inhabitants of the Town, who do not subscribe to this Society, cannot be admitted for the Evening.

IV. Members who wish to introduce Gentlemen-Strangers, can only do it with the Approbation of the Managers for the Evening, to whom they are to be introduced, so as to meet with proper Attention.

V. Gentlemen introducing Strangers, will be accountable for their Admission-Tickets.

VI. The Society will assemble at Six o'Clock, the Ladies will draw for their Places before Seven—Any Lady coming after that Time, will be placed at the Foot of either Set, as the Managers please.

VII. No Precedence to be admitted of, except Brides, their Attendants, and Strangers, and that for one Dance only.

VIII. The Ladies of each Set to take their Places immediately, when called upon by the Managers, under the Penalty of being placed wherever the Managers choose.

IX. Ladies who do not intend to dance, are requested not to draw.

X. No Lady will be entitled to a Place, without producing her Number; and if any Number be wanting, the Lady must take the Bottom of the Dance, and her Place will be given to the Lady producing the next succeeding Number.

XI. In the Dance, the Couple, at the Head of the Set, will observe to begin when the Couple whose Place was next above them, have gone down Three Couple, or must descend so as to preserve this Order, without dancing.

XII. The Lady calling a Dance, will take Place at the Foot of the Set, when the Dance is finished.

XIII. No Person, who has carried down a Dance, will be permitted to sit down till the Dance is finished; nor is any Gentleman or Lady to dance out of his or her Place, without the Consent of the Managers, under the Penalty of dancing no more that Evening.

XIV. Not more than one Cottilion to be danced during the Evening, without the Consent of the Managers, and that immediately after Supper.

XV. Gentlemen in Boots will, on no Account, be permitted to enter the Dancing-Room.

XVI. The Music to be under the entire Direction of the Managers, for the Evening; and it is particularly requested of the Ladies and Gentlemen, not to attempt to alter the Tune or Figure of a Dance fixed upon by the Lady who calls it.

XVII. That a Majority of the Subscribers have Power to expel those, whose Conduct may render them unworthy of continuing Members of this Society; and displacing Managers, Impropriety of Behaviour.

BALTIMORE, *November* 25, 1791.

Broadside of the rules of the Baltimore *Amicable Society* (November 25, 1791). Courtesy, Maryland Historical Society, Baltimore.

those seeking a distinctively American literary past, across the ocean to England.

Scholarship of the past twenty years has paid concerted attention to sentimental fiction and has largely rejected the earlier scathing indictments of these novels. Further, most critics have come to agree that the sentimental and the gothic are not easily separated in early American fiction. Even the most gothic of American novels has sentimental elements, and vice versa. Concomitantly, studies by such critics as Alan Axelrod, Jane Tompkins, Cathy N. Davidson, Robert S. Levine, Michael Warner, Larzer Ziff, Bill Christophersen, Steven Watts, Christopher Looby, Julia Stern, Edward Watts, and Teresa Goddu have illustrated that Brown was very much a man of his times with regard to his interest in political, economic, and social issues.[1] Although most of the aforementioned critics discuss Brown alongside other writers of the early Republic, only Davidson, Stern, and Edward Watts locate his fiction within an extensive context of work by other *novelists*. Reading Brown's fiction alongside the work of his contemporaries reveals striking convergences, as I will argue in this chapter, and enriches our understanding of both Brown's novels and the novel in general. Like the novels of Judith Sargent Murray and Hannah Foster, among others, Brown's fiction voices qualms about the mode of social behavior appropriate to citizens of the new Republic, the difficulty of assessing the characters of strangers in an economically and geographically mobile society, the anxiety of the bourgeois for acceptance by the social elite, and the inadequacy of traditional American institutions to contend with socially transgressive or criminal conduct. These novels represent a distinctive fictional take on a larger cultural crisis of representation and misrepresentation that encompassed both social and economic exchange.[2] At the same time, they participate in a broad reconstruction of social authority as their fictions struggle to find ways to accommodate the civic imperatives of republicanism to modern capitalist behavior.

In a broader context, eighteenth-century America was a time and place fascinated by criminal conduct, and numerous literary forms attest to this fascination: criminal confessions, printed execution sermons, and rogue's autobiographies, whether based in fact, like that of Stephen Burroughs, or fictional, like Daniel Defoe's *Moll Flanders*, were immensely popular steady sellers.[3] These stories, concerned not only with crime and transgression, but also with madness and evil, attest to a fascination with the darker side of human nature at precisely a time during the Enlightenment when there was incredible optimism about the ability of humans to shape their own characters and regulate their behavior in a positive fashion, subjects that I discussed in chapter 1. Yet as I suggested in the previous chapter, the American mythology of self-creation has a darker side, and this darker side manifested itself in fiction not only in the figure of the speculator, but also in the rake and the rogue. My subject in this chapter, the novel's preoccupation with the rakish gentleman-like stranger, speaks to the growing failure of traditional social bulwarks such as the family and the community to control male individuals who lacked either innate virtue or the self-discipline necessary to control their selfish, anti-social impulses. While these novels may critique individuals for their selfishness and greed, they also critique a culture that was failing in some sense to control or discipline its male members, a fact that was exacerbated by the unprecedented mobility—social, economic, and geographical—of post-Revolutionary society.[4] Early American fiction is filled with female orphans, as numerous critics have noted, but it is also populated by male characters who are likewise orphans or estranged from their families;[5] these absent families mark the breakdown of authority in traditional communities.[6] Estranged from family life, these fictional rakes, masquerading as "gentlemen strangers"— a label used by the Baltimore Amicable Society during the 1790s to designate those men whose manners and genteel appearance marked them as members of polite society and hence potentially welcome at the society's assemblies—have the persuasive rhetoric, physical presence, polished manners, and material accouterments that mark them as members of the gentry class.[7] This appearance of wealth and mastery of polite behavior guaranteed acceptance as the American culture depicted in fiction shifted from an economy of virtue, which placed a premium on individual character, to an economy of credit, in which the presumption of worth was extended based on one's credit status; the fluidity of credit likewise entailed increased fluidity among and into the social elite. The unqualified acceptance of strangers appearing to number among the elite classes also suggests bourgeois anxiety for acceptance by the elite. *Story of Margaretta*, *The Coquette*, and *Arthur Mervyn* thus illustrate for us how some novelists, while welcoming the new economic opportunities available in a modern capitalist society, at the same time feared the dangers entailed when communities become overly dependent upon money in order to establish relationships and categorize individuals.

Not entirely comfortable with this economy of credit, seeking alternatives to the family as a means of social control, and capitalizing on popular interest in transgressive behavior, early American novelists frequently explore the ability of external institutions such as the prison to effect self- and social control. Numerous American novels written during the early Republic era, including Brown's *Arthur Mervyn* and *Wieland*, Sarah Wood's *Dorval*, "Adelio's" *A Journey to Philadelphia*, George Watterson's *The Lawyer*, and Murray's *Story of Margaretta*, have at their heart the prison, for just as treatment of the mentally ill was being reformed during this time, so were criminal punishment and prevention being reconsidered.[8] Fiction imaginatively participated in this reformation, and thus the prison and prison scene are near constants in novels from this era, common tropes that unite sentimental and gothic fiction, both British and American.[9] By going beyond the closed prison door to create what Michel Foucault might call a different "modality" of power—public exposure—for fiction and its authors, novelists create voyeuristic narrative spectacles at a time when there was a move away from using spectacles as a form of punishment for criminals.[10] The anonymous work *The Gambler* attempts to explain and rationalize some of the era's fascination with prisons. Written in first person, *The Gambler* is ostensibly narrated by an American who is visiting England and wants to learn the character of the nation. The narrator explains: "I sought for an acquaintance with private manners, but as I was not ennobled, nor nobly or powerfully recommended, and had never conceived the idea of procuring letters of introduction to the people of a nation reputed to be hospitable, excepting a few days on my first landing, I found no access to society but in their coffee-houses and taverns, where the variety and multitude forbade every impression at discrimination—and left no impression of a comprehensible character on my mind" (4). Unable to grasp a sense of the character of the nation—despite, or perhaps because of, the teeming masses of people he faces—the narrator instead seeks out the worst that Britain has to offer, "those abodes of misery, their prison and their hospitals, so numerous and indicative of a state of society as contradictory, as the appearance of those anomalous crowds that animate their public streets and places of amusement" (4). What he finds inside one of these "mansions of misfortune" is a broken man imprisoned along with his family for gambling debts (6), and the narrator rationalizes that the worst aspects of a society will tell us more about it than its best. That may indeed be the truth, but the titillation of the scandalous in all likelihood also sold books, while at the same time the anti-British slant of this particular scenario potentially appealed to patriotic American interests. Almost invariably these American excursions into the prison have similar dual purposes: education of the moral sense and entertainment, the outcomes of public punishment (at least for the viewers) all over again.

While early American fiction is fascinated with transgressions of all sorts, masculine economic behavior was of particular concern, especially with regard to credit, debt, and the effects of credit on social relationships. The American novel's obsession with prison and the popular topics of debt and bankruptcy likely grew out of the financial panics of the 1790s. An increase in bankruptcies was a contributing factor to these panics, for as the individual burden of debt increased over the course of the eighteenth century, so did the rate of defaults. Persistent narrative critique of the laws governing debt, insolvency, and bankruptcy suggests that novelists were also critiquing the breakdown of a system of doing business that prior to the 1790s depended upon trust derived from community ties and personal relationships. An increasingly impersonal, commercial economy dependent upon the legal system supplanted this more personal economy despite the apparent ineffectiveness of contemporary policies regarding debt. The legal system was in many ways a poor substitute for the order and hierarchy formerly established by personal relationships and community ties, as it made no distinction between those who were unlucky and those who practiced deliberate fraud, just as it was relatively ineffective at deterring bankruptcy.[11] In the world of the novel, this impersonal credit economy and the impersonal social relations it fostered ultimately enable economic fraud and other social deceptions.

Conduct Literature, Politeness, and Republican Virtue

As I discussed in chapter 1, the vast majority of female conduct books prevalent in the American colonies and in the newly formed United States emphasize self-reflection and self-discipline as central concerns of female behavior. Although conduct works such as *Advice from a Lady of Quality to Her Children*, Robert Dodsley's *The Economy of Human Life* (1809), and John Hamilton Moore's *The Young Gentleman and Lady's Monitor and English Teacher's Assistant* (1792) were intended for an audience of both young men and women, most advice and conduct books were specifically gendered to reflect the different situations of and expectations for young men and women. With the exception of pietistic conduct books such as George Burder's *The Closet Companion*, male advice literature placed much less importance on self-reflective behavior, instead emphasizing social conduct.

Until several decades into the nineteenth century, reprints of British and continental texts dominated male conduct literature in America. One of the central tenets of these works was the proper mode of social conduct, or "politeness." Lawrence Klein has written extensively about the origins and development of politeness in Britain. Quoting Abel Boyer's *The English Theophrastus* (1702), Klein explains: "The kernel of the phenomenon was given in a simple phrase: 'the art of pleasing in company.' As such, 'politeness' encompassed technique, norm, and social environment: it was the set of attitudes, strategies, skills, and devices that an individual could command to gratify others and thus render the social realm truly sociable" (190).[12] Further, "'Politeness' was the art of sociability . . . an art involving self-presentation, inter-subjectivity, and self-love. Social status was not something granted, but rather something up for grabs" (191). Klein argues that "Virtue was insufficient without 'politeness,' without the techniques of social success. . . . It was this social competence, this capacity to 'appear to advantage in the World,' that made virtues (such as '*Honesty*, *Courage*, or *Wit*') visible or attractive to the world at large: the true worth of virtues could be realized only when they became 'socialized' in this manner" (190).

Prior to the Revolution, politeness held sway among literary and cultural elites, who saw themselves as part of a larger Anglo-European community of letters, while frequent reprintings of British conduct texts served to consolidate the importance of this mode of social behavior. David Shields wonderfully evokes in *Civil Tongues* the sociable and intellectual delights of this polite society as rendered in pre-Revolutionary belles lettres and social spaces. Yet, after the Revolution, politeness became increasingly controversial, given the long-standing association of politeness with aristocratic British culture. Michael Warner has likewise noted the tendency to identify themselves as "polite" among coteries of American belletrists, yet he also notes the loyalist tendencies among these same literary coteries.[13] This association with all things British rendered politeness suspect among republicans. Klein identifies the crux of American concerns about politeness when he suggests, "If 'politeness' amounted to a presentational competence at virtue, it might easily move beyond supplementing virtue to supplanting it" (190). He also contends that politeness as a mode of social behavior depended upon "the creation of an image, not the manifestation of the soul"

(191). Politeness depended upon the calculated, self-conscious creation of appearance, whereas civility and virtue were thought, relatively speaking, to be innate and natural. As Ann Murry, author of *Mentoria, or, The Young Ladies Instructor*, a popular British text reprinted in the United States, explains, "Civility consists of good offices performed by impulse or instinct, whilst those which are classed under politeness are produced by reflection, and proceed more from the head than the heart."[14] The studiedness of politeness as a code of social behavior was thus on a collision course with popular conceptions of republican virtue in the post-Revolutionary era.

The contested status of appropriate republican behavior is readily apparent in the content of any of the popular "libraries" or compendiums of male advice literature reprinted throughout the early national period. While collections like *The Young Gentleman's Parental Monitor* (1792) and *The Gentleman's Pocket Library* (1794) include such excerpts as Lord Chesterfield's advice to his son on manners (popularly advertised as "Principles of Politeness"), they also include information about economic issues, most commonly supplementing their collections of social conduct literature with Benjamin Franklin's "The Way to Wealth," a text which, incidentally, is not included in any of the dozens of female conduct works I have surveyed. Making money is a decidedly gendered objective. As Sarah E. Newton explains in *Learning to Behave*,

> Still framing all conduct advice from the high moral ground of religious principle and moral character, advice books published after the American Revolution implicitly acknowledge that young men must gingerly and cautiously face a society of change. For this new world young men required advice on the value of openness and honesty in republican behavior (an implied contrast with the decadence of the European character), on the import of rationality in selecting and pursuing goals, and on proper preparedness through education and books and through study and application. (44)

For Americans, it was no longer enough for conduct and advice books to discuss social conduct. To remain relevant, books had to emphasize economic virtue and success—how to make steady economic advancement in a way that would mutually benefit the individual and his community. Economic advice thus came to coexist alongside more traditional conduct literature.

At the same time, politeness was under open attack from a variety of critics. Politeness was a prime target of critics of luxury in the Sans Souci

Club debate, which I discussed in the previous chapter in the context of luxury and trade. This lingering suspicion of politeness in American thought derives in part from the close association between this mode of behavior and British and continental elites. Drawing upon this association, Samuel Adams, writing as "The Observer" in the Massachusetts *Centinel*, argues that politeness—a central tenet of the club—was antithetical to republican virtue. He labels it "an Assembly so totally repugnant to virtue, as in its very name (*Sans Souci*, or *free and easy*) to banish the idea by throwing aside every necessary restraint—those being esteemed the politest, who are the most careless;—and the most genteel and accomplished, who can, like the figures at a masquerade, mix in each scene, however devoid of delicacy, it is therefore to be hoped the citizens of a free republic, will unanimously exert themselves to give a check to so injurious an institution" (quoted in Wood, *The Rising Glory* 139). Supporters of the Tea Assembly conceded that politeness was indeed a valued feature of their gatherings, but they also argued that politeness was not incompatible with virtue, a claim that Adams and his partisans were not willing to grant.[15] The satirical play *Sans Souci, Alias, Free and Easy, or, an Evening's Peep into a Polite Circle*, often attributed to Mercy Otis Warren, pillories the politeness and alleged decadence of Sans Souci Club members. The generically named "Republican heroine" ridicules characters who subscribe to politeness—as well as fashion and gambling, which the writer sees as associated with politeness—and mocks those Americans who aspire to "the manners of Europe."[16] "Jemmy Satirist," one of those aspirants to polite society, utterly rejects any concept of republican virtue or austerity, blasphemously redefining independence to mean "independence of every restraint which can mar the pleasures and amusements of life"—a definition from which readers are obviously intended to recoil in horror (19).

Despite widespread criticism of politeness and persuasive arguments about the inconsistency of politeness with republican virtue, reprintings of popular works containing polite texts outlived the public debates of the 1780s. The pervasive critique of politeness in early American fiction beginning in the 1790s, then, at the same time conduct anthologies included texts advocating politeness, suggests not that politeness became less controversial as a mode of behavior, but rather that the staging ground for this cultural contest shifted and the issues altered. Novels illustrate the dangerous deceptions that polished behavior and the appearance of wealth enable when communities institute an economy of credit and appearance.

"A Mere Proteus": The Rake's Progress in American Sentimental Fiction

Like the economic speculator, the rake most often appears in a decidedly American context, taking advantage of the peculiar freedoms and trust offered by the American social system with no regard to the effect on others. In part, the Americanization of the rake is suggestive of social problems of particular concern during the early Republic, problems such as the rise in illegitimate births in the decades following the Revolution and increased public misgivings about gambling and debt. However, his opportunistic nature most clearly identifies the rake, for he successfully establishes social positions in communities where, despite continual praise of virtue, worth is predicated upon class and money—precisely the hypocrisy Sanford sets out to expose in *The Coquette*. Depictions of the rake castigate the shallow nature of American society, a society that had thrown off inherited titles, only to predicate social standing on equally shaky ground. These Gentleman-Strangers, such as Courtland of *Story of Margaretta* and Sanford of *The Coquette*, not only are tolerated due to their grace, social elegance, and illusion of wealth, but actually are encouraged; indeed the rake's cachet depends upon his politeness and social sophistication, which distinguish him from his less sophisticated but more virtuous contemporaries. Boyer and Sanford of *The Coquette* perfectly illustrate this scenario, just as do Edward Hamilton and Sinisterus Courtland of *Story of Margaretta*.

In *Story of Margaretta*, for example, the Gleaner knows from the first that Sinisterus Courtland is a scoundrel, despite his urbane manners, but his pleasing appearance attracts Margaretta. Although the Gleaner and his wife are displeased that the Worthington family allowed their adopted daughter to form an attachment to Courtland during her visit with them, they do not reject him outright, because they fear that Margaretta will find the mystique of the forbidden even more attractive. Instead, the Gleaner warns Courtland: "You are no stranger to me. Sir; your *amours*, your *improvidence*, the *ruined state of your finances*, &c. &c" (89). Nonetheless, they allow Courtland's courtship of Margaretta to continue under their careful supervision, rather than foolishly—as they see it—forbidding Margaretta to see Courtland. The Gleaner explains their thinking this way:

> Should we refuse, to this pretender, that uniform civility, with which we have distinguished every stranger, the wound thereby given to the feelings of Margaretta, might very possibly add to the strength of her attachment; and the idea of

his suffering upon her account, interesting her gratitude, would still more have endeared him to her; while, in the inmost recesses of her soul, accusing us of injustice, she would syllogistically have concluded, that error in one particular involved a possibility of a mistake in another. And it would, in truth, have been in a very high degree absurd, to have denied his claim to common attentions, merely because he had eyes for the charms of a person, whom our partiality induced us to think, had merit sufficient to captivate every beholder. (74–75)

The Gleaner's decision makes sense in terms of their overall pattern of psychological manipulation of Margaretta. Further, he maintains that by permitting this courtship, "we also made ourselves witnesses of every movement, precluding all necessity for, and possibility of, clandestine views" (75). As my discussion in chapter 2 illustrates, secret relationships and clandestine meetings render young women particularly vulnerable. What Margaretta's parents depend on is their mentoring of Margaretta and her training in epistolary correspondence—training that prompts her to confess to her mother her attraction to Courtland, even though she suspects that they will disapprove. As she explains, "You have accustomed me, dearest lady, to unbosom myself to you, and though this is my first separation from you, yet the epistolary correspondence, with which I have for such a length of time, though continued under your roof, been indulged, hath given me the habit of expressing myself to you in this way, with the utmost freedom" (67).

Margaretta's ultimate rejection of Courtland and her marriage to the worthy Edward Hamilton demonstrate the success of her parents' pedagogical and parenting strategies. The education that Mr. and Mrs. Vigillius have given their daughter is in some ways like that of Rousseau's *Émile*. Just as Rousseau advocates in his guise as tutor, their pedagogical method is to allow Margaretta latitude to make her own decisions. Her choices are always so carefully shaped by them, however, that she has only the illusion of free choice; if she is rational and sensible as they have educated her to be, she will always agree with their suggestions. Thus she eventually concludes that Courtland is unworthy of her and rejects him in time to save herself from marriage to this corrupt, mercenary scoundrel.

Although the decision Margaretta's parents make thus seems logical, rational, and thoughtful, the problem with their pedagogical method—and one that seems utterly to have escaped them—is that their tolerance of Courtland enables his continued social acceptance. Without precisely the kind of social license that people such as the Worthington and Vigillius families grant him, he would have been unable to prey upon Frances Wellwood who, like Margaretta, is an orphan, but not nearly so fortunate in her education or guardianship. Consequently, Courtland seduces Frances, keeps her as his mistress, and wastes her fortune. Unable to pay his extensive debts, he is jailed. The Gleaner promises to assist Courtland, but he will do so only on the condition that Courtland marry Frances and legitimize their three children. The situation in which Courtland is involved can be neatly resolved only after Courtland is imprisoned and thus has lost his social status—the very quality that enabled his seductions by granting him access to wealthy, unprotected young women like Frances Wellwood and protected him from retribution. If it is difficult to determine if Murray herself perceived the ironic implication of the Gleaner's rationalist pedagogy—that a learning situation carefully controlled for one young woman could spell disaster for another young woman without the benefits of such mentorship, but it certainly escapes the Gleaner's narrative persona.

Hannah Foster's *The Coquette* likewise features a rake, Major Peter Sanford, whose social status augments his seductive abilities and protects him from the consequences of his actions. Through Sanford, perhaps the best known rake of early American fiction, Foster scourges early American society for essentially commodifying young women and for tolerating male scoundrels, while the same society severely castigates young women for the slightest misstep. Sanford vividly illustrates the kind of fawning tolerance extended on the basis of social status, manners, and sex. As Fritz Fleischmann puts it, "Class privilege [for Sanford] sustains gender privilege to the point where republican assertions of virtue ring hollow" (322). Although American society of the time obviously was purged of inherited titles, Foster plays upon the importance of other sorts of titles denoting class and social status in *The Coquette*. Virtually all of the men depicted in this novel hold some sort of professional title guaranteeing them social rank: *Major* Sanford, *Captain* Pribble, *Colonel* Farrington, *General* Richman, *Reverend* Boyer, *Reverend* Haly, and even Eliza's deceased father, *Reverend* Wharton. The mark of officers or educated gentleman, these titles are awarded for being part of an educated class or rank, and yet they also exist as social markers independent of the professions, ensuring their holders social acceptance wherever they go.[17]

With the marker of rank, polished manners, and the appearance of wealth as his social passport, Sanford is for the most part enthusiastically accepted by the New England gentry, who consciously see themselves as participants in a polite society and do not inquire too carefully into his situation or antecedents. While this polite society creates a space for women to participate in semi-public life, as Dietmar Schloss has noted,[18] the rules that guide this society's social interactions also render them vulnerable to the machinations of gentleman strangers. Indeed a conspiracy of silence surrounds Sanford—and the rake figure in general—in a way that it does not surround the erring female, who, like Eliza, becomes the subject of public speculation. How Sanford acquired his military title is unclear; the reader of *The Coquette* is privy to certain information, nonetheless, and Sanford himself asserts in a letter to his friend Deighton that he once had money, but his profligate style of living has squandered it (72). No other correspondents know this fact, however, and Eliza, like her neighbors, assumes throughout much of their acquaintance that he is rich, frequently praising his "liberal fortune" (60), "a fortune sufficient to ensure the enjoyments of all the pleasing varieties of social life" (52). As she later writes her friend Lucy, "He lives in all the magnificence of a prince" (86).

Eliza first meets Sanford while visiting with her cousins, General and Mrs. Richman. Although the Richmans much later will roundly condemn Sanford, they initially sanction him by encouraging Eliza to enjoy his company when he invites her to a ball. Eliza explains to Mrs. Richman, "I have not much acquaintance with this gentleman, madam; but I suppose his character sufficiently respectable to warrant an affirmative answer" (14). Mrs. Richman enigmatically replies, "He is a gay man, my dear, to say no more, and such are the companions we wish, when we join a party avowedly formed for pleasure" (14). Only after Eliza has accepted his invitation does she perceive that "something disapprobating appeared in the countenances of both my friends" (14). The Richmans disapprove of Sanford, but they give Eliza no substantive reason for that disapproval, which seems to be neglectful behavior for the hosts of a young lady; Eliza is so mystified by their equivocal behavior that she labels it a "secret" that she must attempt to "extract" from Mrs. Richman (15).

The Richmans receive Sanford into their home with no great joy, but they nonetheless tolerate him and his attendance on Eliza because of his social rank. Reverend Boyer first seriously questions Sanford's character; in asking Mrs. Richman about her toleration of Sanford, he queries "—is his character unexceptionable? Will a lady of delicacy associate with an immoral, not to say profligate man?" (16). With her hypocrisy exposed, Mrs. Richman defends her judgment by claiming, "The rank and fortune of Major Sanford . . . procure him respect" (16). As Sharon M. Harris notes, "Sanford's acceptance by society in Hartford discredits any idea that propriety—'virtue'—is requisite for a man's social acceptance" (10). Mrs. Richman qualifies her acceptance of Sanford, however, by claiming: "His specious manners render him acceptable in public company; but I must own that he is not the person with whom I wish my cousin to be connected, even for a moment" (17). Yet Mrs. Richman justifies her reluctance to forbid Eliza to accompany Sanford by explaining, "I forbore to destroy her expected happiness, by acquainting her with my disapprobation of her partner" (17).

What Mrs. Richman understands—and Eliza does not—is that there are at least two sets of standards that women must negotiate: those of company or public behavior and those of private behavior with one's intimates. Public behavior entails a certain performativeness, whereby one's actions may directly contradict what one knows and believes to be right. As Jeffrey H. Richards notes, "the American woman as figured in sentimental novels seems trapped in a world where all life is performance. The problem she faces is to determine where playacting stops and acting in earnest begins" ("The Politics of Seduction," 238–39). Lucy Freeman understands the stage-like quality of public life and reminds Eliza of this fact in light of her coquetry with Boyer and Sanford; she admonishes Eliza, "Remember that you are *acting for life* (emphasis added); and that your happiness in this world, perhaps in the next, depends on your present choice!" (59).

As a whole, *The Coquette* dramatizes Eliza's naivete concerning the disconnect between private and public behaviors. Even though Mrs. Richman privately abhors Sanford, standards of politeness—that index to gracious social behavior—dictate that she publicly tolerate what she cannot privately condone. Eliza fails to understand the distinction here, and she asserts to Lucy Freeman that "The entertainment for which I was prepared [the ball] was such as virtue would not disapprove, and my gallant was a man of fortune, fashion, and for ought I knew, unblemished character" (19). Mrs. Richman treats Sanford civilly precisely because he is a "gentleman," suggesting that Sanford embodies the surface qualities of politeness; her own qualified sanction of him allows him access to her home and bolsters his position in the social hierarchy. She nonetheless lambastes those women who do not understand that Sanford is to be only grudgingly accorded social respect, by reason of his social standing: "It is perfectly astonishing to me, that the virtuous part of my sex will countenance, caress, and encourage those men, whose profession it is to blast their reputation, destroy their peace, and triumph in their infamy!" (51). Although she may not "caress" Sanford, Mrs. Richman seems ironically unaware of her own culpability in countenancing Sanford in social situations, tacitly encouraging his pursuit of Eliza by permitting him to visit the Richman household. Much later, after Eliza's death, Lucy Freeman Sumner sheds further light on the Richmans' culpability in Eliza's downfall. Critics often quote from her letter to Julia Granby, in which she relates the moralistic words of advice that she wishes to be "engraved upon every heart" of the "American fair," but they seldom discuss the closing lines of this advice; after admonishing women to beware of the rake, she warns, "To associate, is to approve; to approve, is to be betrayed!" (167, 168). Eliza is indeed betrayed—not only by Sanford, but also by the Richmans. By associating with Sanford and allowing him to associate with them, the Richmans tacitly grant him social approval, and they must also bear some responsibility for Eliza's subsequent unhappiness, social ruin, and death—especially given Mrs. Richman's suspicion of Sanford's true character.

When Mrs. Richman and Eliza eventually discuss Sanford's character, after he has flattered Eliza with "ease, politeness, and attention," Mrs. Richman reveals her hypocrisy (20). Mrs. Richman claims she objects to Sanford because "he is deficient in one of the great essentials of the character, and that is, *virtue*" (20). She goes on to assert that Sanford is a "professed libertine," practiced in "the arts of seduction" (20). Eliza immediately queries, "O, why was I not informed of this before?" (20). Mrs. Richman explains that she put Eliza's pleasure first, relying on Eliza's own virtue to protect her. She nonetheless asserts that Sanford "ought to be banished from all virtuous society" (20). Even so, when Eliza wonders if she should "refuse him admission, if he call, in compliance with the customary forms," Mrs. Richman decisively tells her, "By no means" (20). The Richmans thus expect Eliza to be able to navigate the arcane rules of a society that tolerates a "professed libertine" like Sanford, allowing him access to vulnerable young women who should subtly discourage him, yet who must do so without "any breach of the rules of politeness" (20)—a very Clarissa-like dilemma, and one Foster draws to our attention when Mrs. Richman warns Eliza against becoming another Clarissa to Sanford's Lovelace (38).

Understandably troubled by this task, Eliza broaches the issue of character with Sanford; yet each time she does so, he draws upon his rhetorical power to shift the terms of value from character to social class. When Eliza explains to Sanford her cousin's reservations about his character, his defensive response is to pull rank—to assert his superior social status: "You intimate that my company is not agreeable to them; but I know not why. Surely my rank in life is as elevated; and my knowledge of, and acceptance in the world, are as extensive as General Richman's" (36). By invoking and reminding Eliza of his rank, Sanford shrewdly plays upon Eliza's desire for status.[19] Further, Sanford understands that Mrs. Richman would like private notions of virtue to take precedence over social worth as estimated by the world, so he seeks to create intimacy through an appearance of utter candor. He claims: "I plead guilty to the charge, madam, which they have undoubtedly brought against me, of imprudence and folly in many particulars; yet of malignancy and vice I am innocent. Brought up in affluence; inured from my infancy to the gratification of every passion; the indulgence of every wish, it is not strange, that a life of dissipation and gaiety should prove alluring to a youthful mind, which had no care but to procure what it deemed enjoyment. In this pursuit I have perhaps deviated from the rigid rules of discretion, and the harsher laws of morality" (37). In this scene, just as Sanford skillfully displaces the terms of value from virtue to social rank, so he seemingly alters their relationship from potential seduction to a "friendship" based on charity and frankness. This claim of friendship and his humble, self-reflective "confession" enable Sanford to circumvent the distinction between public, social acquaintances and intimate, private friendships. By requesting a boon from Eliza, Sanford grants to her a special kind of social power. Further, his "confession" reinforces his social status (and his difference from Reverend Boyer) by confirming his genteel upbringing with its emphasis on the gratification of the self and the passions.[20]

By purchasing the seat of Captain Pribble in Hartford, about a mile from Eliza's mother's house, Sanford consolidates his social image and guarantees himself continued contact with Eliza. Hearing of his prospective purchase, Lucy Freeman Sumner writes to Eliza, telling her that "Many of our gentry are pleased with the prospect of such a neighbor. As an accomplished gentlemen, say they, he will be an agreeable addition to our social parties; and as a man of property, and public spirit, he will be an advantage to the town" (31). Lucy disagrees with this assessment, claiming: "I am far from supposing him a desirable acquisition in either of these respects. A man of a vicious character cannot be a good member of society. In order to that, his principles and practice must be uncorrupted: in his morals, at least, he must be a man of probity, and honor. Of these qualifications, if I mistake not, this gallant of yours cannot boast" (31). Lucy does not observe a split between the polite world and private life, requiring of any she would wish to label social acquaintances the same standards that she would require of her intimate friends. As she learns more of Sanford's character, she becomes ever more scathing in her condemnation of him, more so than any other character. She tells Eliza:

> I look upon the vicious habits, and abandoned character of Major Sanford, to have more pernicious effects on society, than the perpetrations of the robber and the assassin. These, when detected, are rigidly punished by the laws of the land. If their lives be spared, they are shunned by society, and treated with every mark of disapprobation and contempt. But to the disgrace of humanity and virtue, the assassin of honor; the wretch, who breaks the peace of families, who robs virgin innocence of its charms, who triumphs over the ill placed confidence of the inexperienced, unsuspecting, and too credulous fair, is received, and caressed, not only by his own sex, to which he is a reproach, but even by ours, who have every conceivable reason to despise and avoid him. (63)

Lucy's point is that regardless of the havoc the rakish seducer wreaks upon a community, he usually escapes relatively unscathed, unlike his victims. It is worth noting here the way that class and race implicitly and explicitly inform Lucy's concerns. "Fair," a category to which Lucy has frequent recourse, refers not to women in general, but specifically to white women, and in this case bourgeois white women; Lucy, and by extension Hannah Foster, are not alone in their privileging of bourgeois white women, for their concerns dominate the early novel. Despite the reservations of Lucy Freeman Sumner and the more qualified reservations of the Richmans, Sanford continues to be accorded considerable social respect among the very bourgeois families upon whom he preys, prompting him to write to Deighton, "I am very much courted and caressed by the family of Mr. Lawrence, a man of large property in this neighborhood" (34). After he moves to Hartford, Lucy regretfully tells Eliza that "he has been called upon and welcomed by most of the neighboring gentry" (62).

Despite Lucy Freeman Sumner's avowed disapproval of him, Sanford insinuates himself into her wedding festivities, vividly illustrating the power of masculine politeness and wealth and the limits of female social power. Eliza accounts for his presence by considering the structure of social relationships: "As all the neighboring gentry were invited, Mr. Freeman would, by no means, omit Major Sanford, which his daughter earnestly solicited" (71). Lucy's wedding is very much a "public" wedding, as opposed to the private weddings and engagements that wreak so much havoc in the novels that I discuss in chapter 2. However, the participation of women in such public weddings merely establishes their rank and legal status; it does not necessarily entail their empowerment (or even their financial protection, as Sanford's wife later discovers), and hence Lucy's wishes are little valued.[21] Mr. Freeman, like the Richmans, upholds a code of behavior that privileges polite social behavior and wealth above individual virtue. As Lucy explains, Sanford's "profuseness... bribe[s] the unthinking multitude to show him respect" (62). Sanford himself explains his continued social success by exclaiming to Deighton, "What deference is always paid to equipage! They may talk of this virtue, their learning, and what not; but without either of them, I shall bear off the palm of respect from those, who have them, unadorned with gold, and its shining appendages" (117). These "shining appendages" to which he refers are the accouterments of wealth like his fashionable phaeton and his newly purchased seat, assets which make him more attractive to Eliza and which Boyer lacks. Sanford understands that these accouterments are the keys to social success among the bourgeois eager for the society of the elite; as he demonstrates, "Show and equipage are my hobby-horse" (35). "Show and equipage"—smoothness of social manners and the appearance of wealth—enable him to maintain his place in a social echelon that still privileges class and wealth regardless of revolutionary rhetoric. Even Selby acknowledges this social reality in a letter to Reverend Boyer discussing Sanford, whom he grudgingly labels "in the modern sense of the phrase... *much of a gentleman*, that is, a man of show and fashion" (43).

Choice of a marriage partner is a prerogative of Sanford's rank as a seemingly wealthy gentleman, an ability to choose to which Eliza aspires. She consistently argues that she wants choice—especially concerning *whom* she will marry and *when* she will marry. Although displeased with her father's choice of the Reverend Mr. Haly as a husband for her, she grudgingly acquiesces, for, as Gillian Brown points out, Eliza herself is something of a gambler, who "calculated that her agreement would pose a low 'risk' to her 'future happiness'" (5). "Seeing, from their 'first acquaintance, his declining health,' Eliza 'was the more encouraged' to chance the engagement to Haley [sic]. Her speculation proves successful when both her father and fiancé die before the marriage can take place."[22] A similar speculative desire motivates her to postpone an engagement to Boyer, on the chance that someone better suited to Eliza's desires might happen along. Brown argues that *The Coquette* dramatizes Eliza's power to consent, which she exercises in both positive and negative senses through her coquetry. However, as Brown acknowledges, "Foster's narrative of the coquette's difficulties in pursuing her desires reveals that having agency is not enough" (126). Eliza has agency, but she exercises this agency in a scope circumscribed by her economic status, limited legal rights, and eighteenth-century customs; coquettish behavior only reinforces Eliza's limited ability to make choices for herself.

While Eliza aspires to the same power to choose a partner afforded to bourgeois and elite men, much of Sanford's attractiveness stems from a different sort of power—the *illusion* of power he seems to offer Eliza over him. As I have mentioned, he has already pointed out to Eliza that she has the power to admit him (or not) to her friendship. Pressing Eliza to reject an engagement to Boyer, Sanford tells her, "But it is from your lips only that I can hear my sentence! You must witness its effects! To what lengths my despair may carry me, I know not! You are the arbitress of my fate!" (90). Eliza may lack financial capital, but Sanford willingly acknowledges her sociability and sexual allure, capital of another sort, but which he values differently from money. This illusion of power—of having *him* in romantic thralldom to *her*—has a potent appeal to Eliza. Unfortunately, Eliza's power is indeed illusive, for it lasts only as long as it is untested. Although Sanford continues to love Eliza after he seduces her, she nonetheless loses social value in his eyes; as he tells Deighton, "[T]he idea of being thus connected with a woman whom I have been able to dishonor would be rather hard to surmount. It would hurt even my delicacy, little as you may think me to possess, to have a wife whom I know to be seducible" (157). That part of Sanford's valuation of Eliza rests not with her interior, intrinsic qualities but rather with her reputation should not be surprising, for Sanford has consistently demonstrated that he views women as commodities. Earlier in the novel, he speaks of his pursuit of Miss Laurence, another of his potential brides, by saying she "might easily be obtained"—just as he would purchase a home, a horse, or a carriage (72). The difference, however, is that in marriage, in addition to the intrinsic and status-enhancing value a bride brings to a marriage, the groom is paid for his purchase via his bride's dower.

Sanford's social and romantic successes are all predicated upon maintaining the illusion that women have equal power in his relationships with them. In fact, he boasts to his friend Deighton, "I am a mere Proteus, and can assume any shape that will best answer my purpose" (22). In his ability to shape himself to whatever pleases his viewers, auditors, and readers, he is not unlike Eliza, who has earlier gloried in her power to be "perfectly adapted to the tastes of my gallant [Boyer]" (12). The difference between Sanford and Eliza is in the degree of their deceit: While Eliza has displayed for Boyer only certain facets of herself, Sanford continuously operates under this principle of protean social deceit, frequently reiterating to his friend Deighton that individuals who are taken in by his smooth social skills, grand appearance, or promises of love deserve exactly what they get. Sanford admits no blame in his unhappy marriage to Nancy, yet another heiress. After breaking Eliza's commitment to Boyer, Sanford evades his creditors by taking a trip south, which Sanford explains is necessary for "the prospect of making a speculation, by which I hope to mend my affairs"; there, he meets and marries the spoiled Nancy, who is "visibly captivated by [his] external appearance" (96, 115). Sanford gains five thousand pounds in this marriage, and Nancy "must blame herself," Sanford claims, if she gets a profligate husband who loves another (115). In the typical seduction novel, readers might expect the seducer to manifest the most desire, but this is not the case with Sanford. He desires Eliza more than any other woman, as he explains to Deighton, but there is an element of vengefulness intertwined with this desire, as he continually iterates his desire to seek revenge against the female sex (18, 34). Sanford is also the object *of* desire, for Nancy, Miss Laurence, and Eliza Wharton project their own desires onto Sanford, and his powerful seductive abilities are predicated upon understanding and fulfilling (however temporarily) the desires of his victims, whether for love, companionship, riches, or status, or some mixture of them.

Despite Sanford's morally reprehensible and illegal acts—marriage to a woman he does not love for purely mercenary reasons and the adulterous seduction of the woman he does profess to love—he acts with relative impunity, aside from the guilt he later feels over Eliza's death. Although Eliza's friends are distraught over the circumstances of her elopement and death, neither General Richman nor Eliza's brother seeks vengeance or recompense of any sort from Sanford. Sanford's estate is eventually attached, but that action results from his financial profligacy, not his social or sexual behavior, however criminal it seems to Eliza's friends. Sexual transgressions may still be illegal, but they are no longer treated as crimes, per se, and the social world of *The Coquette* ultimately privileges property over people. Although Julia Granby reviles Sanford for his role in Eliza's downfall, what she denounces is not Sanford as an individual, but rather his "base arts" (163)—those tools that give the protean character its power. With no legal recourse, Julia argues instead for a new set of values for her community, which she hopes will share her view that although Eliza lost her life bearing Sanford's illegitimate child, she lost "what was still dearer ... reputation and virtue" (163). She wishes that the "base arts" (163) of men like Sanford would "be exposed, and stamped with universal ignominy! Nor do I doubt but you [Lucy Freeman Sumner and the reader, as well] will join with me in execrating the measures by which *we* have been robbed of so valuable a friend; and *society*, of so ornamental a member" (164). Despite Julia's attempt to criminalize the actions of the polite, adulterous seducer by describing the loss of Eliza as the "robbery" of her friends, thereby suggesting a crime against property, the power of the community remains limited. Sanford is free to move "where the name of Sanford is unknown" (166) and take with him what he brought to Connecticut: his rank and social polish. What has the most power over Sanford, as I proposed in chapter 1, is Eliza's image, installed within him in place of his conscience, an image that will continue to haunt him since he hid within his house to protect his property from attachment, rather than seeking her out to beg her forgiveness.

Dangerous Deceptions:
Arthur Mervyn

It makes sense now to turn to *Arthur Mervyn*, for *Arthur Mervyn* draws upon many of the themes that I have discussed in earlier chapters: madness, seduction, suicide, the sea trade, unscrupulous economic behavior, and the difficulty of "reading" character, among others. This lengthy list suggests the broad scope of the novel, and indeed, *Arthur Mervyn* twines together many of the thematic and tropical threads that unite early American fiction as a body of work. While Brown's experimentation with virtually every trope important to early American fiction makes the novel attractive to contemporary critics, it also tends to make the novel confusing and less than coherent from the standpoint of plot. Undoubtedly the work's inchoate nature also owes something to Brown's erratic attention to the actual composition process.[23] Regardless, the over-the-top excesses and sly humor of *Arthur Mervyn* render it one of the more engaging—and engaged—novels of the early national period.

Narrated by multiple narrators and framed as a potential legal defense for its title character, *Arthur Mervyn* is by far the most economically involved of Brown's novels, detailing the adventures of Arthur Mervyn, a young countryman, amidst the economic machinations of members of the Philadelphia commercial class, whose schemes make and lose immense fortunes. The intense foregrounding of economic issues in this novel has led one critic to claim, "In no other novel before the Civil War are we so assaulted by the sheer immediacy and pervasiveness of a commercial society."[24] Thousands of pounds and dollars quickly change hands as characters engage in economic transactions involving bills of exchange, mortgages, debts, bankruptcy, counterfeiting, and insurance swindles—all of which in some way are founded on the sea trade. The advent of a yellow fever epidemic further confounds matters, with the physical corruption of the epidemic paralleling and heightening the moral rot already pervading the city. Brown's preface to *Arthur Mervyn* signals this correspondence: "The evils of pestilence by which this city has lately been afflicted will probably form an aera in its history. The schemes of reformation and improvement to which they will give birth, or, if no efforts of human wisdom can avail to avert the periodical visitations of this calamity, the change in manners and population which they will produce, will be, in the highest degree, memorable. They have already supplied new and copious materials for reflection to the physician and the political economist" (3). His union of the physician and the political economist—one who heals the body and one who cures or at least diagnoses economic ills—suggests that the pestilence afflicting the city is not only the yellow fever, but also a sickness of the spirit that leads individuals to cheat and connive against their countrymen in relentless pursuit of wealth.

Teresa Goddu has recently argued in *Gothic America* that the more dangerous disease pervading *Arthur Mervyn* is not yellow fever, but commerce that depends upon the slave trade. As Goddu puts it, "*Arthur Mervyn* articulates its culture's central contradiction and greatest fear: that a republic with a commercial society at its core cannot remain healthy" (31). In grappling with the proper role of commerce, *Arthur Mervyn* fits squarely with other American novels of the time. While Rebecca Rush, Sally Wood, and other authors ultimately portray the East India trade as a virtuous means of amassing capital and a viable alternative to inheriting wealth, Brown's portrayal of commerce in *Arthur Mervyn* is not so sanguine, which is not surprising given that much of the commerce taking place in this novel has at its base dependence on slave labor. Clearly it was much easier for Rush and Wood to reconcile themselves to commerce with Asia than to justify a trade that, while it brought economic benefits to the United States, also brought wholesale misery to an entire people. In a reading of *Arthur Mervyn* that converges in interesting ways with my own reading of the larger body of work that is early American fiction, Goddu argues that medicine, represented in the novel by Dr. Stevens, offers a possible cure to both yellow fever and commerce: "Adhering to the 'moral treatment' that gained ascendancy in the 1790s from the age's optimism in reform and that urged patients to minister to themselves and form internal self-control, Stevens believes that he can restore Arthur to good health through narrative" (39).

Indeed, like the female characters in epistolary fiction, Arthur will later claim he finds self-discipline through the act of writing. Overwrought by anxiety at his impending wedding to Achsa Fielding, Mervyn turns to writing to calm and discipline himself. He explains, "The pen is a pacifyer. It checks the mind's career; it circumscribes her wanderings. It traces out, and compels us to adhere to one path. It ever was my friend. Often it has blunted my vexations; hushed my stormy passions; turned my peevishness to soothing.... It may temper my impetuous wishes; lull my intoxication; and render my happiness supportable: And, indeed, it has produced partly this effect already. My blood, within the few minutes thus employed, flows with less destructive rapidity. My thoughts range themselves in less disorder—" (414). Whether Arthur is truly able to cure himself of the poisonous influence of urban commercial life is debatable, as I will argue, but certainly confessional writing plays as large a role in this novel as it does in any of the epistolary novels that I discussed in chapter 1.

Notwithstanding its overt focus on economic issues, *Arthur Mervyn* is also about the difficult, perhaps impossible, process of uncovering the truth of human interactions. Midway through his narrative, while on a temporary hiatus in the country at the Hadwin farm, Mervyn entertains himself translating the elder Lodi's manuscript from Italian, a language that Mervyn does not know, into English via Latin, a language that he does know. This challenging, seemingly impossible, process of translation serves as a meta-narrative for the process of interpreting Arthur Mervyn the character and *Arthur Mervyn* the text. Mervyn explains, "I had no grammar or vocabulary to explain how far the meanings and inflections of Tuscan words varied from the Roman dialect. I was to ponder on each sentence and phrase; to select among different conjectures the most plausible, and to ascertain the true, by patient and repeated scrutiny" (126). Mervyn's theory of translation might well be a prescription for the task of any literary critic seeking to make sense of this jigsaw puzzle of a novel. Despite the obvious difficulties of this interpretive dilemma, Mervyn believes it "to be within the compass of [his] powers" (126). He explains, moreover, "The detail of my progress would be curious and instructive. What impediments, in the attainment of a darling purpose, human ingenuity and patience are able to surmount; how much may be done by strenuous and solitary efforts; how the mind, unassisted, may draw forth the principles of inflection and arrangement; may profit by remote, analogous, and latent similitudes, would be forcibly illustrated by my example" (126). This interpretative task likewise parallels Mervyn's attempt to understand the motives for others' actions. Despite Mervyn's initial optimism, however, he apparently leaves his translation unfinished after finding twenty thousand dollars hidden between the pages of the manuscript.

What does this event suggest for our understanding of Mervyn and his narrative? At the least, this twenty thousand dollars literally symbolizes how the language of economics pervades the text and controls its characters. Nonetheless, we are still left with these questions: Is it possible for one individual to "read" the characters of others simply by studying their features and rhetoric, even when they wear masks of social polish? Dr. Stevens, Mervyn's mentor and surrogate father, believes it is possible, and Mervyn himself at times claims to share this belief, but *Arthur Mervyn* challenges the existence of the transparent countenance and the value of the "penetrating eye" in evaluating physiognomy. If the eye can no longer be trusted to evaluate character, and the extension of virtue based on credit and politeness proves to be dangerous, then what principle shall organize social relations? This debate assumes crucial importance given the volatile economic relationships found in Philadelphia and the confusion wrought by the yellow fever plague, both of which serve to bring into contact people who might not otherwise meet. In such circumstances, how do we conduct ourselves? What system will we use to order social relations? *Arthur Mervyn* resolves none of these questions decisively, but its portrayal of the family under assault and the threatening nature of alternative institutions representing the state suggest Brown's anxieties about post-Revolutionary America.

"Gentleman Strangers": Arthur Mervyn and Thomas Welbeck

Arthur Mervyn

Like *The Coquette*, *Arthur Mervyn* plays upon the tensions between public or social life and private life—how we behave in social situations or business relations versus how we behave among our families and intimate acquaintances. Mervyn himself collapses this distinction, behaving consistently as if he has an intimate acquaintance with whomever he comes into contact, behavior that puzzles its recipients. Yet at the same time, *Arthur*

Mervyn tensely debates the relative merits of public exposure through the creation of perfectly transparent self versus the delusive benefits but ultimate dangers of the masked, opaque, secretive self. Mervyn himself continually acts impetuously, with little apparent forethought or explanation of his actions, yet he frets when these actions become the subject of wonderment and contention, and he risks being misunderstood, his actions misinterpreted. Mrs. Althorpe, for instance, a former neighbor of Mervyn's, can attribute his bizarre behavior toward her and his family—and his father, in particular—only to depravity or folly (230–37). Mrs. Althorpe describes Mervyn as a strange being, whose singular behavior "betrayed a mixture of shrewdness and folly, of kindness and impudence, which justified, perhaps, the common notion that his intellects were unsound" (236).

Despite Mervyn's curious behavior, he has a mesmerizing, persuasive, even seductive manner, with the ability to convey a compelling aura of virtuous innocence despite the unsavory circumstances in which he is continually discovered. A variety of evidence sustains this reading of Mervyn's character. He himself boasts of his rhetorical skill in his verbal skirmish with Philip Hadwin, Eliza's brutal and scheming uncle. Despite Hadwin's dire threats of whippings and hanging for Mervyn's complicity in burning Mr. Hadwin's will, Mervyn's rhetoric and behavior—which he himself describes as "at once damnably tough and devilishly pliant" (308)—enable him to soothe Hadwin's rage, enough so that Hadwin cannot decide whether the vicious rumors he has heard of Mervyn's deceitfulness and depravity are true. He knows only that Mervyn is "*a queer sort of chap*" (309). Several other characters express their amazement that a supposedly naive young man from the country should be so confident and self-possessed.

Mervyn's aura of innocence is powerful, we know, for it induces a variety of people to open their homes to him, and in the case of Dr. Stevens, even to risk exposing his family to yellow fever. When Dr. Stevens confronts Mervyn with the inconsistent portraits he has received of him, Mervyn explains, "I am not surprised or afflicted at the misconceptions of my neighbors, with relation to my own character. Men must judge from what they see: they must build their conclusions on their knowledge" (340)—an explanation deriving from sensationalist philosophy. Given Mervyn's own obsessive, Caleb Williams-like probing into the affairs of others—curiosity that leads Welbeck to label Mervyn "the author . . . of horrors without number and name" (337)—his initial refusal to explain his own actions appears all the more strange. Instead of being angered or nonplused at the neighbors' judgments, Mervyn claims:

It was not me whom they hated and despised. It was the phantom that passed under my name, which existed only in their imagination, and which was worthy of all their scorn and all their enmity. . . .

They thought me slothful, incurious, destitute of knowledge, and of all thirst of knowledge, insolent and profligate. They say that in the treatment of my father, I have been ungrateful and inhuman. I have stolen his property, and deserted him in his calamity. Therefore they hate and revile me. It is well: I love them for these proofs of their discernment and integrity. Their indignation at wrong is the truest test of their virtue. (340–41)

After this curiously dispassionate discourse, Mervyn finally elucidates the various circumstances upon which his neighbors judged his character and found him wanting. He explains, for instance, that his refusal to work (after he has repeatedly avowed to Stevens his desire to become a gentleman farmer) stemmed not from disrespect of his father, but rather from respect for his mother's wishes concerning his delicate health. His violence toward his father in the tavern, when he rebukes him and snatches away his glass, ensued not from "want of filial respect and duty," but from precisely those traits—his desire to help his father "resist temptation" (344). Appearances, then, are not what they seem, according to Mervyn. He manages to justify even the time he spent with Betty Lawrence (who soon became his stepmother), claiming that she never seduced him, but rather that he learned a great deal about the world from her: "Her intercourse has instructed me in what some would think impossible to be attained by one who had never haunted the impure recesses of licentiousness in a city. The knowledge, which residence in this town for ten years gave her audacious and inquisitive spirit, she imparted to me" (345). Mervyn's slyly humorous phrasing in this passage is rife with double entendres, but his audience attends to his claims without grasping the innuendo. And, despite the misunderstandings that arise from his adventures with Welbeck, Mervyn likewise claims to value them, for "knowledge of Welbeck has been useful" to him and has helped eliminate Mervyn's "ignorance of the world" (357). Repeatedly, we see Mervyn explaining but offering no concrete proof to substantiate his actions.

Yet Mervyn's behavior—his utter unwillingness to explain his conduct at the time of its occurrence—still seems curious, especially since he himself claims that the only way one individual can judge another is upon the basis of visible displays of character—in other words, appearances. Mervyn likewise contradicts his own comportment when he claims, "The internal and undiscovered character of another, weighed nothing with me in the question, whether they should be treated with frankness or reserve. I felt no scruple on any occasion, to disclose every feeling and every event. Any one who could listen, found me willing to talk.... I *claimed* the kindness and sympathy of every one" (397). As Michael Warner argues in *The Letters of the Republic*, "Disclosing information, making things public, is understood as ensuring a civic source of validity" (166). Certainly Mervyn talks and talks and talks once he befriends Dr. Stevens. Ultimately at stake here is not his willingness to talk or disclose information, but rather his frankness and forthrightness.

After struggling to extricate himself from several half-truths he has told to Dr. Stevens, Mervyn vows to tell his whole story to Achsa Fielding in such a manner that she cannot fail to believe him; he explains that "All this was done with sincerity and fervor, with gestures, actions, and looks, in which I felt as if my whole soul was visible" (397). Here Mervyn strives for transparence, a trope which, as I explore in chapter 1, suggests a manner of bearing oneself characterized by openness and frankness. Mervyn, like the characters and authors of other early American novels, consciously associates this transparence with women. Despite his friends' qualms about the character of Achsa Fielding, Mervyn believes that he literally can read goodness on her face—that her innermost nature is represented not merely by her physiognomy, but by her very expressions. In describing his interactions with Achsa, he claims, "I placed myself before her, and fixed my eyes steadfastly upon her features. There is no book in which I read with more pleasure, than the face of woman. *That* is generally more full of meaning, and of better meaning too, than the hard and inflexible lineaments of man . . ." (403). When speaking to Achsa, Mervyn strives to convey the same openness that he believes is innate to women. He maintains that "My eyes glistened as I spoke. In truth, I am in that respect, a mere woman" (398).[25] Certainly, writers of advice literature advocated openness and candor as aspects of "natural" conduct or behavior. John Bennett, author of the popular work *Letters to a Young Lady*, too, associated transparence with young women, proposing that "An *unstudied* openness and simplicity of manners are the strongest symptoms of a guiltless heart, and a virtuous intention. Those young people are generally the most amiable, that are the most undisguised. Having nothing to *conceal,* they have studied no *art*."[26] Yet for Mervyn, openness has a performative aspect, for he is conscious of striving to convey this transparence, as he says, "with gestures, actions, and looks" (397). This begs the question: If openness is studied, how can it be "natural"?

Given that many republican thinkers disliked politeness for its performative, studied nature, the similar performativeness of Mervyn's virtuous openness is troubling in light of his professed republican principles. As I suggested in the previous chapter, Franklin's theory of character also has a certain performative aspect, but his emphasis on performance is an emphasis on *doing*, on active and visible virtue; it is not enough to *be* good, one must *do* good. Mervyn's performative practice of character seems quite different from Franklin's, in that Mervyn projects vastly more than he achieves; there is a tremendous gap between his stated intentions and the results of his actions.[27] Rather than focusing on politeness, Mervyn instead strives for an appearance of openness and transparency, but this conscious desire to convey transparency represents its antithesis. To strive for openness undermines the very existence of this seemingly natural mode of conduct. Despite the republican rhetoric of virtue that Mervyn voices on occasion, he is an apt apprentice for Welbeck, lending weight to his claim that he learned many lessons from him. Mervyn emphasizes his changeability—his ability to reshape himself according to his audience—late in the novel when he speaks of how he became "wax" in Achsa Fielding's hands: "without design and without effort, I was always of that form she wished me to assume" (428). In his own way, Mervyn is as much a "Proteus" as is Welbeck or *The Coquette's* Sanford.

Despite Mervyn's new policy of openness and probity in his conduct, he continues to engage in thoughtless, inexplicable behavior. Given his circumstances—he has no money, he has lost the protective cloak of family, and he must depend upon untested new friends and strangers—his behavior becomes less eccentric than it is irrational. As Jay Fliegelman asserts about late eighteenth-century America in *Declaring Independence*, "In a world where appearance and public perception constitute a primary reality, character becomes synonymous with public estimation or reputation (which Franklin called 'dearer to you than perhaps your life'), less a fixed indwelling moral nature than a fluid and vulnerable social identity" (124–25). Elizabeth Jane Wall Hinds suggests that under such circumstances, "one is not so much a being but a series of action designed from within and without to participate in public life" (72). "Arthur Mervyn," then, is not Arthur Mervyn the interior individual, but Arthur Mervyn the social actor. Along similar lines, Larzer Ziff argues that, in commercial Philadelphia, "A man is as good as the amount of trust he can command rather than the amount of property he possesses" (70). Thus for the impoverished Mervyn to allow himself to become the subject of speculation in a city in which his reputation can make or break his fortune is dangerous.

Mervyn's character literally becomes his fortune when a warrant is issued for Mervyn's arrest as a possible accomplice of Welbeck, based on Wortley's suspicions, but at Jamieson and Thetford's instigation. Although Stevens has frequently defended Mervyn, Wortley dismisses Mervyn's explanations as "unworthy of the least credit" (226). Upon learning of the warrant, Stevens begs his friend to tell him what he knows saying, "Facts? Let me know them, I beseech you. If Mervyn has deceived me, there is an end to my confidence in human nature. All limits to dissimulation, and all distinctions between vice and virtue will be effaced. No man's word, no force of collateral evidence shall weigh with me an hair" (248–49). Unmoved by his friend's dramatic assertion, Wortley merely replies, "It was time . . . that your confidence in smooth features and fluent accents should have ended long ago" (249). Wortley disdains the value of the senses and denies that possession of a "penetrating eye" enables one accurately to read the countenance, explaining, "Till I gained from my present profession, some knowledge of the world . . . I was equally wise in my own conceit; and, in order to decide upon the truth of any one's pretensions, needed only a clear view of his face and a distinct hearing of his words. My folly, in that respect, was only to be cured, however, by my own experience, and I suppose your credulity will yield to no other remedy" (249). Mrs. Wentworth likewise questions the value of judging another based upon his or her countenance. Still suspicious even after Mervyn has told her of the death of her nephew Clavering, Mrs. Wentworth declines to enter his scheme to "rescue" Clemenza from the Villars household. She tells Mervyn, "[T]here must be other proofs besides an innocent brow and a voluble tongue, to make me give full credit to your pretensions" (363). Once again illustrating how economic metaphors pervade this novel, both Wortley and Mrs. Wentworth use the language of money: credit here suggests both credence or belief, as well as the literal credit or cash that they risk on this belief. While Wortley and the elderly Mrs. Wentworth might not be vulnerable to traditional seduction, for them, and maybe any dweller in this commercial city, perhaps the greater danger stems from confidence men and economic fraud.

Even Dr. Stevens, Mervyn's mentor, at several points queries the reliability of using the senses to judge another by virtue of his or her appearance. He questions, "Surely the youth was honest. His tale could not be the fruit of invention; and yet, what are the bounds of fraud? Nature has set no limits to the combinations of fancy. A smooth exterior, a show of virtue, and a specious tale, are, a thousand times, exhibited in human intercourse by craft and subtlety. Motives are endlessly varied, while actions continue the same; and an acute penetration may not find it hard to select and arrange motives, suited to exempt from censure any action that an human being can commit" (229). Stevens's use of the word "penetration" here is a curious inversion of a common figure of speech; in early American fiction, the trope of "penetration" usually describes social discernment, an ability ascribed to virtuous, astute individuals such as Julia Granby of *The Coquette*, whose sterling character and penetrating eye empower her to discern Sanford's dishonesty; this is the same "penetration" that eventually aids Margaretta of *Story of Margaretta* to see through Courtland's polite facade. Yet in this instance, Stevens attributes this trait instead to the one who would commit fraud.

Despite his worrisome suspicion that it is Mervyn who possesses the penetrating eye—a penetrating eye that would enable him to spot his dupes and victims—Stevens retracts his conjectures, claiming,

> Had I heard Mervyn's story from another, or read it in a book, I might, perhaps, have found it possible to suspect the truth; but, as long as the impression, made by his tones, gestures and looks, remained in my memory, this suspicion was impossible. Wickedness may sometimes be ambiguous, its mask may puzzle the observer; our judgment may be made to faulter and fluctuate, but the face of Mervyn is the index of an honest mind. Calm or vehement, doubting or confident, it is full of benevolence and candor. He that listens to his words may question their truth, but he that looks upon his countenance when speaking, cannot withhold his faith. (229–30)

Consequently, Stevens must defend himself from accusations that he was beguiled by Mervyn's rhetoric and oratorical performance, a performance in which *how* he expresses himself, what he "reveals" of himself during his discourse, is at least as important as *what* he says.[28] Stevens recognizes that it is the combination of Mervyn's compelling voice along with his elocution and benevolent countenance that persuade him of Mervyn's truthfulness. This potent combination of the visual and the oral that Stevens experiences exonerates him if Mervyn's written tale fails to convince his readers; we only read about Mervyn's adventures, and at some remove, since Stevens transcribes part of them.

Mervyn himself muses at length on this issue of appearances, telling himself that it would be useless for him to publish—meaning to expose—Thetford's economic fraud, for "by whom will my single testimony be believed, in opposition to that plausible exterior, and, perhaps, to that general integrity which Thetford has maintained? To myself it will not be unprofitable. It is a lesson on the principles of human nature; on the delusiveness of appearances; on the perviousness of fraud; and on the power with which nature has invested human beings over the thoughts and actions of each other" (137). The question that numerous critics have posed is precisely *how* Mervyn profits from this lesson and others he has learned from Betty Lawrence and Thomas Welbeck. Do they enable him to protect himself in a commercial society, or do they provide another sort of instruction—how to inveigle oneself into economic power over others? Mervyn's seeming triumph at the end of the novel through his impending marriage to the wealthy widow Achsa Fielding further discomfits critics, since so much ambiguity surrounds what would be, in a more conventionally sentimental text, a reward congruent with Mervyn's previous suffering and virtue. (Although perhaps this "reward" is indeed fitting, since Achsa's virtue is likewise questioned by other characters). Mervyn's persistent adherence to self-interest, even while pursuing larger goals of benevolence, troubles his critics, both within and without the text. W. B. Berthoff, for instance, claims that "His benevolence is selfish, acquisitive, in no way disinterested" (431). Brown's own comment in a February 1799 letter to his brother, James Brown, that "Arthur is a hero whose virtue, in order to be productive of benefit to others, and felicity to himself, stands in no need of riches" further complicates the issue.[29] There is no easy resolution to this question of Mervyn's moral virtue, and the text itself provides reams of contradictory information. In labeling Mervyn "a fictional palindrome, an enigma who reads true from opposite vantage points simultaneously," Bill Christophersen aptly sums up the problematic issue of Arthur's conduct (91).

Thomas Welbeck

Arthur Mervyn is perhaps the most geographically mobile of all early American novels. Characters move with dizzying rapidity not only between the country and the city and among Charleston, Baltimore, and Philadelphia, but also across the ocean from Jamaica to the United States, and between the United States and Europe. In such a highly mobile society, appearances take precedence, despite their sometimes-delusive nature. Welbeck, like Sanford, Courtland, and numerous other American rogues, rapidly gains social acceptance based upon his genteel public behavior and his appearance of immense wealth. In an endless deferral of value, Philadelphians foolishly credit Welbeck with virtue based on the wealth credited to him, which is itself a fraud. Similarly, even Mrs. Villars and her daughters, a family of prostitutes, are able to pass themselves off as genteel for a brief time. Dr. Stevens explains that Mrs. Villars and her three daughters were "well trained in the school of fashion, and elegant in person, manners, and dress. They had lately arrived from Europe, and for a time, received from their neighbors that respect to which their education and fortune appeared to lay claim" (221). Both Welbeck and a kinsman of Dr. Stevens fall victim to these delusive appearances and are unable to escape before the Villars bankrupt them. As the Villars incidents illustrate, the problem here is that a fortune, in and of itself, is considered a firm enough basis in commercial Philadelphia to command "respect." That this was the case in Arthur Mervyn's fictional Philadelphia suggests the degree to which Brown saw America as prostituting its republican ideals in pursuit of traffic in human souls.

Welbeck immediately takes advantage of the gullibility and greed of this financially driven city, presenting Philadelphians with an affluent image. After taking the money that the deceased Lodi entrusted to Welbeck for his sister, Clemenza, Welbeck had traveled to Philadelphia, rented an opulent home, and purchased all its furnishings from the Claverings, a respectable, if troubled, family removing to Europe. The stupendous luxury of Welbeck's enormous, marble-laden mansion dazzles Mervyn; he is awed by the "pictured walls, glossy hangings, gilded sofas, mirrors that occupied from cieling [*sic*] to floor, carpets of Tauris, and the spotless and transcendent brilliancy of coverlets and napkins" (334). Mervyn immediately and, as it happens, correctly, imagines to himself when he sees this enormous mansion that "This fair inheritance had fallen to one who, perhaps, would only abuse it to the purposes of luxury" (47). Whereas Mervyn's admiring description of the mansion suggests his aesthetic appreciation of its furnishings, for Welbeck this mansion merely represents an "unproductive" or "symbolic expenditure," to use Georges Bataille's terms.[30] Welbeck uses this luxurious setting to suggest to Philadelphia society that he does not need to use his money productively. He intends to use this mansion as an entree into Philadelphia society, while cultivating an air of mystery in order to obscure his true identity. He later explains to Mervyn that "There was no difficulty in persuading the world that Welbeck was a personage of opulence and rank.... The facility with which mankind are mislead in their estimate of characters, their proneness to multiply inferences and conjectures will not be readily conceived by one destitute of my experience. My sudden appearance on the stage, my stately reserve, my splendid habitation and my circumspect deportment were sufficient to intitle me to homage" (95). For residents of this post-Revolutionary commercial city, money, not a title, establishes rank, which has no relationship to virtuous character. If virtue retains any lingering importance, it is because it is something that is *imputed* to him who possesses rank. Mervyn himself initially suffers from this same problem of inferences, and part of the lesson that he must learn is "to discern the illusions of power and riches, and [to abjure] every claim to esteem that was not founded on integrity" (200).

Welbeck thrives upon the respect accorded to him because of his wealth, and all his actions are guided by the surface image he wishes to present to the world. As he reveals to Mervyn, "The artifices that were used to unveil the truth, and the guesses that were current respecting me, were adapted to gratify my ruling passion" (95). Welbeck's "ruling passion" is his value of the world's opinion of him; he explains that "The esteem of mankind was the spring of all my activity, the parent of all my virtue and all my vice" (89). For the wealthy man (unlike the poor Mervyn, or any woman), being the subject of "guesses" or curious speculation *increases* his value, for this positive publication, this social circulation, heightens his image. Pursuit of this esteem drives Welbeck to tremendous extravagance with Lodi's money, and Mervyn fears that should Welbeck gain control of the remainder of his money, "The same dependence on the world's erroneous estimation, the same devotion to imposture, and thoughtlessness of futurity" would result (199). As Teresa Goddu has commented, "For Welbeck, reputation—public credit—replaces all private value" (35). Proteus-like, Welbeck even adapts his demeanor and personality to suit the expectations of genteel company. When he is in the presence of company and hence "on-stage," Welbeck becomes virtually a different person, Mervyn notes, "on whom his entrance into this company appeared to operate like magic. His eye sparkled; his features expanded into benign serenity; and his wonted reserve gave place to a torrent-like and overflowing elocution" (73). What others see of Welbeck is not merely the mask of the social man, but rather a full-fledged theatrical performance of gentility and sociability designed to enhance his reputation.

The performance that Welbeck executes, allied to his luxurious lifestyle, prompts Thetford and others to style Welbeck the "Nabob" and treat him accordingly. When Mrs. Thetford wisely questions the existence of Welbeck's wealth, Thetford, willing and accustomed to deal in surfaces, tautologically replies, "Mark how he lives" (40). Yet this fraudulent display of excessive wealth exposes Welbeck himself to an enormously complicated fraud engineered by Thetford. Thetford and his brother defraud Welbeck of his shipping investment based on what they assume about his wealth—that he is so wealthy that the loss of "thirty thousand [will be] nothing" (40). Ruled by greed, they fail to consider that Watson, who captains the ship, will also suffer when the British impound it for carrying planted contraband. Justifying his deceit, Thetford, whose own home is also luxurious beyond Mervyn's comprehension, claims, "Besides, this man is not what he ought to be. He will some time or other, come out to be a grand impostor. He makes money by other arts than bargain and sale. He has found his way, by some means, to the Portuguese treasury" (40–41). Welbeck's immense wealth, then, makes him subject to fraud precisely because he is wealthy and, as Mervyn understands, "because he was imagined to have acquired this opulence by other than honest methods" (78). Thetford, merely suspecting that Welbeck has acquired his money dishonestly, becomes his judge and jury, sentencing Welbeck to become a victim of fraud. Although Mervyn frequently speculates about the philanthropic good he could accomplish if only he had money, those characters in *Arthur Mervyn* who do have wealth above the bourgeois level of financial security are thieves and frauds (Thetford and Welbeck), prostitutes (Mrs. Villars), or unpleasant and unscrupulous liars (Mrs. Maurice).

"Mansions of Misfortune"

Arthur Mervyn sketches a near-apocalyptic view of urban American life in the 1790s, with a city under assault from the physical corruption of the plague and the moral corruption of economic fraud. In Brown's Philadelphia, greed, crippling debt, seduction, and violence effect the breakdown of numerous families, thereby destabilizing an urban culture that has already allowed money to substitute for good character. Given the state of near-collapse of Brown's fictional Philadelphia, it is not surprising that he would turn his attention to institutions such as the prison and the hospital, arms of the state that were substituting with mixed success for the order that the family and church would have promoted in earlier times. Present in the narrative almost constantly, whether in fact or in Mervyn's imagination, the hospital and the prison alternately suggest fantasies of power and of powerlessness, nightmarish versions of the institutions that were struggling to deal with post-Revolutionary social problems.[31]

Mervyn, whose mere presence in the city seems to be a source of anxiety for him, constantly and self-consciously ponders sickness and suffering, crime and punishment. During his brief interlude at the Hadwin farm,

Mervyn romantically imagines various calamities that might befall him in the city, especially fantasies of sickness and imprisonment. As he says of the yellow fever in Philadelphia, "A certain sublimity is connected with enormous dangers, that imparts to our consternation or our pity, a tincture of the pleasing" (130). He points out, however, that at that time in his life, he himself was in no danger from the fever and thus could "personate the witnesses and sufferers of this calamity" at his leisure; "This employment was not enjoined upon me by necessity, but was ardently pursued, and must therefore have been recommended by some nameless charm" (130).

Yet Mervyn reacts with horror at the mention of the hospital at Bush-Hill, considering it "a contagious and abhorred receptacle" that, in the absence of family, torments sufferers (149).[32] Mervyn is not the only one who fears the hospital. Thetford's serving girl, who suffered from an ailment other than the fever, "resigned herself to despair" upon being sent to the hospital: "In going to the hospital, she believed herself led to certain death, and to the sufferance of every evil which the known inhumanity of its attendants could inflict" (159). Wallace, whom Thetford likewise sends to the hospital, lives to tell of its horrors, although he claims that when Thetford forced the servant girl to be admitted to the hospital, he sent her to "execution" (172). Further, when Wallace recalls his own forced admission to the hospital, he labels Thetford a "murderer" and recalls how he begged the attendants "to procure a respite from my sentence. They were deaf to my intreaties, and prepared to execute their office by force" (172). He describes his conveyance to the hospital as torture, claiming, "To be disjointed and torn piece-meal by the rack, was a torment inexpressibly inferior to this" (173). The scene of the hospital that Wallace paints is reminiscent of Bedlam, filled with suffering overlaid by maniacal laughter. But in Bush-Hill, in an inversion of order, it is not the patients who laugh maniacally; it is the attendants, whose apartments are "the scenes of carrousals and mirth," of "debauchery and riot" (173). "Execution," "sentence," "the rack," "debauchery"—Wallace's language seems more appropriate to describe a prison than a hospital. Despite the eventual reforms of the plague hospital detailed in Mathew Carey's *A Short Account of the Malignant Fever, lately prevalent at Philadelphia*, the hospital in Brown's nightmarish vision of Philadelphia—a horrific, yet necessary, substitute for the loving care of families torn apart by greed, disease, and fear—is not a place of succor, but a perverse institution of punishment for physical corruption, heightening the tensions of the city, rather than alleviating them. Mervyn expends much energy evading hospitalization, but his *fear* of being hospitalized—whether from the plague, or from the blow to his head—is a very real fear given the absence of a caring family to nurse him, and this fear overshadows much of his sojourn in the city.

Paralleling his anxiety about being hospitalized, Mervyn also has fear-inspiring yet masochistic fantasies of being imprisoned, and he must confront the imprisonment of several acquaintances, as well as his father's death while imprisoned for debt. The prospect of being thought a criminal horrifies yet fascinates Mervyn, but he continues to act in ways that invite misapprehension, such as his habit of bursting into other people's homes without knocking, as he does in the homes of Mrs. Watson, Mrs. Wentworth, and Mrs. Villars, actions which he rationalizes by claiming his "*purposes* were not dishonest" (emphasis added) (182). Yet time after time, he titillates himself with the thought that he might be apprehended for crimes sometimes imagined and other times accidental. However, just as he eventually exposes himself to yellow fever and succumbs, so does he ultimately and deliberately engage in criminal behavior.

Arriving in Philadelphia destitute, without family or friends, Mervyn first fears being arrested for indigence. After wandering through the darkness of the city in the company of a mysterious young man who Mervyn will later learn is the mischievous Wallace, Susan Hadwin's fiancé, Arthur is locked in a dark room in an equally dark house. Fearful of voluntarily revealing himself to the occupants of the house, Mervyn ponders: "[W]hat would be the consequence" of being found in a locked room in a dark house? "Should I not be arrested as a thief and conveyed to prison?" (35). Mervyn eventually emerges undiscovered from the prison-like closet that he calls his "perilous asylum" (41), but he does not escape his fears of imprisonment. "Terrors of imprisonment and accusation" likewise haunt Mervyn when he assists Welbeck in burying the unfortunate Watson's body (113). Welbeck's lengthy absence from the cellar prompts him to fear that Welbeck has deliberately abandoned him to "be pursued by the most vehement suspicions and, perhaps, hunted to my obscurest retreat by the ministers of justice" (111–12). With justification, he fears not only prosecution for his actual crimes—concealing a murder and abetting a murderer—but also being thought guilty of murder. According to his narrative, Mervyn is innocent; nonetheless, he ponders that "my tale however circumstantial or true, will scarcely suffice for my vindication. My flight will be construed into a proof of incontestable guilt" (112).

Even after Mervyn locates Welbeck in another part of the cellar and realizes his error, both continue to use juridical language. As he accompanies

Welbeck to the river, Mervyn ponders his complicity in aiding Welbeck and tells himself, "I had acted long enough a servile and mechanical part; and been guided by blind and foreign impulses. It was time to lay aside my fetters, and demand to know whither the path tended in which I was importuned to walk" (114). Although Mervyn gains no satisfaction from Welbeck, Welbeck's earlier comment, "I shall quickly place myself beyond the reach of inquisitors and judges . . ." (108), prepares Mervyn to view Welbeck's plunge into the Schuylkill River as a suicide. Welbeck's use of legalistic terms such as "inquisitors and judges" suggests his disdain for the legal system, but certainly his comment might apply equally to the inquisitorial Mervyn. Once again unable to locate Welbeck after he has jumped into the river, Mervyn realizes that he had become so deeply involved in Welbeck's affairs as to be guilty by association, and he thus makes no attempt to expose Welbeck's crime, or to exonerate himself. Haunted by his culpability in concealing Watson's death, Mervyn temporarily retires to the Hadwin farm, where he fantasizes about the diseases of the city.

Welbeck's reappearance in Philadelphia sets into motion more fantasies of imprisonment embedded in Mervyn's anxieties about credit and credibility. After Mervyn discovers that Welbeck did not drown in the river, Welbeck once more deceives Mervyn by telling him that the money hidden in Lodi's manuscript is counterfeit. Welbeck claims that he saved himself from drowning in order to prevent anyone from using the money, because he feared being the cause of an innocent person's conviction for counterfeiting (208). Welbeck's explanation prompts Mervyn again to imagine himself as an innocent victim, this time innocent in truth, since he could not have known those particular bills were counterfeits. He momentarily agonizes over how he had "tottered on the brink of destruction! If I had made use of this money, in what a labyrinth of misery might I not have been involved! My innocence could never have been proved. . . . My career would have found an ignominious close; or, if my punishment had been transmuted into slavery and toil, would the testimony of my conscience have supported me?" (209). For Mervyn, it is not enough to know that he is innocent, because that self-knowledge could not have sustained him. The false credit of the counterfeit bills would have destroyed any worth credited to him because of his virtue. In a frenzy of contriteness for a crime he does not commit, Mervyn burns the bills as Welbeck watches in horror, since he has apparently lied about their counterfeit status.[33] As Edward Watts has pointed out, Mervyn's inability here to distinguish between the real banknotes and Welbeck's false story "undermines his claim to reliable interpretive skills, and thus casts doubt on his entire narrative" (109).[34] Ironically, Mervyn's determination to be credible by burning the suspect bank notes indirectly leads to Welbeck's imprisonment; destitute after Mervyn burns the money, Welbeck is caught passing stolen bills. Mervyn then finally sees the inside of a prison, when he visits Welbeck at the urging of Clemenza Lodi.

Structurally, the prison functions in virtually the same fashion as the hospital at Bush-Hill, for instead of creating order it encourages disorder. The scene in the debtors' prison in Prune Street is at the center of *Arthur Mervyn*. Originally constructed in 1773 as a workhouse, by the 1790s the Prune Street building was used as a debtors' prison for the Walnut Street Jail. The Walnut Street Jail had been the site of considerable reform by the early 1790s, but the prison scene in *Arthur Mervyn* bears little relation to contemporary reform theories of what a prison should do and be.[35] Rather than creating order and fostering an environment in which prisoners would have the opportunity for quiet contemplation of their errors, Brown's Prune Street prison instead encourages uproarious mirth and dissipation. Mervyn describes the prison by saying, "Never had I smelt so noisome an odour, or surveyed faces so begrimed with filth and misery. The walls and floors were alike squallid and detestable. It seemed that in this house existence would be bereaved of all its attractions; and yet those faces, which could be seen through the obscurity that encompassed them, were either void of care or distorted with mirth" (334). Similarly horrified by the depraved levity of the prison, Dr. Stevens describes the main apartment as being "filled with pale faces and withered forms. The marks of negligence and poverty were visible in all; but few betrayed, in their features or gestures, any symptoms of concern on account of their condition. Ferocious gaiety, or stupid indifference, seemed to sit upon every brow" (253–54). Undaunted by their imprisonment, this "promiscuous" crowd smokes, drinks, and plays cards in a carnivalesque atmosphere. Both Mervyn and Stevens are struck by the irrational gaiety with which most of the prisoners comport themselves. Although contemporary reform theories advocated that prison should be a place of last resort to encourage self-discipline, clearly this prison fails its inhabitants, although not in all respects. For Mervyn, the mere thought of prison and imprisonment is an effective deterrent; his imaginative constructions of accusations, of crimes he did not commit, of punishments, and of imprisonment serve as checks for his conduct, although they do not completely prevent his transgressive behavior. For Mervyn, then, the prison as an institution serves the deterrent role the state intends it to.

When Mervyn finally locates Welbeck, who is ill and resting in a private chamber, Mervyn elevates himself from contemplating his own possible criminality to judging that of Welbeck. On the basis of five days' acquaintance with Welbeck and the brief interlude during which they grapple over the Lodis's money, Mervyn claims for himself a superior understanding of Welbeck and hence the right to judge him. In an apostrophe to the still unseen Welbeck, Mervyn explains: "Mankind will pursue thee to the grave with execrations. Their cruelty will be justified or palliated, since they know thee not. They are unacquainted with the goadings of thy conscience and the bitter retributions which thou art daily suffering: they are full of their own wrongs, and think only of those tokens of exultation and complacency which thou wast studious of assuming in thy intercourse with them. It is I only that thoroughly know thee, and can rightly estimate thy claims to compassion" (333). Given that Mervyn has excused himself of all manner of trespasses and minor crimes with the justification that his own "purposes were not dishonest" (182), it is no small irony that he esteems himself fit to judge Welbeck. Mervyn continues his imaginary conversation with Welbeck, asking him, "Is it rational to cherish the hope of thy restoration to innocence and peace? Thou art no obdurate criminal; hadst thou less virtue, thy compunctions would be less keen" (333). Clearly Mervyn's fantasies of benevolence temporarily overcome his rationality: Welbeck is a thief many times over, an adulterous seducer, a counterfeiter, and a murderer. Mervyn wisely gives up his daydreams of holding Welbeck in his benevolent thrall when Welbeck glares malignantly at the man he has accused of being the "author" of his problems; he quickly revises his plan to instead use Welbeck as a negative exemplar. He thinks, "Let me gain, from contemplation of thy misery, new motives to sincerity and rectitude" (334).

The "use" to which Mervyn puts Welbeck irks him even more, given that it is his exposure within the prison that subjects him to Mervyn's presence. He demands of him: "How dare you thrust yourself upon my privacy? Why am I not alone? Fly! and let my miseries want, at least, the aggravation of beholding their author" (337). Welbeck dreads exposure of his guilt and the shattering of his golden image more than death or punishment, but imprisonment renders him powerless to protect this image. Similarly, when Watson confronted Welbeck about the seduction of his sister, Welbeck claimed, "I dreaded not his violence. The death that he might be prompted to inflict, was no object of aversion. It was poverty and disgrace, the detection of my crimes, the looks and voice of malediction and upbraiding, from which my cowardice shrunk" (103). Welbeck tells Mervyn that the only further harm he can do is to "betray the secrets that are lodged in thy bosom, and rob me of the comfort of reflecting that my guilt is known but to one among the living" (338).[36]

Mervyn cannot legally turn Welbeck into a public exemplar, for to do so would be to expose himself to prosecution. Instead, his alternative method of dealing with Welbeck's intransigence is through publication. As I pointed out earlier, Welbeck has already accused Mervyn of being the "author" of his problems—suggesting both that Mervyn is the cause of his troubles and that his authorship, or publication, of Welbeck's story along with his own furthers his persecution of Welbeck. While Welbeck sees Mervyn's behavior as *persecution*, Mervyn himself might well consider it *prosecution*—Welbeck's just deserts for rejecting Mervyn's benevolent intentions. As Warner points out in *The Letters of the Republic*, for Mervyn, "Disclosure bears a punitive character"—not for the discloser, but for the characters about whom information is being disclosed (166). Disclosure becomes associated with the power of the legal system "because of the close identification of the public and the legitimate in representational polity, for the consequence of that identification is that the secret and the hidden automatically appear as illegitimate" (167). Welbeck's greatest fear has been of public exposure, while Mervyn has feared that, lacking credibility, the hospital or prison will be his fate. It is Welbeck, however, who ends up imprisoned, ill, and exposed.

Ironically, Welbeck dies not from the plague—that disease has run its course in Philadelphia—but rather from exposure. The publication of his crimes permanently shatters the public image into which he has invested so much ego.[37] Welbeck regards imprisonment as an evil to be endured, but he cannot tolerate the exposure to which prison subjects him. Mervyn's threat to bring Clemenza Lodi to visit Welbeck elicits a bizarre, violent outburst. He tells Mervyn: "[K]eep her from a prison. Drag her to the wheel or to the scaffold; mangle her with stripes; torture her with famine; strangle her child before her face, and cast it to the hungry dogs that are howling at the gate; but—keep her from a prison" (336). He also reacts violently upon learning that Mervyn has told Dr. Stevens about him, exclaiming, "[G]ood God! what mean you? Headlong and rash as you are, you will not share with this person your knowledge of me?" (258). After Mervyn informs him that he had already told Stevens everything, despite his promise to keep Welbeck's secrets, Welbeck's countenance "betrayed a mixture of incredulity and horror" (258). Surprisingly, his horror stems from his real sense of betrayal. He asks Mervyn, "Hast thou shut every avenue to my return to honor? Am I known to be a seducer and assassin? To have meditated all crimes, and to have perpetrated the worst?" (259). Welbeck certainly problematizes honor, if a seducer and murderer could still hope to be known as an "honorable" man in commercial Philadelphia. Ultimately, Welbeck concludes, "Infamy and death are my portion. I know they are reserved for me; but I did not think to receive them at thy hands" (259).

The irony of Welbeck's imprisonment—and a scathing indictment of the urban commercial world through which he moves—is that he is not arrested for a physical crime against a person. He is not arrested for adultery, for fornication, or even for Watson's murder, but for crimes against property. While he was rich and hence respected, no crime was too great to conceal behind his public display of opulence. Later, poor and friendless, he is arrested for economic fraud in Baltimore when, bankrupt and unable to return to his home, he tries to pass off Mrs. Maurice's bills of exchange as his own. Bankruptcy per se is not as fully explored in early American fiction as it would later be in Victorian novels such as *Dombey and Sons* (1848), *Vanity Fair* (1848), *The Mill on the Floss* (1860), and *Middlemarch* (1872).[38] Nonetheless, the larger issues of debt and economic fraud greatly concerned American novelists, given the complex web of financial interdependence that arose in the new Republic as a result of international trade and widespread land, currency, and commodity speculation. Impersonal financial relationships supplanted the family, religious, and civic ties that once bound communities together—ties made conspicuous in *Arthur Mervyn* by their absence.

In Brown's post-Revolutionary Philadelphia, neither religion nor civic ties unite communities. Instead, money both binds people together and tears them apart, while fraud and economic failure endanger families and the larger community, as the disappearance of Watson suggests. Until Mervyn carries Watson's papers to his widow and her brother, they tremble on the verge of insolvency, and only the unusual generosity of their creditors saves them from debtors' prison; Mrs. Maurice likewise faces bankruptcy until Mervyn returns her stolen bills of exchange, while Miss Carleton must work as a scrivener in order to support herself and free her brother from debtors' prison.

Regardless of the reason for debt in the early national era, the moral implications of being unable to pay one's debts are unavoidable, whether insolvency came about more or less accidentally through misfortune, bad business dealings or speculation, or whether it was the result of gambling or fraud. Yet those who bear the greatest burden of this fiscal irresponsibility are inevitably female relations (wives, daughters, or siblings), for debt, like gambling and speculation, poses a threat to the home and the domestic circle; at the same time, unlike Miss Carleton, most women were unprepared to assume the financial burdens of a family. Like foreign trade, debt illustrates both the permeability of the private sphere and its dependence on commerce. Both the home and domestic life are shockingly vulnerable to the vicissitudes of commercial enterprise. Even wealthy women are not exempt from this threat; indeed, their wealth perhaps renders them more vulnerable. This situation holds true for *Arthur Mervyn*, where Welbeck first seduces Clemenza Lodi and then steals her money, leaving her pregnant, impoverished, and friendless; it also holds true in *Story of Margaretta*, where Courtland squanders Frances Wellwood's inheritance, and in *The Coquette*, where Sanford wastes his wife's dowry, forcing her to return to her parents when his property is attached.

Read in the context of work by other early American writers, Charles Brockden Brown's fiction reveals striking similarities. *The Coquette*, *Story of Margaretta*, and *Arthur Mervyn* all voice misgivings about the impact of changing economic conditions on social relations and the inadequacy of traditional American institutions to contend with socially transgressive or criminal conduct. As Hans Robert Jauss has written in *Toward an Aesthetic of Reception*,

> A literary work, even when it appears to be new, does not present itself as something absolutely new in an informational vacuum, but predisposes its audience to a very specific kind of reception by announcements, overt and covert signals, familiar characteristics, or implicit allusions. It awakens memories of that which was already read, brings the reader to a specific emotional attitude, and with its beginning arouses expectations for the 'middle and end,' which can then be maintained intact or altered, reoriented, or even fulfilled ironically in the course of the reading according to the specific rules of the genres or type of text.[39]

Certainly Brown's work—and *Arthur Mervyn* in particular—did not emerge from an "informational vacuum." Although Brown's vision of commerce dependent on the slave trade is much darker than those of novelists who explore the promise of the East India trade, Brown shared the interests and anxieties of his fellow novelists with regard to changing social and economic relationships in the early Republic, the social difficulties wrought by increasing geographical mobility, and the substitution of credit for individual worth in social relationships. As liberalism in the guise of economic individualism gained sway in America, Brown and his fellow novelists used fiction to intervene into public discourse on masculine economic behavior. Participating in a broad reconstitution of social authority, their fictions struggled, sometimes unsuccessfully, to find ways to accommodate modern capitalist behavior without sacrificing the virtuous ethos of republicanism. If Brown's fiction differs in any significant way from that of other early American writers, it is through his play with the "rules of the genre," through his refusal or failure to provide a decisive resolution—whether positive or negative—to these vexing issues.

Epilogue

*Looking Forward to
Antebellum Fiction*

IT IS MORE THAN a little ironic that Samuel Richardson's *Pamela*, the first novel to be printed in America—an epistolary novel at that and one that challenged the British class system—was so resoundingly rejected as a model by American writers. *Pamela* won rare praise from American readers ranging from Jonathan Edwards to Abigail Adams,[1] but American-authored fiction of the late eighteenth century systematically counters *Pamela* and its prescription that "reformed rakes make the best husbands," for neither rakes, nor their wives, nor their mistresses fare well in American fiction. Perhaps most ironic is how American fiction, written and published in the land where "all men are [said to be] created equal," so diligently reinscribes the class boundaries that *Pamela* transgressed. If fiction presents us with an America imagined, then it is an America that by and large reflects its creators—white men and women of the middling and upper classes—and the world they inhabited, a world in which they could only briefly and tentatively imagine sharing their social and legal privileges (no matter how dubious) with people unlike themselves, even if this sharing occurred only in fiction.

The poor, immigrants, servants, slaves, and Native Americans—the subjects of so much nineteenth-century fiction—hover on the margins of this world, as critics such as Cynthia Jordan, Teresa Goddu, and Julia Stern have ably demonstrated, yet for the most part they lack the subjectivity and affect claimed by bourgeois white men and women. Without this interiority, the Sanchos and Queen Mabs of early American fiction never become fully realized, truly sympathetic, characters; instead, many of them function as stock comic figures, as does Teague O'Regan in Hugh Henry Brackenridge's *Modern Chivalry*.[2] As Elizabeth Barnes asserts in *States of Sympathy*, "In its eighteenth-century context, 'sympathy' connotes identification: not feeling for a person, from a distance, but with or alongside of a person."[3] Claudia L. Johnson, writing in *Equivocal Beings* about Anne Radcliffe's gothic novel *The Mysteries of Udolpho*, describes the corollary to this phenomenon when she discusses the self-centered Madame Montoni, aunt of the heroine. Johnson explains, "Madame Montoni reminds us that sentimentality enforces and mystifies certain social priorities by a converse operation of desensitization. It ensures the stable continuance of certain arrangements unconflictually by privileging the feelings of some and excluding from sympathy the feelings of those whose interests fall outside dominant values. Far from granting all persons access to the dignity of interiority by virtue of their capacity for feeling, sentimentality always entails exclusion" (107). "Stable" is not a word that aptly describes the social, legal, or cultural situation of the early Republic, but certainly the first twenty-five years of sentimental fiction produced in the United States privileges the feelings and social, sexual, and economic dilemmas of white men and women of the middling to upper classes. It is this process of exclusion, in concert with the repetition of certain tropes, that grants validity to the concerns of people who, if not precisely ordinary, were neither of exalted social status nor politically powerful. Fiction gave these writers a forum through which they could express their anxieties about a multitude of issues: the weakening of the cultural imperative toward civic virtue as the country moved politically from republicanism to liberalism, the loosening of family and communal authority over young people, and related concerns about female sexuality, marriage, inheritance, and the accumulation of capital. Emphasizing these concerns, making sure that they assumed priority in the American imagination, entailed excluding or, at the least, minimizing, concerns of people unlike themselves. While not always literally invisible in the American novel prior to 1814, the poor, immigrants, servants, slaves, and Native Americans suffer from what Ann Jessie Van Sant labels a "complex invisibility," whereby a group of people may be "seen without being noticed" (40), without registering on viewers or readers as humans with individual concerns. Only by generating sympathy could these individuals be *made* individuals, and only by being made individuals could they generate sympathy.

In the later years of the early Republic, the decades post-1800, economic issues began to bridge the concerns between the middle class and the poor, with novelists extending both interiority and sympathy to the industrious poor; rather than trace the rapid accumulation of capital against a fluid social background, the novel begins to explore the impact of the extended *absence* of capital. The phrase "industrious poor," which resonates in the writing of the day, does not indicate merely those individuals who have temporarily lost wealth and social position, the restoration of which are common subjects of the early novel. Rather, the "industrious poor" encompasses those humble poor on the periphery who understand their place in the social hierarchy and who yet aspire to the core emerging bourgeois values. Sentimentalized philanthropy and benevolence first enable the extension of sympathy to those individuals. As Philip Fisher persuasively argues, "The presence of sentimentality is most obvious at precisely those places where an essential extension of the subject matter of the novel is taking place. Just where new materials, new components of the self, new types of heroes and heroines, new subjects of mood and feeling occur: at exactly those places will the presence of sentimentality be most marked" (93). In sentimental novels such as Martha Read's *Monima; or The Beggar Girl* (1802), Sarah Savage's *The Factory Girl* (1814), and Susanna Rowson's *Lucy Temple* (1828), the worthy poor appear as subjects for philanthropy and the extension of sympathy.[4] Although the poor, beginning to be both more visible and individualized in the novel, first enable American fiction writers to envision a broader scope of subjects, this scope gradually expands throughout the 1820s to imagine subjectivity and interiority for other formerly excluded groups of people, especially Native Americans. The mere presence of sentiment and sympathy, however, does not entail equality; at times, sentiment and sympathy may merely reinscribe the differences between authors and their characters, for the poor, slaves, servants, immigrants, and Native Americans were not yet citizens in the fullest sense, even as they increasingly became part of the national imaginary.[5] Likewise, they were not bourgeois, yet we see in fiction the imposition of bourgeois values—especially self-discipline and self-reflective behavior—onto members of these formerly excluded groups, as their admission price, one might say, to the national imaginary.

Although not unproblematic, this expansion of the national imaginary via attention to the poor and their work marks the transition from early American fiction to antebellum fiction. Sarah Savage's 1814 novel *The Factory Girl* is an especially appropriate work to signal the end of the early novel's preoccupation with issues relevant primarily to the middle and upper classes. Mary Burnam, the heroine of *The Factory Girl*, works in a cotton factory, teaches Sunday school to the children employed in the factory, and practices benevolence to those less fortunate. Although she herself is poor, Burnam adopts the bourgeois tenets of economic and emotional self-discipline promulgated throughout early American fiction. Grounded in the values of an earlier period through its wholesale rejection of gambling even in as benign a form as a lottery, the religiously evangelical novel *The Factory Girl* yet hearkens to new settings and subjects—the working poor and industrialization—topics that would feature prominently in later sentimental novels of the nineteenth century such as Maria Cummins's *The Lamplighter*.

As new types of individuals come to concern novelists in the decades following 1814, the anxieties about the regulation of sexual and economic desire that I have discussed throughout this work similarly transform, moving from the foreground to the background as slavery, Indian conflict, and poverty come to preoccupy American writers. The economic speculator of the early Republic, for example, slowly morphs into the prankster and confidence man, losing perhaps some of his suavity but none of his slickness, appearing in Southwest humor, Melville's *The Confidence Man*, and much later as the Duke and the King in *Adventures of Huckleberry Finn*. The vulnerability of the domestic sphere to the economic machinations of unregulated men likewise remains a preoccupation of the novel and indeed underlies the most important sentimental novel of the antebellum period, *Uncle Tom's Cabin*.

Perhaps better than any other nineteenth-century novel, *Uncle Tom's Cabin* illustrates in complex ways how this role reversal occurred. Economic speculation serves as the genesis of the plot of the novel by threatening the domestic tranquillity of the Shelby farm in *Uncle Tom's Cabin* and necessitating the sale of Harry Harris and Uncle Tom, an event that sets into motion the tragedies and triumphs of the novel. The narrator of *Uncle Tom's Cabin* makes this point clear when she explains that Mr. Shelby had "speculated largely and quite loosely; had involved himself deeply, and his notes to a large amount had come into the hands of Haley," the slave trader.[6] In condemning economic speculation, the narrator reiterates the language of the writers of the early national period. It is greed that drives Mr. Shelby to speculate, with "the prospect of sudden and rapid gain" taking precedence over "the interests of the helpless and unprotected" (7). Economic speculation and debt in this novel not only threaten the destruction of the white domestic sphere, but do, in fact, destroy the happy domestic environment of Uncle Tom, Aunt Chloe, and their children. Economic speculation also threatens the physical bodies of the slaves, whom Stowe successfully incorporates into the domestic sphere of their white owners, individualizing them through interiority and, consequently, sympathy, albeit a sympathy that at times merely reinforces the privileged status of their white owners.[7] This situation differs markedly from the novels of the early national era, wherein slaves and servants are at once a part of and yet distinct from the domestic sphere; certainly in novels such as *Kelroy* or *Arthur Mervyn*, they are exempt from the kind of interest and sympathy evoked on behalf of their owners and employers. In the reformist novels of the mid-nineteenth century, however, both the bodies and minds of slaves and servants become preoccupations of novelists.

There is one final, monumental way in which Stowe's *Uncle Tom's Cabin* plays upon themes important to writers of the early national era, and that is with regard to the relationship between madness and sexual transgression. Economic speculation and slavery threaten not merely the domestic happiness and physical bodies of slaves, but also their very sanity and religious salvation. Cassie, beautiful, black, and unchaste, hovers on the brink of madness throughout the novel. We learn she has been the victim of circumstances, sold into slavery as the mistress of a white man after the death of her white father, and sold again, along with her two children, to clear her lover's gambling debts. Cassie then becomes the mistress of a succession of men, terminating in the loathsome Simon Legree. Her sexual liaisons are never conscious, rational choices for Cassie, for she does not really have any options. She even defends herself to Tom when she tells him, "But it can't be that the Lord will lay sin to our account . . . he won't charge it to us, when we're forced to it; he'll charge it to them that drove us to it" (313). Nonetheless, her belief that forced depravity does not count as sin does not prevent Cassie from descending into madness, which leads her to stab Butler, her second lover, with a bowie knife, to murder a third child to save him from a life of slavery, and to contemplate the murder of Legree. As Tom tells her, the fact that they are slaves and cannot always control their fates "won't keep us from growing wicked . . . it won't make much odds to me how I come so; it's the *bein' so*,—that ar's what I'm a dreadin'" (313). Sandra M. Gilbert and Susan Gubar have famously, and compellingly, traced Cassie's madness to Stowe's fascination with Charlotte Brontë and *Jane Eyre*, as Cassie literally becomes the madwoman in the attic during her cat-and-mouse escape with Emmeline from Simon Legree.[8] Of course for Bertha Mason Rochester, *Jane Eyre's* madwoman in the attic, madness and sexuality are similarly intertwined. The connection to *Jane Eyre* aside, Cassie is one more in a long train of American literary characters whose sexual unchasteness, even if not by choice, has led her to the brink of madness.

While Stowe's novel brought welcome attention to the plight of female slaves, her project was not entirely liberatory. As Stowe strives in *Uncle Tom's Cabin* to expose the evils of slavery and racial prejudice, the moral economy of the novel simultaneously exposes the entangled nature of race and class in nineteenth-century America. For as Stowe's treatment of Cassie reveals, the expansion of the national imaginary to include slaves brought with it the extension of bourgeois requirements for female self-regulation onto individuals who, by virtue of their slave status, were unable to be self-regulating.[9]

The greatness of *Uncle Tom's Cabin* owes in large part to its sympathetic treatment of slaves in a nation perplexed by slavery and longing to understand how to feel for, and toward, southern slaves. The greatness of *Uncle Tom's Cabin* and its tremendous popularity in the nineteenth century also have to do, I propose, with Stowe's brilliant repackaging of themes and tropes that had been important to American writers and part of the horizon of expectations for readers for six decades, with an attendant shift in perspective from bestowing sympathy only to middle-class white characters to extending sympathy to and privileging the interiority of those previously excluded from both the polity and the national imaginary. At the same time, *Uncle Tom's Cabin* suggests the expanding moral authority of female bourgeois authors, who, like their counterparts during the early national era, sought a space for themselves in public discourse.

Notes

Introduction

1. First published in *The Monthly Magazine* in 1799, "Walstein's School of History: From the German of Krants of Gotha" is reprinted in *The Rhapsodist and Other Uncollected Writings by Charles Brockden Brown*, ed. Harry Warfel (New York: Scholars' Facsimiles & Reprints, 1943), from which the above quotation is drawn, 152. Norman S. Grabo and Jane Tompkins, among others, argue that this sketch contains a précis of *Arthur Mervyn* in its description of Engel's fictional historical work, "Olivo Ronsica." While there are indeed obvious similarities between "Olivo Ronsica" and *Arthur Mervyn*, I am more concerned with what Brown has to say generally about relations between individuals. See Grabo, *The Coincidental Art of Charles Brockden Brown* (Chapel Hill: University of North Carolina Press, 1981), 87–89 and 126, and Tompkins, *Sensational Designs: The Cultural Work of American Fiction 1790–1860* (New York: Oxford University Press, 1985), 64.

2. For a comprehensive overview of a century of criticism, see Winfried Fluck's essay "From Aesthetics to Political Criticism: Theories of the Early American Novel," in *Early America Re-Explored: New Readings in Colonial, Early National, and Antebellum Culture*, ed. Klaus H. Schmidt and Fritz Fleischmann (New York: Lang, 2000), 225–68.

3. Grabo quotes this same evocative passage from "Walstein's School of History" in his introduction to *Edgar Huntly*, applying it specifically to that novel. There, he interprets "sex" to mean "marriage." See Grabo, Introduction, *Edgar Huntly* (1799. New York: Penguin, 1988), xiii.

4. Ernest Renan, "What is a Nation?" in *Nation and Narration*, ed. Homi K. Bhabha, trans. Martin Thom (London and New York: Routledge, 1990), 8–22.

5. My thinking here about the economy underlying social relations is informed, in part, by Pierre Bourdieu, *Outline of a Theory of Practice*, trans. Richard Nice (1972. New York and Cambridge: Cambridge University Press, 1977), especially 171–83.

6. The novel as a genre is an excellent site through which to trace the ongoing conversation between republicanism and liberalism in the early Republic. In an indispensable review essay, Daniel T. Rodgers outlines the evolution of these terms. Rodgers identifies the work of Bernard Bailyn, Gordon Wood, and J. G. A. Pocock as pivotal in formulating the republican paradigm, the overriding feature of which is a concern for the collective good over that of the individual. Mediating between Wood and Pocock, Rodgers argues that "the heart of Wood's republicanism was the preeminence of the public good; not *public*, but *civic* was the key term in Pocock's construct. It was on the field of civic action, if anywhere, that time, fortune, and corruption might be withstood. 'Virtue,' which Wood read as self-denial, Pocock read as public self-activity—in which 'personality,' undergirded by sufficient property to give it independence, threw itself (for its own 'perfection' and the survival of the republic) into citizenship, patriotism, and civic life." See Rodgers, "Republicanism: The Career of a Concept," *Journal of American History* 79.1 (1992): 19. Especially useful in assessing republicanism in light of race and gender is Pauline Schloesser's *The Fair Sex: White Women and Racial Patriarchy in the Early American Republic* (New York and London: New York University Press, 2002). In general, I see the early novel as neither exclusively republican nor liberal but rather struggling, as a genre, to find ways to accommodate liberal individualism without sacrificing republican ideals.

7. See James A. Henretta, *The Evolution of American Society, 1700–1815* (Lexington, Mass.: Heath, 1973), 23–31, and Carroll Smith-Rosenberg, "Subject Female: Authorizing American Identity," *American Literary History* 5.3 (1993): 483–84.

8. Ann Douglas discusses clerical disestablishment in *The Feminization of American Culture* (New York: Doubleday, 1977), 17–43.

9. For information about subscription costs for circulating libraries, see Herbert Ross Brown, *The Sentimental Novel in America 1789–1860* (Durham, N.C.: Duke University Press, 1940), 23–24, and Robert B. Winans, "The Growth of a Novel-Reading Public in Late-Eighteenth-Century America," *Early American Literature* 9.3 (1975): 267–75.

10. For a discussion of the changing status of authorship in early and antebellum America, see William Charvat, *The Profession of Authorship in America, 1800–1870*, ed. Matthew J. Bruccoli (Columbus: Ohio State University Press, 1968) and Grantland S. Rice, *The Transformation of Authorship in America* (Chicago: University of Chicago Press, 1997). Especially interesting is Rice's discussion of copyright (70–96). For information about evolving printing technologies and transportation networks, see Ronald J. Zboray, *A Fictive People: Antebellum Economic Development and the American Reading Public* (New York: Oxford University Press, 1993), especially Chapters 1–5.

11. See G. Harrison Orians, "Censure of Fiction in American Romances and Magazines: 1789–1810," *PMLA* 52 (1937): 195–214; Cathy N. Davidson, *Revolution and the Word: The Rise of the Novel in America* (New York: Oxford University Press,

1986), especially 38–54; and Michael T. Gilmore, "The Novel," in *The Cambridge History of American Literature*, ed. Sacvan Bercovitch (New York: Cambridge University Press, 1994), 621.

12. Orians, 202.

13. Winans, 267; Orians, 209–10; see also James D. Hart, *The Popular Book: A History of America's Literary Taste* (New York: Oxford University Press, 1950), 54.

14. Keith J. Fennimore, *Short Stories from Another Day: Eighteenth Century Periodical Fiction* (East Lansing: Michigan State University Press, 1989), 1.

15. Winans, 273.

16. In the late colonial and early national periods, borrowers consistently favored the novel. Ross W. Beales and James N. Green claim that "The two surviving catalogues of colonial circulating libraries, for Boston and Annapolis, show that fiction accounted for 14 percent and 25 percent of the holdings, respectively; by 1783 the Annapolis library was 42 percent fiction. But almost two-thirds of the Bradford collection was fiction (none of it printed in America), and the *rate of circulation* for the genre was also much higher. Of 617 books borrowed in April 1772, an astonishing 86 percent were fiction, while plays and verse were another 7 percent, leaving only 7 percent nonfiction." See Beales and Green, "Libraries and Their Uses," in *A History of the Book in America: The Colonial Book in the Atlantic World*, ed. Hugh Amory and David D. Hall (Cambridge and New York: Cambridge University Press, 2000), 403. By 1800, Winans points out, fiction made up approximately 50 percent of the stock of the circulating libraries he surveyed. Sales and borrowing records "suggest that the proportion of fiction among the books actually taken home from bookstore or library exceeded the proportion of fiction in the catalogues of those institutions" (271).

17. In *Not All Wives*, Karin Wulf explores the lives of unmarried women in eighteenth-century Philadelphia. She notes that, in the post-Revolutionary era, at the same time that the number of single women was increasing in Philadelphia, their public representation in non-fictional print materials was declining. In fact, she sees during this time "erasure of unmarried women" from such public documents as tax roles, part of a process through which "property was no longer the marker of civic status and responsibility, but had been superseded by gender as the crucial determinant of membership in the polity." See Wulf, *Not All Wives: Women of Colonial Philadelphia* (Ithaca, N.Y., and London: Cornell University Press, 2000), 205.

18. See Teresa A. Goddu, *Gothic America: Narrative, History, and Nation* (New York: Columbia University Press, 1997); Julia A. Stern, *The Plight of Feeling: Sympathy and Dissent in the Early American Novel* (Chicago and London: University of Chicago Press, 1997); and Cynthia S. Jordan, *Second Stories: The Politics of Language, Form, and Gender in Early American Fictions* (Chapel Hill and London: University of North Carolina Press, 1989). Jordan distinguishes between the surface narratives of certain early American texts and their conflicting secondary plot lines and subtexts. She argues that Benjamin Franklin, Hugh Henry Brackenridge, and Charles

Brockden Brown, among others, "believed with varying degrees of optimism that language could be used to maintain a patriarchal social order in the new nation. The narrative fictions they wrote to promote such a belief, however, are curiously doubled: their promotional surface narratives are constantly threatened by evidence of opposing views, and that evidence constitutes a rival second story which the authors try to suppress or defuse but which they find increasingly difficult to hold in check" (x).

19. Jeffrey Rubin-Dorsky, "The Early American Novel," in *The Columbia History of the American Novel*, ed. Emory Elliott (New York: Columbia University Press, 1991), 6–9.

20. For a representative collection of short fiction published in America, see Keith J. Fennimore, *Short Stories from Another Day: Eighteenth Century Periodical Fiction*. One short "novel" that also appeared in several periodical publications was the anonymous work *Amelia; or, the Faithless Briton*, which I discuss at length in chapter 2.

21. Useful in tracking the publication of short fiction is Edward W. R. Pitcher's *Fiction in American Magazines Before 1800: An Annotated Catalogue* (Lexington, Ky.: Union College Press in conjunction with Antoca Press, 1993).

22. Kenneth Silverman notes the initial magazine publication of *The Foresters* and *Amelia* in his *A Cultural History of the American Revolution* (New York: Crowell, 1976), 497–98.

23. Steven Watts, *The Republic Reborn: War and the Making of Liberal America, 1790–1820* (Baltimore: Johns Hopkins University Press, 1987), 166–72 and passim.

24. For a comprehensive overview of the condemnation of fiction during the early national period, with generous excerpts from periodicals, see Orians; for information specifically on the shift in public opinion concerning the novel, see 196–97.

25. Novels are not history, per se, and certainly I do not read them as such. Nonetheless, novels illuminate important aspects of cultural history, for they not only reflect and delineate aspects of their culture but, along with other modes of discourse, also help shape its social reality. Early American literature has long been a field in which non-literary works have figured as viable subjects of criticism, a circumstance that undoubtedly stems from the paucity of productions in the traditional literary genres, particularly during the early colonial period. Diaries, personal narratives, sermons, promotional tracts, etc., have thus assumed positions of greater importance in this field of study than they held in nineteenth-century American literature. The early national period, however, forms a sort of gray area between early American and nineteenth-century literature. Scholarly criticism of writing from this period is much more likely than that of the seventeenth or early eighteenth century to separate texts into the literary and the non-literary and consequently to privilege the literary.

26. Larzer Ziff, *Writing in the New Nation: Prose, Print, and Politics in the Early*

United States (New Haven, Conn., and London: Yale University Press, 1991), 193. From a different perspective, Tony Bennett has argued in *Formalism and Marxism* that "literary" and "non-literary" are purely critical distinctions, created by the act of literary criticism, for "written texts do not organize themselves into the 'literary' and the 'non-literary'. . . . Far from reflecting a somehow natural or spontaneous system of relationships between literary texts, literary criticism organizes those texts into a system of relationships which is the product of its own discourse and of the distinctions between the 'literary' and the 'non-literary' which it operates." See Bennett, *Formalism and Marxism* (London: Methuen, 1979), 7.

There is some evidence, however, that suggests literariness was becoming increasingly important for writers residing in the United States following the Revolution, when many writers chose to redirect their attention away from international conflict to domestic issues and to the self-conscious production of "culture"; they were aided in this process by the increasing accessibility of print. Concerned with creating a distinctive American literary culture, many writers deliberately turned their attention to the production of literary genres such as fiction, poetry, drama, and the essay, valuing these types of writing as "culture" itself.

27. Walter L. Reed, *An Exemplary History of the Novel: The Quixotic Versus the Picaresque* (Chicago: University of Chicago Press, 1981), 5.

28. A number of critics have discussed in general terms the relationships between fiction and other modes of discourse. Bakhtin, for example, speaks of "fiction's special relationship with extraliterary genres, with the genres of everyday life and with ideological genres." Bakhtin's point, like that which Walter Reed made much later, is that the early novel is profoundly concerned with social reality and thus necessarily with those other fictions that make up our reality. Bakhtin writes of the novel: "In its earliest stages, the novel and its preparatory genres had relied upon various extraliterary forms of personal and social reality, and especially those of rhetoric. . . . And in later stages of its development the novel makes wide and substantial use of letters, diaries, confessions, the forms and methods of rhetoric associated with recently established courts and so forth. Since it is constructed in a zone of contact with the incomplete events of a particular present, the novel often crosses the boundary of what we strictly call fictional literature—making use first of moral confession, then of philosophical tract, then of manifestoes that are openly political, then degenerating into the raw spirituality of confession. . . ." Bakhtin goes on to assert that "every specific situation is historical." Arguing that fiction is an especially valuable site in which to identify social and cultural change, he claims, "These symptoms of change appear considerably more often in the novel than they do elsewhere, as the novel is a developing genre; they are sharper and more significant because the novel is in the vanguard of change." See M. M. Bakhtin, *The Dialogic Imagination*, ed. Michael Holquist, trans. Caryl Emerson and Michael Holquist (Austin: University of Texas Press, 1981), 33.

29. For a different way of thinking about nationalism and the development of a

national culture, see David Waldstreicher's *In the Midst of Perpetual Fetes: The Making of American Nationalism, 1776–1820* (Chapel Hill and London: University of North Carolina Press, 1997). Waldstreicher examines various reporting media as well as broadsides and ballads in order to explore the role of public celebrations in creating national identity. He argues against consensus, claiming that *conflict* produces nationalism.

30. Cathy N. Davidson, *Revolution and the Word*, 13.

31. Linda K. Kerber addresses this issue in *Women of the Republic: Intellect and Ideology in Revolutionary America*, rev. ed. (New York: Norton, 1986), 279–83.

32. Catherine La Courreye Blecki and Karin A. Wulf, *Milcah Martha Moore's Book: A Commonplace Book from Revolutionary America* (University Park: Pennsylvania State University Press, 1997). Evidence from commonplace books suggests that poetry was the central medium of manuscript culture. Blecki explains, "Our research in the commonplace books, copybooks, and miscellanies of eighteenth-century colonial Pennsylvania reveal[s] that, aside from the Bible, poetry was the primary medium for educating women to read and write, followed by short prose pieces, letters, and for Quakers, personal testimonies. Women's manuscripts show that they frequently question and answer traditional ideas of women's roles and, as the political and historical entries in *Moore's Book* reveal, women were already discoursing on these topics in writing before the sentimental novel appeared" (80). In the latter respect, Blecki challenges Davidson's assertion that sentimental fiction was the first medium that both educated women and allowed them a space for political discussions. For support of Blecki's claim, see the political poetry of Hannah Griffitts in *Milcah Martha Moore's Book*.

In *A Cultural History of the American Revolution*, Silverman likewise notes the centrality of poetry to political discourse in colonial America; he explains that "local" poetry—especially satire that addressed local or regional political concerns—had great appeal to American writers (49–55).

33. Rice explains: "As the tradition of civic authorship—mediated more and more by the impersonal relations of a commercial print culture—was increasingly rendered powerless to engage the state in any direct and meaningful way, for the reasons I have suggested in earlier chapters, writers were forced to adopt a social rather than a political role in their efforts to leverage cultural authority" (139). Here, Rice refers to the tension he traces in the eighteenth century between evolving notions of authorship; he specifically addresses the changing role of the American author from civic commentator to the author as a producer of ideas in a competitive literary marketplace.

34. Edward Watts, *Writing and Postcolonialism in the Early Republic* (Charlottesville: University Press of Virginia, 1998), 22. Watts's introductory chapter is useful to understand how the process of decolonization is represented in a certain segment of the early novel, including *Modern Chivalry, The Gleaner, The Algerine Captive, Arthur Mervyn,* and *The Lawyer,* all novels with problematic, self-conscious

narration. He explains: "By withholding or denying the authorial guidance that dictated interpretive acts in the republican public sphere, these authors cut the reader adrift from the institutionalized forms of authority imposed by the republican elite. Without externally imposed textual meaning, the reader must trust and empower his or her own interpretive skills. This liberation of the reader—or rather this implication that the reader free him or her self—parallels the growth of democratic individualism chronicled by Sharp, Wood, and Steven Watts. Their focus on individual authorial voices, then, allows their texts to become microcosms for the larger conflict over the nature of American identity taking place around them" (23). Watts does not claim that his thesis applies to the genre of early American fiction in its entirety, and indeed, Blythe Forcey has made an argument about the novel diametrically opposed to Watts's. Forcey argues that Susanna Rowson moves away from epistolarity in *Charlotte Temple* precisely so that, through her narrator, she can maintain authorial control of how readers interpret her novel. That both Watts's and Forcey's arguments are persuasive is further proof of the attractiveness of the novel to writers across the political spectrum. See Forcey, "*Charlotte Temple* and the End of Epistolarity," *American Literature* 63.2 (1991): 225–41.

35. Marion Rust, "'Into the House of an Entire Stranger': Why Sentimental Doesn't Equal Domestic in Early American Fiction," *Early American Literature* 37.2 (2002): 297–99.

36. See Richard Beale Davis, *A Colonial Southern Bookshelf: Reading in the Eighteenth Century* (Athens: University of Georgia Press, 1979), 12–13.

37. James N. Green points out that *Pamela* was so long and Franklin so busy with other, more lucrative printing projects, that it took him two years to complete his printing of *Pamela*. Green speculates that abridgements became popular in part because of the economics of printing and concludes that, "given how quickly they [novels] went in and out of fashion, it was less risky to import them." See Green, "English Books and Printing in the Age of Franklin," in *A History of the Book in America: The Colonial Book in the Atlantic World*, ed. Hugh Amory and David D. Hall (Cambridge and New York: Cambridge University Press, 2000), 268. For more information about how costs and profitability affected whether novels were imported versus printed in America, see Robert B. Winans, "Bibliography and the Cultural Historian: Notes on the Eighteenth-Century Novel," in *Printing and Society in Early America*, ed. William L. Joyce, David D. Hall, Richard D. Brown, and John B. Hench (Worcester, Mass.: American Antiquarian Society, 1983), 174–85.

38. Leonard Tennenhouse, "The Americanization of Clarissa," *The Yale Journal of Criticism* 11.1 (1998): 184–86. Tennenhouse argues that the editing process leading to these abridged versions makes them "American," in that it de-emphasizes the original epistolary nature of these texts and instead emphasizes the physical bodies of both Pamela and Clarissa. In the resulting texts, "Englishness" can continue to be reproduced (190), an argument that supports Tennenhouse's claim that while the former English colonists might have desired political and economic liberty, "it

is not nearly so clear that these same people wanted cultural independence" (182). Tennenhouse's point is well taken, but the persistent appeals by writers during the early national era for the development of an American literary culture suggest that at least some segments of American society longed for a distinctively American culture.

39. Janet Todd, *Sensibility: An Introduction* (London and New York: Methuen, 1986), 2. Todd distinguishes between sentiment and sensibility by pointing out that "A 'sentiment' is a moral reflection, a rational opinion usually about the rights and wrongs of human conduct; the early eighteenth-century [British] novel of sentiment is characterized by such generalized reflections" (7). Explicitly sentimental fiction, then, explores issues of virtue and morality, particularly through the evocation of emotion.

40. Although the sentimental bent of much early American fiction recently reprinted might seem to suggest otherwise, not all early American novels are sentimental; Jeremy Belknap's *The Foresters* and Francis Hopkinson's *A Pretty Story*, for example, are both satirical political allegories. Yet even non-sentimental works frequently invoke the sentimental, even if only to parody it, as does Tabitha Tenney in her satirical novel *Female Quixotism* or Hugh Henry Brackenridge in *Modern Chivalry*.

41. Sharon M. Harris, ed. *Redefining the Political Novel: American Women Writers, 1797–1901* (Knoxville: University of Tennessee Press, 1995), xiv. For further discussion of the permeability of the domestic sphere in early American fiction, see Karen A. Weyler, "Sally Sayward Barrell Keating Wood," *Legacy: A Journal of American Women Writers* 15.2 (1998): 204–12. Marion Rust calls into question the traditional demarcation of domestic and public spaces in criticism of the early novel and argues against the equation of sentimentality with domesticity in her essay "'Into the House of an Entire Stranger': Why Sentimental Doesn't Equal Domestic in Early American Fiction."

42. See Lillie Deming Loshe, *The Early American Novel* (New York: Columbia University Press, 1907) and Herbert Ross Brown, *The Sentimental Novel in America, 1789–1860* (Durham, N.C.: Duke University Press, 1940).

43. Elizabeth Barnes, *States of Sympathy: Seduction and Democracy in the American Novel* (New York: Columbia University Press, 1997), 2.

44. As much as I admire Stern's splendid readings of individual novels, I think she over-generalizes about early American fiction as a body of work when she labels the early American novel "a gothic formulation devoted to channeling the voices of the socially dead" (12). While this point is well-taken with regard to the five novels on which *The Plight of Feeling* focuses, early American fiction as a genre comprises dozens, perhaps close to one hundred texts, the politics of many of which differ radically from those she examines.

45. See, for example, *The Vain Cottager; or, the History of Lucy Franklin* (New Haven, Conn.: For Increase Cooke and Co., from Sidney's Press, 1807).

46. Both Tompkins and Fisher complicate sentimentality by crediting it with complex ideological underpinnings while at the same time they attempt to expose these underpinnings. Further, both view mid-nineteenth-century American sentimentality as a democratizing, humanizing mode of discourse. Tompkins argues in *Sensational Designs* that "The power of a sentimental novel to move its audience depends upon the audience's being in possession of the conceptual categories that constitute character and event. That storehouse of assumptions includes attitudes toward the family and toward social institutions; a definition of power and its relation to individual human feeling; notions of political and social equality; and above all, a set of religious beliefs that organizes and sustains the rest" (126–27). Fisher similarly proposes that "the political content of sentimentality is democratic in that it experiments with the extension of full and complete humanity to classes of figures from whom it has been socially withheld. The typical objects of sentimental compassion are the prisoner, the madman, the child, the very old, the animal, and the slave." See Fisher, *Hard Facts: Setting and Form in the American Novel* (New York: Oxford University Press, 1995), 99. Both Tompkins and Fisher emphasize the relationship between sentimentality and democratic equality, yet differ in their emphases. Tompkins, with an avowedly feminist agenda, is interested in the different forms of power that women wield in *Uncle Tom's Cabin* through sentimental relations. Fisher, on the other hand, is more interested in the political radicalism of the sentimentality in *Uncle Tom's Cabin* and how sentimentality enabled readers to extend compassion and sympathy to slaves and others less privileged than themselves. While Tompkins and Fisher have illuminated our understanding of nineteenth-century sentimental writings and sparked an avalanche of critical responses by arguing that these texts seek equality through sympathy, sentimental fiction of the early Republic differs in important ways. While it would be unwise to apply wholesale theories of antebellum sentimentality to the early novel, understanding both eighteenth- and nineteenth-century sentimentality is crucial to trace the slow accommodation of republicanism to liberalism in the American novel as bourgeois subjectivity developed.

47. As Michael Warner explains in *The Letters of the Republic: Publication and the Public Sphere in Eighteenth-Century America* (Cambridge: Harvard University Press, 1990), phrases like "we the people" seem inclusive, but they actually depended upon the understood assumption that they excluded women, people of color, etc., and awarded other rights by virtue of class and education (111–12; 173–74). While I argue that sentimental discourse valorizes the individual—particularly the white, female, middle-class individual—I do not mean to claim any broad democratizing powers for sentimental fiction of the early Republic era, since sentimental fiction systematically locates Native Americans, blacks, and certain immigrant groups on the margins, if at all, until the second and third decades of the nineteenth century.

48. A quick overview of several texts will illustrate my point. Children are pres-

ent in many fictional narratives, but usually as the product of illegitimate unions, as is the case in Hannah Foster's *The Coquette* and the anonymous work *Amelia: or, the Faithless Briton*. We feel sympathy for the mothers, rather than for the children, whose names we never learn, a deliberate narrative strategy. Old Deb, also called "Queen Mab," a displaced Delaware Indian in Charles Brockden Brown's *Edgar Huntly*, is not a figure of equality to the white settlers (although Edgar's disinheritance seems to echo the displacement of her tribe from their traditional lands), but rather a symbol of the savagery to which Huntly descends. In *Kelroy*, Rebecca Rush expediently tosses the slave Sancho out of a tree and off a cliff to enable his master, Dunlevy, to meet Emily Hammond, whom he will later marry, a point Dana Nelson makes in her introduction to *Kelroy*. Upon seeing the badly injured, swooning Sancho, Emily utters "an involuntary exclamation of compassion" (138), an expression of sympathy that directs Dunlevy's attention away from his suffering servant and toward Emily, a more compelling subject for *his* sympathy. See Dana D. Nelson, *Kelroy* (New York: Oxford University Press, 1992), xx–xxi. In *The Plight of Feeling*, Stern points to another brief episode featuring a slave that operates under a similar dynamic. In *The Power of Sympathy*, the young Harrington speaks with a female slave while visiting Charleston. After observing her scarred back, Harrington erupts into praise for her heroic endurance of her suffering; as Stern explains, Harrington's delight in his own gratifying expression of sympathy "erases the palpable suffering of the African American bondwoman" (25). Sympathy in this instance does not create a lasting sense of equality; rather, it serves to validate the feelings of the observer and presumably of the reader.

49. One need only consider the early novelistic treatment of slaves, for example, and then contrast how much more richly and sympathetically their plight is evoked in other genres such as Philip Freneau's poem "To Sir Toby" or J. Hector St. John de Crèvecoeur's *Letters from an American Farmer* to understand their peripheral standing in the early novel.

50. According to my count, women authored at least thirty percent of all novels written and published in the United States prior to 1814; in all likelihood that percentage is considerably higher, assuming that women authored any of the many texts published anonymously during this period. It would likewise be higher if one were to include texts by expatriate writers such as Helena Wells, author of *Constantia Neville; or, the West Indian* and *The Step-Mother*, who published her novels in London. Regardless, this percentage of female-authored texts is higher than in any other field of print, excluding pedagogical, conduct, and captivity literature.

51. Marion Rust makes a similar point in her discussion of William Cobbett's (aka Peter Porcupine) attack on Susanna Rowson's works. She writes, "By subjecting a widely published female author to ridicule in a manner that conflates the acts of writing and public speaking, Cobbett indicates the threat that women and other disenfranchised groups were seen to pose to a tenuous American social order, and thus the climate of anxiety and hostility within which authors such as Rowson

were operating." See Rust, "'Into the House of an Entire Stranger': Why Sentimental Doesn't Equal Domestic in Early American Fiction," 298.

52. Fredric Jameson, *The Political Unconscious: Narrative as a Socially Symbolic Act* (Ithaca, N.Y.: Cornell University Press, 1981), 106.

53. Nancy Armstrong and Leonard Tennenhouse, *The Imaginary Puritan: Literature, Intellectual Labor, and the Origins of Personal Life* (Berkeley: University of California Press, 1992), 147–48; 251, note 13.

Chapter 1
A Manner Unquestionably More Agreeable

1. See, for example, Godfrey Frank Singer's *The Epistolary Novel: Its Origins, Development, Decline, and Residuary Influence* (Philadelphia: University of Pennsylvania Press, 1933); Robert Adams Day's *Told in Letters: Epistolary Fiction before Richardson* (Ann Arbor: University of Michigan Press, 1966); Ruth Perry's *Women, Letters, and the Novel* (New York: AMS, 1980); Janet Gurkin Altman's comparative study *Epistolarity: Approaches to a Form* (Columbus: Ohio State University Press, 1982); and Sarah Marino's unpublished dissertation, "'Almost Infinite Variations': Eighteenth-Century Epistolary Fictions," University of North Carolina, 1994.

2. Herbert Ross Brown provides an overview of early American epistolary fiction in *The Sentimental Novel in America 1789–1860* (52–73), but only recently have critics again addressed the importance of letters in early American fiction. In *The Plight of Feeling*, Julia Stern discusses the role of epistolarity and pseudoepistolarity with regard to *The Power of Sympathy*, *The Coquette*, *Charlotte Temple*, and *Wieland*. She sees the epistolary mode in these novels as "a powerful conjunction of the performative, vocal, and textual dynamics" (16) and claims that "the letter form bridges the acoustic and the textual, creating a dialectic of voice against vision that infuses the novels of the Federalist period with a uniquely affective charge" (17). Textual interruptions and failed communication in these letters embody for Stern the deeply divided nature of post-Revolutionary American social and political culture.

Three other useful essays are Sarah Emily Newton's "Wise and Foolish Virgins: 'Usable Fiction' and the Early American Conduct Tradition," *Early American Literature* 25.2 (1990): 139–67; Claire Pettengill's "Sisterhood in a Separate Sphere: Female Friendship in Hannah Webster Foster's *The Coquette* and *The Boarding School*," *Early American Literature* 27.3 (1992): 185–203; and, W. M. Verhoeven's "'Persuasive Rhetorick': Representation and Resistance in Early American Epistolary Fiction," in *Making America / Making American Literature: Franklin to Cooper*, ed. A. Robert Lee and W. M. Verhoeven (Amsterdam and Atlanta: Rodopi, 1996): 123–64. Newton argues that there is an important intersection between the conduct book and epistolary fiction which led to the development of the hybrid genre of the "conduct novel," or what Henri Petter called in *The Early American Novel* (Columbus: Ohio State University Press, 1971) "usable fiction" (63). Pettengill makes a case for the significance of epistolary fiction, arguing that through it we can trace the developing ideology of separate spheres. Verhoeven examines American epistolary fiction in light of Richardson's achievement in *Clarissa*, arguing that *The Power of Sympathy* and *The Coquette* "constitute a regression from Richardson's rhetorical command of the sentimental novel of letters," while *Jane Talbot* "continues where Richardson left off, thus creating America's first authentic counter-discourse" (129).

Blythe Forcey, on the hand, declares epistolarity a non-issue in American fiction in her essay "*Charlotte Temple* and the End of Epistolarity." Forcey argues that Susanna Rowson's authorial narrative interventions in the place of letters were crucial in limiting and controlling the varieties of readings possible for *Charlotte Temple*, an important function in an increasingly diverse nation. However, Forcey overstates her case when she argues that "Lacking the support of such narrative guidance, the epistolary novel [as a genre] could not make the successful crossing to the New World" (228) and later that "the epistolary novel never acquired much of a foothold in the New World" (240).

In fact, epistolary fiction was popular in the British colonies and the early United States with both readers and writers. In *Golden Multitudes*, Frank Luther Mott includes *Pamela* and *Clarissa* among his brief list of best sellers (meaning sales equivalent to 1 percent of the population) before the Revolution, and *The Coquette* after the Revolution (304). Approximately 30 percent of the American novels published before 1814 are epistolary, while a large number of others include a significant epistolary component or use letters as framing devices. Although less popular as a mode for adult fiction during the nineteenth century, epistolary fiction continued to be popular among writers of juvenile fiction. Singer's bibliography in *The Epistolary Novel* provides a starting place for a bibliography of American epistolary fiction, but he overlooks a number of early American titles, among them *The Boarding School* and *Story of Margaretta*.

3. David S. Shields, *Civil Tongues and Polite Letters in British America* (Chapel Hill: University of North Carolina Press, for the Institute of Early American History and Culture, 1997), 318, 319.

4. Abigail Adams, quoted by Kevin J. Hayes in *A Colonial Woman's Bookshelf* (Knoxville: University of Tennessee Press, 1996), 112.

5. Historically, "sensibility" has been associated generally with sensation and the capacity of the body to express feelings, while "sentiment" has been associated with the mind, in relationship to thoughts and reflections. For further definitions of sentiment and sensibility and examples of varying historical usage in European and British writing, see Janet Todd, *Sensibility*, 6–9, and Ann Jessie Van Sant, *Eighteenth-Century Sensibility and the Novel* (New York: Cambridge University Press, 1993), 4–14. Todd claims about "sensibility": "Little used before the mid-eighteenth-century... it came to denote the faculty of feeling, the capacity for extremely refined emotion and a quickness to display compassion for suffering" (7).

6. John Mullan, *Sentiment and Sociability: The Language of Feeling in the Eighteenth Century* (New York: Clarendon, 1988), 201.

7. The concepts of self-control and discipline were likewise popular in Britain, lending themselves to the titles of novels by Mary Brunton. Her novel *Self-Control*, first published in Britain in 1810–11, was reprinted in two different American editions in 1811, one in Philadelphia, and one in New York. *Discipline* was first published in Britain in 1815 and reprinted the same year in Boston and Philadelphia. While Brunton's novels are not epistolary, they do emphasize the importance of self-examination and discipline.

Self-Control is the story of Laura Montreville's love triangle with Colonel Hargrave and De Courcy. Laura has self-control, but rejects Colonel Hargrave, whom she loves passionately, because he lacks the ability to control his desires and passions. As the omniscient narrator explains, Laura is a model of rectitude who regularly examines her conduct in minute detail as part of her daily devotions, a relentless process of searching her conscience for the slightest errors. As the narrator later describes her, "Young as she was, however, she had long been a vigilant observer of her own actions" (207). Despite her model behavior, Laura continually "reproached," "upbraided," and "accused" herself for not demonstrating even more self-control (100).

Ellen Percy, the spoiled daughter of a wealthy businessman, narrates the story of her experiences in *Discipline*. *Discipline* is in many ways a conversion narrative, for Ellen undergoes a profound spiritual conversion—not merely to Christianity, but also to an empathetic awakening to the sorrows of other human beings. Her retrospective narration focuses on her previous lack of discipline and on how she learns to practice self-denial. Her reward for her self-sacrifice is marriage to a man whose good qualities she can now appreciate. Both *Discipline* and *Self-Control* are much more profoundly and explicitly Christian than any of the American novels I will discuss, all of which secularize the issue of self-examination for the larger interests of civil society.

8. Davidson addresses this issue in *Revolution and the Word*, 47–49.

9. Any scholarly work that uses terms such as "discipline" and "control" must be indebted to Michel Foucault's *Discipline and Punish: The Birth of the Prison*, as indeed I am. While Foucault is more interested in the technology and mechanisms of power used for discipline in prisons and other institutions, his ideas about surveillance readily translate to a discussion of epistolary fiction as I am reading it, into what he would call a "reciprocal, hierarchized observation." As he explains, "A relation of surveillance, defined and regulated, is inscribed at the heart of the practice of teaching, not as an additional or adjacent part, but as a mechanism that is inherent to it and which increases its efficiency." See Foucault, *Discipline and Punish: The Birth of the Prison*, trans. Alan Sheridan (1975. New York: Vintage, 1979), 176.

10. In *The Fair Sex: White Women and Racial Patriarchy in the Early American Re-

public, Pauline Schloesser points out that "Only *white* women of the property-owning classes enjoyed moral authority in republican discourses" (7). Further, as she explains, the "fair sex," a phrase that appears often in early American fiction (see, for example, *The Coquette*), specifically excluded women of color. Schloesser concludes, "Fair sex ideology supported the development of racial patriarchy by giving white women a sense of subjectivity in a world that legally subjected them to white men" (8).

11. Davidson discusses education and the novel throughout *Revolution and the Word*, especially in chapter 4, entitled "Literacy, Education, and the Reader."

12. J. Paul Hunter addresses the seventeenth-century origins of what he calls the "guide tradition" and its influence on the early English novel in *Before Novels: The Cultural Contexts of Eighteenth-Century English Fiction* (New York: Norton, 1990). Self-examination, he argues, stemming from both the Catholic and Protestant religious traditions, was an important element in the guide tradition (285–88). Nancy Armstrong discusses the influence of the female conduct book, a genre related to but distinct from the guide tradition, on the English novel in *Desire and Domestic Fiction: A Political History of the Novel* (New York: Oxford, 1987).

13. Culturally, Hitchcock is perhaps even more important than my brief description of him suggests. His fiction was well-known to Martha Washington, to whom his *Memoirs of the Bloomsgrove Family* is dedicated; further, prior to its publication, this novel circulated in manuscript form through a network of salons associated with Washington's Republican Court. I am indebted to David S. Shields for this information.

14. Enos Hitchcock, *A Discourse on Education, Delivered at the Meeting-House on the West Side of the River, in Providence, November 16, 1785* (Providence: Wheeler, 1785), 6.

15. Franklin E. Court discusses at length the influence of Scottish Common Sense philosophy on the American educational system in *The Scottish Connection: The Rise of English Literary Study in America* (Syracuse, N.Y.: Syracuse University Press, 2001), especially in chapters 1 and 3. See also Henry May, *The Enlightenment in America* (New York: Oxford University Press, 1976), 346–50.

16. As Lawrence Cremin notes in *American Education: The Colonial Experience 1607–1783* (New York: Harper, 1970), "The colonists were thoroughly familiar with the *Essay* and the *Thoughts*, which circulated briskly in all regions and were commonly referred to in letters and periodicals; and the *Conduct* was available in one or another of the editions of the *Collected Works*, first published in 1714. Yet, in the realm of learning as in the realm of piety, Locke was even better known through a burgeoning popular literature that reflected—or at least coincided with—some of his most characteristic views; and, indeed, toward the end of the century, that literature was increasingly wont to attribute commonplaces to him, whether or not they were his. A flood of pamphlets, periodicals, almanacs, children's books, and manuals of advice deliberately undertook to instruct the public in the precepts of

'Lord Bacon, the incomparable Mr. Newton, and the great Mr. Locke,' as the litany went; and, while the Lockean views that came through such popularizations were almost as often imputed as they were properly inferred, there is no denying that such popularizations did give enormous circulation to certain aspects of Locke's corpus" (365).

17. Gillian Brown, *The Consent of the Governed: The Lockean Legacy in Early American Culture* (Cambridge and London: Harvard University Press, 2001), 36.

18. Gillian Brown discusses Hannah Foster's *The Coquette* and Tabitha Tenney's *Female Quixotism* at length. See *The Consent of the Governed*, chapters 5 and 6.

19. James L. Axtell, Introduction, *The Educational Writings of John Locke* (London: Cambridge University Press, 1968), 58.

20. John Locke, *Some Thoughts Concerning Education* (1693. *The Educational Writings of John Locke*, ed. James L. Axtell [London: Cambridge University Press, 1968]), 42, 146.

21. Jay Fliegelman, *Prodigals and Pilgrims: The American Revolution against Patriarchal Authority, 1750–1800* (New York: Cambridge University Press, 1982), 12. Fliegelman traces the influence of Lockean educational thought on the evolution of parent-child relationships throughout the eighteenth century. See chapter 1: "Educational Theory and Moral Independence," 9–35.

22. Habit was essential, in Rush's view, to produce "republican machines," for virtue itself would become habit; that this virtue was mechanistic did not detract from its benefits, in Rush's eyes. Melvin Yazawa discusses Rush's views on habit in *From Colonies to Commonwealth: Familial Ideology and the Beginnings of the American Republic* (Baltimore: Johns Hopkins University Press, 1985), 162–65.

23. Cremin points out that Watts's *Logic* was "widely used in the colonial colleges and academies as an explicitly Lockean introduction to the systemic study of logic" (368–69). Cremin further argues that *"The Improvement of the Mind* may well have been the single most popular tract on the subject in circulation in eighteenth-century America, standing in relation to the *Logick* much as Locke's *Of the Conduct of the Understanding* stood in relation to the *Essay*" (370).

24. Isaac Watts, *Logic: Or, the Right Use of Reason, in the Inquiry after Truth. With a Variety of Rules to Guard Against Error in the Affairs of Religion and Human Life, As Well as in the Sciences*, 2nd American ed. (Newburyport, Mass.: Barrett, 1796), 4.

25. Isaac Watts, *The Improvement of the Mind: or a Supplement to the Art of Logic. In Two Parts. To Which is Added, a Discourse on the Education of Children and Youth* (Exeter, N.H.: Lamson & Odiorne for West, 1793), 72.

26. See Albert O. Hirschman, *The Passions and the Interests: Political Arguments for Capitalism before Its Triumph* (Princeton: Princeton University Press, 1977), especially 14–20.

27. The Reverend John Bennett, *Strictures on Female Education; Chiefly as It Relates to the Culture of the Heart. In Four Essays. By a Clergyman of the Church of England* (Norwich, Conn.: Ebenezer Bushnell, 1792), 58, 62.

28. John Walker, *The Teacher's Assistant in English Composition; or Easy Rules for Writing Themes and Composing Exercises on Subjects Proper for the Improvement of Youth of Both Sexes at School* (Carlisle, Pa.: Kline, 1804), 132.

29. Hannah More, "Essays," *The Lady's Pocket Library*, ed. Matthew Carey. (Philadelphia: Carey, 1792), 62.

30. Clearly, nothing was thought beyond the power of discipline and habit to control, as Henry May relates concerning Thomas Reid, a key figure in the Scottish Enlightenment. May writes of Reid, "According to his friend and biographer Dugald Stewart, Reid suffered from bad dreams in his early life. He disciplined himself to wake up by insisting, in his dreams, that these were unreal. Finally he arrived at the point of not dreaming at all" (May 344).

31. Samuel Stanhope Smith, quoted in *The Papers of James Madison*, vol. 1: 16 March 1751–16 December 1779, ed. William T. Hutchinson and William M. E. Rachal. (Chicago: University of Chicago Press, 1962–91), 208.

32. Fliegelman's work in *Prodigals and Pilgrims* is particularly useful here, for by tracing the influence of Lockean pedagogy on parent-child relationships, he demonstrates how rhetoric about parental tyranny was applied to the situation between Great Britain and the colonies and was used to justify the rupture between them. After this "fortunate fall," however, education and cultivation of good habits were considered essential to creating a virtuous Republic.

33. Here I am referring to more formal epistolary fiction, with correspondence carried on between two or more individuals, rather than texts that merely use letters as framing devices, such as Charles Brockden Brown's *Wieland* and *Edgar Huntly*.

34. For an excellent discussion of the interplay of gender and genre in *The Gleaner* as a whole, see Kristin Wilcox's essay "The Scribblings of a Plain Man and the Temerity of a Woman: Gender and Genre in Judith Sargent Murray's *The Gleaner*," *Early American Literature* 30 (1995): 121–44. Wilcox explores the multiple layers of narration and argues that "the masquerade of genre enacts a literary space between the serial essay and the forms of fiction current at the time, an imaginary public space within which the Gleaner moves as freely as any real-life white, propertied male of the period" (123).

35. In *Women, Letters, and the Novel*, Perry notes that numerous British novels involve correspondence between members of the same household. See chapter 4: "Separation and Isolation in Epistolary Fiction," especially pp. 107–10. The significant difference between these British works she discusses and American fiction, however, is that the British letter writers are often estranged from or imprisoned by family members. The estrangement of the eponymous heroine of Samuel Richardson's *Clarissa* from her family illustrates this difference.

36. Judith Sargent Murray, *Story of Margaretta, The Gleaner. A Miscellaneous Production by Constantia* (1798. Schenectady, N.Y.: Union College Press, 1992), 60.

37. Brodhead, *Cultures of Letters: Scenes of Reading and Writing in Nineteenth-*

Century America (Chicago: University of Chicago Press, 1993), 73–74. In *Domesticity with a Difference*, Nicole Tonkovich notes a similar phenomenon occurring in women's boarding schools. Speaking of Catharine Beecher's own boarding school education, Tonkovich describes how, in 1814, students each week read aloud from their personal journals, in which they were to describe their adherence to or violation of school rules. In this way, each student was made responsible for her own self-surveillance. Tonkovich concludes that "such self-assessment and self-reporting undoubtedly accomplished the effect for which it was intended—to maintain a system of institutional discipline—but it also surely taught those who wrote such journals how to write in prescribed forms and afforded them the opportunity to invent publicly acceptable personae that were linked by convention to the gendered body that voiced them." See Tonkovich, *Domesticity with a Difference: The Nonfiction of Catharine Beecher, Sarah J. Hale, Fanny Fern, and Margaret Fuller* (Jackson: University Press of Mississippi, 1997), 9. Tonkovich also discusses at length later nineteenth-century manifestations of loving discipline, or "disciplinary intimacy," as she calls it, especially at Beecher's Hartford Female Seminary (160–68).

38. Jürgen Habermas, *The Structural Transformation of the Public Sphere: An Inquiry into a Category of Bourgeois Society*. 1962. Trans. Thomas Burger with Frederick Lawrence (Cambridge: MIT Press, 1989), 49.

39. Adam Smith, *The Theory of Moral Sentiments* (1759. Ed. E. G. West. Indianapolis: Liberty, 1976), 203–4.

40. *Lady Pennington's Unfortunate Mother's Advice to Her Daughter*, in *The Lady's Pocket Library*, ed. Matthew Carey. (Philadelphia: Carey, 1792), 150.

41. *Parental Legacies, Consisting of Advice from a Lady of Quality to Her Children. Delivered in the Last Stage of a Lingering Illness. Translated from the French, by S. Glasse, D.D. F.R.S. Chaplain in Ordinary to his (British) Majesty* (Boston: Bumstead, 1804), 122–23.

42. See, for example, Cathy N. Davidson, "Mothers and Daughters in the Fiction of the New Republic," in *The Lost Tradition: Mothers and Daughters in Literature*, ed. Cathy N. Davidson and E. M. Broner (New York: Frederick Ungar, 1980), 115–27, and Michelle Burnham, *Captivity and Sentiment: Cultural Exchange in American Literature, 1682–1861* (Hanover, N.H., and London: University Press of New England, 1997), 70–71; 77–78.

43. Sally Sayward Barrell Keating Wood, *Dorval; or the Speculator. A Novel, Founded on Recent Facts* (Portsmouth, N.H.: Printed at the Ledger Press by Nutting & Whitelock, for the author, 1801), iv.

44. In British America, these manuals began to appear very early in the eighteenth century, and they continued to be popular throughout the early national era. Some important examples of these letter books printed in America include: *The Young Secretary's Guide: or, a Speedy Help to Learning* (1703) (at least twenty-two editions of this work alone appeared during the first half of the eighteenth century); *The Complete Letter-Writer* (1790); *The Scrivener's Guide* (1797); *The American*

Letter-Writer (1793); *The American Academy of Compliments; or the Complete American Secretary* (1796); *The New Universal Letter-Writer; or, Complete Art of Polite Correspondence* (1800); and *The Fashionable Letter Writer, or Art of Polite Correspondence* (1818). Often these works appeared in identical or only slightly differing format under similar titles.

45. *The Complete Letter-Writer. Containing Familiar Letters on the Most Common Occasions in Life. Also, a Variety of Elegant Letters for the Direction and Embellishment of Style. On . . . Business, Duty, Amusement, Love, Courtship, Marriage, Friendship, & Other Subjects. . . .* 2nd edition. (Boston: Folsom, 1790), 8.

46. Richardson, quoted in Bruce Redford, *The Converse of the Pen: Acts of Intimacy in the Eighteenth-Century Familiar Letter* (Chicago: University of Chicago Press, 1986), 1.

47. *The American Letter-Writer: Containing a Variety of Letters on the Most Common Occasions in Life* (Philadelphia: McCullough, 1793), 3.

48. Hugh Blair, *Lectures on Rhetoric and Belles Lettres*. 2 vols. 2nd American ed. (Philadelphia: Carey, 1793), 224, 127.

49. Gustafson, *Eloquence is Power: Oratory and Performance in Early America*, 169–70; for a discussion of Gannett's exceptionalism, see 246–57.

50. Several novels register concern about the power of seductive rhetoric. Clara, in Charles Brockden Brown's *Wieland*, finds Carwin's voice to be mesmerizing. Likewise, in *The Coquette*, readers learn that it is Sanford's seductive voice (not a personal letter) that persuades Eliza to consider the disadvantages of being a clergyman's wife. Although Eliza admits, "My heart did not approve his sentiments," she adds, "my ear was charmed with his rhetoric, and my fancy captivated by his address" (36). Realizing Eliza's susceptibility, Mrs. Richman warns her: "[S]uffer not your ear to be charmed by the syren voice of flattery" (38). W. M. Verhoeven suggests, in fact, that the primary difference between the courting of Eliza by Boyer and Sanford is that "Boyer insists on communicating with Eliza in writing, whereas Sanford chooses the ephemeral medium of light-hearted conversation and witty small-talk" (143). As an epistolary courtship sanctioned by Eliza's family and friends, Boyer's letters suggest stable representations of his intentions, while Sanford's speeches and address are, to the contrary, ephemeral, unstable, and, consequently, unsanctioned.

51. Eliza Leslie, *The Young Ladies' Mentor; or, Extracts in Prose and Verse, for the Promotion of Virtue and Morality* (Philadelphia: Johnson, 1803), iv.

52. Susanna Rowson, *A Present for Young Ladies* (Boston: John West & Co., 1811), 27.

53. Carla Mulford, Introduction, *The Power of Sympathy and The Coquette*, ed. Carla Mulford (New York: Penguin, 1996), xxxi.

54. William Hill Brown, *The Power of Sympathy*, ed. William S. Osbourne (New Haven, Conn.: College and University Press, 1970), 33. All subsequent references are to this edition.

55. Melvin Yazawa explains that in the post-Revolutionary era, "dependence was despised by republicans, and dependent persons became objects of suspicion because they were seen as easy targets of corruption." See Yazawa, 141.

56. For a different reading of Harrington's death, see Stern's *The Plight of Feeling*. Stern argues that the younger Harrington's death results from his democratic liberalism, as part of the "reactionary subtext" of *The Power of Sympathy* (27).

57. Sukey Vickery, *Emily Hamilton, a Novel* (Worcester: Isaiah Thomas, 1803), 18.

58. Lori Merish, *Sentimental Materialism: Gender, Commodity Culture, and Nineteenth-Century American Literature* (Durham, N.C.: Duke University Press, 2000), 83–84.

59. Hannah Foster, *The Coquette; or, the History of Eliza Wharton* (1797. Ed. Cathy N. Davidson. New York: Oxford University Press, 1986), 83. All subsequent references are to this edition.

Frank Shuffelton has persuasively argued that we need to understand American novels as written for an audience of American readers, who bring a unique cultural context to these works. Eliza's downfall in *The Coquette*, he claims, speaks to the decline of the "brotherly watch," the guidance and discipline provided by church members to erring members in order to maintain consistent community morals and standards. As he explains, "The aim of the brotherly watch was to bring about the sinner's repentance and reconciliation with the community, but for Eliza there is no reconciliation" (220). And he concludes, "[T]his is not to say that Mrs. Foster's primary conscious concern in this novel was to portray the consequences of the failure of the traditional brotherly watch, but that she inhabited a world undergoing radical social and political changes, a world where the decriminalizing of sin was a symptom both of the loosening of moral bonds which had held traditional New England society together and of the confusion of the appropriate roles of public and private life" (221). See "Mrs. Foster's Coquette and the Decline of the Brotherly Watch," *Studies in Eighteenth-Century Culture* 16 (1986): 211–24. While I am of course deeply sympathetic to Shuffelton's argument about understanding the context in which American fiction was produced, the English, French, and American secular advice literature that I discuss throughout this chapter also seems important in understanding *The Coquette*.

60. See Rice, *The Transformation of Authorship in America*, 162–68, and Adam Goldgeier, "The Coquette Composed," *Constructions* (1990): 1–14.

61. Bruce Burgett explains Eliza's silence in this way: "Having eschewed marriage, she lacks the conjugal home that generates and shelters the audience-oriented subjectivities of her middle-class correspondents. The corrosive effects of this lack are confirmed by Foster's narrative: childbirth (out of wedlock) and death (in a public tavern) collapse the writing and sexed body by 'disclos[ing]' the involuntary effects of Eliza's 'intercourse' with Sanford" (146). See Burgett, *Sentimental Bodies: Sex, Gender, and Citizenship in the Early Republic* (Princeton, N.J.: Princeton University Press, 1998), 106.

62. See Dorothy Z. Baker, "'Detested be the Epithet!': Definition, Maxim, and the Language of Social Dicta in Hannah Webster Foster's *The Coquette*," *Essays in Literature* 23.1 (1996): 53; Ian Finseth, "'A Melancholy Tale': Rhetoric, Fiction, and Passion in *The Coquette*," *Studies in the Novel* 33.2 (2001): 137; and John Paul Tassoni, "'I Can Step Out of Myself a Little': Feminine Virtue and Female Friendship in Hannah Foster's *The Coquette*," in *Communication and Women's Friendships: Parallels and Intersections in Literature and Life*, ed. Janet Doubler Ward and JoAnna Stephens Mink (Bowling Green, Ohio: Bowling Green State University Popular Press, 1993), 104, 107.

63. Donna R. Bontatibus, *The Seduction Novel of the Early Nation: A Call for Socio-Political Reform* (East Lansing: Michigan State University Press, 1999), 76.

64. For a different interpretation of the importance of scrutiny in *The Coquette*, see David Waldstreicher's "'Fallen Under My Observation': Vision and Virtue in *The Coquette*," *Early American Literature* 27 (1992): 204–18.

65. Leonard Cassuto, "The Seduction of American Religious Discourse in Foster's *The Coquette*," in *Reform and Counterreform: Dialectics of the Word in Western Christianity Since Luther*, ed. John C. Hawley (Berlin and New York: Mouton de Gruyter, 1994), 105.

66. Fritz Fleischmann, "Concealed Lessons: Foster's *Coquette* and Brockden Brown's 'Lesson on Concealment,'" in *Early America Re-Explored: New Readings in Colonial, Early National, and Antebellum Culture*, ed. Klaus H. Schmidt and Fritz Fleischmann (New York: Peter Lang, 2000), 320. Sanford himself echoes Eliza's use of this phrase after Boyer's rejection of her; she writes to Lucy: "Oh my friend, I am undone! I am slighted, rejected . . ." (Foster 105).

67. Newton describes conduct novels as a hybrid of fiction and conduct book, thus producing texts that "[embed] principles and ideals in narrative matrices that make the process of deciding to do right or wrong plausibly human and alive" (140).

68. Pettengill examines the trope of sisterhood in light of the "separate spheres" ideology in "Sisterhood in a Separate Sphere: Female Friendship in Hannah Foster's *The Coquette* and *The Boarding School*." Rather than "sisterhood," which implies a sense of equality among these women, I emphasize the more hierarchical "monitor" or mentor aspects, which better reflects these two novels' emphases on self-examination and regulation.

Gwendolyn Audrey Foster also discusses the issue of female friendship in *The Boarding School*, arguing that Foster uses the epistolary form "to create a mythic feminist community" (60), a claim that seems somewhat anachronistic. See Foster, "The Dialogic Margins of Conduct Fiction: Hannah Webster Foster's *The Boarding School*," *Journal of the American Studies Association of Texas* 25 (1994): 59–72.

69. Hannah Foster, *The Boarding School; or, Lessons of a Preceptress to Her Pupils* (Boston: Thomas and Andrews, 1798), 7, 6.

70. In terms of style and content, *The Boarding School* bears a striking resem-

blance to Susanna Rowson's 1794 novel *Mentoria*. *Mentoria* consists of a one-sided correspondence between a former governess named Helena, who adopts the pen name Mentoria, and her now-grown pupils. There is no formal plot or character development in this novel; rather, it might be best described as a short story cycle, united by Mentoria's persona. Since her former pupils are motherless, Mentoria continues to monitor their behavior, gently rebuking them for their failings by telling instructive stories. These stories range in length from two to seventy pages; some appear to be "borrowed" from other texts. Each story features individuals from Mentoria's circle of acquaintances, friends, and relatives. As a result, her circle ironically emerges as a hotbed of filial disobedience, seductions, false-marriages, and near-incest, painting a world of nearly unmitigated depravity—or at any rate a social world where young women face threats not only from young men, but also from depraved female acquaintances, and whose only hope of salvation is family or a devoted mentor.

71. James Fordyce, *Sermons to Young Women* (Philadelphia: Dobson, 1787), 273.

72. Nell Irvin Painter, "Representing Truth: Sojourner Truth's Knowing and Becoming Known," *Journal of American History* 81.2 (1994): 467.

73. Sally Sayward Barrell Keating Wood, *Dorval; or the Speculator. A Novel, Founded on Recent Facts* (Portsmouth, N.H.: Printed at the Ledger Press by Nutting & Whitelock, for the author, 1801), 35.

74. Barker-Benfield describes the development of the Lockean nerve paradigm in detail in *The Culture of Sensibility: Sex and Society in Eighteenth-Century Britain* (Chicago: University of Chicago Press, 1992), 1–23.

75. For information about separate, sequenced instruction for reading and writing skills, see David D. Hall, *Worlds of Wonder, Days of Judgment: Popular Religious Belief in Early New England* (New York: Knopf, 1989), 31–38, and E. Jennifer Monaghan, "Literacy Instruction and Gender in Colonial New England," in *Reading in America: Literature and Social History*, ed. Cathy N. Davidson (Baltimore: Johns Hopkins University Press, 1989), 53–80.

76. Jeffrey H. Richards, "The Politics of Seduction: Theater, Sexuality, and National Virtue in the Novels of Hannah Foster," in *Exceptional Spaces: Essays in Performance and History*, ed. Della Pollock (Chapel Hill: University of North Carolina Press, 1998), 239.

77. See Joan Shelley Rubin, *The Making of Middlebrow Culture* (Chapel Hill and London: University of North Carolina Press, 1992), Chapter 1, especially 1–15.

Chapter 2
Unlawful Embraces

1. Benjamin Rush, *Medical Inquiries and Observations upon the Diseases of the Mind* (1812. New York: Hafner, 1962), 44. Although not published until 1812, *Medical Inquiries and Observations upon the Diseases of the Mind* was based upon thirty

years of medical experience and very much reveals its origins in eighteenth-century thought. In the decades before the publication of this work, Rush promulgated his theories through teaching, lectures, and essays.

2. As social historians have demonstrated, spousal affection was becoming increasingly important in everyday life as well. In "Eighteenth-Century Family and Social Life Revealed in Massachusetts Divorce Records," in *A Heritage of Her Own: Toward a New Social History of American Women*, ed. Nancy F. Cott and Elizabeth H. Pleck (New York: Simon and Schuster, 1976), Cott notes that, prior to 1765, divorce petitions did not mention loss of spousal affection; however, after 1765, although by itself not grounds for a divorce, loss of romantic spousal affection became an increasingly important issue in petitions (123). In *Women of the Republic*, Kerber also notes an increase in the mention of spousal affection in post-Revolutionary Connecticut divorce petitions (175). Merril D. Smith addresses the issue of romantic marital expectations in *Breaking the Bonds: Marital Discord in Pennsylvania, 1730–1830* (New York: New York University Press, 1991), especially 69–75.

3. Another useful study is Klaus Dörner's *Madmen and the Bourgeoisie: A Social History of Insanity and Psychiatry* (1969. Trans. Joachim Neugroschel and Jean Steinberg. Oxford: Blackwell, 1981). Dörner uses a comparative approach to describe the origins and evolution of British, French, and German psychiatric treatments for the insane.

4. Albert Deutsch, *The Mentally Ill in America: A History of Their Care and Treatment from Colonial Times* (New York: Doubleday, 1937), 52–53.

5. Generally, madness is depicted rather differently in more overtly Gothic fiction, such as Charles Brockden Brown's *Wieland* and *Edgar Huntly*. In these novels, madness is not merely a trope; the violent manias of such characters as Wieland and Clithero provide the action for the plot rather than a source for the moral denouement, as episodes of insanity do in sentimental fiction. In much sentimental fiction, madness is an expedient means of exposing moral failings; in this fashion, it became a convenient and recognizable trope that readers could easily decipher, since it operates similarly in a number of novels.

6. When reflecting on the "new" canon of early American fiction that has expanded in the past twenty years to include not only Charles Brockden Brown's four "major" novels (*Edgar Huntly*, *Wieland*, *Arthur Mervyn*, and *Ormond*), but also Susanna Rowson's *Charlotte Temple* and Hannah Foster's *The Coquette*, it is useful to remember Raymond Williams's comments on canons and traditions: "Most versions of 'tradition' can be quickly shown to be radically selective. From a whole possible area of past and present, in a particular culture, certain meanings and practices are selected for emphasis and certain other meanings and practices are neglected or excluded. Yet, within a particular hegemony, and as one of its decisive processes, this selection is presented and usually successfully passed off as 'the tradition,' 'the significant past.' What has then to be said about any tradition is that it is in this sense an aspect of *contemporary* social and cultural organization, in the in-

terest of the dominance of a specific class. It is a version of the past which is intended to connect with and ratify the present. What it offers in practice is a sense of *predisposed continuity*." See Williams, *Marxism and Literature* (New York: Oxford University Press, 1977), 115–16.

7. See Loshe, *The Early American Novel*, and Brown, *The Sentimental Novel in America, 1789–1860*.

8. Davidson, *Revolution and the Word*, 66, 73. Davidson also discusses these issues at length in chapter 4: "Literacy, Education, and the Reader." Many contemporary figures of cultural authority, as politically diverse as Thomas Jefferson and Timothy Dwight, as well as numerous anonymous writers of newspaper reviews, considered sentimental fiction potentially subversive and iniquitous, especially for female readers; they regarded the very nature, subject matter, and status of fiction as topics of grave concern. See Thomas Jefferson, *The Writings of Thomas Jefferson*, ed. Paul Leicester Ford (New York: Putnam's, 1892–99), vol. X, 104; and Timothy Dwight, *Travels in New England and New York* (New Haven, Conn.: Dwight, 1821), vol. I, 515–18. See also Orians, "Censure of Fiction in American Romances and Magazines: 1789–1810."

9. Davidson specifically cites novels by Helena Wells and Sally Wood as embodying this problem. I discuss Wood's *Dorval; or the Speculator* at length later in this chapter.

10. M. M. Bakhtin, *The Dialogic Imagination*, ed. Michael Holquist, trans. Caryl Emerson and Michael Holquist (Austin: University of Texas Press, 1981), 39.

11. There seems to me to be some question about the extent to which a genre itself (as opposed to individual texts) can be considered truly subversive once it has entered into mainstream culture through publishing and book trade networks and circulating libraries. Further, widespread newspaper and journal reviews of fiction, despite their condemnation of the genre, would seem to neutralize to some degree the potential subversiveness of those works through their acknowledgment of the power of fiction—especially during the course of the early national era, as publishing and distribution networks became better established and novel reading and ownership became more widespread. I am not arguing that fiction loses its power, but rather that *its power loses its subversive edge*.

12. Luce Irigaray, *This Sex Which Is Not One*, trans. Catherine Porter with Carolyn Burke (Ithaca, N.Y.: Cornell University Press, 1985), 184.

13. By "private" and "public" spheres, I refer to the distinctions that Jürgen Habermas makes in *The Structural Transformation of the Public Sphere*, whereby certain concerns fall under the aegis of the conjugal family within the private realm, while others, such as matters of public opinion, belong to the public area of the private realm. Still other concerns, like laws, fall into the sphere of public authority. As I argue in this chapter, the distinctions between the public and private spheres in the early Republic were fluid, particularly concerning the regulation of female behavior and sexuality.

14. For more on marriage as an economic transaction, see Bourdieu, *Outline of a Theory of Practice*, 172.

15. Norman Dain, *Concepts of Insanity in the United States, 1789–1865* (New Brunswick: Rutgers University Press, 1964), 15.

16. Dain, 4–5. For more information on the evolution of moral treatment and the rise of institutions in post-1825 America, see Ruth B. Caplan's *Psychiatry and the Community in Nineteenth-Century America: The Recurring Concern with the Environment in the Prevention and Treatment of Mental Illness* (New York: Basic, 1969). Mary Ann Jimenez's *Changing Faces of Madness: Early American Attitudes and the Treatment of the Insane* (Hanover, N.H.: University Press of New England, 1987) discusses the medicalization of insanity as a disease, as well as the rise of moral treatment in America, focusing particularly on Massachusetts. For a fascinating and very readable account of moral treatment in nineteenth-century England, see Elaine Showalter, *The Female Malady: Women, Madness, and English Culture, 1830–1980* (New York: Pantheon Books, 1985). As Showalter cautions, however, although there continued to be considerable international exchange with regard to medical theories and treatment of insanity over the course of the nineteenth century, treatment practices and cultural attitudes toward madness varied greatly from country to country (6).

17. Vincenzo Chiarugi, an Italian contemporary of Rush, Pinel, and Tuke, was also an advocate during the 1770s and 1780s for humane treatment of the mentally ill, but he was much less influential in America.

18. Dain, *Concepts of Insanity in the United States, 1789–1865*, 22–24. Citing Nathan G. Goodman and James E. Gibson, Dain estimates that Rush taught three thousand students during his thirty years of teaching and private practice. See Goodman, *Benjamin Rush, Physician and Citizen 1746–1813* (Philadelphia: University of Pennsylvania Press, 1934), 192; see also Gibson, "Benjamin Rush's Apprenticed Students," *Transactions and Studies of the College of Physicians of Philadelphia* 4th series, 14 (1946): 127–32.

19. Hugh P. Greely, "Early Wisconsin Medical History," *Wisconsin Medical Journal* 20 (1922): 564. Quoted in Dain, 38.

20. For a fictional treatment of mania, see Charles Brockden Brown's *Wieland*, in which, in the grip of religious mania, Theodore Wieland murders his wife, children, and a family friend.

21. Several published treatises discuss the effects of passions such as grief on the body and the mind, including Henry Rose's *An Inaugural Dissertation on the Effects of the Passions upon the Body* (Philadelphia: Woodward, 1794) and Alexander Anderson's *An Inaugural Dissertation on Chronic Mania* (New York: Swords, 1796).

22. For a discussion of Rush's understanding of the moral faculties, see Yazawa, 158–65.

23. In *Democracy and Punishment: Disciplinary Origins of the United States* (Madison: University of Wisconsin Press, 1987), Thomas L. Dumm notes that the prison

reforms instituted at Philadelphia's Walnut Street Jail in the 1790s closely parallel the reforms taking place in the treatment of mental patients. The central point of these penal reforms was a movement away from the desire to humiliate prisoners by making them public spectacles toward a policy of isolating prisoners in solitary confinement as the first step in the rehabilitation process. Prisoners were removed from the public eye, yet under the constant surveillance and control of prison guards. Such a system was designed to promote order, rationality, and contemplation for the purpose of producing self-regulating republican machines (101–105). Rush's work undoubtedly influenced these penal reforms, as he believed that the same environmental controls would benefit both criminals and the mentally ill, once again demonstrating his and other reformers' continued (albeit unintentional) conflation of these two groups.

24. See Richard H. Brodhead, especially chapter 1, "Sparing the Rod: Discipline and Fiction" in *Cultures of Letters: Scenes of Reading and Writing in Nineteenth-Century America* (Chicago: University of Chicago Press, 1993).

25. In *Worlds of Wonder, Days of Judgment: Popular Religious Belief in Early New England* (New York: Alfred A. Knopf, 1989), David D. Hall discusses the public, ritualistic nature of seventeenth- and eighteenth-century religious and civil confession, which served to relieve sinners of the burden of their transgressions (172–78). The confessional nature of late eighteenth-century sentimental fiction represents the increasing secularization of this behavior.

Cornelia Hughes Dayton explores the confessional urges of Sarah Grosvenor in a fascinating real-life case of fornication and attempted abortion that had fatal consequences. Dayton notes that "an inward gaze, a strong consciousness of sin and guilt, a desire to avoid conflict and achieve reconciliation—these are the impulses expressed in women's intimate talk in the weeks before Sarah died" (40). Dayton argues that this confessional impulse was decidedly gendered, for the men involved in this episode, "at least when presenting themselves before legal authorities, adopted secular voices and learned self-interested strategies" (42). See "Taking the Trade: Abortion and Gender Relations in an Eighteenth-Century New England Village," *William and Mary Quarterly* 48.1 (1991): 19–49.

26. See William E. Nelson, "Emerging Notions of Modern Criminal Law in the Revolutionary Era: An Historical Perspective," *New York University Law Review* 42 (1967): 450–82. His study, which concentrates on Middlesex County, Massachusetts, reports startling findings. Immediately before the Revolution, during the period from 1760 to 1774, 210 women were prosecuted for fornication in Middlesex County (452). In 1786, a change in the statutes regarding fornication allowed women guilty of this crime simply to appear before a magistrate and pay their fines without being subject to prosecution. Nelson concludes that even this penalty was no longer enforced after 1791. Further, during the 1790s, women were able to file paternity suits against the fathers of their illegitimate children without themselves risking punishment. The enforcement of adultery statutes was similarly weakened;

even though divorces were regularly granted after the Revolution for reason of adultery, spouses were seldom criminally punished (455–57). Several other studies support Nelson's findings.

In *A Midwife's Tale: The Life of Martha Ballard, Based on Her Diary, 1785–1812* (New York: Knopf, 1990), Laurel Thatcher Ulrich notes similar findings in Lincoln County, Maine, with regard to evidence of fornication: "Between 1785 and 1797 Martha delivered 106 women of their first babies. Of these infants, forty, or 38 percent, were conceived out of wedlock" (155–56). Ulrich also notes similar findings with regard to a statistical decline in the prosecution of fornication (148–49). In spite of this decline, women vastly outnumber men in terms of prosecutions. Ulrich observes, however, "that women are overrepresented on county court dockets may have less to do with a decline of interest in prosecuting men for fornication than with the voluntary nature of paternity proceedings," since women first had to give evidence of fornication and an out of wedlock birth "in order to establish an action for paternity against a man" (153).

See also Nancy F. Cott, "Eighteenth-Century Family and Social Life Revealed in Massachusetts Divorce Records," 107–35; and Cott, "Divorce and the Changing Status of Women in Eighteenth-Century Massachusetts," in *The American Family in Social-Historical Perspective*, ed. Michael Gordon, 2nd ed. (New York: St. Martin's, 1978), 115–39. Cott demonstrates that there truly was a sexual double standard when it came to marital sexual infidelity. The differing rates of male and female divorce petitions granted on the basis of adultery suggest that women were judged much more harshly than were men and that male marital infidelity was more likely to be dismissed. These statistics begin to change after the Revolution ("Divorce and the Changing Status of Women," 122–26). Cornelia Hughes Dayton also notes this sexual double standard in mid-eighteenth-century New England. She suggests that not only were men no longer being punished for the crime of fornication, but that "the sexually irresponsible activities of men in their youth would not be held against them as they reached for repute and prosperity in their prime" (22). The legal origins of this double standard for sexual conduct apparently date to the mid-seventeenth century, as Carol F. Karlsen proposes in *The Devil in the Shape of a Woman: Witchcraft in Colonial New England* (New York: Norton, 1987). Karlsen argues that "the tendency to hold women more responsible than men for violations of sexual norms, which would become more obvious over the rest of the century, dates from the mid-1640s" (195–96). See also 198–202.

In *Breaking the Bonds*, Smith notes that in post-Revolutionary Pennsylvania, women were "slightly more successful than men in winning divorces on adultery grounds when they did petition" (85). Nonetheless, Smith also notes the continuance of a sexual double standard; women were occasionally charged with adultery after a pregnancy, particularly when local officials became concerned that the child might be a charge on the community.

27. Ellen K. Rothman, "Sex and Self-Control: Middle-Class Courtship in America, 1770–1870," in *The American Family in Social-Historical Perspective*, ed. Michael Gordon, 3rd ed. (New York: St. Martin's, 1983), 394–95. See also Ellen K. Rothman, *Hands and Hearts: A History of Courtship in America* (New York: Basic, 1984), especially chapter 1.

28. Daniel Scott Smith, "Parental Power and Marriage Patterns: An Analysis of Historical Trends in Hingham, Massachusetts," *Journal of Marriage and the Family* 35 (1973): 419–28. Smith acknowledges that it is difficult to generalize about the rest of the country based upon the study of one town; however, fertility patterns in Hingham are consistent with those at the national level. Further, Jane Turner Censer's study of upper class North Carolina families during the early nineteenth century supports Smith's conclusions. Censer, too, found an increase in the number of marriages by women out of birth order. See Censer, *North Carolina Planters and Their Children, 1800–1860* (Baton Rouge: Louisiana State University Press, 1984), 89–91. Significantly, Smith also argues that illegitimacy rates parallel rates of premarital sex. While there are currently no statistics available about the rate of illegitimate births in America during this time, most historians concur with Smith that the number of illegitimate births probably increased as well.

29. Daniel Scott Smith and Michael S. Hindus, "Premarital Pregnancy in America 1640–1971," *Journal of Interdisciplinary History* 5 (1975): 561. This statistic is particularly dramatic when compared to the years before and after this period. For the period from 1721–1760, 22.5 percent of first births to married women occurred before the ninth month of marriage; for the period from 1801–1840, the figure was 23.7 percent (561). Robert A. Gross notes similar findings in his study of Concord in *The Minutemen and Their World* (New York: Hill and Wang, 1976). Gross concludes that 41 percent of all first births between 1760 and 1774 were the result of prenuptial conceptions (217, note 59). Smith and Hindus hypothesize that this spike is related to "the disintegration of the traditional, well-integrated rural community to the beginnings of economic and social modernization" (559).

Religious revivalism of the nineteenth century probably was instrumental in lowering premarital pregnancy rates (551). Further, Smith and Hindus propose that "sexual restraint was compatible with the norms of thrift and abstinence required of the upwardly striving young capitalist.... Having internalized the mechanism of delayed gratification in terms of his economic life, the nineteenth-century American male would not risk the consequences of a marriage precipitated by a premarital pregnancy" (552). Given that it is beyond the scope of their study, Smith and Hindus do not consider the role of fiction in the development of bourgeois subjectivity. While fiction represents this development, it also simultaneously encouraged the regulation of sexual behavior.

30. Since fictional mothers and illegitimate children infrequently survive birth, seldom is accountability after birth an issue for either mother or father. Mrs. P. D.

Manvill's *Lucinda; or the Mountain Mourner*, 2nd ed. [with additions] (Ballston Spa, N.Y., 1810) provides a notable exception. After Melvin Brown rapes Lucinda, she bears an illegitimate daughter. In order to keep her from being committed "to the care of the public" (99), her parents have to provide bail or demonstrate that moving her would be dangerous to her health. Her parents successfully petition to keep her at home until her death. The novel ends once the magistrate confronts Brown to make him accountable for his actions and forces him to pay for the care of his child. *Lucinda* also differs from other early American seduction novels in its religiosity: Lucinda ponders, for example, whether illegitimate children have the opportunity to go to heaven and continually worries about the state of her soul.

31. Although violations of adultery and fornication statutes are seldom prosecuted today, as of 1989, twenty-five states and the District of Columbia still prohibited adultery, while thirteen states and the District of Columbia prohibited fornication. See Richard Green, "*Griswold's* Legacy: Fornication and Adultery as Crimes," *Ohio Northern University Law Review* 16 (1989): 545–49. Many statutes remained on the books in unaltered form for decades, even centuries. For example, until 1973, the statutory punishment for adultery in New Hampshire was whipping and the wearing of the letters "AD" on one's clothing. See "The Scarlet Legislature: For Adulterers Only," *Student Lawyer* (May 1987), 6–7. Needless to say, this punishment had not been enforced for several centuries, but the fact that it remained on the statute books is an indication of how states began deliberately turning a blind eye toward so-called "domestic" crimes during the late eighteenth century.

32. Hayden White suggests that all "narrativity, whether of the fictional or factual sort, presupposes the existence of a legal system against or on behalf of which the typical agents of a narrative account militate. And this raises the suspicion that narrative in general, from the folktale to the novel . . . has to do with the topics of law, legality, legitimacy, or, more generally, authority" (13). See White, "The Value of Narrativity in the Representation of Reality," in *The Content of the Form* (Baltimore: Johns Hopkins University Press, 1987), 1–25.

33. Davidson discusses death and childbirth in *Revolution and the Word*, 116.

34. Buchan, 285, and Thomas Parran, *Shadow on the Land: Syphilis* (New York: Reynal and Hitchcock, 1937), 75.

35. See Edward B. Vedder, *Syphilis and Public Health* (Philadelphia: Lea, 1918), 97. Vedder's statistics differ for men and women. He estimates that syphilis was demonstrable among 20–25 percent of white males admitted to insane asylums, but probably present in 25–35 percent of that population. Syphilis was demonstrable in white women in 10–23 percent of the inmate population, but probable in 15–30 percent (97). Parran estimates that by 1937, before the widespread use of penicillin to treat syphilis but after the improvement of alternate treatments for the disease, the number of the syphilitic insane dropped to 10 percent of the total admissions to state psychiatric institutions (301).

36. Philip Ricord's *Illustrations of Syphilitic Disease* (Philadelphia: Hart, 1852)

contains a somewhat useful bibliography of works on syphilis, dating from the first appearance of the disease through 1850. This bibliography is more comprehensive for British and European titles than American ones, for it provides only a partial listing of American titles and frequently excludes the most important reprints of British works. Some of the more important early works on syphilis published in the United States and intended for a scientific audience include John Hunter's *A Treatise on the Venereal Disease* (1787; 1791); Benjamin Bell's *A Treatise on Gonorrhoea Virulenta and Lues Venerea* (1795); Thomas T. Hewson's *A Complete Treatise on Syphilis* (1815); and Richard Carmichael's *An Essay on the Venereal Diseases Which Have Been Confounded with Syphilis, and the Symptoms Which Exclusively Arise from That Poison* (1817).

37. Sally Sayward Barrell Keating Wood, *Amelia; or, the Influence of Virtue* (Portsmouth, N.H.: Printed at the Oracle Press, by William Treadwell, 1802), 241–42; Caroline Matilda Warren Thayer, *The Gamesters; or Ruins of Innocence* (Boston: Thomas & Andrews, 1805), 304. April London notes similar literary descriptions of venereal disease in the eighteenth-century British novel. See "Avoiding the Subject: The Presence and Absence of Venereal Disease in the Eighteenth-Century English Novel," in *The Secret Malady: Venereal Disease in Eighteenth-Century Britain and France*, ed. Linda E. Merians (Lexington: University Press of Kentucky, 1996), 213–27. This anthology of essays contains several other useful discussions of the historical and medical contexts of venereal disease, as well as its treatment in literary texts.

38. Popular in America, William Hogarth's print series *The Rake's Progress*, which depicts the imprisonment and ultimate death of the Rake in Bedlam, likewise suggests syphilitic insanity resulting from debauched behavior.

39. That Elizabeth should use the word "commerce" in *Dorval* is intriguing, for as I argue in the following chapter, commerce and economics in general are central concerns of this novel. Through her secretive "commerce," Elizabeth inadvertently gives away without the recompense of marriage her virtuous reputation, the only marketable commodity (along with virginity) that most women of her time individually possessed, independent of family wealth.

40. By way of contrast, Aurelia, secure in the knowledge of her own virtue, suffers from hysteria when she learns of Elizabeth's elopement. Aurelia brooded "over these accumulated evils, till her blood became congealed. It ceased to flow with its usual calmness. Her pulse stopped, and a suffocating sensation, more dreadful than fainting, came over her" (104). This juxtaposition of hysteria with madness emphasizes the physical manifestations of hysteria, while accenting the correlation between transgressive behavior and madness. Hysteria, it seems, is an appropriate state for a virtuous woman.

41. Samuel Relf, *Infidelity, or the Victims of Sentiment; a Novel, in a Series of Letters* (Philadelphia: W. W. Woodward, 1797), 18.

42. Susanna Rowson, *Charlotte: A Tale of Truth* and *Charlotte's Daughter; or, the*

Three Orphans, ed. Ann Douglas (1794 and 1828; New York: Penguin, 1991), 122. All subsequent references to *Charlotte Temple* and *Lucy Temple* are from this edition and will be cited parenthetically in the text.

For a very different, psychoanalytic reading of *Charlotte Temple* and of this scene in particular, see Julia Stern, "Working through the Frame: *Charlotte Temple* and the Poetics of Maternal Melancholia," *Arizona Quarterly* 49.4 (1993): 1–32. Stern does not believe that Charlotte's intense grief is brought about by her regret for her actions, since Stern argues that she is an "emotional infant" and hence "not an agent in her own life" (15). Rather, Stern claims, "Separated perhaps too early from the loving blanket of maternal care, betrayed by a false surrogate mother-figure [Madam La Rue], and seduced and forsaken by a brutally indifferent male object, Charlotte Temple is undone by the grief of these successive abandonments" (22). Stern elaborates on her argument in *The Plight of Feeling: Sympathy and Dissent in the Early American Novel*, 31–69.

43. This paradigm works similarly in other novels by these same authors. For example, in Rowson's 1794 epistolary novel *Mentoria; or, the Young Lady's Friend*, Mentoria relates the story of Marian, whose father abandoned her and her mother when she was an infant. Years later, when she has been seduced and is near starvation, her father, who does not recognize her, tries to persuade her to become his mistress. When he realizes the incestuous nature of his transgression, he suffers "a sudden fit of insanity," complete with incoherent ravings about his lost daughter (23). Unfairly, he recovers from this fit, but Marian dies, illustrating once more how Rowson tends to visit the crimes of the father upon his children.

Wood, however, emphasizes in *Julia, and the Illuminated Baron* (Portsmouth, N.H.: Charles Peirce, 1800) that the innocent may suffer but will remain in full possession of their "reason," while those guilty of sexual transgression inevitably verge on madness. On her deathbed, Leonora, a nun who eloped from a convent with her lover, raves wildly. The narrator describes the "wildness of her fine eyes" as a "picture of beauty in ruins; and those ruins brought on, by the stings of a wounded conscience; and a heart corroded by guilt" (168). Leonora explains in a posthumous letter that "my reason and my misery could not exist together; as there was no remedy for the latter, the former fell a sacrifice; and for several years, I was a confirmed maniac," "a poor distracted creature" (180). After witnessing the death of her aunt Leonora, Julia grieves, but "she found herself innocent and in full possession of her reason, and she sent humble gratitude to heaven, for both these blessings" (170).

44. Lucinda, the title character of the 1807 novel *Lucinda; or, the Mountain Mourner*, is perhaps the most blameless of all. Raped and impregnated by a vengeful rejected suitor, Lucinda later accepts a coerced offer of marriage from him but dies before he can be forced to marry her. Lucinda crazily sings her way to the grave, but not before expressing intense guilt at leaving her impoverished parents with another mouth to feed.

45. Shirley Samuels, "Infidelity and Contagion: The Rhetoric of Revolution," *Early American Literature* 22.2 (1987): 187. Samuels elaborates on this relationship between the family and the state in the introduction to *Romances of the Republic: Women, the Family, and Violence in the Literature of the Early American Nation* (New York: Oxford University Press, 1996), 3–22. Jay Fliegelman also discusses the connection between the family and the state throughout *Prodigals and Pilgrims: The American Revolution against Patriarchal Authority, 1750–1800*. In particular, he argues, "the problems of family government addressed in the fiction and pedagogy of the period—of balancing authority with liberty, of maintaining a social order while encouraging individual growth—were the larger political problems of the age translated into the terms of daily life" (5).

46. Exploring Charlotte's passivity, Marion Rust has argued that *Charlotte Temple* "is *not* really a novel of seduction, in the sense of being a document that provides sexual titillation under cover of pedagogic censure. Instead, far from depicting Charlotte's overweening desire, the novel portrays the fatal consequences of a woman's inability to want anything enough to motivate decisive action." See Rust, "What's Wrong with Charlotte Temple?" *William and Mary Quarterly*, 3rd series, 10.1 (2003): 103.

47. Lucy Franklin of *The Vain Cottager: or, the History of Lucy Franklin* (1807) is one of the few unmarried, sexually active women in early American fiction who does not die. Instead, this novel has a rehabilitative theme: Lucy continues to live in the same community, but her narrative punishment is to watch her true love marry her virginal younger sister. The renewed respect of the townspeople is Lucy's only compensation for her lost love.

Likewise, the title character of Leonora Sansay's *Laura* (Philadelphia: Bradford & Inskeep, 1809) lives on after bearing a child out of wedlock; Laura's fiancé is killed in a duel defending her honor hours before they are to marry. Although she lives, more beautiful and brilliant than ever, the novel concludes with this grim envoi: Laura's "life was an exemplification of this truth:—'that perpetual uneasiness, disquietude, and irreversible misery, are the certain consequences of fatal misconduct in a woman; however gifted, or however reclaimed'" (181).

48. David Perkins, *Is Literary History Possible?* (Baltimore: Johns Hopkins University Press, 1992), 111.

49. Janice A. Radway, *Reading the Romance: Women, Patriarchy, and Popular Literature*, rev. ed. (Chapel Hill: University of North Carolina Press, 1991), 196. See also Fredric Jameson, "Reification and Utopia in Mass Culture," *Social Text* 1 (1979): 135–37.

50. Mulford explains in the Introduction to *The Power of Sympathy and The Coquette*, "If republican principles were to succeed . . . they needed to be inculcated not only at the level of government but also within the culture as a whole" (xvi).

51. In *Imagined Communities: Reflections on the Origin and Spread of Nationalism* (London: Verso, 1983), Benedict Anderson argues that vernacular print culture was

essential in establishing "imaginary communities" of widely separated individuals; these "imaginary communities" in turn enabled the rise of modern nationalism. Anderson emphasizes the importance of newspapers as a part of vernacular print culture. Nancy Armstrong and Leonard Tennenhouse extend Anderson's thesis, but suggest that fiction was perhaps the more important medium in creating modern communities. See *The Imaginary Puritan*, especially 141–48.

52. John Zomchick, *Family and the Law in Eighteenth-Century Fiction: The Public Conscience in the Private Sphere* (Cambridge: Cambridge University Press, 1993), 4.

53. See Ulrich, chapter 4, especially 159–60.

54. For more on unproductive expenditure, see Georges Bataille, "The Notion of Expenditure," in *Visions of Excess: Selected Writings, 1927–1939*, ed. Allan Stoekl, trans. Allan Stoekl, with Carl R. Lovitt and Donald M. Leslie, Jr. (Minneapolis: University of Minnesota Press, 1985), 116–29.

55. Rush, "Introductory Lecture on the Certainty of Medicine," quoted in Yazawa, 149.

56. Medical practitioners were in turn influenced by artistic treatments of insanity. Indeed, Rush's *Medical Inquiries and Observations upon the Diseases of the Mind* is remarkable today both for the fluidity with which he moves between science and art and for the manner in which he juxtaposes poetry and quotations from Shakespeare's *King Lear* as medical "evidence" alongside his own observations. Similarly, Samuel Coates, a manager of the asylum at the Pennsylvania Hospital from 1785 to 1825, kept a memorandum book in which he noted case histories of patients at the hospital. His narratives are themselves dramatized in a manner reminiscent of contemporary sentimental fiction. See Coates's memorandum book, "Cases of Several Lunatics in the Pennsylvania Hospital," 1785–1825, located in the archives of the Pennsylvania Hospital.

Chapter 3
A Speculating Spirit

1. See Gordon S. Wood, *The Creation of the American Republic, 1776–1787* (New York: Norton, 1993), especially chapter 10.

2. As Jeffrey H. Richards points out in *Theater Enough: American Culture and the Metaphor of the World Stage, 1607–1789* (Durham, N.C.: Duke University Press, 1991), the association between public theater and "British frivolity and corruption" led to the suppression of theater during the Revolutionary War era. Even post-Revolutionary drama continues to express concern about the linkage between British manners and luxury, especially in such works as Royal Tyler's *The Contrast*. See Richards, *Theater Enough*, 265–79.

3. Although Christopher J. Berry in *The Idea of Luxury* suggests that luxuries are created by both their scarcity and the status of being desired by many, much anx-

iety about luxury in the writings of the early Republic centers around financial costs and the moral impact of owning such goods. The anonymous author of *Of Commerce and Luxury* (Philadelphia: Lang, 1791), for example, defines luxury as "the abuse of riches: it consists in an extravagance for fantastical superfluities, disproportioned to the situation and abilities of him that spends." See *Of Commerce and Luxury*, 23. This work is frequently attributed to John Mills (d. 1784?). Although the Philadelphia edition claims to be reprinted from a British edition, I have been unable to locate an edition prior to the 1791 American edition. See also Christopher J. Berry, *The Idea of Luxury: A Conceptual and Historical Investigation* (New York: Cambridge University Press, 1994), 4–6.

4. J. Hector St. John de Crèvecoeur, *Letters from an American Farmer and Sketches of Eighteenth-Century Life* (New York: Penguin, 1986). See letter 4, "Description of Nantucket," in which he likens luxury to an epidemic (125) and letter 9, "Description of Charles Town," in which he scathingly denounces the luxurious lifestyles of the planters, merchants, and lawyers of Charleston.

5. For more information about republican conceptions of female virtue, see Ruth H. Bloch, "The Gendered Meanings of Virtue in Revolutionary America," *Signs* 13.1 (1987): 37–58, especially 52. Also useful is Jan Lewis's essay, "The Republican Wife: Virtue and Seduction in the Early Republic," *William and Mary Quarterly* 44.4 (1987): 689–721.

6. Here I want to emphasize the phrase "virtuous commerce." The international commerce this chapter discusses is the East India trade, not the international slave trade, which flourished for most of the period under discussion.

7. Anne Dalke notes in passing the frequency with which wealth is inherited in early American fiction. Discussing *Margaretta*, Dalke argues that "opportunity is open in this novel only to those already well-to-do. No man rises here by his own efforts: De Burling's failure in trade is marked, and he and his father-in-law both succeed finally by means of inherited wealth. Upward mobility is possible in this book only through inheritance." See Dalke, "Original Vice: The Political Implications of Incest in the Early American Novel," *Early American Literature* 23.2 (1988): 199. Ultimately, the same might be said of several other novels, including *Moreland Vale; or, the Fair Fugitive* and *The Fortunate Discovery*. In these novels, the male characters struggle to earn a virtuous living either through trade or a professional occupation, but the conclusions of both novels hinge upon a denouement of newly-discovered British patrimonies with inherited wealth. A number of other novels, however, explore possibilities for earning wealth through virtuous economic practices.

For further discussion of economic desire as a driving force for narrative, see chapter 2 of Peter Brooks's *Reading for the Plot: Design and Intention in Narrative* (Cambridge: Harvard University Press, 1992).

8. Charles Brockden Brown, *Arthur Mervyn: or, Memoirs of the Year 1793*, 2 vols. 1799/1800. (Kent, Ohio: Kent State University Press, 1980), 57–58.

9. Although numerous studies discuss economic issues in Brown's novels, several are especially valuable. The most comprehensive of these studies is Elizabeth Jane Wall Hinds's *Private Property: Charles Brockden Brown's Gendered Economics of Virtue* (Newark: University of Delaware Press, 1997). Hinds argues that Brown's fiction epitomizes the dramatic changes facing Americans during the 1790s, changes embodied by the shift in American economic life from a land-based economy, dependent on patronage and characterized by vertical power relations, to an economy dependent upon paper money and credit and characterized by relatively horizontal power relations. Hinds explicitly discusses the issue of Edgar Huntly's disinheritance, arguing that Edgar perceives his economic potential to be "family- and land-based rather than entrepreneurial or labor-based. Edgar never considers making money; he merely bemoans his lack of inheritance" (141). He longs for an Old World economic system of landed inheritance supported by a system of patronage, a system that Hinds labels as "incompatible with capitalist goals" (144). Bitter about his progressive disinheritances, Edgar seeks revenge, but revenge cannot return what he never truly possessed.

Hinds sees Arthur Mervyn, however, as a rising capitalist. Untroubled by the moral ambiguities of Mervyn's actions, Hinds reads his character as innately virtuous and benevolent, but nonetheless calculating. "What Arthur gains," Hinds explains, "is the experience necessary to convert his natural propensity for benevolence into exchangeable currency. His virtue, then, joins forces with a will-to-wealth to the end of a specifically capitalist success" (69). In an original reading of this book vis-à-vis Adam Smith's *Wealth of Nations*, Hinds argues that Mervyn successfully manipulates what she calls the "'specter' . . . a useful term for the indwelling, ghostly image of public approval for the early capitalist citizen: this representation manufactures a public self for the individual, acting as a mirror both of the public world—with its ordinances and reputations; in short, with its system of credit and credibility—*and* of the individual subject measured within and against that public arena" (72). Thus, for Brown, masculine virtue is not merely exercised—it is *performed*, and this performance itself is crucial for success in public, commercial life. Further, Mervyn's narrative skill—necessary to convince others of the justice and benevolence of his actions—becomes in a sense his capital, as he must gauge the standards of his listeners in order to produce a persuasive version of his story. For other useful discussions of *Arthur Mervyn*, see Bill Christophersen, *The Apparition in the Glass: Charles Brockden Brown's American Gothic* (Athens: University of Georgia Press, 1993), especially 111–15, and Alan Axelrod, *Charles Brockden Brown: An American Tale* (Austin: University of Texas Press, 1983), 134–59.

Also helpful is the first chapter of Steven Watts's *The Romance of Real Life: Charles Brockden Brown and the Origins of American Culture* (Baltimore: Johns Hopkins University Press, 1994). Watts explores interactions between the novel and "the shaping of capitalist culture in America," arguing that the novel "promoted the consolidation of liberal hegemony not only in class and cultural terms, but in psychological terms as well. By constructing and disseminating what Raymond Williams has aptly called 'structures of feeling,' American fictional texts helped establish the growing dominance of bourgeois values by the late 1700s and early 1800s. They did so in part, of course, by promoting values of individualism, material ambition, self-control, and privatization" (24–25).

10. There is considerable disagreement among historians as to the extent to which republicans embraced agricultural pursuits at the expense of trade. The United States of the 1780s and 1790s that Drew R. McCoy portrays in *The Elusive Republic* is one of constant tension between those generally aligned in the Jeffersonian Republican camp, who favored agricultural pursuits combined with limited domestic manufactures of necessary items such as clothing and household furnishings, opposed to Alexander Hamilton and the Federalists, who favored increased foreign commerce and more sophisticated domestic manufactures like those in England. There was, however, considerable division within these general groupings. Further, there was fluidity even between groups, as some who held a general orientation towards Jeffersonian Republicanism favored trade as a means of disposing of excess agricultural produce and also as a way of staving off further development of domestic manufacturing; this position gained adherents throughout the 1790s. See McCoy, *The Elusive Republic: Political Economy in Jeffersonian America* (Chapel Hill: University of North Carolina Press, 1980), 188; also useful is chapter 3: "Commerce and the Independent Republic." Steven Watts makes a similar argument, although he sees even more fluidity across party lines than does McCoy; see Watts, *The Republic Reborn: War and the Making of Liberal America, 1790–1820* (Baltimore: Johns Hopkins University Press, 1987), 12–14 and 329–30.

By way of contrast, however, in *Capitalism and a New Social Order: The Republican Vision of the 1790s* (New York: New York University Press, 1984), Joyce Appleby argues that the Jeffersonian Republicans were far more interested in commerce than most scholars credit. She points to the anticapitalist bias of most historians and suggests that this bias and a tendency to view capitalism as a monolithic system "have obscured the role that the expectation of commercial growth played in the social thought of the Jeffersonian Republicans" (46). She concludes that "Where Republicans differed from Federalists was in the moral character they gave to economic development.... Capitalism thus disclosed itself in a benign and visionary way to Republicans who drew from its dynamic operation the promise of a new age for ordinary men" (49–50). Appleby extends this thesis in chapters 2 and 12 of *Liberalism and Republicanism in the Historical Imagination* (Cambridge: Harvard University Press, 1992), where she examines what she sees as the agrarian, yet decidedly progressive and commercial, vision Jefferson had for the United States, in which grain sold in the transatlantic market would provide funds for European manufactured goods.

11. *Moreland Vale; or the Fair Fugitive*, [by the author of *The Fortunate Discovery*], (New York: printed by L. Nichols and Co. for Samuel Campbell, 1801), 144.

12. Despite this exaltation of agricultural life, few novels actually portray the life of the gentleman farmer. Enos Hitchcock's 1793 bildungsroman *The Farmer's Friend, or the History of Mr. Charles Worthy* is a notable exception.

13. Sarah Savage's *The Factory Girl*, which depicts the female protagonist reeling cotton in a mill, is the only early American novel to portray any type of advanced manufacturing. Although Hamilton and some of the Federalists advocated sophisticated manufactures in the United States, most writers of fiction regarded such development unfavorably, since it would require a dense urban population working for low wages, as in England.

Thomas B. Lovell discusses at length the topics of virtuous and productive labor—crucial issues in justifying female labor in factories—and uses *The Factory Girl* to call into question historiography about the development of the separate spheres ideology. Despite the narrative's defense of factory work, I argue that it still demonstrates considerable anxiety about the issue of female work outside the home, as well as the danger of "mixing" with workers of unknown virtue within the factory. Nevertheless, *The Factory Girl* also features a significant subplot involving the dangerous seductions entailed by playing the lottery; clearly virtuous work—even if carried out in a factory—is preferable to gambling. See Lovell, "Separate Spheres and Extensive Circles: Sarah Savage's *The Factory Girl* and the Celebration of Industry in Early Nineteenth-Century America," *Early American Literature* 31.1 (1996): 1–24.

14. The historiography of attitudes toward Anglo-American commerce is extensive. For my purposes, some of the most helpful writers on the subject are J. G. A. Pocock, Carroll Smith-Rosenberg, and Drew McCoy, whose works are representative of scholarly opinion on the subject. Pocock's work is a good starting point, as he considers the attitudes of the British gentry toward trade during the early part of the eighteenth century in *The Machiavellian Moment: Florentine Political Thought and the Atlantic Republican Tradition* (Princeton, N.J.: Princeton University Press, 1975), 440–61. Carroll Smith-Rosenberg discusses the contested nature and definitions of republicanism in the eighteenth century. She claims that "the man of trade occupied a more ambivalent position within classical-republican discourse. The value of the gentry's land, the source of the gentry's political dependence, depended on trade, and hence on the actions of the traders and on events occurring in London and in ports around the world. Their independence thus circumscribed by men and processes beyond their control or ken, the gentry responded with nervous suspicion. Trade, they wrote each other, was productive, linked to England's and their own prosperity. But trade also 'introduces luxury . . . and extinguishes virtue.' It depended on credit which hung upon opinion and the passions of hope and fear. It was cathected with desire. It might seduce independent men away from the simple ways of their fathers. It could entrap them in an endless web of debt and ruin" (164). See "Domesticating 'Virtue': Coquettes and Revolutionaries in Young America," in *Literature and the Body: Essays on Popula-*

tions and Persons, ed. Elaine Scarry (Baltimore: Johns Hopkins University Press, 1986), 160–84. McCoy explores this ambivalence in chapter 3, "Commerce and the Independent Republic," 76–104.

15. T. H. Breen, "Narrative of Commercial Life," *William and Mary Quarterly* 50.1 (1993): 471–501. Breen discusses these issues in several other essays as well, including "'Baubles of Britain': The American and Consumer Revolutions of the Eighteenth Century," *Past and Present* 119 (1988): 73–104, and "An Empire of Goods: The Anglicization of Colonial America, 1690–1776," *Journal of British Studies* 25.4 (1986): 467–99. Breen also notes the importance of consumer goods in creating a shared cultural identity; see "'Baubles of Britain,'" 79–87.

16. Jackson Turner Main, *The Social Structure of Revolutionary America* (Princeton, N.J.: Princeton University Press, 1965), 190–92.

17. Stuart M. Blumin discusses the status of merchants throughout the second chapter of *The Emergence of the Middle Class*. In particular, he argues, "Respect accrued to the genteel *rentier*, but no less dignified (in America, at least), than large-scale landlording and the traditional professions of aristocratic or genteel younger sons (the military, law, and the clergy) was the pursuit of long-distance trade. Nonmanual work on a smaller scale, such as keeping a retail store (often called 'dealing,' 'trading,' or 'mongering'), was significantly less respectable, while work with one's hands, even in a skilled and valuable craft, was distinctly degrading" (30). For further information, see *The Emergence of the Middle Class: Social Experience in the American City, 1760–1900* (New York: Cambridge University Press, 1989), 17–65. As I will argue, Blumin seems to overstate the case for the respectability of foreign trade during the early Republic era.

18. Pelatiah Webster, "A Dissertation," in *Political Essays on the Nature and Operation of Money, Public Finances, and Other Subjects: Published during the American War, and Continued up to the Present Year, 1791* (Philadelphia: Crukshank, 1791), 219.

19. This tolerance arose from self-interest: American shipping provided an essential backup service for British merchants, especially during the Napoleonic war (Goldstein 24–25; Furber 240–45). British law, however, expressly prohibited American ships from participating in the opium trade, although some did so anyway. For more on American participation in the opium trade, see Goldstein 46–70.

20. Numerous studies examine the import-export trade with East India and China. For a sampling, see Foster Rhea Dulles, *The Old China Trade* (Boston: Houghton Mifflin, 1930), 40–49; Holden Furber, "The Beginnings of American Trade with India, 1784–1812," *The New England Quarterly* 11.2 (1938): 235–65; Goldstein, *Philadelphia and the China Trade*, 30; Thomas M. Doerflinger, *A Vigorous Spirit of Enterprise: Merchants and Economic Development in Revolutionary Philadelphia* (Chapel Hill: University of North Carolina Press, 1986), 291–97; Philip Chadwick Foster Smith, *The Empress of China* (Philadelphia: Philadelphia Maritime Museum, 1984). Also useful is app. 1, vol. 7 of *The Papers of Robert Morris*, ed. John Catanzariti et al. (Pittsburgh: University of Pittsburgh Press, 1995), which contains

correspondence with detailed annotations about Morris's trading ventures. Also, the Peabody-Essex Museum in Salem, Massachusetts, has a remarkable collection of goods imported from China and East India, as well as an extensive library of materials on the East India and China trade.

21. David Waldstreicher, in *In the Midst of Perpetual Fetes*, speaks of the importance of gentility in displays of republican identity. Although he does not discuss post-Revolutionary tea-drinking per se, the uses of tea that I describe above perform a function similar to those he describes in "The Constitution of Federal Feeling," especially 67–85.

22. Shields discusses the importance of the tea table and the relationship between tea tables and the development of salons in *Civil Tongues*, 99–140; see especially 114.

23. Rebecca Rush, *Kelroy, a Novel*, ed. Dana D. Nelson (1812. New York: Oxford University Press, 1992), 156.

24. Profits for voyages varied widely, depending on the goods exported to China, the amount of competition for goods in Canton, and the timing of the return to American ports with Chinese goods. By the mid-1820s, increased competition caused the China trade to flatten out, and there were fewer opportunities for individual profit, as the trade became dominated by large firms who established permanent American agents in Canton and eliminated the need for supercargoes (Dulles 113–14).

25. See Philip Freneau, *Poems Written between the Years 1768 and 1794* (Monmouth, N.J.: printed at the press of the author, 1795), 291.

26. See "On Commerce and Luxury" in *The Time Piece* (17 November 1797 and 20 November 1797), which Freneau abstracted from *Of Commerce and Luxury*.

27. For Smith's critique of the French physiocrat system, see vol. 3, book 4, chapter 9 of *An Inquiry into the Nature and Causes of the Wealth of Nations*, rev. ed., 3 vols. (Philadelphia: Dobson, 1789), 7–42.

28. Thomas Cooper, *Political Arithmetic* ([Philadelphia]: 1798), 14.

29. John Taylor, *An Enquiry Into the Principles and Tendency of Certain Public Measures* (Philadelphia: Dobson, 1794), 78.

30. For a brief overview of nonfictional literary critiques (especially poetic ones) of luxury, see Silverman, *A Cultural History of the American Revolution*, 504–19.

31. Reprinted in Gordon S. Wood, ed. *The Rising Glory of America 1760–1820*, rev. ed. (Boston: Northeastern University Press, 1990), 144. Subsequent references to the debate over the Boston Tea Assembly are quoted from *The Rising Glory*, chapter 9 ("The Problem of Luxury") and will be indicated parenthetically in the text.

32. In *Card Sharps, Dream Books, & Bucket Shops: Gambling in Nineteenth-Century America* (Ithaca, N.Y.: Cornell University Press, 1990), Ann Vincent Fabian argues that in the mid- to late nineteenth century, "Gambling . . . became a 'negative analogue,' the one form of gain that made all other efforts to get rich appear normal, natural, and socially salubrious" (5). Thus, she argues, because gambling in

a narrowly defined sense was damned, speculative economic practices became rehabilitated and normalized.

This rehabilitation had not yet begun in the 1790s, however. Instead, land speculation is linked to gambling, and both are described in unmitigatedly negative terms. Indeed, the relationship between gambling and speculation makes activities such as the East India trade appear virtuous by comparison, since it productively (at least for those engaged in commerce) linked an imperialist project with the interests of the bourgeois.

33. *St. Hubert; or, Mistaken Friendship* (District of Columbia: Wood, 1800), iii–iv.

34. In *Enlightenment and the Shadows of Chance: The Novel and the Culture of Gambling in Eighteenth-Century France* (Baltimore: Johns Hopkins University Press, 1993), Thomas M. Kavanagh points out that in early- to mid-eighteenth-century France, gambling was frequently characterized as the "unleashing of potentially uncontrollable passions threatening the individual's sovereign exercise of reason" (35–36). Discussing Jean Barbeyrac's *Traité du Jeu* (Amsterdam: Humbert, 1709), Kavanagh explains, "To gamble was to risk losing all self-control, to create a situation in which one literally did not know what one would do next. Trying to analyze gambling's power to inspire such disarray in otherwise rational individuals, Barbeyrac hypothesized that gambling should be understood not as a single passion but as a monstrously self-perpetuating synthesis of antithetical passions—desire and fear, hope and disappointment, joy and regret, anger and hatred" (61). Although most of Kavanagh's discussion of gambling is relevant only to the particular social structure of eighteenth-century France, he nonetheless sheds fascinating light on the relationship between gambling and social class. Chapter 2, "Gambling as Social Practice," is especially interesting.

35. Caroline Matilda Warren Thayer, *The Gamesters; or Ruins of Innocence. An Original Novel, Founded in Truth* (Boston: Thomas & Andrews, 1805), 190–91.

36. Evermont, the narrator of Jessee L. Holman's *The Prisoners of Niagara, or Errors of Education* (Frankfort, Ky.: William Gerard, 1810) goes so far as to label gambling, even social gambling, "a species of swindling; and the pick pocket and gambler are equally entitled to their gains: they are instigated by the same passion of indolent avarice, and pursue the same object of unrewarded gain; their only difference is, that gambling is tolerated by custom, and practiced by the proud and powerful" (263).

37. Speculation itself was at the center of political controversy between the Jeffersonian Republicans and the Federalists. As McCoy explains, "While supporters of a bankruptcy law generally viewed speculation as the necessary basis for economic growth, Republicans tended to consider it a dangerous activity to be discouraged, not promoted. Perhaps this fear of the social and moral repercussions of uncontrolled speculation was the strongest fear the Jeffersonians had, especially in the wake of a speculative fever in the early months of 1798 that resulted in a wave of defaults and insolvencies" (183).

Jefferson frequently discussed the issue of speculation in his correspondence. In an August 17, 1785, letter to Nathaniel Tracy, Jefferson writes: "It is much to be wished that every discouragement should be thrown in the way of men who undertake to trade without capital. . . . The consumers pay for it in the end, and the debts contracted, and bankruptcies occasioned by such commercial adventurers, bring burthen and disgrace on our country. No man can have a natural right to enter on a calling by which it is at least ten to one he will ruin many better men than himself." See *The Papers of Thomas Jefferson*, ed. Julian P. Boyd (Princeton, N.J.: Princeton University Press), 8:399.

38. Timothy Dwight, *Travels in New England and New York*, 4 vols., ed. Barbara Miller Solomon with Patricia M. King (Cambridge: Belknap Press of Harvard University Press, 1969), 1:158.

39. Originally published in pamphlet form in 1779, *A Second Essay on Free Trade* is reprinted in *Political Essays on the Nature and Operation of Money, Public Finances, and Other Subjects: Published during the American War, and Continued up to the Present Year, 1791* (Philadelphia: Crukshank, 1791); the quotation is from p. 37.

40. Solomon Aiken, *The Rise and Progress of the Political Dissension* (Haverhill, Mass.: Allen, 1811), 13.

41. "Plan for a Nobility," *National Gazette* 7 May 1792. Also in the *National Gazette*, in "Detached Reflections from a Correspondent" (3 November 1793), Freneau claims that "a speculating spirit, if prevalent, is always dangerous in any country." Freneau also wrote satiric poetry about greedy land speculators. See "The Projectors," in *Poems Written between the Years 1768 and 1794*, 224–25.

42. A.W., *A Dandy Song* ([Boston]: 1807).

43. Stephen Burroughs, *Memoirs of Stephen Burroughs*, ed. Philip F. Gura (Boston: Northeastern University Press, 1988), 351, 345.

44. Hezekiah N. Woodruff, *The Danger of Ambition Considered, in a Sermon Preached at Scipio, N.Y., the Lord's Day, August 12, 1804: Occasioned by the Death of General Alexander Hamilton, Who Fell in a Duel with Aaron Burr, Vice-President of the United States of America, on the 11th Day of July, 1804* (Albany, N.Y.: Webster, 1804), 7.

45. John Adams, *Discourses on Davila*, in *The Works of John Adams*, ed. Charles Francis Adams (Boston: 1851), vol. 6: 233–34.

46. Juvenile works, in particular, praise industry, rather than ambition, which is not surprising since these works generally feature the working class or the worthy poor as inspirational models. Clearly honest industry was seen as a more suitable goal for the poor than ambition, which was stimulated by overweening pride. A sampling of such juvenile works published in America in multiple editions includes: *The Instructive Story of Industry and Sloth*, an allegorical tale comparing two households; Maria Edgeworth's *Idleness and Industry Exemplified in the History of James Preston and Lazy Lawrence*, a story comparing the behavior of two children; and *Dame Partlet's Farm: Containing an Account of the Great Riches She Obtained by*

Industry . . ., a tale of a poor widow who through industry obtains a farm. The anonymous work *The Little Islanders: or, Blessings of Industry*, a brief novel in which the children of titled parents imitate Crusoe and thereby learn habits of industry, crosses class lines in an interesting way and provides a notable exception to the advocacy of industry for the poor.

Not until the mid- to late nineteenth century does ambition supplement or supplant industry as a central tenet of male conduct and advice literature, as Sarah E. Newton notes in *Learning to Behave: A Guide to American Conduct Books before 1900*, 53–54.

47. Benjamin Franklin, *The Autobiography of Benjamin Franklin*, ed. Leonard W. Labaree et al. (New Haven, Conn.: Yale University Press, 1964), 149.

48. The most comprehensive source of information about Rebecca Rush is Dana D. Nelson's profile of her in the recently reprinted edition of *Kelroy*, in which Nelson details her painstaking, but largely unfruitful, research into Rush's life. See Nelson, Introduction, *Kelroy, a Novel*, by Rebecca Rush (New York: Oxford University Press, 1992), xi–xxiv. For more information about Wood, see Karen A. Weyler, "Profile: Sally Sayward Barrell Keating Wood," *Legacy: A Journal of American Women Writers* 15.2 (1998): 204–12.

49. Kathryn Zabelle Derounian convincingly argues that *Kelroy* is a hybrid of the romance and the novel of manners, since Rush pits two essentially romantic characters, Emily and Kelroy, against the social reality of the novel of manners as represented by Mrs. Hammond, who is, above all, the shallow product of materialistic cultural expectations. See Derounian, "Lost in the Crowd: Rebecca Rush's *Kelroy*," *American Transcendental Quarterly* 47–48 (1980): 117–26.

50. Steve Hamelman addresses Mrs. Hamilton's aphasia at some length via a deconstructive reading of the various silences and failures of speech in *Kelroy*. See "Aphasia in Rebecca Rush's *Kelroy*," *South Atlantic Review* 62.2 (1997): 88–110.

51. For a contemporary, nonfiction discussion of the scrip problem, see Pelatiah Webster's exuberantly titled *A Plea for the Poor Soldiers: Or, an Essay to Demonstrate that the Soldiers and Other Public Creditors, Who Really and Actually Supported the Burden of the Late War, Have Not Been Paid, Ought to Be Paid, Can Be Paid and Must Be Paid*, reprinted in Webster's *Political Essays on the Nature and Operation of Money, Public Finances, and Other Subjects: Published During the American War, and Continued up to the Present Year, 1791*, 306–43.

52. Indeed, through her opposition to gambling and excessive luxury, Aurelia emerges as an advocate of near-spartan republicanism. As part of a discussion about the dangers of fashion, Aurelia argues that "I have often thought . . . we should be better and happier for sumptuary laws. If we were obliged by the legislature not to alter the mode of our dress but once in ten years, it would save a great deal of trouble, needless expense, and waste of time" (80).

53. At this time, the Yazoo purchase was the linchpin in frontier land speculation, because those lands, which compose the present-day states of Alabama and

Mississippi, bordered the Mississippi River; their purchase would open that part of the country up to profitable trade. The land in question was under dispute, however, since Spain, various Indian tribes, and the states of Georgia and South Carolina claimed it. Induced by bribes, the Georgia legislature sold thirty million acres to four separate companies for five hundred thousand dollars—about one and a half cents per acre. As A. M. Sakolski explains in *The Great American Land Bubble* (New York: Harper, 1932), "Georgia did not guarantee title against other claimants, and disclaimed responsibility for the acts or claims of the Indians" (133). Following these sales, there was tremendous speculation of shares; many purchasers bought these shares on credit and soon amassed speculative fortunes, which they lost just as quickly when land values stabilized. Outraged Georgians soon protested the sale of what they viewed as their land and demanded that the legislature repudiate the act authorizing the sale of the land. Although Georgia offered to refund payments, most purchasers did not take advantage of this offer and instead continued to speculate in shares of this land. The claims on this property were not settled until 1815, at which time the settlement benefited wealthy speculators who were able to buy shares cheaply and gamble on a future profit at the time of settlement.

54. Edward W. Said, *Culture and Imperialism* (New York: Knopf, 1993), 64. The entire second chapter of *Culture and Imperialism* is useful for understanding the economically imperial (yet anti-colonialist) orientation of the United States in the early national era. Also useful for thinking about the United States and imperialism is Amy Kaplan's "'Left Alone with America': The Absence of Empire in the Study of American Culture," *Cultures of United States Imperialism*, ed. Amy Kaplan and Donald E. Pease (Durham, N.C., and London: Duke University Press, 1993): 3–21. Kaplan points out that "[I]mperialism as a political or economic process abroad is inseparable from the social relations and cultural discourses of race, gender, ethnicity, and class at home.... Foregrounding imperialism in the study of American cultures shows how putatively domestic conflicts are not simply contained at home but how they both emerge in response to international struggles and spill over national boundaries ..." (16). Said's and Kaplan's comments help us understand the centrality of international trade in forging American nationalism and enabling American bourgeois subjectivity, especially when triangulated against British colonialist policy and the East Indies.

55. In *Imagined Communities: Reflections on the Origin and Spread of Nationalism*, Benedict Anderson addresses the importance of vernacular print culture in the formation of "imaginary communities," which he claims contributed to the rise of modern nationalism.

56. William E. Lenz, *Fast Talk and Flush Times: The Confidence Man as a Literary Convention* (Columbia: University of Missouri Press, 1985), 1.

57. Several works on confidence men discuss Franklin and Stephen Burroughs as such. In particular, see Gary Lindberg, *The Confidence Man in American Literature* (New York: Oxford University Press, 1982), chapter 3, "Benjamin Franklin and the

Model Self." Also useful is Daniel E. Williams, "In Defense of Self: Author and Authority in *The Memoirs of Stephen Burroughs*," *Early American Literature* 25.2 (1990): 96–122. The fact that Burroughs's work moves easily between fact and what appears to be fiction helps it bridge the differences among the genres of autobiography, polemical political tracts, and fiction; while Burroughs is certainly concerned with the creation of self, it is not the ideal, public self modeled by Franklin, but rather a fluid self more closely akin to that of the confidence man.

Chapter 4
Gentleman Strangers and Dangerous Deceptions

1. See Alan Axelrod, *Charles Brockden Brown: An American Tale* (Austin: University of Texas Press, 1983); Tompkins, *Sensational Designs: The Cultural Work of American Fiction 1790–1860*; Davidson, *Revolution and the Word: The Rise of the Novel in America*; Robert S. Levine, *Conspiracy and Romance: Studies in Brockden Brown, Cooper, Hawthorne, and Melville* (New York: Cambridge University Press, 1989); Warner, *The Letters of the Republic: Publication and the Public Sphere in Eighteenth-Century America*; Ziff, *Writing in the New Nation*; Christophersen, *The Apparition in the Glass: Charles Brockden Brown's American Gothic*; Steven Watts, *The Romance of Real Life: Charles Brockden Brown and the Origins of American Culture*; Christopher Looby, *Voicing America: Language, Literary Form, and the Origins of the United States* (Chicago: University of Chicago Press, 1996); Stern, *The Plight of Feeling: Sympathy and Dissent in the Early American Novel*; Edward Watts, *Writing and Postcolonialism in the Early Republic*; and Goddu, *Gothic America: Narrative, History, and Nation*. In her introduction to *Gothic America*, Goddu provides a succinct overview of how American writers and literary critics have employed the gothic; see 1–12.

2. For a useful overview of political anxieties over issues of representation, see Waldstreicher, *In the Midst of Perpetual Fetes*, 60–78.

3. Ziff points out that by 1900 thirty editions of Burroughs's *Memoirs* had appeared (59). For recent work on criminal conduct, see Daniel E. Williams, ed., *Pillars of Salt: An Anthology of Early American Criminal Narratives* (Madison: Madison House, 1993) and Daniel A. Cohen, *Pillars of Salt, Monuments of Grace: New England Crime Literature and the Origins of American Popular Culture, 1674–1860* (New York: Oxford University Press, 1993).

4. Cornelia Hughes Dayton addresses the issue of social fluidity and the greater leeway given to young men who violated social codes throughout "Taking the Trade: Abortion and Gender Relations in an Eighteenth-Century New England Village."

5. Terence Martin made this point in "Social Institutions in the Early American Novel," *American Quarterly* 9.1 (1957): 72–84. Speaking of the importance of the family in American fiction, he argues, "Danger arises only when one is alienated in

some way from the family group. Conversely, an immoral and decadent person is generally without family ties (decadence is at once the cause and the result of alienation); he has either broken away from family relationships, or, as is sometimes the case, he may appear never to have been a part of any family group. And in sentimental fiction the lone character is very often suspect" (77).

6. James Henretta discusses the social and economic implications of population growth in late eighteenth-century New England and the mid-Atlantic states and argues that, by the end of the eighteenth century, population pressures reduced the amount of land available for inheritance. Consequently, Henretta argues, "Unable to settle all of their male offspring on the already subdivided family estate, fathers lost a vital measure of control over the lives of their children" (26). Early American fiction mirrors this historical development, frequently exploring the strain placed on family relations when parents could no longer provide economically secure futures for their children.

7. See *Amicable Society Rules* (Baltimore: W. Goddard and J. Angell, 1791). In discussing the figure of the rake in *The Power of Sympathy*, *The Coquette*, and *Charlotte Temple*, Gareth Evans notes the European influence on the rake and the tendency for this rake to be "an un-American and unrepublican purveyor of the corrupt 'European' morals that threaten to destroy America" (44). See Evans, "Rakes, Coquettes and Republican Patriarchs: Class, Gender and Nation in Early American Sentimental Fiction," *Canadian Review of American Studies* 25.3 (1995): 41–62. Certainly American depictions of the rake do emphasize this character type's British origins, but there are important differences in the way the American rake is depicted. Social, economic, and geographical mobility enable the rake to move freely in American society.

8. While to some extent drawing upon gothic conventions, the prevalence of criminal conduct and the omnipresent prison scene in early novels also reflect concern in the late eighteenth-century transatlantic community with penal reform and new theories of punishment. Reformist thinkers like Cesare Beccaria strongly influenced such Americans as Benjamin Franklin, Thomas Jefferson, and John Adams in their reasoning about the need for a humane, rational system of punishments, proportional to the crime committed. Beccaria and his followers' ideas about reform stem from the notion of harnessing and cultivating the passions, rather than repressing them, and in this sense were consistent with current pedagogical theories. See, for example, Cesare Beccaria, *On Crimes and Punishments and Other Writings* (1765. New York: Cambridge University Press, 1995); Marcello Maestro, *Cesare Beccaria and the Origins of Penal Reform* (Philadelphia: Temple University Press, 1973); and Adolph Caso, *America's Italian Founding Fathers* (Boston: Branden Press, 1975).

9. The prison is likewise a central trope in British fiction. John Bender's *Imagining the Penitentiary: Fiction and the Architecture of the Mind in Eighteenth-Century England* (Chicago: University of Chicago Press, 1987) credits the novel with help-

ing create the state of mind and feeling that led to the modern penitentiary and modern conceptions of punishment. Bender writes, "Fabrications in narrative of the power of confinement to reshape personality contributed to a process of cultural representation whereby prisons were themselves reconceived and ultimately reinvented" (1). Further, "These penitentiaries assumed novelistic ideas of character and re-presented the sensible world (both to their inmates and to the public at large) in order to alter motivation and, ultimately, to reconstruct the fictions of personal identity that underlie consciousness" (2).

10. The past several decades have produced extensive literature regarding eighteenth-century penal reform. For a sampling of some of the most important works on this subject, see Michel Foucault, *Discipline and Punish: The Birth of the Prison* and Michael Ignatieff, *A Just Measure of Pain: The Penitentiary in the Industrial Revolution, 1750–1850* (New York: Pantheon Books, 1978). Of particular interest to scholars of the early Republic are David Rothman, *The Discovery of the Asylum: Social Order and Disorder in the New Republic* (Boston: Little, 1971) and Michael Meranze, *Laboratories of Virtue: Punishment, Revolution, and Authority in Philadelphia, 1760–1835* (Chapel Hill: University of North Carolina Press, 1996).

11. My thinking about debt, insolvency, and bankruptcy has been influenced by Peter J. Coleman's *Debtors and Creditors in America: Insolvency, Imprisonment for Debt, and Bankruptcy, 1607–1900* (Madison: State Historical Society of Wisconsin, 1974). Especially useful is chapter 18, "Imprisonment for Debt." Debtor-creditor relationships were immensely complicated in the years after the Revolution, with each state passing individual and often conflicting laws, for it was unclear whether Congress had the constitutional authority to pass federal laws governing these relationships.

Coleman notes that there was an increase in the rate of defaults over the course of the eighteenth century disproportionate to the increase in population, with a particularly high rate of defaults in the decades after the Revolution. He speculates: "As lending and borrowing became commonplace, credit pervaded every facet of life from the wide-ranging operations of the largest merchants to the simplest purchases of humble farmers. Moreover, as more and more people came to confuse the over-all success of colonization with their own capacities to prosper, they assumed a larger burden of debt than their prospects warranted. As a result, the incidence of default grew at a faster pace than did the population itself" (251). Meanwhile, the transition to impersonal debtor-creditor relationships contributed to an increase in arrests and imprisonments for debt. Coleman notes, however, that "The poor were the chief victims. About sixty percent of [those imprisoned for debt] owed no more than ten dollars" (254). Nonetheless, the imprisonment of public figures such as William Duer and Robert Morris drew attention to the debtors' prisons, while penal reformers and critics of the debtor laws—and novelists, as well, I will argue—drew attention to ineffective policies. Coleman suggests that a certain amount of the criticism of debtor laws actually "fed the effort to cut the ties to the Anglo-Saxon legal heritage, especially in the common law, and strengthened the attack on imprisonment for debt by branding it as an Old World anachronism which had no place in a republican society of virtuous, free men" (257). Significant revisions of debtor laws occurred between 1811 and Reconstruction, during which time most eastern states prohibited imprisonment for debt except in cases of suspected fraud (256).

12. All quotations from Klein in this and the following paragraph are from "The Third Earl of Shaftesbury and the Progress of Politeness," *Eighteenth-Century Studies* 18 (1985): 186–214. Klein suggests in this essay that critics of politeness in eighteenth-century Britain were concerned about the relationship between politeness and the seductiveness of luxury, a concern that would resonate in America. Also useful is Klein's "Berkely, Shaftesbury, and the Meaning of Politeness," *Studies in Eighteenth-Century Culture* 16 (1986): 57–68.

13. Warner notes, "Strikingly, but perhaps not coincidentally, a vastly disproportionate number of colonial belletrists, from Byles to the Tuesday Club to William Smith's Philadelphia Circle, showed loyalist sympathies during the imperial crisis. The connection seemed logical to the more radically republican Americans at the time, since until the last quarter of the century the republican paradigm classed politeness with the corrupt insubstantiality of persons in aristocratic society" (133).

14. Ann Murry, *Mentoria, or, the Young Ladies Instructor* (New York: Moore, 1812), 47.

15. For more information about "politeness" as a central issue of the Sans Souci Club dispute, see Wood, *The Creation of the American Republic, 1776–1787*, 422–23, and *The Rising Glory of America*, 137–53.

16. *Sans Souci, Alias, Free and Easy, or, an Evening's Peep into a Polite Circle* (Boston: Warden and Russell, 1785), 22. A second edition appeared in the same year. The attribution to Warren is tentative and seems to be suggested by the fact that a Mrs. W———n appears among the cast voicing republican sentiments.

17. *The Coquette* is not singular in its use of titles in this fashion; titles in early American fiction are often used to indicate a general (but fallacious) presumption of honor. For example, the father of Amelia in *Amelia; or, the Faithless Briton* naively assumes that the rank of Doliscus, a British officer and nobleman, will ensure that he treats Amelia honorably.

18. Dietmar Schloss has argued for an essentially positive representation of politeness in the novel. See Schloss, "Republicanism and Politeness in the Early American Novel," *Early America Re-Explored: New Readings in Colonial, Early National, and Antebellum Culture*, ed. by Klaus H. Schmidt and Fritz Fleischmann (New York: Peter Lang, 2000), 269–90.

While I concur with Schloss's argument that modern criticism has overemphasized the role of democratic individualism in the early American novel as a genre (270), I read this rendering of polite society much more ambivalently. It is true that polite society as depicted in *The Coquette* creates a space for women's public voices.

However, the Richmans, models of polite society, allow Sanford unlimited access to Eliza, despite their reservations about his reputation and intentions. Further, when given the opportunity, they *retreat* from the polite world, preferring, as Eliza notes, their own company and the intimacy of the private, domestic environment. I see similar ambivalence about politeness and polite society expressed throughout early American fiction, given the ease with which credit economies enable men of dubious virtue to enter such society.

19. In this instance as in others, Sanford proves himself a master rhetorician. As Jay Fliegelman argues in *Declaring Independence*, quoting James Burgh from *The Art of Speaking*, "The creation of desire, that 'internal act, which, by influencing the will, makes one proceed to action,' was in the view of virtually all the period's rhetoricians the ultimate purpose of all oratory" (32). Wilbur Samuel Howell, quoting Hugh Blair, similarly argues that eloquence is "The Art of Persuasion" (654). See Howell, *Eighteenth-Century British Logic and Rhetoric* (Princeton, N.J.: Princeton University Press, 1971).

20. In *The Protestant Temperament: Patterns of Child-Rearing, Religious Experience, and the Self in Early America* (New York: Knopf, 1977), Philip Greven notes that "the genteel were notably indifferent to most of the issues that concerned both evangelicals and moderates, feeling very comfortable about themselves and indeed experiencing a sense of self-confidence that set them apart from most people. They were far more at ease with themselves, their desires, and their pleasures than were others, for they lived without the burdens of conscience and guilt that so often shaped the sensibilities and the self of evangelicals and moderates. . . . Self-assertion rather than self-control or self-suppression was to be the central theme of many of their lives, thus revealing just how different they were from those who were moderates or evangelicals" (14).

21. In a wonderfully thought-provoking essay, Lawrence E. Klein questions how the terms "private" and "public" have been used in recent scholarship concerned with eighteenth-century culture. He suggests that, too often, "the concerns of analysts of the nineteenth century are imposed on the eighteenth" (105); thus scholars overlook the fluidity in the meaning and usage of "private" and "public" in the eighteenth century. In considering these overlapping public spheres, Klein further argues that there are many "public" spheres in which women participated, including legal, civic, economic, and cultural venues. See Klein, "Gender and the Public/Private Distinction in the Eighteenth Century: Some Questions about Evidence and Analytic Procedure," *Eighteenth-Century Studies* 29.1 (1995): 97–109. Lucy Freeman Sumner's marriage is one of those events that straddles the boundary between private and public event; her wedding is public in the sense that it is an event taking place openly, with participation more open perhaps than she would like.

22. See Gillian Brown, *The Consent of the Governed*, 124.

23. For a detailed discussion of the composition of *Arthur Mervyn*, see Norman S. Grabo's "Historical Essay" in the Kent State University Press edition of the novel.

24. James H. Justus, "Arthur Mervyn, American," *American Literature* 42.3 (1970): 315. Justus adds, "It is possible, I think to read *Arthur Mervyn*, despite its hero's homilies, as a novel about the generative power of money, its power to promote both greed and benevolence, crime and charity. It is the single undeniable requirement for the society to which Arthur aspires" (314).

Certainly economic issues are not absent from Brown's other works; indeed, debt and other economic concerns figure prominently in a number of his works, including Constantia Dudley's poverty in *Ormond*, Edgar Huntly's lack of an inheritance or means to support himself, and the debt for which Bredloe in "The Man at Home" is liable, to name just a few.

25. Mervyn is in many ways an androgynous character. His facility with feminine occupations such as knitting and his disinterest in masculine pursuits astonish Mrs. Althorpe. She contends, "Persons of his age are rarely fond of work, but then they are addicted to company, and sports, and exercises. They ride, or shoot, or frolic; but this being moped away his time in solitude, never associated with other young people, never mounted an horse but when he could not help it, and never fired a gun or angled for a fish in his life" (233).

Further, as I describe earlier, Mervyn, like the female characters of epistolary fiction, espouses similar beliefs about the virtue of writing in pursuit of self-discipline, calling the pen "a pacifyer" (414). In this context, Welbeck's forgery, his maimed hand, and his resultant inability to write take on new meaning and speak to his inability to discipline himself. One wonders if Marney in Rebecca Rush's 1812 novel *Kelroy*, likewise a forger with a maimed hand, owes anything to Welbeck.

26. John Bennett, *Strictures on Female Education; Chiefly as It Relates to the Culture of the Heart. In Four Essays. By a Clergyman of the Church of England* (Norwich, Conn.: Ebenezer Bushnell, 1792), vol. 2, 48–49.

27. For a different view of the relationship between Charles Brockden Brown and Benjamin Franklin, and between Franklin and Mervyn, see Alan Axelrod's extended discussion in chapter 6 of *Charles Brockden Brown: An American Tale*.

28. As Fliegelman explains about late eighteenth-century American rhetoric in *Declaring Independence*, "Speaking ... [became] less a form of argumentative or expository communication than a revelation of 'internal moral dispositions' and passions registered by vocal tones, physical 'exertions,' and facial expressions that are received in unmediated form by the sympathetic 'social' nature of the auditor" (30).

29. Brown likewise promises in this letter that Mervyn will marry Eliza Hadwin, who will inherit her father's estate after he dies—none of which happens except for the death of Mr. Hadwin. See William Dunlap, *The Life of Charles Brockden Brown*, vol. 2 (Philadelphia: Parke, 1815), 98.

30. See Bataille, 118–20.

31. For a different take on institutions during the early Republic era, see Shirley Samuels, *Romances of the Republic: Women, the Family, and Violence in the Literature*

of the Early American Nation, chapter 1: "Plague and Politics in 1793: *Arthur Mervyn*," 23–43. Whereas I argue that *Arthur Mervyn* delineates the failure of social institutions, Samuels claims that the novel "documents the rise of institutions of social order—and particularly the institution of the family—that counter the linked threats of revolution, contagion, and political and sexual infidelity" (30). She contends that Mervyn's fantasies about reconstructing a family for himself suggest Brown's particular interest in "a restored family as a restored form of institutional order. Without a family, Arthur feels like and is treated as a displaced person, a refugee without connections who can be fitted into any available slot. Not until he has carefully collected a father, a mother, and a sister, can he train for a career and take his place in a world which is now placed around him" (32).

Brown leaves Arthur's family arrangement dangerously tenuous, however, deferring his marriage until after the close of the novel. Further, every family in the novel, excepting the Stevens family, is devastated in one way or another: the Mervyn family is ravaged by inherited disease, seduction, and alcoholism; the Hadwin family is destroyed by the plague, immoderate grief, and greed; the Lodis are devastated by violence and seduction; the Watsons are destroyed by seduction and murder; the entire Thetford family is wiped out by yellow fever after the greedy father refuses to leave his business in the city; and Achsa Fielding's family is crushed by debt, suicide, and seduction. Indeed, internal threats deriving from greed, lust, or fear ultimately are as destructive to these families as are (and perhaps even more so than) external threats such as the plague. This mass destruction of families suggests to me that the weakening of traditional social controls, represented in part by the breakdown of the family itself, enables dangerous characters like Welbeck to thrive initially. For that matter, the breakup of his own family enables Mervyn to escape to Philadelphia, where he himself eventually thrives.

32. Despite his horror, Mervyn also fantasizes about taking charge of the hospital. This is a fantasy of benevolence, but Mervyn's benevolence in this instance, as in most instances found in early American fiction, is also a fantasy of power. Martha Read's *Monima, or the Beggar Girl* (New York: P. R. Johnson, for L. N. Ralston, 1802) provides an interesting counterpoint to this view of philanthropy as a way to reinscribe social relations.

33. In *Sensational Designs*, Jane Tompkins advises readers to consider the larger consequences of burning this currency, given the contemporary shortage of hard currency. Welbeck's crimes—stealing and lying about the counterfeit status of Lodi's money—affect more than Lodi's sister, Clemenza: they threaten the already weak local and national economies (76–77).

34. As Edward Watts sees it, the question of Mervyn's reliability is the key to the novel: "By inviting heteroglossic interpretations of Arthur, Brown brings to the readership the need for rigorous critical thought and self-examination, asking them to see in themselves what Stephen Slemon calls 'the ambivalent, the mediated, the conditional, and the radically compromised' nature of Second World ex-

perience (10) instead of the stable but false world and text of the republic" (121). By refusing to control the process of interpretation, Watts argues, writers of the early Republic "cut the reader adrift from the institutionalized forms of authority imposed by the republican elite" (23). Consequently, the individual reader must independently interpret texts, a process we see enacted and reenacted with *Arthur Mervyn*.

35. In chapter 5, "The Dynamics of Discipline," Meranze discusses hygienic and moral reforms, as well as the physical separation of the prisoners. See especially 173–89.

36. Welbeck fears punishment and disgrace far more than death, and he would rather die than "be subjected to the necessity of honest labor" (199). After Watson discovers the whereabouts of Welbeck, who had seduced Watson's married sister, Welbeck explains to Mervyn: "To be a fugitive from exasperated creditors, and from the industrious revenge of Watson, was an easy undertaking; but whither could I fly, where I should not be pursued by the phantoms of remorse, by the dread of hourly detection, by the necessities of hunger and thirst? In what scene should I be exempt from servitude and drudgery? Was my existence embellished with enjoyments that would justify my holding it, encumbered with hardships, and immersed in obscurity?" (103). Welbeck's initial comments suggest to Mervyn that he regrets the actions that he has committed. Then Welbeck spoils this regretful pretense by adding, "In what scene should I be exempt from servitude and drudgery?" and questioning whether a life lived in "obscurity" is worth living, again suggesting his driving concern with esteem.

37. In *Declaring Independence*, Fliegelman briefly considers the relationship between punishment and public exposure. He writes, "On the dangers of excessive public exposure, Jefferson reports in his *Autobiography* on a reformist experience to replace, for a certain class of criminals, capital punishment with hard labor conducted in public: 'Exhibited as a public spectacle, with shaved heads and mean clothing, working on the high roads, produced in the criminals such a prostration of character, such an abandonment of self-respect, as, instead of reforming, plunged them into the most desperate and hardened depravity of morals and character.'" Fliegelman concludes, "To transform an individual into a public spectacle is itself a crime" (122).

38. For an extended discussion of bankruptcy in the British novel, see Barbara Weiss, *The Hell of the English: Bankruptcy and the Victorian Novel* (Lewisburg, Pa.: Bucknell University Press, 1986). Imprisonment for debt in America in all likelihood held considerably less stigma than Weiss argues it had in nineteenth-century England, perhaps because British bankruptcy laws originated from the criminal codes developed during the reign of Henry VIII to punish fraudulent or crooked traders.

39. Hans Robert Jauss, *Toward an Aesthetic of Reception*, trans. Timothy Bahti (St. Paul: University of Minnesota Press, 1982), 23.

Epilogue

1. Kevin J. Hayes summarizes American readers' responses to the four-volume *Pamela* in *A Colonial Woman's Bookshelf*, 103–14.

2. In a discussion of *Kelroy*, Jeffrey H. Richards has pointed out that, rather than bestow sympathy, members of the elite class often threatened servants and social inferiors with violence. Pointing to the diary of Elizabeth Drinker, Richards suggests that this violence was not limited to fiction. See Richards, "Decorous Violence: Manners, Class, and Abuse in Rebecca Rush's *Kelroy*," in *Over the Threshold: Intimate Violence in Early America*, ed. Christine Daniels and Michael V. Kennedy (New York and London: Routledge, 1999): 202–16. *Kelroy* is not the only novel in which servants are treated with violence or contempt. Teague O'Regan, the poor Irish servant or "bogtrotter," in Hugh Henry Brackenridge's *Modern Chivalry* is, literally, a comic whipping boy for Captain Farrago and the narrator. While American slaves and servants are not at this time the stock comic characters found frequently in the eighteenth-century British novel, they are often used for comic purposes or to reveal some facet of the white, middle-class subject of the novel. Teague O'Regan's various occupational adventures—as an actor, a politician, a philosopher, etc.—as he and his employer, Captain Farrago, tour the newly-formed United States are all designed to puncture the pretensions of these groups and expose the hypocrisy, greed, and social snobbery rampant in the early Republic.

3. Elizabeth Barnes, "Affecting Relations: Pedagogy, Patriarchy, and the Politics of Sympathy," *American Literary History* 8.4 (1996): 606–7.

4. Martha Read's *Monima, or the Beggar Girl* is a fascinating early fictional examination of poverty. Monima is not born poor but rather is the daughter of a formerly wealthy French family of high social status. Although her marriage at the conclusion of the novel to Sonnetton, her "benefactor," restores Monima's social position, the humiliation she endures from her poverty is unmatched in early American fiction. Sentiment and sensibility sustain this novel, and after her marriage, Monima becomes "the soother of the afflicted, the mother to the orphan, the supporter of the oppressed, and the indulgent friend to the sufferer of sensibility" (464). For a discussion of sentiment and benevolence in this novel, see Joseph Fichtelberg, "Friendless in Philadelphia: The Feminist Critique of Martha Meredith Read," *Early American Literature* 32.3 (1997): 205–21.

5. As Michael Warner points out in *The Letters of the Republic*, "You can be a member of the nation, attributing its agency to yourself in imaginary identification, without being a freeholder or exercising any agency in the public sphere. Nationalism makes no distinction between such imaginary participation and the active participation of citizens. In republicanism that distinction counted for everything" (173). In this sense, there was a hollow core at the center of nineteenth-century liberalism, whereby the affinity individuals may have felt for the United States as a nation was not always politically or socially rewarded.

6. Harriet Beecher Stowe, *Uncle Tom's Cabin*, ed. Elizabeth Ammons (New York: Norton, 1994), 8.

7. Lori Merish discusses at length how "white maternal care," or sentimental ownership, is used to create sympathy for black slaves (154); Merish argues that Stowe "(re)constructs black slaves as gendered 'subjects' by situating them within the sentimental bonds of domestic intimacy" (156). See *Sentimental Materialism*, 152–59.

8. Sandra M. Gilbert and Susan Gubar, *The Madwoman in the Attic: The Woman Writer and the Nineteenth-Century Literary Imagination* (New Haven, Conn., and London: Yale University Press, 1979), 533–35.

9. The oppressiveness of such bourgeois values is nowhere made more clear than in a work about—and by—another slave, Harriet Jacobs, who in *Incidents in the Life of a Slave Girl* torturously justifies her deviation from white, middle-class sexual mores. On the other hand, Stowe clearly saw *free* blacks as capable of adopting such bourgeois values, as evidenced by her portrayal of the peaceful, disciplined domestic environment that Eliza and George establish once they have escaped to Canada, where George seeks to improve himself and his family by self-study.

Bibliography

Adams, John. *Discourses on Davila* in *The Works of John Adams*. Ed. Charles Francis Adams. Boston: Little, Brown, 1851.
Aiken, Solomon. *The Rise and Progress of the Political Dissension*. Haverhill, Mass.: Allen, 1811.
Altman, Janet Gurkin. *Epistolarity: Approaches to a Form*. Columbus: Ohio State University Press, 1982.
Amelia; or, the Faithless Briton. Boston: Spotswood and Wayne, 1798.
The American Letter-Writer: Containing a Variety of Letters on the Most Common Occasions in Life. Philadelphia: McCullough, 1793.
Amicable Society Rules. Baltimore: W. Goddard and J. Angell, 1791.
Anderson, Alexander. *An Inaugural Dissertation on Chronic Mania*. New York: Swords, 1796.
Anderson, Benedict. *Imagined Communities: Reflections on the Origin and Spread of Nationalism*. London: Verso, 1983.
Appleby, Joyce. *Capitalism and a New Social Order: The Republican Vision of the 1790s*. New York: New York University Press, 1984.
——. *Liberalism and Republicanism in the Historical Imagination*. Cambridge: Harvard University Press, 1992.
Armstrong, Nancy. *Desire and Domestic Fiction: A Political History of the Novel*. New York: Oxford University Press, 1987.
Armstrong, Nancy, and Leonard Tennenhouse. *The Imaginary Puritan: Literature, Intellectual Labor, and the Origins of Personal Life*. Berkeley: University of California Press, 1992.
Axelrod, Alan. *Charles Brockden Brown: An American Tale*. Austin: University of Texas Press, 1983.
Axtell, James L. Introduction. *The Educational Writings of John Locke*. London: Cambridge University Press, 1968.
Baker, Dorothy Z. " 'Detested be the Epithet!': Definition, Maxim, and the Lan-

guage of Social Dicta in Hannah Webster Foster's *The Coquette*." *Essays in Literature* 23.1 (1996): 58–68.

Bakhtin, M. M. *The Dialogic Imagination*. Ed. Michael Holquist. Trans. Caryl Emerson and Michael Holquist. Austin: University of Texas Press, 1981.

Barker-Benfield, G. J. *The Culture of Sensibility: Sex and Society in Eighteenth-Century Britain*. Chicago: University of Chicago Press, 1992.

Barnes, Elizabeth. "Affecting Relations: Pedagogy, Patriarchy, and the Politics of Sympathy." *American Literary History* 8.4 (1996): 597–614.

———. *States of Sympathy: Seduction and Democracy in the American Novel*. New York: Columbia University Press, 1997.

Bataille, Georges. "The Notion of Expenditure." In *Visions of Excess: Selected Writings, 1927–1939*. Ed. Allan Stoekl. Trans. Allan Stoekl with Carl R. Lovitt and Donald M. Leslie, Jr. Minneapolis: University of Minnesota Press, 1985. 116–29.

Beales, Ross W., and James N. Green. "Libraries and Their Uses." In *A History of the Book in America: The Colonial Book in the Atlantic World*. Ed. Hugh Amory and David D. Hall. Cambridge and New York: Cambridge University Press, 2000. 399–404.

Beccaria, Cesare. *On Crimes and Punishments and Other Writings*. 1765. Ed. Richard Bellamy. Trans. Richard Davies with Virginia Cox and Richard Bellamy. New York: Cambridge University Press, 1995.

[Belknap, Jeremy.] *The Foresters, an American Tale: Being a Sequel to the History of John Bull the Clothier. In a Series of Letters to a Friend*. 1792. Upper Saddle River, N.J.: Gregg Press, 1970.

Bender, John. *Imagining the Penitentiary: Fiction and the Architecture of the Mind in Eighteenth-Century England*. Chicago: University of Chicago Press, 1987.

Bennett, John. *Letters to a Young Lady*. 2 vols. Hartford, Conn.: Hudson, 1791.

———. *Strictures on Female Education; Chiefly as It Relates to the Culture of the Heart. In Four Essays. By a Clergyman of the Church of England*. Norwich, Conn.: Ebenezer Bushnell, 1792.

Bennett, Tony. *Formalism and Marxism*. London: Methuen, 1979.

Berry, Christopher J. *The Idea of Luxury: A Conceptual and Historical Investigation*. New York: Cambridge University Press, 1994.

Berthoff, W. B. "Adventures of the Young Man: An Approach to Charles Brockden Brown." *American Quarterly* 9 (1957): 421–34.

Blair, Hugh. *Lectures on Rhetoric and Belles Lettres*. 2 vols. 2nd American ed. Philadelphia: Carey, 1793.

Blecki, Catherine La Courreye, and Karin A. Wulf. *Milcah Martha Moore's Book: A Commonplace Book from Revolutionary America*. University Park: Pennsylvania State University Press, 1997.

Bloch, Ruth. "The Gendered Meanings of Virtue in Revolutionary America." *Signs* 13.1 (1987): 37–58.

Blumin, Stuart M. *The Emergence of the Middle Class: Social Experience in the American City, 1760–1900*. New York: Cambridge University Press, 1989.

Bontatibus, Donna R. *The Seduction Novel of the Early Nation: A Call for Socio-Political Reform*. East Lansing: Michigan State University Press, 1999.

Bourdieu, Pierre. *Outline of a Theory of Practice*. 1972. Trans. Richard Nice. New York and Cambridge: Cambridge University Press, 1977.

Brackenridge, Hugh Henry. *Modern Chivalry*. Ed. Claude M. Newlin. New York: American Book Company, 1937.

Breen, T. H. " 'Baubles of Britain': The American and Consumer Revolutions of the Eighteenth Century." *Past and Present* 119 (1988): 73–104.

———. "An Empire of Goods: The Anglicization of Colonial America, 1690–1776." *Journal of British Studies* 25.4 (1986): 467–99.

———. "Narrative of Commercial Life: Consumption, Ideology, and Community on the Eve of the American Revolution." *William and Mary Quarterly* 50.1 (1993): 471–501.

Brodhead, Richard H. *Cultures of Letters: Scenes of Reading and Writing in Nineteenth-Century America*. Chicago: University of Chicago Press, 1993.

Brooks, Peter. *Reading for the Plot: Design and Intention in Narrative*. Cambridge: Harvard University Press, 1992.

Brown, Charles Brockden. *Arthur Mervyn: or, Memoirs of the Year 1793*. 2 vols. 1799–1800. Kent, Ohio: Kent State University Press, 1980.

———. *Edgar Huntly; or, Memoirs of a Sleep-Walker*. 1799. Kent, Ohio: Kent State University Press, 1984.

———. "The Man at Home." 1798. In *The Rhapsodist and Other Uncollected Writings by Charles Brockden Brown*. Ed. Harry R. Warfel. New York: Scholars' Facsimiles and Reprints, 1943.

———. *Ormond, or, the Secret Witness*. 1799. Kent, Ohio: Kent State University Press, 1982.

———. "Walstein's School of History." 1799. In *The Rhapsodist and Other Uncollected Writings by Charles Brockden Brown*. Ed. Harry R. Warfel. New York: Scholars' Facsimiles and Reprints, 1943.

Brown, Gillian. *The Consent of the Governed: The Lockean Legacy in Early American Culture*. Cambridge and London: Harvard University Press, 2001.

Brown, Herbert Ross. *The Sentimental Novel in America 1789–1860*. Durham, N.C.: Duke University Press, 1940.

Brown, William Hill. *The Power of Sympathy*. 1789. Ed. William S. Osbourne. New Haven, Conn.: College and University Press, 1970.

Brunton, Mary. *Discipline*. 1815. London: Pandora, 1986.

———. *Self-Control*. 1810–11. London: Pandora, 1986.

Buchan, William. *Domestic Medicine; or the Family Physician*. 17th ed. Halifax, N.C.: Hodge, 1801.

Burder, George. *The Closet Companion: or, an Help to Serious Persons, in the Important Duty of Self-Examination. Intended to be Kept in the Christian's Usual Place of Retirement, in Order to Remind Him of, as Well as to Assist Him in, This Work.* Hartford, Conn.: Hosmer, 1810.

Burgett, Bruce. *Sentimental Bodies: Sex, Gender, and Citizenship in the Early Republic.* Princeton, N.J.: Princeton University Press, 1998.

Burnham, Michelle. *Captivity and Sentiment: Cultural Exchange in American Literature, 1682–1861.* Hanover, N.H., and London: University Press of New England, 1997.

Burroughs, Stephen. *Memoirs of Stephen Burroughs.* 1798. Ed. Philip F. Gura. Boston: Northeastern University Press, 1988.

Caplan, Ruth B. *Psychiatry and the Community in Nineteenth-Century America: The Recurring Concern with the Environment in the Prevention and Treatment of Mental Illness.* New York: Basic, 1969.

Carey, Mathew, ed. *The Lady's Pocket Library, Containing 1. Miss More's Essays. 2. Dr. Gregory's Legacy to his Daughters. 3. Lady Pennington's Unfortunate Mother's Advice to Her Daughter. 4. Marchioness of Lambert's Advice of a Mother to her Daughter. 5. Mrs. Chapone's Letter on the Government of the Temper. 6. Swift's Letter to a Young Lady Newly Married. 7. Moore's Fables for the Female Sex.* Philadelphia: Carey, 1792.

———. *A Short Account of the Malignant Fever, Lately Prevalent at Philadelphia.* Philadelphia: Carey, November 14, 1793.

Caso, Adolph. *America's Italian Founding Fathers.* Boston: Branden Press, 1975.

Cassuto, Leonard. "The Seduction of American Religious Discourse in Foster's *The Coquette.*" *Reform and Counterreform: Dialectics of the Word in Western Christianity Since Luther.* Ed. John C. Hawley. Berlin and New York: Mouton de Gruyter, 1994. 105–18.

Censer, Jane Turner. *North Carolina Planters and Their Children, 1800–1860.* Baton Rouge: Louisiana State University Press, 1984.

Charvat, William. *The Profession of Authorship in America, 1800–1870.* Ed. Matthew J. Bruccoli. Columbus: Ohio State University Press, 1968.

Christophersen, Bill. *The Apparition in the Glass: Charles Brockden Brown's American Gothic.* Athens: University of Georgia Press, 1993.

Coates, Samuel. "Cases of Several Lunatics in the Pennsylvania Hospital." 1785–1825. Archives of the Pennsylvania Hospital.

Cohen, Daniel A. *Pillars of Salt, Monuments of Grace: New England Crime Literature and the Origins of American Popular Culture, 1674–1860.* New York: Oxford University Press, 1993.

Coleman, Peter J. *Debtors and Creditors in America: Insolvency, Imprisonment for Debt, and Bankruptcy, 1607–1900.* Madison: State Historical Society of Wisconsin, 1974.

The Complete Letter-Writer. Containing Familiar Letters on the Most Common Occa-

sions in Life. Also, a Variety of Elegant Letters for the Direction and Embellishment of Style. On . . . Business, Duty, Amusement, Love, Courtship, Marriage, Friendship, and Other Subjects. . . . 2nd ed. Boston: Folsom, 1790.

Cooper, Thomas. *Political Arithmetic*. [Philadelphia]: 1798.

Cott, Nancy F. "Divorce and the Changing Status of Women in Eighteenth-Century Massachusetts." *The American Family in Social-Historical Perspective*. Ed. Michael Gordon. 2nd ed. New York: St. Martin's, 1978. 152–39.

———. "Eighteenth-Century Family and Social Life Revealed in Massachusetts Divorce Records." In *A Heritage of Her Own: Toward a New Social History of American Women*. Ed. Nancy F. Cott and Elizabeth H. Pleck. New York: Simon and Schuster, 1979. 107–35.

Court, Franklin E. *The Scottish Connection: The Rise of English Literary Study in Early America*. Syracuse, N.Y.: Syracuse University Press, 2001.

Cremin, Lawrence A. *American Education: The Colonial Experience 1607–1783*. New York: Harper and Row, 1970.

Cutbush, Edward. *An Inaugural Dissertation on Insanity*. Philadelphia: Poulson, 1794.

Dain, Norman. *Concepts of Insanity in the United States, 1789–1865*. New Brunswick, N.J.: Rutgers University Press, 1964.

Dalke, Anne. "Original Vice: The Political Implications of Incest in the Early American Novel." *Early American Literature* 23.2 (1988): 188–201.

Dame Partlet's Farm: Containing an Account of the Great Riches She Obtained by Industry . . . . Philadelphia: Johnson, 1806.

Davidson, Cathy N. *Revolution and the Word: The Rise of the Novel in America*. New York: Oxford University Press, 1986.

———. "Mothers and Daughters in the Fiction of the New Republic." *The Lost Tradition: Mothers and Daughters in Literature*. Ed. Cathy N. Davidson and E. H. Broner. New York: Frederick Ungar, 1980. 115–27.

Davis, Richard Beale. *A Colonial Southern Bookshelf: Reading in the Eighteenth Century*. Athens: University of Georgia Press, 1979.

Day, Robert Adams. *Told in Letters: Epistolary Fiction before Richardson*. Ann Arbor: University of Michigan, 1966.

Dayton, Cornelia Hughes. "Taking the Trade: Abortion and Gender Relations in an Eighteenth-Century New England Village." *William and Mary Quarterly* 48.1 (1991): 19–49.

Derounian, Kathryn Zabelle. "Lost in the Crowd: Rebecca Rush's *Kelroy*." *American Transcendental Quarterly* 47–48 (1980): 117–26.

Deutsch, Albert. *The Mentally Ill in America: A History of Their Care and Treatment from Colonial Times*. New York: Doubleday, 1937.

Dilworth, H. W. *The Complete Letter-Writer: or, Young Secretary's Instructor. Containing a Great Variety of Letters . . . . . to Which Are Prefixed, Plain Instructions for Writing Letters on All Occasions*. New York: Duyckinck, 1795.

Dodsley, Robert. *The Economy of Human Life*. London: Printed for Sherwood, Neely, and Jones, et al., 1809.

Doerflinger, Thomas. *A Vigorous Spirit of Enterprise: Merchants and Economic Development in Revolutionary Philadelphia*. Chapel Hill: University of North Carolina Press, 1986.

Dörner, Klaus. *Madmen and the Bourgeoisie: A Social History of Insanity and Psychiatry*. 1969. Trans. Joachim Neugroschel and Jean Steinberg. Oxford: Blackwell, 1981.

Douglas, Ann. *The Feminization of American Culture*. New York: Doubleday, 1977.

Dulles, Foster Rhea. *The Old China Trade*. Boston: Houghton Mifflin, 1930.

Dumm, Thomas L. *Democracy and Punishment: Disciplinary Origins of the United States*. Madison: University of Wisconsin Press, 1987.

Dunlap, William. *The Life of Charles Brockden Brown*. 2 vols. Philadelphia: Parke, 1815.

Dwight, Timothy. *Travels in New England and New York*. 4 vols. 1822. Ed. Barbara Miller Solomon with Patricia M. King. Cambridge: Belknap Press of Harvard University Press, 1969.

Edgeworth, Maria. *Idleness and Industry Exemplified in the History of James Preston and Lazy Lawrence*. Philadelphia: Johnson, 1803.

Evans, Gareth. "Rakes, Coquettes and Republican Patriarchs: Class, Gender and Nation in Early American Sentimental Fiction." *Canadian Review of American Studies* 25.3 (1995): 41–62.

Fabian, Ann Vincent. *Card Sharps, Dream Books, and Bucket Shops: Gambling in Nineteenth-Century America*. Ithaca: Cornell University Press, 1990.

Fennimore, Keith J. *Short Stories from Another Day: Eighteenth Century Periodical Fiction*. East Lansing: Michigan State University Press, 1989.

Fichtelberg, Joseph. "Friendless in Philadelphia: The Feminist Critique of Martha Meredith Read." *Early American Literature* 32.3 (1997): 205–21.

Fidelity Rewarded: or, The History of Polly Granville. Boston: Young and Minns, 1796.

Finseth, Ian. "'A Melancholy Tale': Rhetoric, Fiction, and Passion in *The Coquette*." *Studies in the Novel* 33.2 (2001): 125–59.

Fisher, Philip. *Hard Facts: Setting and Form in the American Novel*. New York: Oxford University Press, 1985.

Fleischmann, Fritz. "Concealed Lessons: Foster's *Coquette* and Brockden Brown's 'Lesson on Concealment.'" *Early America Re-Explored: New Readings in Colonial, Early National, and Antebellum Culture*. Ed. Klaus H. Schmidt and Fritz Fleischmann. New York: Peter Lang, 2000. 309–48.

Fliegelman, Jay. *Declaring Independence: Jefferson, Natural Language, and the Culture of Performance*. Stanford, Calif.: Stanford University Press, 1993.

———. *Prodigals and Pilgrims: The American Revolution against Patriarchal Authority, 1750–1800*. New York: Cambridge University Press, 1982.

Fluck, Winfried. "From Aesthetics to Political Criticism: Theories of the Early American Novel." *Early America Re-Explored: New Readings in Colonial, Early National, and Antebellum Culture*. Ed. Klaus H. Schmidt and Fritz Fleischmann. New York: Peter Lang, 2000. 225–68.

Forcey, Blythe. "*Charlotte Temple* and the End of Epistolarity." *American Literature* 63.2 (1991): 225–41.

Fordyce, James. *Sermons to Young Women*. Philadelphia: Dobson, 1787.

The Fortunate Discovery. Or, the History of Henry Villars [by the author of *Moreland Vale*]. New York: Printed by R. Wilson for Samuel Campbell, 1798.

Foster, Gwendolyn Audrey. "The Dialogic Margins of Conduct Fiction: Hannah Webster Foster's *The Boarding School*." *Journal of the American Studies Association of Texas* 25 (1994): 59–72.

Foster, Hannah. *The Boarding School; or, Lessons of a Preceptress to Her Pupils*. Boston: Thomas and Andrews, 1798.

———. *The Coquette; or, the History of Eliza Wharton*. 1797. Ed. Cathy N. Davidson. New York: Oxford University Press, 1986.

Foucault, Michel. *Discipline and Punish: The Birth of the Prison*. 1975. Trans. Alan Sheridan. New York: Vintage, 1979.

———. *Madness and Civilization: A History of Insanity in the Age of Reason*. 1965. Trans. Richard Howard. New York: Vintage, 1973.

Franklin, Benjamin. *The Autobiography of Benjamin Franklin*. Ed. Leonard W. Labaree et al. New Haven, Conn.: Yale University Press, 1964.

Freneau, Philip. "Chronology of Facts." *National Gazette*. May 31, 1792.

———. "Detached Reflections from a Correspondent." *National Gazette*. November 3, 1793.

———. "On Commerce and Luxury." Abstract printed in *The Time Piece*. November 17, 1797 and November 20, 1797.

———. "Plan for a Nobility." *National Gazette*. May 7, 1792.

———. *Poems Written between the Years 1768 and 1794*. Monmouth, N.J.: 1795.

Furber, Holden. "The Beginnings of American Trade with India, 1784–1812." *The New England Quarterly* 11.2 (1938): 235–65.

The Gambler, or the Memoirs of a British Officer. 2nd ed. Washington City, 1802.

The Gentleman's Pocket Library. Boston: Spotswood for Rice, 1794.

Gibson, James E. "Benjamin Rush's Apprenticed Students." *Transactions and Studies of the College of Physicians of Philadelphia* 4th series, 14 (1946): 127–32.

Gilbert, Sandra M., and Susan Gubar. *The Madwoman in the Attic: The Woman Writer and the Nineteenth-Century Literary Imagination*. New Haven, Conn., and London: Yale University Press, 1979.

Gilmore, Michael T. "The Novel." In *The Cambridge History of American Literature*. Ed. Sacvan Bercovitch. New York: Cambridge University Press, 1994. 620–43.

The Glass; or Speculation: A Poem: Containing an Account of the Ancient, and Genius of the Modern, Speculators. New York: Printed for the author, 1791.

Goddu, Teresa A. *Gothic America: Narrative, History, and Nation*. New York: Columbia University Press, 1997.
Goldgeier, Adam. "The Coquette Composed." *Constructions* (1990): 1–14.
Goldstein, Jonathan. *Philadelphia and the China Trade, 1682–1846: Commercial, Cultural, and Attitudinal Effects*. University Park: Pennsylvania State University Press, 1978.
Goodman, Nathan G. *Benjamin Rush, Physician and Citizen, 1746–1813*. Philadelphia: University of Pennsylvania, 1934.
Grabo, Norman S. *The Coincidental Art of Charles Brockden Brown*. Chapel Hill: University of North Carolina Press, 1981.
———. "Historical Essay." *Arthur Mervyn: or, Memoirs of the Year 1793*. 1st and 2nd parts. Kent, Ohio: Kent State University Press, 1980.
———. Introduction. *Edgar Huntly*. New York: Penguin, 1988.
Green, James N. "English Books and Printing in the Age of Franklin." In *A History of the Book in America: The Colonial Book in the Atlantic World*. Ed. Hugh Amory and David D. Hall. Cambridge and New York: Cambridge University Press, 2000. 248–98.
Green, Richard. "*Griswold's* Legacy: Fornication and Adultery as Crimes." *Ohio Northern University Law Review* 16.3 (1989): 545–49.
Greven, Philip. *The Protestant Temperament: Patterns of Child-Rearing, Religious Experience, and the Self in Early America*. New York: Knopf, 1977.
Griffith, William. *The Scrivener's Guide; Containing Concise Precedents of Acquittances . . .* Newark, N.J.: Woods, 1797.
Gross, Robert A. *The Minutemen and Their World*. New York: Hill and Wang, 1976.
Gustafson, Sandra. *Eloquence Is Power: Oratory and Performance in Early America*. Chapel Hill and London: University of North Carolina Press, for the Omohundro Institute of Early American History and Culture, 2000.
Habermas, Jürgen. *The Structural Transformation of the Public Sphere: An Inquiry into a Category of Bourgeois Society*. 1962. Trans. Thomas Burger with Frederick Lawrence. Cambridge: MIT Press, 1989.
Hall, David D. *Worlds of Wonder, Days of Judgment: Popular Religious Belief in Early New England*. New York: Alfred A. Knopf, 1989.
Hamelman, Steve. "Aphasia in Rebecca Rush's *Kelroy*." *South Atlantic Review* 62.2 (1997): 88–110.
Hansen, Klaus P. "The Sentimental Novel and Its Feminist Critique." *Early American Literature* 26.1 (1991): 39–54.
Harris, Sharon M. "Hannah Webster Foster's *The Coquette*: Critiquing Franklin's America." Harris 1–22.
———. "Introduction: Literary Politics and the Political Novel." Harris vii–xxiii.
———, ed. *Redefining the Political Novel: American Women Writers, 1797–1901*. Knoxville: University of Tennessee Press, 1995.

Hart, James D. *The Popular Book: A History of America's Literary Taste*. New York: Oxford University Press, 1950.
Haslam, John. *Observations on Madness and Melancholy*. 1809. New York: Arno, 1976.
Hayes, Kevin J. *A Colonial Woman's Bookshelf*. Knoxville: University of Tennessee Press, 1996.
Henretta, James A. *The Evolution of American Society, 1700–1815*. Lexington, Mass.: Heath, 1973.
Hinds, Elizabeth Jane Wall. *Private Property: Charles Brockden Brown's Gendered Economics of Virtue*. Newark: University of Delaware Press, 1997.
Hirschman, Albert O. *The Passions and the Interests: Political Arguments for Capitalism before Its Triumph*. Princeton, N.J.: Princeton University Press, 1977.
Hitchcock, Enos. *A Discourse on Education, Delivered at the Meeting-House on the West Side of the River, in Providence, November 16, 1785*. Providence, R.I.: Wheeler, 1785.
———. *The Farmer's Friend, or the History of Mr. Charles Worthy*. Boston: Thomas and Andrews, 1793.
Holman, Jessee L. *The Prisoners of Niagara, or Errors of Education*. Frankfort, Ky.: William Gerard, 1810.
Hopkinson, Francis. *A Pretty Story: Written in the Year of Our Lord 1774, by Peter Grievous, Esq., A.B.C.D.E.* Philadelphia: Dunlop, 1774.
Howell, Wilbur Samuel. *Eighteenth-Century British Logic and Rhetoric*. Princeton, N.J.: Princeton University Press, 1971.
Hunter, J. Paul. *Before Novels: The Cultural Contexts of Eighteenth-Century English Fiction*. New York: Norton, 1990.
Ignatieff, Michael. *A Just Measure of Pain: The Penitentiary in the Industrial Revolution, 1750–1850*. New York: Pantheon Books, 1978.
The Instructive Story of Industry and Sloth. Hartford, Conn.: Babcock, 1798.
Irigaray, Luce. *This Sex Which Is Not One*. Trans. Catherine Porter with Carolyn Burke. Ithaca, N.Y.: Cornell University Press, 1985.
Jameson, Fredric. *The Political Unconscious: Narrative as a Socially Symbolic Act*. Ithaca, N.Y.: Cornell University Press, 1981.
———. "Reification and Utopia in Mass Culture." *Social Text* 1 (1979): 130–48.
Jauss, Hans Robert. *Toward an Aesthetic of Reception*. Trans. Timothy Bahti. St. Paul: University of Minnesota Press, 1982.
Jefferson, Thomas. *The Writings of Thomas Jefferson*. Ed. Paul Leicester Ford. New York: Putnam's, 1892–99.
———. *The Papers of Thomas Jefferson*. Ed. Julian P. Boyd. Princeton, N.J.: Princeton University Press, 1950–.
Jimenez, Mary Ann. *Changing Faces of Madness: Early American Attitudes and the Treatment of the Insane*. Hanover, N.H.: University Press of New England, 1987.

Johnson, Claudia L. *Equivocal Beings: Politics, Gender, and Sentimentality in the 1790s: Wollstonecraft, Radcliffe, Burney, Austen*. Chicago: University of Chicago Press, 1995.

Jordan, Cynthia S. *Second Stories: The Politics of Language, Form, and Gender in Early American Fictions*. Chapel Hill and London: University of North Carolina Press, 1989.

Justus, James H. "Arthur Mervyn, American." *American Literature* 42.3 (1970): 304–24.

Kaplan, Amy. " 'Left Alone with America': The Absence of Empire in the Study of American Culture." In *Cultures of United States Imperialism*. Ed. Amy Kaplan and Donald E. Pease. Durham, N.C., and London: Duke University Press, 1993. 3–21.

Karlsen, Carol F. *The Devil in the Shape of a Woman: Witchcraft in Colonial New England*. New York: Norton, 1987.

Kavanagh, Thomas M. *Enlightenment and the Shadows of Chance: The Novel and the Culture of Gambling in Eighteenth-Century France*. Baltimore: Johns Hopkins University Press, 1993.

Kerber, Linda K. *Women of the Republic: Intellect and Ideology in Revolutionary America*. 1980. New York: Norton, 1986.

Klein, Lawrence. "Berkeley, Shaftesbury, and the Meaning of Politeness." *Studies in Eighteenth-Century Culture* 16 (1986): 57–68.

———. "Gender and the Public/Private Distinction in the Eighteenth Century: Some Questions about Evidence and Analytic Procedure." *Eighteenth-Century Studies* 29.1 (1995): 97–109.

———. "The Third Earl of Shaftesbury and the Progress of Politeness." *Eighteenth-Century Studies* 18 (1985): 186–214.

Lenz, William E. *Fast Talk and Flush Times: The Confidence Man as a Literary Convention*. Columbia: University of Missouri Press, 1985.

Leslie, Eliza. *The Young Ladies' Mentor; or, Extracts in Prose and Verse, for the Promotion of Virtue and Morality*. Philadelphia: Johnson, 1803.

Levine, Robert S. *Conspiracy and Romance: Studies in Brockden Brown, Cooper, Hawthorne, and Melville*. New York: Cambridge University Press, 1989.

Lewis, Jan. "The Republican Wife: Virtue and Seduction in the Early Republic." *William and Mary Quarterly* 44.4 (1987): 689–721.

Lindberg, Gary. *The Confidence Man in American Literature*. New York: Oxford University Press, 1982.

The Little Islanders; or, Blessings of Industry. Philadelphia: Johnson and Warner, 1809.

Locke, John. *Some Thoughts Concerning Education*. 1693. *The Educational Writings of John Locke*. Ed. James L. Axtell. London: Cambridge University Press, 1968.

London, April. "Avoiding the Subject: The Presence and Absence of Venereal Disease in the Eighteenth-Century English Novel." *The Secret Malady: Venereal*

Disease in Eighteenth-Century Britain and France. Ed. Linda E. Merians. Lexington: University Press of Kentucky, 1996. 213–27.

Looby, Christopher. *Voicing America: Language, Literary Form, and the Origins of the United States.* Chicago: University of Chicago Press, 1996.

Loshe, Lillie Deming. *The Early American Novel.* New York: Columbia, 1907.

Lovell, Thomas B. "Separate Spheres and Extensive Circles: Sarah Savage's *The Factory Girl* and the Celebration of Industry in Early Nineteenth-Century America." *Early American Literature* 31.1 (1996): 1–24.

Madison, James. *The Papers of James Madison.* Vol. 1: 16 March 1751–16 December 1779. Ed. William T. Hutchinson and William M. E. Rachal. Chicago: University of Chicago Press, 1962–1991.

Maestro, Marcello. *Cesare Beccaria and the Origins of Penal Reform.* Philadelphia: Temple University Press, 1973.

Main, Jackson Turner. *The Social Structure of Revolutionary America.* Princeton, N.J.: Princeton University Press, 1965.

Mandeville, Bernard. *The Fable of the Bees.* Ed. F. B. Kaye. 2 vols. Oxford: Clarendon, 1924.

Manvill, Mrs. P. D. *Lucinda, or the Mountain Mourner.* 1807. 2nd ed. (with additions). Ballston Spa, N.Y., 1810.

Marino, Sarah. " 'Almost Infinite Variations': Eighteenth-Century Epistolary Fictions." Diss. University of North Carolina at Chapel Hill, 1994.

Martin, Terence. "Social Institutions in the Early American Novel." *American Quarterly* 9.1 (1957): 72–84.

May, Henry F. *The Enlightenment in America.* New York: Oxford University Press, 1976.

McCoy, Drew. *The Elusive Republic: Political Economy in Jeffersonian America.* Chapel Hill: University of North Carolina Press, 1980.

Meranze, Michael. *Laboratories of Virtue: Punishment, Revolution, and Authority in Philadelphia, 1760–1835.* Chapel Hill: University of North Carolina Press, for the Institute of Early American History and Culture, 1996.

Merians, Linda E., ed. *The Secret Malady: Venereal Disease in Eighteenth-Century Britain and France.* Lexington: University Press of Kentucky, 1996.

Merish, Lori. *Sentimental Materialism: Gender, Commodity Culture, and Nineteenth-Century American Literature.* Durham, N.C.: Duke University Press, 2000.

Monaghan, E. Jennifer. "Literacy Instruction and Gender in Colonial New England." In *Reading in America: Literature and Social History.* Ed. Cathy N. Davidson. Baltimore: Johns Hopkins University Press, 1989.

Moore, John Hamilton. *The Young Gentleman and Lady's Monitor, and English Teacher's Assistant: Being a Collection of Select Pieces from Our Best Modern Writers: Calculated to Eradicate Vulgar Prejudices and Rusticity . . . Rectify the Will, Purify the Passions . . .* New York: Gaine, 1792.

More, Hannah. "Essays." *The Lady's Pocket Library.* Ed. Matthew Carey. Philadelphia: Carey, 1792.

Moreland Vale; or the Fair Fugitive [by the author of *The Fortunate Discovery*]. New York: Printed by L. Nichols and Co. for Samuel Campbell, 1801.

Morris, Robert. *The Papers of Robert Morris.* Ed. John Catanzariti et al. vol. 7. Pittsburgh: University of Pittsburgh Press, 1995.

Mott, Frank Luther. *The Golden Multitudes: The Story of Best Sellers in the United States.* New York: Macmillan, 1947.

Mulford, Carla. Introduction. *The Power of Sympathy and The Coquette.* Ed. Carla Mulford. New York: Penguin, 1996. ix–li.

Mullan, John. *Sentiment and Sociability: The Language of Feeling in the Eighteenth Century.* New York: Clarendon, 1988.

Murray, Judith Sargent. *Story of Margaretta. The Gleaner. A Miscellaneous Production by Constantia.* 1798. Schenectady, N.Y.: Union College Press, 1992.

Murry, Ann. *Mentoria, or, the Young Ladies Instructor.* New York: Moore, 1812.

Nelson, Dana D. Introduction. In *Kelroy, a Novel.* By Rebecca Rush. New York: Oxford University Press, 1992. xi–xxiv.

Nelson, William E. "Emerging Notions of Modern Criminal Law in the Revolutionary Era: An Historical Perspective." *New York University Law Review* 42 (1967): 450–82.

The New Universal Letter-Writer: or, Complete Art of Polite Correspondence.... Philadelphia: Hogan, 1800.

Newton, Sarah E. *Learning to Behave: A Guide to American Conduct Books before 1900.* Westport, Conn.: Greenwood, 1994.

———. "Wise and Foolish Virgins: 'Usable Fiction' and the Early American Conduct Tradition." *Early American Literature* 25.2 (1990): 139–67.

Of Commerce and Luxury. Reprint from the London edition. Philadelphia: Lang, 1791.

Orians, G. Harrison. "Censure of Fiction in American Romances and Magazines: 1789–1810." *PMLA* 52.1 (1937): 195–214.

Painter, Nell Irvin. "Representing Truth: Sojourner Truth's Knowing and Becoming Known." *Journal of American History* 81.2 (1994): 461–92.

Parental Legacies, Consisting of Advice from a Lady of Quality to Her Children. Delivered in the Last Stage of a Lingering Illness. Translated from the French, by S. Glasse, D.D. F.R.S. Chaplain in Ordinary to his (British) Majesty. And a Father's Legacy to His Daughters. By the Late Dr. Gregory, of Edinburgh. Also, a number of interesting and valuable extracts from new publications, and other works of merit. Boston: Bumstead, 1804.

Parran, Thomas. *Shadow on the Land: Syphilis.* New York: Reynal and Hitchcock, 1937.

Parrish, Joseph. *An Inaugural Dissertation on the Influence of the Passions upon the Body in the Production and Cure of Diseases.* Philadelphia: Kimber, 1805.

Patterson, Mrs. *The Unfortunate Lovers, and Cruel Parents: A Very Interesting Tale Founded on Fact*. 17th ed. N.p.: John and Callendar, 1797.

Perkins, David. *Is Literary History Possible?* Baltimore: Johns Hopkins University Press, 1992.

Perry, Ruth. *Women, Letters, and the Novel*. New York: AMS, 1980.

Pettengill, Claire C. "Sisterhood in a Separate Sphere: Female Friendship in Hannah Webster Foster's *The Coquette* and *The Boarding School*." *Early American Literature* 27.3 (1992): 185–203.

Petter, Henri. *The Early American Novel*. Columbus: Ohio State University Press, 1971.

Pinel, Philippe. *A Treatise on Insanity*. 1806. Trans. D. D. Davis. New York: Hafner, 1962.

Pitcher, Edward W. R. *Fiction in American Magazines before 1800: An Annotated Catalogue*. Lexington, Ky.: Union College Press in conjunction with Antoca Press, 1993.

Pocock, J. G. A. *The Machiavellian Moment: Florentine Political Thought and the Atlantic Republican Tradition*. Princeton, N.J.: Princeton University Press, 1975.

Quétel, Claude. *History of Syphilis*. Baltimore: Johns Hopkins University Press, 1990.

Radway, Janice A. *Reading the Romance: Women, Patriarchy, and Popular Literature*. Rev. ed. Chapel Hill: University of North Carolina Press, 1991.

[Read, Martha]. *Monima, or the Beggar Girl*. New York: P. R. Johnson for L. N. Ralston, 1802.

Redford, Bruce. *The Converse of the Pen: Acts of Intimacy in the Eighteenth-Century Familiar Letter*. Chicago: University of Chicago Press, 1986.

Reed, Walter L. *An Exemplary History of the Novel: The Quixotic Versus the Picaresque*. Chicago: University of Chicago Press, 1981.

Relf, Samuel. *Infidelity, or the Victims of Sentiment; a Novel, in a Series of Letters*. Philadelphia: W. W. Woodward, 1797.

Renan, Ernest. "What is a Nation?" In *Nation and Narration*. Ed. Homi K. Bhabha. Trans. Martin Thom. London and New York: Routledge, 1990. 8–22.

Rice, Grantland S. *The Transformation of Authorship in America*. Chicago: University of Chicago Press, 1997.

Richards, Jeffrey H. "Decorous Violence: Manners, Class, and Abuse in Rebecca Rush's *Kelroy*." In *Over the Threshold: Intimate Violence in Early America*. Ed. Christine Daniels and Michael V. Kennedy. New York and London: Routledge, 1999. 202–16.

———. "The Politics of Seduction: Theater, Sexuality, and National Virtue in the Novels of Hannah Foster." In *Exceptional Spaces: Essays in Performance and History*. Ed. Della Pollock. Chapel Hill: University of North Carolina Press, 1998. 238–57.

———. *Theater Enough: American Culture and the Metaphor of the World Stage, 1607–1789*. Durham: Duke University Press, 1991.

Ricord, Philip. *Illustrations of Syphilitic Disease.* Trans. Thomas F. Betton. Philadelphia: Hart, 1852.

Rodgers, Daniel T. "Republicanism: The Career of a Concept." *Journal of American History* 79.1 (1992): 11–38.

Rose, Henry. *An Inaugural Dissertation on the Effects of Passion upon the Body.* Philadelphia: Woodward, 1794.

Rothman, David. *The Discovery of the Asylum: Social Order and Disorder in the New Republic.* Boston: Little, 1971.

Rothman, Ellen K. *Hands and Hearts: A History of Courtship in America.* New York: Basic, 1984.

———. "Sex and Self-Control: Middle-Class Courtship in America, 1770–1870." In *The American Family in Social-Historical Perspective*. 3rd. ed. Ed. Michael Gordon. New York: St. Martin's, 1983. 393–410.

Rousseau, Jean-Jacques. *Émile.* Trans. Barbara Foxley. New York: Dutton, 1966.

Rowson, Susanna. *Charlotte Temple and Lucy Temple.* 1791 and 1828. Ed. Ann Douglas. New York: Penguin, 1991.

———. *Mentoria; or the Young Lady's Friend.* 2 vols. Philadelphia: Printed for Robert Campbell by Samuel Harrison Smith, 1794.

———. *A Present for Young Ladies.* Boston: John West and Co., 1811.

Rubin, Joan Shelley. *The Making of Middlebrow Culture.* Chapel Hill and London: University of North Carolina Press, 1992.

Rubin-Dorsky, Jeffrey. "The Early American Novel." In *The Columbia History of the American Novel.* Ed. Emory Elliott. New York: Columbia University Press, 1991. 6–25.

Rush, Benjamin. *Medical Inquiries and Observations upon the Diseases of the Mind.* 1812. New York: Hafner, 1962.

[Rush, Rebecca]. *Kelroy, a Novel.* 1812. Ed. Dana D. Nelson. New York: Oxford University Press, 1992.

Rust, Marion. " 'Into the House of an Entire Stranger': Why Sentimental Doesn't Equal Domestic in Early American Fiction." *Early American Literature* 37.2 (2002): 281–309.

———. "What's Wrong with Charlotte Temple?" *William and Mary Quarterly*, 3rd series, 10.1 (2003): 99–118.

Said, Edward W. *Culture and Imperialism.* New York: Knopf, 1993.

St. Hubert; or, Mistaken Friendship. District of Columbia: Wood, 1800.

St. John de Crèvecoeur, J. Hector. *Letters from an American Farmer and Sketches of Eighteenth-Century Life.* New York: Penguin, 1986.

Sakolski, A. M. *The Great American Land Bubble.* New York: Harper, 1932.

Samuels, Shirley. "Infidelity and Contagion: The Rhetoric of Revolution." *Early American Literature* 22.2 (1987): 183–91.

———. *Romances of the Republic: Women, the Family, and Violence in the Literature of the Early American Nation.* New York: Oxford University Press, 1996.

Sans Souci, Alias, Free and Easy, or, an Evening's Peep into a Polite Circle. Boston: Warden and Russell, 1785.

[Sansay, Leonora.] *Laura.* Philadelphia: Bradford & Inskeep, 1809.

[Savage, Sarah]. *The Factory Girl.* Boston: Munroe, Francis and Parker, 1814.

"The Scarlet Legislature: For Adulterers Only." *Student Lawyer* (May 1987): 6–7.

Schloesser, Pauline. *The Fair Sex: White Women and Racial Patriarchy in the Early American Republic.* New York and London: New York University Press, 2002.

Schloss, Dietmar. "Republicanism and Politeness in the Early American Novel." In *Early America Re-Explored: New Readings in Colonial, Early National, and Antebellum Culture.* Ed. Klaus H. Schmidt and Fritz Fleischmann. New York: Peter Lang, 2000. 269–90.

Shields, David S. *Civil Tongues and Polite Letters in British America.* Chapel Hill: University of North Carolina Press, for the Institute of Early American History and Culture, 1997.

Showalter, Elaine. *The Female Malady: Women, Madness, and English Culture, 1830–1980.* New York: Pantheon Books, 1985.

Shuffelton, Frank. "Mrs. Foster's Coquette and the Decline of the Brotherly Watch." *Studies in Eighteenth-Century Culture* 16 (1986): 211–24.

Silverman, Kenneth. *A Cultural History of the American Revolution: Painting, Music, Literature, and the Theatre in the Colonies and the United States from the Treaty of Paris to the Inauguration of George Washington, 1763–1789.* New York: Crowell, 1976.

Singer, Godfrey Frank. *The Epistolary Novel: Its Origins, Development, Decline, and Residuary Influence.* New York: Russell and Russell, 1963.

Smith, Adam. *An Inquiry into the Nature and Causes of the Wealth of Nations.* 1776. Rev. ed. 3 vols. Philadelphia: Dobson, 1789.

———. *The Theory of Moral Sentiments.* 1759. Ed. E. G. West. Indianapolis: Liberty, 1976.

Smith, Daniel Blake. *Inside the Great House: Planter Family Life in Eighteenth-Century Chesapeake Society.* Ithaca, N.Y.: Cornell University Press, 1980.

Smith, Daniel Scott. "Parental Power and Marriage Patterns: An Analysis of Historical Trends in Hingham, Massachusetts." *Journal of Marriage and the Family* 35 (1973): 419–28.

——— and Michael S. Hindus. "Premarital Pregnancy in America 1640–1971: An Overview and Interpretation." *Journal of Interdisciplinary History* 5 (1975): 537–70.

Smith, Merril D. *Breaking the Bonds: Marital Discord in Pennsylvania, 1730–1830.* New York: New York University Press, 1991.

Smith, Philip Chadwick Foster. *The Empress of China.* Philadelphia: Philadelphia Maritime Museum, 1984.

Smith-Rosenberg, Carroll. "Domesticating 'Virtue': Coquettes and Revolutionaries in Young America." In *Literature and the Body: Essays on Populations and Persons*. Ed. Elaine Scarry. Baltimore: Johns Hopkins University Press, 1986. 160–84.

———. "Subject Female: Authorizing American Identity." *American Literary History* 5.3 (1993): 481–511.

Stallybrass, Peter, and Allon White. *The Politics and Poetics of Transgression*. London: Methuen, 1986.

Stern, Julia A. *The Plight of Feeling: Sympathy and Dissent in the Early American Novel*. Chicago and London: University of Chicago Press, 1997.

———. "Working through the Frame: *Charlotte Temple* and the Poetics of Maternal Melancholia." *Arizona Quarterly* 49.4 (1993): 1–32.

Stowe, Harriet Beecher. *Uncle Tom's Cabin; or, Life Among the Lowly*. 1852. Ed. Elizabeth Ammons. New York: Norton, 1994.

Sullivan, James. *The Path to Riches: An Inquiry into the Origin and Use of Money . . .* Boston: Edes, 1792.

Tassoni, John Paul. " 'I Can Step Out of Myself a Little': Feminine Virtue and Female Friendship in Hannah Foster's *The Coquette*." In *Communication and Women's Friendships: Parallels and Intersections in Literature and Life*. Ed. Janet Doubler Ward and JoAnna Stephens Mink. Bowling Green, Ohio: Bowling Green State University Popular Press, 1993. 97–111.

Taylor, John. *An Enquiry into the Principles and Tendency of Certain Public Measures*. Philadelphia: Dobson, 1794.

Tennenhouse, Leonard. "The Americanization of Clarissa." *The Yale Journal of Criticism* 11.1 (1998): 177–96.

Tenney, Tabitha Gilman. *Female Quixotism*. 1801. Ed. Jean Nienkamp and Andrea Collins. New York: Oxford University Press, 1992.

Thayer, Caroline Matilda Warren. *The Gamesters; or Ruins of Innocence. An Original Novel, Founded in Truth*. Boston: Thomas and Andrews, 1805.

Todd, Janet. *Sensibility: An Introduction*. London and New York: Methuen, 1986.

Tompkins, Jane. *Sensational Designs: The Cultural Work of American Fiction 1790–1860*. New York: Oxford University Press, 1985.

Tonkovich, Nicole. *Domesticity with a Difference: The Nonfiction of Catharine Beecher, Sarah J. Hale, Fanny Fern, and Margaret Fuller*. Jackson: University Press of Mississippi, 1997.

Ulrich, Laurel Thatcher. *A Midwife's Tale: The Life of Martha Ballard, Based on Her Diary, 1785–1812*. New York: Knopf, 1990.

The Vain Cottager; or, the History of Lucy Franklin. New Haven, Conn.: For Increase Cooke and Co., from Sidney's Press, 1807.

Van Sant, Ann Jessie. *Eighteenth-Century Sensibility and the Novel*. New York: Cambridge University Press, 1993.

Vedder, Edward B. *Syphilis and Public Health*. Philadelphia: Lea, 1918.

Verhoeven, W. M. "'Persuasive Rhetorick': Representation and Resistance in Early American Epistolary Fiction." In *Making America / Making American Literature: Franklin to Cooper*. Ed. A. Robert Lee and W. M. Verhoeven. Amsterdam and Atlanta: Rodopi, 1996. 123–64.

[Vickery, Sukey]. *Emily Hamilton, a Novel*. Worcester: Isaiah Thomas, 1803.

W., A. *A Dandy Song*. [Boston: 1806].

Wakefield, Priscilla. *Mental Improvement: or the Beauties and Wonders of Nature and Art. In a Series of Instructive Conversations*. 1st American ed., from 3rd London ed. New Bedford, Mass.: Greene, 1799.

Waldstreicher, David. "'Fallen under My Observation': Vision and Virtue in *The Coquette*." *Early American Literature* 27.3 (1992): 204–18.

———. *In the Midst of Perpetual Fetes: The Making of American Nationalism, 1776–1820*. Chapel Hill and London: University of North Carolina Press, for the Omohundro Institute of Early American History and Culture, 1997.

Walker, John. *The Teacher's Assistant in English Composition; or Easy Rules For Writing Themes and Composing Exercises on Subjects Proper for the Improvement of Youth of Both Sexes at School*. Carlisle, Pa.: Kline, 1804.

Warner, Michael. *The Letters of the Republic: Publication and the Public Sphere in Eighteenth-Century America*. Cambridge: Harvard University Press, 1990.

Watts, Edward. *Writing and Postcolonialism in the Early Republic*. Charlottesville and London: University Press of Virginia, 1998.

Watts, Isaac. *The Improvement of the Mind: or a Supplement to the Art of Logic. In Two Parts. To Which is Added, a Discourse on the Education of Children and Youth*. Exeter, N.H.: Lamson and Odiorne for West, 1793.

———. *Logic: Or, the Right Use of Reason, in the Inquiry after Truth. With a Variety of Rules to Guard against Error in the Affairs of Religion and Human Life, as Well as in the Sciences*. 2nd American ed. Newburyport, Mass.: Barrett, 1796.

Watts, Steven. *The Republic Reborn: War and the Making of Liberal America, 1790–1820*. Baltimore: Johns Hopkins University Press, 1987.

———. *The Romance of Real Life: Charles Brockden Brown and the Origins of American Culture*. Baltimore: Johns Hopkins University Press, 1994.

Webster, Pelatiah. *A Plea for the Poor Soldiers: Or, an Essay to Demonstrate That the Soldiers and Other Public Creditors, Who Really and Actually Supported the Burden of the Late War, Have Not Been Paid, Ought to Be Paid, Can Be Paid and Must Be Paid*. 1790. In *Political Essays*. Philadelphia: Crukshank, 1791. 306–43.

———. *Political Essays on the Nature and Operation of Money, Public Finances, and Other Subjects: Published During the American War, and Continued up to the Present Year, 1791*. Philadelphia: Crukshank, 1791.

———. *A Second Essay on Free Trade*. 1779. In *Political Essays*. Philadelphia: Crukshank, 1791. 27–49.

Weems, Mason Locke. *God's Revenge against Gambling: Exemplified in the Misera-*

ble Lives and Untimely Deaths of a Number of Persons of Both Sexes, Who Had Sacrificed Their Health, Wealth, and Honor at Gaming Tables*. Augusta: Hobby and Bunce, 1810.

Weiss, Barbara. *The Hell of the English: Bankruptcy and the Victorian Novel*. Lewisburg, Pa.: Bucknell University Press, 1986.

Wells, Helena. *Constantia Neville; or, the West Indian*. 2nd ed. 2 vols. London, 1800.

———. *The Step-Mother; a Domestic Tale from Real Life*. 2nd ed. 2 vols. London: T. N. Longman, 1798.

Weyler, Karen A. "Profile: Sally Sayward Barrell Keating Wood." *Legacy: A Journal of American Women Writers* 15.2 (1998): 204–12.

White, Hayden. "The Value of Narrativity in the Representation of Reality." In *The Content of the Form*. Baltimore: Johns Hopkins University Press, 1987. 1–24.

Wilcox, Kristin. "The Scribblings of a Plain Man and the Temerity of a Woman: Gender and Genre in Judith Sargent Murray's *The Gleaner*." *Early American Literature* 30 (1995): 121–44.

Williams, Daniel E. "In Defense of Self: Author and Authority in *The Memoirs of Stephen Burroughs*." *Early American Literature* 25.2 (1990): 96–122.

———, ed. *Pillars of Salt: An Anthology of Early American Criminal Narratives*. Madison: Madison House, 1993.

Williams, Raymond. "Base and Superstructure in Marxist Cultural Theory." *New Left Review* 82 (1973): 3–16.

———. *Marxism and Literature*. New York: Oxford University Press, 1977.

Winans, Robert B. "Bibliography and the Cultural Historian: Notes on the Eighteenth-Century Novel." In *Printing and Society in Early America*. Ed. William L. Joyce, David D. Hall, Richard D. Brown, and John B. Hench. Worcester, Mass.: American Antiquarian Society, 1983. 174–85.

———. "The Growth of a Novel-Reading Public in Late-Eighteenth-Century America." *Early American Literature* 9.3 (1975): 267–75.

Wood, Gordon S. *The Creation of the American Republic, 1776–1787*. New York: Norton, 1993.

———, ed. *The Rising Glory of America 1760–1820*. Rev. ed. Boston: Northeastern University Press, 1990.

Wood, Sally Sayward Barrell Keating. *Amelia; or, the Influence of Virtue: An Old Man's Story*. Portsmouth, N.H.: Printed at the Oracle Press, by William Treadwell and Co., 1802.

———. *Dorval; or the Speculator. A Novel, Founded on Recent Facts*. Portsmouth, N.H.: Printed at the Ledger Press by Nutting and Whitelock, for the author, 1801.

———. *Julia, and the Illuminated Baron*. Portsmouth, N.H.: Charles Peirce, 1800.

Woodruff, Hezekiah N. *The Danger of Ambition Considered, in a Sermon Preached at Scipio, N.Y., the Lord's Day, August 12, 1804: Occasioned by the Death of General Alexander Hamilton, Who Fell in a Duel with Aaron Burr, Vice-President of the*

United States of America, on the 11th Day of July, 1804. Albany, N.Y.: Webster, 1804.

Wulf, Karin. *Not All Wives: Women of Colonial Philadelphia*. Ithaca, N.Y., and London: Cornell University Press, 2000.

Yazawa, Melvin. *From Colonies to Commonwealth: Familial Ideology and the Beginnings of the American Republic*. Baltimore: Johns Hopkins University Press, 1985.

The Young Gentleman's Parental Monitor. From the London ed. Hartford, Conn.: Patten, 1792.

The Young Lady's Parental Monitor. Hartford, Conn.: Patten, 1792.

Zboray, Ronald J. *A Fictive People: Antebellum Economic Development and the American Reading Public*. New York: Oxford University Press, 1993.

Ziff, Larzer. *Writing in the New Nation: Prose, Print, and Politics in the Early United States*. New Haven, Conn., and London: Yale University Press, 1991.

Zomchick, John. *Family and the Law in Eighteenth-Century Fiction: The Public Conscience in the Private Sphere*. Cambridge: Cambridge University Press, 1993.

Index

Adams, Abigail, 13, 31, 183
Adams, John, 13, 82; on ambition, 125; and penal reform, 232n8
Adams, Samuel, 117, 148
Adultery and fornication, 24–25, 75–76, 80–81, 102–03, 180; in *The Coquette*, 159; fictional treatment of, 89; in *Laura*, 219n47; legal treatment of, 75–76, 213–14n26, 216n31; and pregnancy in fiction, 215–16n30; prosecutions of, 213–14n26, 216n31; in *Uncle Tom's Cabin*, 187–88; in *The Vain Cottager*, 219n47
Aiken, Solomon, 123
Altman, Janet Gurkin, 199n1
Ambition, 124–26; in Benjamin Franklin's *Autobiography*, 125–26; in *Discourses on Davila*, 125; in *Dorval*, 132; opposed to industry, 228n46
Amelia; or, The Faithless Briton (anon.), 9, 24, 78, 81, 96–100, 103, 192n20; and grief and guilt, 97–98; and insanity, 97, 99; and seduction, 100
Amelia; or, The Influence of Virtue (Sally Sayward Barrell Keating Wood), 70; syphilis in, 91
Amicable Society Rules, 140, 141, 142
Anderson, Alexander, 212n21
Anderson, Benedict, 22, 219n51, 230n55
Anonymous publication, 14
Appleby, Joyce, 222n10

Armstrong, Nancy, 22, 202n12, 220n51
Arthur Mervyn: or, Memoirs of the Year 1793 (Charles Brockden Brown), 26, 108, 143–44, 160–82, 187, 189n1, 194n34, 237–38n34; adultery and fornication in, 180; androgyny in, 236n25; and Arthur's fear of imprisonment, 175–76; benevolence in, 237n32; capitalism in, 222n9; composition history of, 235n23, 236n29; counterfeiting in, 176–77; and debt, 180–81; delusive appearances in, 165–66, 169–72; families in, 237n31; hospital in, 174–75, 237n32; importance of writing in, 162; marriage in, 170; money in, 236n24, 237n33; politeness in, 166; prison in, 173, 177–80; public versus private life in, 163–64; and relationship between credit and reputation, 167–68, 170–73; and self-discipline, 236n25; slave trade in, 161, 181; and social performance, 166–67, 170–73; transparency in, 166–67; and Welbeck's resistance to obscurity, 238n36; writing in, 236n25; yellow fever in, 161
Authorship, changing conceptions of, 190n10, 194n33
Axelrod, Alan, 142, 236n27
Axtell, James L., 36

Bailyn, Bernard, 190n6
Baker, Dorothy Z., 60

Bakhtin, M. M., 22, 78, 193n28
Bankruptcy, 145, 233n11, 238n38
Barker-Benfield, G. J., 72
Barnes, Elizabeth, 17–18, 20, 184
Bataille, Georges, 171, 220n54
Beales, Ross W., 191n16
Beccaria, Cesare, 232n8
Belknap, Jeremy, 9, 196n40
Bender, John, 232–33n9
Bennett, John, 39–40, 63, 166
Bennett, Tony, 193n26
Berry, Christopher J., 220–21n3
Berthoff, W. B., 170
Blair, Hugh, 50, 235n19
Blecki, Catherine La Courreye, 194n32
Bleecker, Ann Eliza, 8, 9. *See also The History of Maria Kittle*
Bloch, Ruth, 221n5
Blumin, Stuart M., 225n17
Boarding School, The (Hannah Foster), 24, 32, 63–68, 71; and conduct fiction, 63; and letters, 63, 66–68, 72; premarital pregnancy in, 68; and reading character, 68; servants in, 68; similarities with Rowson's *Mentoria*, 208–09n70; title page from, 64; and writing, 65–66
Bontatibus, Donna R., 61
Boston Tea Assembly, 117–18; and politeness, 147–48, 234n15
Bourdieu, Pierre, 189n5, 211n14
Bourgeois subjectivity, development of, 2, 3, 10, 19, 24, 27, 30, 73–74, 76–77, 112, 136–37, 142, 185, 188, 197n46
Brackenridge, Hugh Henry, 22, 184, 191n18, 196n40. *See also Modern Chivalry*
Breen, T. H., 109, 225n15
Brodhead, Richard H., 43, 86
Brooks, Peter, 221n7
Brown, Charles Brockden, 1–2, 8, 13, 17, 22, 26, 108, 160, 170, 181–82, 192n18, 236n27, 236n2; critical overview of, 140–42; treatment of money, 236n24. *See also Arthur Mervyn; Edgar Huntly; Ormond; Wieland*
Brown, Gillian, 35–36

Brown, Herbert Ross, 17, 78, 199n2
Brown, William Hill, 9, 17, 24, 32, 52. *See also The Power of Sympathy*
Brunton, Mary, 201n7
Buchan, William, 83, 84, 89, 90–91
Burder, George, 39, 146
Burgett, Bruce, 207n61
Burnham, Michelle, 46
Burrell, William, 90
Burroughs, Stephen, 124–25, 142, 230–31n57, 231n3

Caplan, Ruth B., 82
Carey, Mathew, 45, 174
Cassuto, Leonard, 62
Censer, Jane Turner, 215n28
Channing, William Ellery, 74
Character, nineteenth-century definitions of, 74
Character formation, 33–41. *See also* Reading character
Charlotte's Daughter (Susanna Rowson). *See Lucy Temple*
Charlotte Temple (Susanna Rowson), 11, 17, 24, 60, 71, 81, 94–95, 100, 210n6; frontispiece from, 95; grief in, 218n42; letters in, 194n34; narrative interventions in, 199n2; and passivity of Charlotte, 219n46; sensibility in, 31; syphilis in, 91
Charvat, William, 190n10
Chastity, 3, 79–80, 107
Chesterfield, Lord. *See* Philip Stanhope
Chiarugi, Vincenzo, 212n17
Childbirth, death in, 17, 130, 216n33
Children, illegitimate, 197n48
China trade. *See* East India and China trade
Christophersen, Bill, 142, 170, 222n9
Clarissa (Samuel Richardson), 15, 49, 195n38, 199n2; letters in, 204n35; sensibility in, 31
Coates, Samuel, 220n56
Coleman, Peter J., 233n11
Commerce. *See* East India and China trade; Trade

Complete Letter-Writer, The, 49
Conduct literature, 51, 52, 55; gender distinctions in, 145–47
Conduct novels, 199n2, 208n67
Confession: and fornication, 102–03; and insanity, 86–89; of a religious nature, 213n25
Confidence men, 139, 230–31n57
Cooper, James Fenimore, 11, 20
Cooper, Thomas, 115–16
Copyright law, 5, 190n10
Coquette, The (Hannah Foster), 11, 17, 24, 26, 32, 51, 57–63, 78–80, 100, 143, 149, 151–60, 167, 169, 199n2, 207n59, 207n61, 208n66, 210n6; adultery and fornication in, 159; and death in childbirth, 130; debt in, 181; Eliza as a coquette in, 58; epistolary courtship in, 206n50; friendship in, 60–61, 208n68; letters in, 71–72, 199n2, 206n50; and letter-writing, 60; marriage in, 157–59, 235n21; politeness in, 234–35n18; private versus public behavior in, 153–54; reading character in, 69, 70; rhetoric in, 206n50, 235n19; and Sanford as object of desire, 159; and self-examination, 57, 59, 61–62; social rank in, 152–53, 154–55; speculation in, 157, 159; titles in, 151–52, 234n17
Cott, Nancy F., 210n2
Counterfeiting, 106; in *Arthur Mervyn*, 176–77
Court, Franklin E., 202n15
Credit economy, 26–27, 143–44, 148
Cremin, Lawrence A., 202n16, 203n23
Cutbush, Edward, 82

Dain, Norman, 82, 212n18
Dalke, Anne, 221n7
Dandy Song, A, 124
Davidson, Cathy N., 5, 12, 16–18, 32, 68, 78, 130, 142, 190n11, 211n8, 211n9, 216n33
Davis, Richard Beale, 195n36
Dayton, Cornelia Hughes, 213n25, 231n4
Debt, 145, 180–81, 233n11; and imprisonment for, 233–34n11

Debtors' prison, 177
Derounian, Kathryn Smith, 229n49
Discipline (Mary Brunton), 201n7
Discourse on Education, A (Enos Hitchcock), 33–34
Dodsley, Robert, 145
Dörner, Klaus, 210n3
Dorval; or the Speculator (Sally Sayward Barrell Keating Wood), 24, 26, 78, 81, 91, 103, 108, 110, 127, 130, 131–32, 144, 229n52; and ambition, 132; and East India and China trade, 113, 136–39; and gambling linked to speculation, 134–35; and guilt, 92; hysteria in, 217n40; and insanity, 92; and reading character, 70–71; and republican virtue, 131–32; and speculation, 132–34; writing in, 47–48
Douglas, Ann, 190n8
Dulles, Foster Rhea, 113
Dumm, Thomas L., 212–13n23
Dunlap, William, 236n2
Dwight, Timothy, 103; and criticism of the novel, 211n8; on speculation, 122–23

East India and China trade, 106, 109–10, 111–16, 126; in *Dorval*, 136–39; in *Kelroy*, 128–30; profits from, 112–13, 226n24; scholarly treatments of, 225n20
Economic imperialism, 136–37, 230n54
Economic virtue, 147; defined, 107
Edgar Huntly; or, Memoirs of a Sleep-Walker (Charles Brockden Brown), 108; inheritance in, 222n9, 236n24; madness in, 210n5
Edwards, Jonathan, 183
Emerson, Ralph Waldo, 66, 74
Emily Hamilton, a Novel (Sukey Vickery), 24, 32, 55–57, 59; and friendship, 56; and passion, 55–57; and reading character, 71
Epistolary fiction: popularity of, 29–30, 200n2; role of letters, 199n2; theory of, 23, 73, 86
Evans, Gareth, 232n7

Fabian, Ann Vincent, 226–27n32

Factory Girl, The (Sarah Savage), 10, 26, 109; labor in, 185–86, 224n13
Fair, American, 24, 154, 156, 201–02n10
Family: importance of, 231–32n5; and inheritance, 232n6
Farmer's Friend, The (Enos Hitchcock), 33, 224n12
Female Quixotism (Tabitha Gilman Tenney), 196n40
Fennimore, Keith J., 6
Fichtelberg, Joseph, 239n4
Fiction: criticism of, 5–7, 11, 20, 192n24; by Thomas Jefferson, 211n8; by Timothy Dwight, 211n8. *See also* Novel
Fidelity Rewarded; or, The History of Polly Granville, 110
Finseth, Ian, 60
Fisher, Philip, 19, 20, 197n46
Fleischmann, Fritz, 63, 208n66
Fliegelman, Jay, 37, 46–47, 167, 203n21, 204n32, 219n45, 235n19, 236n28, 238n37
Fluck, Winfried, 189n2
Forcey, Blythe, 194n34, 200n2
Fordyce, James, 69
Foresters, an American Tale, The (Jeremy Belknap), 9, 196n40
Fornication. *See* Adultery and fornication
Fortunate Discovery, The (by the author of *Moreland Vale*), inherited wealth in, 221n7
Foster, Gwendolyn Audrey, 208n68
Foster, Hannah, 17, 24, 26, 32, 51, 57, 63, 142, 151. *See also The Boarding School*; *The Coquette*
Foucault, Michel, 77, 144, 201n9, 233n10
Franklin, Benjamin, 9, 37, 127, 167, 191n18, 230–31n57, 232n8, 236n27; on ambition, 125–26; publication of *Pamela*, 15, 195n37; and "The Way to Wealth," 147
Freneau, Philip, 198n49; and speculation, 228n41; and trade, 114–15

Gambler, or The Memoirs of a British Officer, The (anon.), 26, 118–20, 121, 144–45
Gambling, 24, 106, 110, 227n36; anxieties over, 117–21; in France, 227n34; linked with seduction, 120–21; linked with speculation, 121–22, 134–35, 227n32; nineteenth-century constructions of, 226–27n32
Gamesters; or Ruins of Innocence, The (Caroline Matilda Warren), 121; syphilis in, 91
Gentleman's Pocket Library, The, 147
Gentleman strangers, 143
Gilbert, Sandra M., 187
Gilmore, Michael T., 6, 67
Giraud, James, 90
Glass; or Speculation, The (anon.), 105
Goddu, Teresa A., 8, 142, 161–62, 172, 183, 231n1
God's Revenge against Gambling (Mason Locke Weems), 118, 121; frontispiece from, 119
Goldgeier, Adam, 58
Goldstein, Jonathan, 113
Gothic fiction, 8, 140, 144, 196n44, 231n1; madness in, 210n5
Grabo, Norman S., 189n1, 189n3, 235n23
Green, James N., 191n16, 195n37
Green, Richard, 216n31
Gregory, John, 41, 45, 70
Greven, Philip, 235
Grief: as cause of insanity, 83–84; in *Charlotte Temple*, 218n42
Gross, Robert A., 215n29
Gubar, Susan, 187
Guide tradition. *See* Conduct literature
Guilt, as cause of insanity, 84
Gustafson, Sandra, 13, 50–51

Habermas, Jürgen, 44, 211n13
Hall, David D., 209n75, 213n25
Hamelman, Steve, 229n50
Harris, Sharon M., 16, 152
Hart, James D., 191n13
Haslam, John, 24, 40, 83, 84, 85, 89
Henretta, James A., 190n7
Hinds, Elizabeth Jane Wall, 167, 222n9
Hindus, Michael S., 88, 215n29
Hirschman, Albert O., 39

History of Maria Kittle, The (Ann Eliza Bleecker), 8, 9
Hitchcock, Enos, 5, 13, 33–34, 40, 202n13, 224n12. *See also A Discourse on Education; The Farmer's Friend*
Holman, Jessee L., 227n36
Hopkinson, Francis, 196n40
Horizon of expectations, 188
Howell, Wilbur Samuel, 235n19
Hunter, J. Paul, 202n12
Hysteria, 83, 217n40

Imperialism. *See* Economic imperialism
Improvement of the Mind, The (Isaac Watts), 24, 38–39, 66, 69
Industry, 106, 228n46
Infidelity, 100. *See also* Adultery and fornication
Infidelity, or The Victims of Sentiment (Samuel Relf), 24, 78, 81, 93–94, 100, 103; and guilt, 94
Inheritance, 221n7, 222n9, 232n6
Inquiry into the Nature and Causes of the Wealth of Nations, An (Adam Smith), 115, 226n27
Insanity: failure to control passions as cause of, 40; grief as cause of, 83–84; guilt as cause of, 76, 78, 84; history of, 77–78; self-control as a preventive of, 101; syphilis as cause of, 89–90, 216n35. *See also* Moral treatment
Irigaray, Luce, 80

Jacobs, Harriet, 240n9
Jail. *See* Prison
Jameson, Fredric, 21
Jauss, Hans Robert, 181
Jefferson, Thomas, 82; and criticism of novel, 211n8; and criticism of speculation, 228n37; and penal reform, 232n8, 238n37
Jimenez, Mary Ann, 212n16
Johnson, Claudia L., 184
Jordan, Cynthia S., 8, 183, 191n18
Journey to Philadelphia, A ("Adelio"), 144

Julia, and the Illuminated Baron (Sally Sayward Barrell Keating Wood), 218n43
Justus, James H., 236n24

Kaplan, Amy, 230n54
Karlsen, Carol F., 214n26
Kavanagh, Thomas M., 227n34
Kelroy, a Novel (Rebecca Rush), 26, 108, 113, 127–31, 187, 229n49; aphasia in, 229n50; and East India trade, 128–30; and female economic desire, 130–31; and gambling, 128; and the lottery, 128; and luxury, 127–28; relationship between luxury goods and status in, 127–28; servants in, 239n2; and tea drinking, 112
Kerber, Linda K., 13
Klein, Lawrence, 146–47, 234n12, 235n21

Labor: productive, 224n13; productive versus unproductive, 115–16
Laura (Leonora Sansay), 219n47
Lenz, William E., 230n56
Leslie, Eliza, 51
Letters, personal, 30–31
Letter-writing manuals, 6, 48–50, 205–06n44
Levine, Robert S., 142
Lewis, Jan, 221n5
Liberalism, 184, 190n6, 207n45; and economic individualism, 19, 182; and national imaginary, 239n5; nineteenth-century incarnation of, 27; and transition from republicanism, 10, 19, 184, 197n46
Libraries, circulating, 7, 190n9, 191n16
Lindberg, Gary, 230–31n57
Locke, John, 24, 35–37, 73, 202n16; and importance of habit, 36–37; and influence on American educational thought, 35, 37; and influence on parent-child relationships, 203n21
Logic: Or, the Right Use of Reason (Isaac Watts), 24, 37–38, 66, 203n23
London, April, 217n37
Looby, Christopher, 142
Loshe, Lillie Deming, 17, 78, 96

Lotteries: frontispiece from *The Lottery*, 129; in *Kelroy*, 128
Lovell, Thomas B., 224n13
Lucinda, or the Mountain Mourner (Mrs. P. D. Manvill), 215–16n30, 218n44
Lucy Temple (Susanna Rowson), 24, 81, 95–96, 103, 185; and guilt, 96; treatment of grief, 96
Luxury, 24, 107, 220–21n3, 226n30; compared to an epidemic, 221n4; criticism of, 117; in *Kelroy*, 127–28; and relationship with politeness, 234n12
Luxury goods, 109, 111–12; anxiety over, 115

Madison, James, 41
Main, Jackson Turner, 110
"Man at Home, The" (Charles Brockden Brown), 236n24
Mandeville, Bernard, 39
Mania, 83, 212n20
Manufacturing, 224n13
Manuscript culture, 13
Manvill, Mrs. P. D., 215–16n30, 218n44
Marino, Sarah, 199n1
Marriage: in *Arthur Mervyn*, 170; private, 99; public, 156–57, 235n21
Martin, Terence, 231n5
May, Henry F., 204n30
McCoy, Drew, 109, 223n10, 224–25n14, 227n37
Medical Inquiries and Observations upon the Diseases of the Mind (Benjamin Rush), 74–75, 210n1; and artistic treatments of insanity, 220n56; and grief, 83; and hysteria, 83; and link between insanity and speculation, 123–24; and moral treatment, 84–85. *See also* Benjamin Rush
Melancholy, 83
Mental illness, reform in treatment of, 212–13n23. *See also* Moral treatment
Mentoria; or the Young Lady's Friend (Susanna Rowson), 42, 209n70, 218n43
Meranze, Michael, 233n10, 238n35
Merchants, 109, 139, 225n17; objections to, 116. *See also* Trade

Merians, Linda E., 217n37
Merish, Lori, 57, 240n7
Modern Chivalry (Hugh Henry Brackenridge), 184, 194n34, 196n40, 239n2
Monaghan, E. Jennifer, 209n75
Monima, or the Beggar Girl (Martha Read), 185, 237n32, 239n4
Moore, John Hamilton, 145
Moore, Milcah Martha, 13, 194n32
Moral faculties, 85
Moral preceptors, 41–42
Moral treatment, 82, 84–85, 212n16; fictional treatments of, 92–93
More, Hannah, 40
Moreland Vale; or the Fair Fugitive (by the author of *The Fortunate Discovery*), 108–09, 110; and East India trade, 108, 113, 137; inherited wealth in, 221n7; use of trade goods in, 112
Morris, Robert, 112, 124, 225n20, 233n11
Mott, Frank Luther, 41
Mulford, Carla, 102, 219n50
Mullan, John, 31
Murray, Judith Sargent, 13, 24, 26, 32, 43, 142, 144, 204n34. *See also Story of Margaretta*
Murry, Ann, 147

National culture, creation of, 13, 22–23
National imaginary, 185, 188
Nationalism, 106, 107, 111, 137, 139, 193n29, 220n51, 230n55; literary, 10
Neal, John, 10
Nelson, Dana D., 130, 198n48, 229n48
Nelson, William E., 87, 213–14n26
Newton, Sarah E., 63, 147, 199n2, 208n67, 229n46
Novel, scholarly criticism of, 189n2. *See also* Fiction

Of Commerce and Luxury (anon.), 115, 221n3
Oratory, 50–51; political, 13
Orians, G. Harrison, 5, 190n11
Ormond, or, the Secret Witness (Charles Brockden Brown), 17, 236n24

Painter, Nell Irvin, 70
Pamela (Samuel Richardson), 15, 49; American publication of, 195n37, 195n38; and Locke, 35; praise of, 183; sensibility in, 31
Parental advice literature, 41–46. *See also* Conduct literature
Parental Legacies, 45
Parrish, Joseph, 40, 82
Passions, 91; effect on the body, 212n21; harnessing of, 34, 39–40, 86, 121, 232n8
Penal reform, 177, 212–13n23, 232n8, 238n35, 238n37
Perkins, David, 101
Perry, Ruth, 204n35
Pettengill, Claire C., 199–200n2, 208n68
Petter, Henri, 199n2
Pinel, Philippe, 24, 75, 77, 81, 82, 90, 101
Pitcher, Edward W. R., 192n21
Pocock, J. G. A., 109, 190n6, 224–25n14
Politeness, 146–48, 153; in *Arthur Mervyn*, 166; in *The Coquette*, 234–35n18; and the loyalists, 234n13; in opposition to republican virtue, 147–48; relationship to luxury of, 234n12; and the Sans Souci Club dispute, 234n15
Porcelain, 111–12
Power of Sympathy, The (William Hill Brown), 9, 17, 24, 32, 52–55, 71, 198n48, 199n2; and conduct literature, 52, 55; frontispiece and title page from, 53; Harrington's death, 55, 207n45; reading character in, 69; self-examination in, 52–54
Premarital pregnancy, 88, 215n28, 215n29; fictional treatment of, 54, 68, 215–16n30
Present for Young Ladies, A (Susanna Rowson), 29, 51
Prison, 144, 173, 232–33n9; in *Arthur Mervyn*, 177–80; and reform, 177, 212–13n23, 232n8

Quétel, Claude, 89

Radway, Janice A., 101
Rake, figure of, 149, 151, 232n7

Read, Martha, 185, 237n32, 239n4. *See also Monima*
Reading character, 65, 69–71, 73
Reed, Walter L., 12
Relf, Samuel, 24, 78, 81, 93, 100. *See also Infidelity*
Renan, Ernest, 2
Republicanism, 21, 184, 190n6, 239n5; and capitalism, 222n10; in *Dorval*, 229n52; and speculation, 227n37; and trade, 223n10, 224–25n14; and transition to liberalism, 10, 19, 184, 197n46
Republican mother, 8
Republican virtue: in *Dorval*, 131–32; feminine, 107, 135, 221n5; masculine, 74, 147
Republican wife, 8
Rice, Grantland S., 14, 18, 58, 190n10, 194n33
Richards, Jeffrey H., 73, 153, 220n2, 239n2
Richardson, Samuel, 31, 35, 204n35; on epistolarity, 49. *See also Clarissa*; *Pamela*
Ricord, Philip, 216–17n36
Robert-Fleury, Tony, 75, 77–78, 101
Rodgers, Daniel T., 190n6
Rose, Henry, 212n21
Rothman, David, 233n10
Rothman, Ellen K., 88
Rousseau, Jean-Jacques, 150
Rowson, Susanna, 14, 17, 24, 29, 42, 51, 81, 95, 185, 194n34, 198n51, 199n2, 218n43; and sensibility, 31. *See also Charlotte Temple*; *Lucy Temple*; *Mentoria*
Rubin, Joan Shelley, 74
Rubin-Dorsky, Jeffrey, 8
Rush, Benjamin, 5, 24, 37, 74–75, 78, 87, 90, 94, 103, 126, 220n56; and grief, 83; and hysteria, 83; and influence on students, 82–86, 212n18; and link between insanity and speculation, 123–24; and moral treatment, 84–85; and republican machines, 203n22. *See also Medical Inquiries and Observations upon the Diseases of the Mind*
Rush, Rebecca, 26, 108, 113, 126, 127, 137; biographical information about, 229n48. *See also Kelroy*

Rust, Marion, 14, 196n41, 198n51, 219n46

Said, Edward W., 136, 230n54
St. Hubert; or, Mistaken Friendship (anon.), 120–21, 134
St. John de Crèvecoeur, J. Hector, 106, 107, 221n4
Sakolski, A. M., 229–30n53
Samuels, Shirley, 99–100, 219n45, 236–37n31
Sans Souci, Alias, Free and Easy, or, An Evening's Peep into a Polite Circle, 148, 234n16
Sans Souci Club. *See* Boston Tea Assembly
Sansay, Leonora, 219n47
Savage, Sarah, 10, 26, 109, 185, 224n13. *See also The Factory Girl*
Schloesser, Pauline, 201–02n10
Schloss, Dietmar, 234–35n18
Scott, Sir Walter, 10, 11
Scottish Common Sense philosophy: fear of imagination, 32; influence on American educational thought, 35, 41, 202n15
Seduction: linked with gambling, 120–21; linked to speculation, 134–35
Self-Control (Mary Brunton), 201n7
Self-control, as preventive for insanity, 86
Self-discipline, 2, 8, 21, 24, 30–33, 36–41, 47–48, 52, 55, 57, 62, 63–64, 67–68, 70
Self-examination, 24, 52–54, 202n12
Self-knowledge, 45
Sensibility, 31, 72, 196n39, 200n5
Sentiment, 31, 184–85, 196n39, 200n5; objects of, 197n46
Sentimental fiction, 16–18, 21, 78, 144, 153, 184, 196n40, 197n47; and education, 78; linked with social concerns, 138
Sentimental: defined, 15–16; discourse, 197n47
Servants, 8, 68, 127, 174, 183–84, 239n2
Seventy-Six (John Neal), 10
Shields, David S., 30, 112, 146, 226n22
Showalter, Elaine, 212n16
Shuffelton, Frank, 63, 207n59
Silverman, Kenneth, 194n32, 226n30

Singer, Godfrey Frank, 199n1
Slavery, 8, 28, 186–88
Slaves, 27, 186–88, 198n48, 198n49
Slave trade, 221n6; in *Arthur Mervyn*, 161, 181
Smith, Adam, 24, 30, 32, 39, 115, 226n27; "man within the breast," 44, 63
Smith, Daniel Scott, 88, 215n28, 215n29
Smith, Merril D., 210n2, 214n26
Smith, Samuel Stanhope, 41
Smith-Rosenberg, Carroll, 109, 224–25n14
Sociability, 31, 112
Some Thoughts Concerning Education (John Locke), 24, 35–37
Speculation, 24, 106; and the figure of the speculator, 139; linked with gambling, 121–22, 134–35; linked to seduction, 134–35; and Philip Freneau, 228n41; political treatment of, 227n37; public condemnation of, 122–25; and Stephen Burroughs, 124–25
Spousal affection, 210n2
Stallybrass, Peter, 20–21
Stanhope, Philip, 41–42, 63, 147
Stern, Julia A., 8, 17–18, 19, 61, 142, 183, 196n44, 198n48, 199n2, 206n50, 218n42
Story of Margaretta (Judith Sargent Murray), 24, 26, 32, 71, 143–44, 149–51, 169, 181; letters in, 43, 150
Stowe, Harriet Beecher, 27–28, 240n7, 240n9. *See also Uncle Tom's Cabin*
Sympathy, 184–85, 239n2, 240n7
Syphilis, 89–91, 216n35, 216–17n36; and insanity, 89–90, 216n35

Tassoni, John Paul, 60
Taylor, John, 116
Tea, 112, 226n22
Tennenhouse, Leonard, 22, 195n38, 220n51
Tenney, Tabitha Gilman, 196n40
Thayer, Caroline Matilda Warren, 91, 121. *See also The Gamesters*
Theory of Moral Sentiments, The (Adam Smith), 24, 30, 32; letter writing, 44; "man within the breast," 44

Todd, Janet, 196n39, 200n5
Tompkins, Jane, 19, 20, 142, 189n1, 197n46, 237n33
Tonkovich, Nicole, 205n37
Trade, 109–10; international, 25, 115; objections to, 116; and republicanism, 224–25n14
Transparency, 43, 46, 50, 62, 166–67
Travels in New England and New York (Timothy Dwight), 122–23
Tuke, William, 82

Ulrich, Laurel Thatcher, 102–03, 214n26
Uncle Tom's Cabin (Harriet Beecher Stowe), 19, 27–28, 86, 138, 186–88, 240n9; debt in, 186; fornication linked to insanity in, 187–88; sentiment in, 197n46; slavery in, 186–88; speculation in, 186–87; sympathy in, 240n7
Unfortunate Lovers, and Cruel Parents, The (Mrs. Patterson), 113

Vain Cottager, The (anon.), 196n45, 219n47
Van Sant, Ann Jessie, 184, 200n5
Vedder, Edward B., 216n35
Venereal disease, 217n37. *See also* Syphilis
Verhoeven, W. M., 49, 199n2, 206n50
Vickery, Sukey, 24, 32

Wakefield, Priscilla, 42
Waldstreicher, David, 194n29, 226n21, 231n2
Walker, John, 40
"Walstein's School of History" (Charles Brockden Brown), 1–2, 22, 189n3
Warner, Michael, 142, 166, 179, 197n47, 234n13, 239n5
Warren, Caroline Matilda. *See* Caroline Matilda Warren Thayer
Warren, Mercy Otis, 13, 148, 234n16

Watterson, George, 144
Watts, Edward, 14, 18, 142, 176–77, 194n34, 237–38n34
Watts, Isaac, 24, 37–39, 66, 69, 203n23. *See also The Improvement of the Mind*; *Logic*
Watts, Steven, 10, 142, 222n9, 223n10
Webster, Noah, 103
Webster, Pelatiah, 111, 123, 229n51
Weems, Mason Locke, 118, 119, 121. *See also God's Revenge against Gambling*
Wells, Helena, 198n50, 211n9
White, Allon, 20–21
White, Hayden, 216n32
Wieland (Charles Brockden Brown), 17, 144, 199n2; madness in, 210n5; mania in, 212n20
Wilcox, Kristin, 204n34
Williams, Daniel E., 230–31n57, 231n3
Williams, Raymond, 210n6
Winans, Robert B., 6, 191n16
Wood, Gordon S., 117, 148, 190n6
Wood, Sally Sayward Barrell Keating, 24, 26, 70, 78, 81, 91, 108, 113, 126, 127, 130, 131–30, 137, 144, 196n41, 211n9, 218n43; biographical information about, 229n48; image of, 138; importance of writing to, 47–48. *See also Amelia*; *Dorval*; *Julia*
Woodruff, Hezekiah N., 125
Wulf, Karin, 191n17, 194n32

Yazawa, Melvin, 207n55
Yazoo purchase, 122, 124–25, 229–30n53
Young Gentleman's Parental Monitor, The, 145, 147
Young Lady's Parental Monitor, The, 45

Zboray, Ronald J., 190n10
Ziff, Larzer, 11, 80, 142, 167, 231n3
Zomchick, John, 102